DATE DUE

JE 6 07			
DE 7 09			

DEMCO 38-296

NO EASY WALK
TO FREEDOM

NO EASY WALK TO FREEDOM

Reconstruction and the Ratification of the Fourteenth Amendment

JAMES E. BOND

Westport, Connecticut
London

Library of Congress Cataloging-in-Publication Data

Bond, James Edward, 1943–
    No easy walk to freedom : reconstruction and the ratification of
the Fourteenth Amendment / James E. Bond.
      p. cm.
    Includes bibliographical references and index.
    ISBN 0–275–95703–9 (alk. paper)
    1. United States—Constitutional law—Amendments—14th—
History—19th century. 2. United States—Constitutional law—
Amendments—Ratification—History—19th century. 3. Civil rights—
United States—History—19th century. 4. Afro-Americans—Civil
rights—History—19th century. 5. Southern States—
History—1865–1877. I. Title.
    KF4558 14th.B66 1997
    342.73′085—DC21   96–42481

British Library Cataloguing in Publication Data is available.

Library of Congress Catalog Card Number: 96–42481
ISBN: 0–275–95703–9

First published in 1997

Praeger Publishers, 88 Post Road West, Westport, CT 06881
An imprint of Greenwood Publishing Group, Inc.

Printed in the United States of America

To

Dr. Philip Phibbs

and

the students, staff, and faculty

of the School of Law, 1986–1993,

for making my tenure as dean

the most rewarding professional experience

of my life

Contents

Acknowledgments

This project spanned more than a decade, during most of which I served as dean of the University of Puget Sound School of Law. As one might surmise from the dedication to this book, that deanship entailed very few frustrations. The major one was my inability to get this book written. Most of the primary research had been done by the time I moved to Tacoma in 1986, but it sat boxed for the next seven years, largely untouched except for two month-long, ultimately futile efforts to make some sense of thousands of note cards and barely legible microfilm copies.

When I was finally able to return to the project in the summer of 1993, I discovered to my horror that much of the microfilm copy had deteriorated and was unreadable. Consequently, I had to retrace my research trips to the major libraries in most of the Southern states. The one consolation was that the quality of the reader-printers had improved vastly during the intervening years. The policies regarding their use were as disparate and idiosyncratic as ever, however. Still, the librarians everywhere were unfailingly helpful, and I thank them.

Over the course of this project, I incurred countless other debts. The Earhart Foundation generously funded my research efforts. The Frances and Sidney Lewis Law Center at the Washington and Lee University School of Law kindly allowed me to spend a month there during the summer of 1989; and during that period I did develop a tentative and very general outline of the book. Kelly Kunsch, a public service librarian at the Seattle University School of Law, cheerfully answered my endless pleas for help. Bonnie Speir, my research assistant this past year, determinedly chased down every errant footnote and meticulously proofed the final two drafts. Dee Wakefield and Liz Dorsett, the school's special projects secretaries, typed draft after draft without complaint; and Jill Branham, a former administrative assistant, prepared the camera-ready copy with her usual pleasant dispatch.

And then there were the many colleagues and friends whom I asked to read various drafts: Megan McClintock, an American historian who teaches at the University of Washington (Tacoma); Rhiman Rotz, a college fraternity brother and historian who teaches at the University of Indiana (Gary); Michael Curtis, who followed me as a professor of constitutional law at Wake Forest and who has written brilliantly on the subject of this book; John La Fond, a colleague whose clear and forceful writing style I admire; and David Lips, an attorney whom I came to know and respect as a result of our collaborating on a series of seminars for federal and state judges. To all of these persons I express thanks.

Finally, I want to thank my son Garth and wife Georgana. During the summer of 1986, Garth catalogued the research from two states (Georgia and South Carolina), and for the last eighteen months Georgana has endured file boxes, note cards, and papers stacked on every flat surface in "her" kitchen and dining room. More generally and far more importantly, the unconditional love we share as a family sustains me, and my need to prove myself worthy of their love energizes and motivates me. In that sense, everything I write is for them.

NO EASY WALK
TO FREEDOM

The Remembered Past of the Fourteenth Amendment

The Warren Court "imagined the past and remembered the future."

—Professor Alexander Bickel,
critiquing the Court's attempt to construct the "Egalitarian Society"

The Civil War redefined the American nation, and the legal essence of that re-definition was captured in three constitutional amendments.[1] The first abolished slavery, and the third extended suffrage to all adult males without regard to color. The second—the Fourteenth Amendment—prohibited the states from denying or abridging the fundamental rights of every citizen and required them to grant all persons equal protection and due process. Its first section has in fact become a second American constitution, and its meaning is the preeminent question of contemporary constitutional law.

Although the amendment guarantees both substantive rights and procedural fairness, the three great clauses of Section 1 do not specify either the rights protected or the procedures required.[2] While Section 5 grants Congress the power to enforce Section 1 by "appropriate legislation," it is silent on how, if at all, the federal structure of the government limits that power.[3] The effort to provide that specification and fill that silence has raised two profoundly troubling questions:

- Is the Fourteenth Amendment the new birth of freedom for which Lincoln prayed at Gettysburg or the Jacobin nightmare predicted by its post-Civil War critics?
- Should the amendment's oracle, the Supreme Court, be praised for finally fulfilling the Declaration of Independence's promise of equality and fairness for all or be damned for destroying the republican bulwarks that alone preserve individual liberty?

The answers to these questions divided the Court and the country as early as the *Slaughter-House Cases*.[4] They divide both still.

What ought not to divide either Court or country is the importance of the Southern ratification debates to any understanding of the Fourteenth Amendment.[5] The Fourteenth Amendment embodied the peace terms which the North initially dictated to the South. It was also the platform of the Republican Party in the 1866 congressional elections in the Northern states,[6] and it remained an integral part of Congress's subsequent reconstruction plan for the Southern states. Section 1 in particular was intended to solve a variety of specific problems that had emerged in the South between 1865 and 1866. A contextual understanding of those problems is thus critically important to any understanding of the amendment's original meaning, which became a key question in one of the most wrenching "wars" in the history of American politics.[7]

Indeed, the ratification debate in the South proved that politics is, to confound Clausewitz's dictum, the extension of war by other means. Whatever the verdict of the Civil War battlefield, its practical implementation in the postwar South was uncertain and much disputed. Would the old order survive, or would a new order emerge? Northerners wanted a new order, though they disagreed on the nature of that order. Abolitionists wanted to secure the millennium for which they had shed blood, capitalists wanted to open the South to profitable development, and Republicans wanted to secure the South's allegiance in order to preserve the party's control of the national government. Though many Southerners defended the old order, they, too, were divided over its future. Some Southern whites fought to preserve white supremacy, some fought to protect their economic interests, and some fought to settle old political scores that antedated the Civil War. Indeed, prewar divisions between secessionist Democrats and pro-Union or antiwar Whigs resurfaced even before Lee surrendered; and class and sectional differences within each state exacerbated these divisions. Blacks fought to recover their dignity and secure their freedom. Though this political war began even before the Fourteenth Amendment was promulgated and extended well beyond its ratification, its "capture" was nevertheless one of the principal objects of the "war."

The "war" began because President Johnson and Congress disagreed over how—and how promptly—to restore the Southern states to the Union. Because Congress was in recess when the South fell in the spring of 1865, President Johnson initiated Reconstruction by appointing provisional governors in Alabama, Florida, Georgia, Mississippi, North Carolina, South Carolina, and Texas. He asked each provisional governor to call a convention to repudiate secession, abolish slavery, and ratify the Thirteenth Amendment. The existing, pro-Union governments in occupied Arkansas, Louisiana, Tennessee, and Virginia had already taken these steps; and the governors in those states continued in office. All the state conventions called that fall acquiesced in the president's demand that the South repudiate secession and abolish slavery, and all but Mississippi ratified the Thirteenth Amendment.

Later that fall, elections were held in most of the Southern states to elect governors and state legislatures. A majority of those elected were prewar Whigs who had opposed the war. Meeting amidst social and economic chaos, many of these governments nevertheless adopted laws that significantly limited the rights of the freedmen. Among white Southerners these Black Codes were considered essential to the preservation of social order and the rebuilding of the Southern economy.

Most white Southerners simply dismissed the notion that blacks were entitled to equal rights. One student of Reconstruction in Texas succinctly summarized this attitude:

Psychologically and sociologically, for the Southerner to have accepted the equality of the Negro after 1865 would have been an admission of guilt, not only for the injustice of the slave system but also for the disaster of a war which cost the lives of 600,000 white boys. The face-saving new article of faith had to be a racist social status which would continue the freedman "in his place"—his place of inferiority.[8]

Consequently, these Southerners were reluctant to accept any restoration terms that circumscribed their authority to deal with the freedmen as they thought best. For that reason, among others, they also opposed any significant alteration in the federal structure of the government. Indeed, they clung tenaciously to the doctrine of states' rights.

Many Northerners, however, thought the codes were intended to reenslave the freedmen; and they demanded that the national government intervene to protect the rights of the freedmen. In May 1866 the *New York Evening Post* reported:

In South Carolina and Florida the freedmen are forbidden to bear or keep arms. In South Carolina they are forbidden to work at trades, or to engage in business, unless specially licensed. In Florida it is made a penal offense to teach the freedmen or their children, except a license has first been obtained. In Mississippi all freedmen who are not engaged in labor by the year are compelled to take out a license. . . . In South Carolina it is enacted that the laborer shall be called "servant" and the employer "master."[9]

Congress, dominated by Republicans outraged by these acts, refused to seat Southern congressional delegations, despite the President's proclamation that the Southern states were restored. Moreover, congressional Republicans were alarmed that a resurgent Democracy, strengthened by a restored South, would supplant them as the country's dominant political party. They thus insisted on a restoration that minimized that possibility and insured the freedom of the freedmen. To that end, the Republican majority in Congress struggled throughout the first half of 1866 to reconcile their views and devise a congressional solution to the problems of restoration. It passed the Freedmen's Bureau Bill[10] and the Civil Rights Act,[11] both of which the president angrily vetoed. Though Congress narrowly failed to muster the two-thirds majority needed to override the president's veto of the Freedmen's Bureau Bill, it did overcome his opposition to the Civil Rights Bill. And in June of that year, it approved the Fourteenth Amendment, which the president also denounced.

Congressman O. H. Browning stated the case for the president's plan, dubbed "My Policy":

It is certain that all will be lost unless the states are restored to their constitutional relations to the general government; and every day's delay increases the difficulties of restoration and the dangers of our situation. Will a more favorable or auspicious time ever come? I think not. The people who were in rebellion have ceased their resistance to the government; acknowledged its authority; avowed their wish to remain under its protection, and are living in obedience to its laws. What more can they do? The rest is with us. We fought them four years in the field to make them stay in the Union, and now they have yielded to the demand, and avow a willingness and wish to do all we required, we ought not to fight them in Congress to make them go out.[12]

Carl Schurz, who had toured the South, warned against the president's strategy:

Mark my words: You admit the late rebel States to representation and power in the National Government such as they are, unconditionally, you remove the brakes from the reactionary movement without having first secured and fortified the results of the war by amendments to our Federal Constitution; and I predict the reaction will go so far as to call in question all legislation that was had during the absence from Congress of the eleven rebel States. Whether so atrocious a movement will ultimately succeed will rest with the people; but it is certain that if the President's policy prevails it will be attempted, and the attempt will not be checked before having plunged the Republic into disasters of the wildest confusion.[13]

Congressional radicals and most of their more moderate fellow Republicans shared Schurz's belief that restoration should be delayed until the Southern states met certain conditions.

Northern public opinion appeared initially to be closely divided. Although there was general agreement in the North that the abolition of slavery was a precondition of restoration, there was no similar agreement there, for example, on the status which the newly freed slaves should enjoy or the role the national government should play in protecting that status. Northern whites generally considered blacks inferior, and most Northern states did not allow their black residents to vote or otherwise participate in the public life of the community. Moreover, many—probably a majority—of Republicans still believed in the basic tenets of federalism.[14]

The prevailing division on these questions was dramatized in the late summer and early fall of 1866 when competing national conventions met in Philadelphia. The National Union Convention was organized to rally support behind the president and "My Policy." The Southern Loyalist Convention was organized to drum up support for Congress and the Fourteenth Amendment. Both conventions were elaborately staged; and delegates left their respective conventions buoyed by campaign rhetoric and determined to win the fall elections in the North. The fall elections thus became a referendum on the Fourteenth Amendment, and voters overwhelmingly rejected the president's policy and returned candidates who favored ratification of the Fourteenth Amendment.[15]

While some white Southerners counseled ratification in light of these election results, the vast majority refused. They either clung to the hope that the North would repudiate the radicals and endorse the president; or they calculated that the costs of ratification were too high, whatever penalties Congress might impose. Tennessee did ratify immediately; but every other Southern state, between the last months of 1866 and the first months of 1867, rejected the amendment. This first round of consideration produced governors' messages, committee reports, and widely reported public discussion, much of which focused on the meaning of the Fourteenth Amendment and the consequences of ratifying it.

In March 1867 a determined Congress retaliated against the South's defiant refusal to accept the Fourteenth Amendment. It imposed military Reconstruction,[16] dividing the South into five military districts and establishing new criteria for restoration. Although ratification of the Fourteenth Amendment was included among those criteria, others became more immediately important. First, black males over twenty-one were to be added to the voter rolls; and certain classes of white voters were to be removed from the registration lists. Second, a constitutional convention was to be held in each state; and the resulting constitutions were to be submitted to the voters for their approval. Third, a state could hold elections for state offices once its voters had adopted the new constitution and Congress had approved it. Fourth, the legislature elected under the new constitution had to ratify the Fourteenth Amendment. Only then would Congress pronounce the state restored and seat its congressional delegation.

The campaigns to select convention delegates, the convention deliberations, the referenda on the proposed constitutions, and the concomitant elections of new governors and legislators all once again dramatized the meaning attributed to the Fourteenth Amendment. The new state constitutions themselves provide an additional insight into the original understanding, for everyone agreed that these new constitutions had to conform to the principles of the Fourteenth Amendment. Every one of these constitutions, for example, contained a Bill or Declaration of Rights, whose guarantees necessarily reflected the contemporary understanding of the provisions of the Fourteenth Amendment.

In the summer of 1868, "reconstructed" legislatures in a majority of the Southern states approved the Fourteenth Amendment by only somewhat less overwhelming margins than those by which their "unreconstructed" predecessors had rejected it. The few that did not ratify ratified within a few years. This reconsideration also produced another set of governors' messages (though not committee reports) and was accompanied once again by widespread public discussion. Relentlessly savaged and extravagantly praised, the Fourteenth Amendment was thus endlessly debated for more than two years in the South. Consequently, the ratification debates in the South were the most concentrated and focused since the adoption of the Constitution itself.

A little more than three years after Lee had surrendered the tattered remnants of the Army of Virginia, a new political order appeared to have emerged from the ashes of that defeat. Built on the principles of the Declaration of Independence, the new order promised liberty and equality for all. A white South Carolinian from the upcountry gave poignant voice to this dream when he wrote Governor Robert K. Scott, following Grant's victory in 1868: "I am . . . a native borned S. C. a poor man never owned a Negro in my life. . . . I am hated and despised for nothing else but my loyalty to the mother government. . . . But I rejoice to think that God almighty has given to the poor of S. C. a Gov. to hear to feel to protect the humble poor without distinction to race or color."[17] But the irreconcilables knew how fragile were that promise and that dream. Biding their time, they issued a warning, both chilling and prescient: "These constitutions and governments will last just as long as the bayonets which ushered them into being shall keep them in existence, and not one day longer."[18]

Over the next decade, the Southern states were convulsed by political turmoil; and the actions of the state legislatures during that period also illuminate the contemporary understanding of the Fourteenth Amendment. These legislatures were dominated initially by Republicans who embraced the amendment, albeit with varying degrees of enthusiasm; and they were expected to implement legislative programs consistent with its principles.

- They were asked to fund public schools and therefore had to decide whether these schools would be integrated.
- They were asked to establish militia and therefore had to decide whether blacks and whites would serve together.
- They were asked to pass civil rights acts and therefore had to decide what rights the state was obliged to protect.

Legislative decisions on these matters are especially helpful, for example, in demonstrating the extent to which legislators thought that the Fourteenth Amendment constrained their discretion to fashion public policy on race-sensitive issues; they also reveal how difficult it proved to be to translate the amendment's guarantees into reality. More generally, these decisions underscore the continuing vitality of the federal principle, which permitted the states broad latitude in the exercise of traditional police powers.

This debate on the Fourteenth Amendment did not occur in a vacuum. It was part of an ongoing, continuous political debate about Reconstruction. That debate was multifaceted, of course; but some of the issues upon which it focused involved the very concepts explicitly set out in the Fourteenth Amendment: the privileges and immunities of citizenship, the equal protection of the laws, and due process of law. Among the specific issues which troubled Southerners throughout Reconstruction were these:

- the right to give testimony (could a black testify against a white?);

- the right to serve on a jury (could blacks sit in judgment of whites?);
- the right to vote (could blacks as well as whites vote?);
- the right to serve in the militia (must blacks and whites serve together in the same unit?);
- access to a public education (must blacks and whites be schooled together?); and
- access to public conveyances and accommodations (could blacks sit next to whites?).

Early on, Union military commanders and, later, agents of the Freedmen's Bureau passed on many of these questions, settling disputes and issuing orders.[19] Though their decisions were hardly uniform, they do reflect a generally consistent, liberal commitment to enforcing the rights of the freedmen that the Fourteenth Amendment was intended to secure. The discussion of these specific issues naturally illuminated the community's general understanding of privileges and immunities, equal protection, and due process.

Even more frequently, the Reconstruction debate took up themes implicit in the Fourteenth Amendment: the proper relation of person to person, of person to government, and of state government to national government. For example, Southerners of the day categorized rights as natural, civil, political, or social; and they sharply distinguished among civil, political, and social equality. They also distinguished republican government from democratic government. This broader debate on the philosophical underpinnings of the American political regime is thus a rich secondary source of information about the original understanding of the amendment.[20] Viewed in that light, the Fourteenth Amendment emerged as part of a larger effort to democratize and nationalize the American republic, at least with respect to the protection of individual liberties.

The richness of this discourse may not be fully appreciated by one unfamiliar with the intense political agitation that swept the South during this period. Barbecues and picnics, rallies and parades, resolutions and petitions were the order of the day. Political organizations sprouted like weeds. They often wilted quickly, only to revive later under a new name and with a new mix of members as alliances splintered and reformed.

The newly freed blacks organized. Though they had a clear goal—the preservation of their freedom and dignity—they were by no means of one mind on how to achieve that goal. Ultimately reduced to pawns in the struggle between white patrons, they probably could not have achieved their goal in any case.

Conservatives organized. Though they briefly flirted with an alliance with the freedmen, they soon realized that the terms they offered their former slaves were unacceptable and concentrated instead on the creation of a white man's party. While willing to modernize the old South, they refused to dismantle its aristocratic, racist culture.

Republicans organized. They sought to forge an alliance between blacks and yeoman whites—a poor man's party, financed by Northern capitalists who wanted to develop the South.[21] Once the success of the Republican Party came to depend upon the bloc support of blacks, however, its future was imperiled. If white Republicans could be siphoned off by racist appeals and blacks scared away from the polls, the Republican Party would wither.

The Union Leagues, which rallied blacks in support of the Republican Party, and the Ku Klux Klan, which became the paramilitary arm of the Democratic Party, also flourished during this period. All held meetings and conventions and issued pleas and platforms. These political effusions provide an index to the public's understanding of their rights and the obligation of governments to protect those rights.

The object of all this political activity was plain, and the stakes were great. Each faction wanted to win control of the state governments. After all, everyone understood that those who dominated the state governments would determine, at least initially, how the commands of the Fourteenth Amendment would be implemented. Conservative whites lost the initial skirmishes but in the end won the war. By 1877 they had regained control of every Southern state. They passed themselves off as redeemers, but they broke every promise they made to their black citizens and to the national government in exchange for its acquiescence in their electoral triumph and the removal of federal troops from the South.

For the next seventy-five years, these "redeemed" state governments, aided and abetted by an indifferent national government and a mistaken Supreme Court, ignored the plain commands of the Fourteenth Amendment. Black Americans were thus relegated to a kind of second-class citizenship that those who ratified the Fourteenth Amendment in the South understood it to forbid. Thus, the promise of the amendment was kept to the ear but broken to the hope of the freedmen.

Illuminating as the Southern ratification debates are, they are nevertheless problematic in some aspects. First, the debates are not assembled for easy reference as is the congressional debate. Even today, few states maintain a legislative record like the *Congressional Record*. In the nineteenth century, the practice was so rare as to have been almost nonexistent. Typically, then, the state debates must be pieced together painstakingly from newspaper and other accounts. Some of those accounts are lost. Others are but fragmentary. And in the case of newspapers, the surviving record may not accurately reflect the range of views because there were very few Republican papers, especially during the six-month period following the amendment's submission to the states in June 1866 when it was initially considered. The official documents that do exist—committee reports and governors' messages, for example—are scattered. The construction of a state legislative history for each of the states is thus a daunting task.

Second, the debates did not focus primarily on Section 1, which today is *the* Fourteenth Amendment (along with Section 5, which gives Congress the authority to enforce its provisions by appropriate legislation). Instead, the debates focused on Sections 2 and 3, which dealt respectively with Negro suffrage and apportionment and with the exclusion of rebel leaders from office. While those sections preoccupied Southerners then, today they are "dead letters." So, too, is Section 4, which precluded assumption of the Confederate debt, an issue largely resolved even before the amendment was submitted to the states. In short, the one section which was to become the foundation of so much of modern constitutional law was considered less important than the others—though that fact itself reveals much about the original understanding of its scope.

Third, the debaters usually focused on practical questions of politics, rather than on theoretical questions about the juristic meaning of the amendment's provisions. Strategic questions included the respective merits of submission, compromise, or defiance. Substantive questions included the respective merits of Negro suffrage and the appropriate roles of the state and national governments. While more specific analyses of Section 1 may be found, its meaning must be extracted largely from this general political debate.

Finally, the debate took place in parallel rather than in unison. Admittedly, events at the national level and in the other states affected the debate in each state. State leaders on all sides were in more or less constant communication with their respective allies in Washington. Each faction closely followed events in other states, and the interstate circulation of documents among sympathetic parties was common. Nevertheless, the debate in each state was shaped significantly by factors peculiar to it. The vagaries of political leadership, as well as the history of political factionalism in each state, naturally made a difference. So, too, did the ratio of blacks to whites, which varied from 55 percent to 45 percent in South Carolina to 25 percent to 75 percent in Tennessee.[22] The presence of a relatively large population of well-educated, free blacks in Louisiana and South Carolina influenced the debates there. The presence of Union troops in Arkansas, Louisiana, Tennessee, and Virginia long before the end of the war made a difference in those states, as governments sympathetic to the Union had already been formed there. In some states, specific political issues—like the *ab initio* and division movements in Texas—overshadowed the debate on the Fourteenth Amendment. Thus factors indigenous to the states necessarily complicate the search for an original understanding of the amendment and therefore require a state-by-state analysis of the debate.[23]

In the end, however, these differences did not produce a different understanding of the Fourteenth Amendment. The Southern debates reveal that its most ardent supporters and its fiercest critics shared a common understanding of its core commands. In state after state, those who studied and commented on the amendment raised the same questions and offered the same range of answers. The questions were simple. What rights did Section 1 guarantee blacks, and what powers was the national government given to enforce that guarantee? The answers were more complex and varied. While there was no universal agreement, a common answer does echo through the richly repetitive arguments that were made in every Southern state. Stripped of nuance, the answer was twofold. Section 1 embodied an equality of rights principle that guaranteed blacks the fundamental rights of a citizen and free person and the civil rights necessary to their exercise; Section 5 gave the federal government—principally, though not exclusively, Congress—the authority to intervene if a state failed to protect those rights. The historical context also clarifies two other understandings implicit in that answer. One, no one believed that Section 1 incorporated the Bill of Rights. Two, the proponents of the amendment anticipated that state governments would continue to exercise broad discretion in defining the incidents of the rights which were guaranteed.

Illuminating as this common understanding is, it does not provide definitive answers to every contemporary question about the meaning of the Fourteenth Amendment. This widely shared understanding nevertheless contradicts much of the Supreme Court's current Fourteenth Amendment jurisprudence. If the ratification debates in other states reflect a similar consensus, a major reassessment of that jurisprudence would seem to be required. Almost from the beginning, the Court has erred in its assessment of the original understanding. Pursuing that initial error erratically through the succeeding century, the Court appears to have created an amendment wholly different from the one it is obliged to interpret. If constitutional questions are never settled until they are settled in conformity with the original understanding,[24] many Fourteenth Amendment questions long thought settled must now be reopened.

NOTES

1. See, e.g., Michael Curtis, *No State Shall Abridge: The Fourteenth Amendment and the Bill of Rights* (Durham, N.C.: Duke University Press, 1986); Joseph James, *The Framing of the Fourteenth Amendment* (Macon, Ga.: Mercer University Press, 1984); Jacobus Ten Broeck, *Equal under Law* (New York: Collier, 1965) (originally published in 1951 under the title *The Anti-Slavery Origins of the Fourteenth Amendment*); Howard J. Graham, "The Early Anti-Slavery Backgrounds of the Fourteenth Amendment," *Wisconsin Law Review* (1950): 479, 610.

2. "All persons born or naturalized in the United States, and subject to the jurisdiction thereof, are citizens of the United States and of the State wherein they reside. No State shall make or enforce any law which shall abridge the privileges and immunities of citizens of the United States; nor shall any State deprive any person of life, liberty, or property, without due process of law; nor deny to any person within its jurisdiction the equal protection of the laws." U.S. Constitution, amend. 14, sec. 1.

3. "Congress shall have the power to enforce this amendment by appropriate legislation." U.S. Constitution, amend. 14, sec. 5.

4. *Slaughter-House Cases*, 83 U.S. 36 (1872).

5. The importance of state ratification debates has been acknowledged in other circumstances. The clearest instance, of course, is the ratification of the original Constitution. *The Federalist Papers*, the most frequently consulted source on the original understanding of the Constitution, is a collection of letters to newspapers, designed to influence the ratification vote in New York. Indeed, the views which the federalists and anti-federalists articulated during the ratification debates in the states are considered so illuminating that they have now been collected for ready reference. Alexander Hamilton, James Madison, and John Jay, *The Federalist Papers* (Introduction, Table of Contents, and Index of Ideas by Clinton Rositer) (New York: New American Library, 1961). Morton Borden, *The Antifederalist Papers* (East Lansing: Michigan State University Press, 1965). During oral

argument in the famous case of *McCulloch v. Maryland*, 17 U.S. 316 (1819), counsel for Maryland relied on Chief Justice John Marshall's own comments in the Virginia ratification convention, which he had attended as a delegate.

6. James E. Bond, "The Original Understanding of the Fourteenth Amendment in Illinois, Ohio, and Pennsylvania," *Akron Law Review* 18 (1985): 435, 436 ("Republican papers in these three states commonly ran the text of the 14th Amendment above the masthead on the second page under the heading 'Union Platform.'").

7. See, e.g., Eric Foner, *Nothing but Freedom: Emancipation and Its Legacy* (Baton Rouge: Louisiana State University Press, 1983). Eric Foner, *Reconstruction: America's Unfinished Revolution, 1863–1877* (New York: Harper & Row, 1973). C. Vann Woodward, ed., *Mary Chestnut's Civil War* (New Haven: Yale University Press, 1981). C. Vann Woodward, *The Burden of Southern History* (Baton Rouge: Louisiana State University Press, 1968). C. Vann Woodward, *Origins of the New South* (Baton Rouge: Louisiana State University Press, 1951).

8. Alfred B. Sears, "Presidential Address: Slavery and Retribution," *Southwestern Social Science Quarterly* 41 (1960): 3.

9. Hamilton J. Eckenrode, *The Political History of Virginia during the Reconstruction* (Baltimore: Johns Hopkins University Press, 1904), 43–44.

10. Ch. 200, 14 Stat. 173, 16 July 1866.

11. Ch. 31, 14 Stat. 27, 9 April 1866.

12. *MaComb Eagle*, 19 May 1866.

13. *Columbus Morning Journal*, 5 May 1866.

14. Earl M. Maltz, "Individual Rights and State Autonomy," *Harvard Journal of Law and Public Policy* 12 (1989): 163, 182 ("The [fourteenth] amendment was not seen as a vehicle for reallocating authority between the legislative and judicial branches. . . . While the concept of guaranteeing rights was important to the framers, the proper allocation of authority between the state and federal governments was of equal concern.").

15. During the fall 1866 elections, the Republican or, as it was more commonly called at that time, Union Party adopted the Fourteenth Amendment as its campaign platform. The Democratic Party rejected the Fourteenth Amendment and chose instead to support President Johnson's more lenient reconstruction policy. The Republicans praised the amendment because it would insure peaceful reunion. The Democratic Party denounced the amendment because it would insure continued conflict and disunion. In local party caucuses and conventions, the faithful adopted resolutions extolling or condemning the amendment. Every candidate for state or national office declared himself for or against it. On the stump, these candidates were obliged to explain themselves; and their explanations and the editorial commentary they provoked provide insight into the original understanding. Moreover, major figures in both parties campaigned throughout the North on behalf of their respective platforms. See generally Bond, "The Original Understanding of the Fourteenth Amendment."

16. Ch. 152, 14 Stat. 428, 2 March 1867; Ch. 6, 15 Stat. 2, 23 March 1867.

17. Foner, *Reconstruction*, 345.

18. *Charleston Mercury*, 5 February 1868.

19. See generally George R. Bentley, *A History of the Freedmen's Bureau* (Philadelphia: University of Pennsylvania Press, 1955); Donald G. Nieman, *To Set the Law in Motion: The Freedmen's Bureau and the Legal Rights of Blacks, 1865–1868* (Millwood, N.Y.: KTO Press, 1979); Paul S. Pierce, *The Freedmen's Bureau: A Chapter in the History of Reconstruction* (Iowa City: University of Iowa Press, 1904).

20. See generally Herman Belz, *A New Birth of Freedom: The Republican Party and Freedmen's Rights, 1861–1866* (Westport, Conn.: Greenwood Press, 1976).

21. Eric Foner captures this phenomenon in the following passage:

> In meetings of Union Leagues and the Heroes of America, long-standing class antagonisms and intrastate sectional rivalries were transmuted into the coin of nineteenth-century radicalism. Traditional regional demands, like an end to property qualifications for members of the North Carolina legislature, now merged with a retrospective denunciation of slavery as the foundation of a social order that had held "poor whites . . . as much under bondage" as blacks. Inspired by the hope that "the reign of the would be aristocracy is near at a close," upcountry white Republicanism took on a reforming fervor. "Now is the time," wrote a resident of the Georgia mountains, "for every man to come out and speak his principles publickly [*sic*] and vote for liberty as we have been in bondage long enough." (Foner, *Reconstruction*, 301)

22. John W. Burgess, *Reconstruction and the Constitution* (New York: C. Scribner's Sons, 1982), 146–47 ("Of the eleven states, only South Carolina, Mississippi, and Louisiana contained a black majority; blacks constituted roughly one quarter of the population of Texas, Tennessee, and Arkansas, 40 percent in Virginia and North Carolina, and a bit less than half in Alabama, Florida, and Georgia.").

23. There are very few studies of the state ratification debates on the Fourteenth Amendment. The most thorough is Joseph James's *The Framing of the Fourteenth Amendment* (Macon, Ga.: Mercer University Press, 1984). A political scientist, James concentrates on the political intrigue that surrounded the amendment's ratification rather than on the meaning attributed to its provisions during the ratification process. The best survey of the original understanding of the Fourteenth Amendment at the state level is contained in Charles Fairman's famous law review article, "Does the Fourteenth Amendment Incorporate the Bill of Rights?" *Stanford Law Review* 2 (1949): 5, in which he challenged Justice Hugo Black's incorporation thesis. Although the article focused primarily on the congressional debate and exclusively on the question of incorporation, Fairman did analyze the relevant official state documents on that question. An earlier work by Howard Flack also included some references to the state debates, but the primary focus of the book was, again, on the congressional debate. The most recent is a brief chapter in Curtis, *No State Shall Abridge*, 131–53. While each of these works is meritorious on its own terms, none thoroughly explores the understanding of those politicians and citizens who participated in the state ratification debates.

24. Whether the meaning of the Fourteenth Amendment ought to be fixed by the original understanding of its provisions is also a much disputed issue, at least among academic theorists. See generally Lawrence Tribe, *American Constitutional Law* (Mineola, N.Y.: Foundation Press, 1978), 1–14. The Supreme Court, however, has consistently conceded that the meaning of the Fourteenth Amendment must be derived from the original understanding. In *Brown v. Board of Education*, 345 U.S. 972 (1954), it ordered counsel to answer the following question: "What evidence is there that . . . the state legislatures and conventions which ratified the Fourteenth Amendment contemplated or did not contemplate, understand or did not understand, that it would abolish segregation in public schools?" Moreover, most judges still formally acknowledge that their interpretation of the amendment's language is circumscribed by the intentions of those who drafted and ratified it. Cf. *Richmond v. J. A. Croson Co.*, 488 U.S. 469, 109 S. Ct. 706 (1989); *Adarand Constructors, Inc. v. Federico Pena, et al.*, 115 S. Ct. 2097 (1995).

This was also the view of the framers. See, e.g., Lance Banning, *The Sacred Fire of Liberty: James Madison and the Founding of the Federal Republic* (Ithaca, N.Y.: Cornell University Press, 1996), 371 (quoting Madison as saying he interpreted the Constitution "as understood by the Convention that produced and recommended it and particularly by the state conventions that adopted it").

2

Ratification in Tennessee

If half a nigger can do so well, what would a whole one do?

—Mulatto lawyer from Washington, D.C.,
exhorting a group of black Tennesseans in early 1865
to demand their rights

The last of the Confederate states to secede, Tennessee was the first to be re-stored to the Union. Alone among the Southern states, it ratified the Fourteenth Amendment immediately; it alone escaped congressional Reconstruction. From the beginning, the Joint Committee on Reconstruction had recognized that Tennessee occupied a position different from all the other Confederate states.[1]

What made Tennessee different? When the war ended, it already had an effectively functioning, popularly elected government that supported the Union.[2] In early January 1865, Union loyalists, meeting in Nashville, proposed amendments to the state constitution that abolished slavery, declared secession treason, and invalidated all other rebel legislation. Voters overwhelmingly approved these amendments in February; the following month they elected a legislature and governor.[3] Former Whigs dominated the legislature.[4] The governor—"Parson" Brownlow—advocated such proscriptive policies that Southern conservatives came to view him, along with "Beast" Butler and Thad Stevens, as the unholy trinity of radicalism.[5]

Additionally, the Brownlow government adopted policies and made decisions that impressed Congress. That was their purpose, and they shrewdly anticipated Congress's sentiment on conditions for restoration.[6] They also cemented Republican control of the government and extended basic civil rights to the freedmen in a state where a majority of whites remained attached to the "lost cause," where blacks constituted only a quarter of the population, and where the Unionists were as negrophobic as the former slaveholders.[7]

The debate over these policies and decisions established the context within which Tennessee evaluated the Fourteenth Amendment. In that context, the state's ratification of the amendment was but the penultimate step in its restoration strategy. More importantly, for contemporary purposes, the context illuminates Tennessee's understanding of the Fourteenth Amendment.

Three major groups participated in this two-year dialogue on restoration, and each viewed the Fourteenth Amendment differently. The least influential of the groups—the freedmen—ardently embraced it as a guarantee of the equal rights which they came to believe were their birthright as citizens.[8] Initially, their pleas, though forthright, had been more cautious. On the day the state Constitutional Convention opened in 1865, the "colored citizens of Nashville" petitioned the delegates to abolish slavery, lest their former masters "make every effort to bring them back to bondage." While they did not yet insist on being made citizens, they asserted that they knew "the duties of a good citizen" and avowed their readiness to perform them "cheerfully." They asked only that they "be put in a position in which [they] could discharge them more effectively." Specifically, they prayed for the right to vote and the right to testify in court.[9]

This view reflected the position adopted by the National Convention of Colored Men, which had met in Syracuse, New York, in the fall of 1864. Representatives from Tennessee's small free black community had attended the convention; and upon their return, those from Nashville organized a mock presidential election "to demonstrate the readiness of black Tennesseans to assume the responsibilities of citizenship."[10] Their determination to gain the right to vote was reinforced by Emancipation Day celebrations in Nashville two months later. The principal speaker, a mulatto lawyer from Washington, D.C., urged his black audience to concentrate on self-help and self-development. But he also observed that "no . . . real progress could be made in Tennessee until *all* . . . enjoyed the rights and responsibilities of citizenship."[11]

Still later in 1865, "a number of 'colored gentlemen'" called a State Convention of the Colored People of Tennessee to adopt measures "to . . . secure the 'political liberty and equality in Tennessee of the black man.'"[12] The freedmen had been disappointed that the first session of the 1865 legislature had ignored their pleas for suffrage and protection. These pleas had come in the form of petitions from black Nashville businessmen, who complained that city officials were enforcing antebellum laws that prohibited free blacks from operating any licensed business, and from a group of Knoxville blacks, who asked to be given the chance "to prove themselves" in the jury box and at the ballot box.[13] Although there was much discussion of the issues raised by these petitions, the legislature postponed any action on the "colored question" until its fall session. Frustrated by this inaction and concerned by the racist tenor of much of the discussion that had accompanied the legislative debate on the "colored question,"[14] black Tennesseans now demanded all the rights of citizenship. To that end, this August 1865 convention appointed a central committee "to conduct the fight for the attainment of political privileges and civil rights."[15]

The committee pursued that fight vigorously. While Tennessee blacks welcomed passage of the Civil Rights Act and the Freedmen's Bureau Bill,[16] they concentrated their efforts on securing favorable state legislation when the second session of the legislature opened on October 2, 1865. That session finally agreed to permit Negro testimony in the courts—though the act contained a proviso, declaring "that this act shall not be so construed as to give colored persons the right to vote, hold office or sit on juries in this state."[17]

Later in the session the legislature adopted what amounted to a state civil rights bill. The act provided:

[P]ersons of color have the right to make and enforce contracts, to sue and be sued, to be parties and give evidence, to inherit, to have full and equal benefits of all laws and proceedings for the security of persons and estate, and shall not be subject to any other or different punishment, pains or penalty, for the commission of any act or offence, than such as are prescribed for white persons committing like acts or offences; that all persons of color, being blind, deaf and dumb, lunatics, paupers or apprentices, shall have the full and perfect benefit and application of all laws regulating and providing for white persons, being blind or deaf and dumb or lunatics or paupers or either (in asylums for their benefit) and apprentices.[18]

Several other laws were passed that guaranteed blacks equal treatment, including one which "provided 'that free persons of color may exercise and pursue all or any business not in violation of law, when they may obtain such license under the laws of this State as is applicable to the exercise of such privilege by free white persons.'"[19] Though the legislature once again refused to enfranchise blacks, it had essentially conformed Tennessee's laws to the requirements of the Fourteenth Amendment a month before it was asked to ratify the amendment.

Conservatives had resisted and protested every one of these developments, regarding each in turn as the camel's nose of racial mongrelization and social degradation. For example, Representative H. P. Murphy opposed the Negro testimony bill, explaining that "the two races could not and ought not to live together with equal rights and privileges." He was sure "that the Negro, if given a portion of his rights, would strive to win full equality with the whites." Consequently, Murphy urged that the blacks should be colonized outside the United States "in some place congenial to their nature."[20]

Conservatives detested the Freedmen's Bureau,[21] and they certainly did not welcome the Civil Rights Bill. The latter was denounced as the "opening wedge" in the radical program of "negro equality and amalgamation."[22] Indeed, the Civil Rights Bill was condemned for guaranteeing all manner of rights to blacks, despite its clearly limited scope:

Are we to have negroes representing this government as United States minister at the Courts of France and England? The civil rights bill says that we are.

Shall a negro supercede Grant as General-in-chief of the United States Army? The civil rights bill says that he can do so.

Shall our children see a negro in the Presidential chair? The civil rights bill provides for such a contingency.

Shall the negroes sit in Congress, in the Cabinet and other high stations side by side with white men? The civil rights bill says that he may.

Shall negroes intermingle with our refined ladies in steaming hot theatres, ballrooms and opera houses?—The civil rights bill declares that they must.

Are we to have negroes filling the position of post captains in the United States Navy? The civil rights bill says that we are.

Is this a white man's government for white men? The civil rights bill says that it is not.

Shall the negro intermingle with our daughters, and take an equal place in our household? The civil rights bill says that he shall.

Shall the farms of the great West and the whole country be owned by negroes and white labor made subservient to negro proprietorship?—The civil rights bill provides for this condition of things.

Is the negro five times better than a white man that the former should vote immediately, while the latter has to undergo five years' probation if he brings his skill, labor and money to this country from abroad? The civil rights bill declares that the negro is five times better.[23]

Beyond the rights which it allegedly guaranteed, the Civil Rights Bill was also condemned for giving too much authority to the national government. Thus another observer insisted that the Civil Rights Bill was misnamed, asserting it would "destroy liberty by creating a despotism."[24]

These reactions to the Civil Rights Bill are important for two reasons. First, they illustrate the attitudinal filters through which conservative white Tennesseans would sift the meaning of Sections 1 and 5 of the Fourteenth Amendment. That was especially true because, second, Section 1 of the amendment was widely thought to incorporate not the Bill of Rights, but the Civil Rights Bill.[25]

Conservative Tennesseans had made their general views clear on the occasion of General Washington's birthday when they gathered one thousand strong in Nashville. They declared:

[They were] prepared to aid in extending to the free persons of color such protection as shall secure them the undisturbed enjoyment of all the blessings of freedom; and of conceding to them all the civil and political rights that may be compatible with the best interest of both races. [They] insist, however, that this subject belongs exclusively to the people of the State, and that the same has not been transferred to Congress.[26]

In their formal resolutions, they expanded on the last point:

That the people of the respective States have the right to regulate their own domestic affairs as long as they act consistently with the constitution; hence this opposition to any attempt on the part of Congress to force negro suffrage upon the Southern States, correctly believing that such policy is calculated to widen rather than to heal the breach between the North and South, and to harm rather than benefit the negro.[27]

In other words, conservative Tennesseans would concede civil equality. Even conservatives recognized that blacks should enjoy the government's protection in the exercise of their civil rights—that is, the right to contract and buy and sell. More generally, conservative Tennesseans conceded that all persons should enjoy the protection of the law in their enjoyment of life, liberty, and property.[28] One commentator stated the policy succinctly: Negroes should be put in the same position as the nonvoting white man.[29]

The reason why conservative Tennesseans drew the line at political equality was clear: "[T]he colored race must be held in subordinate position politically; . . . otherwise, the next step must be an indiscriminate social admixture and general decay."[30] The *Nashville Union and American* described that "indiscriminate social admixture" as "mingling . . . at church, in the ballroom, in the theater, in the concert hall, in railroad cars, in the parlor, and at the hotels and watering places."[31] The *Cleveland Banner* described the "general decay" as "miscegenation and amalgamation."[32] The conservative congressman-elect from Memphis stated the position bluntly: "[W]e will not consent to seeing our race degraded to an equality with [the Negro]."[33] Thus it was declared that "the people of the South are willing to extend to the negro the fullest protection to life, liberty and property, but equal political and social privileges, he can no more enjoy here than in the midst of his aristocratic Northern friends."[34]

In short, conservatives objected to the Fourteenth Amendment because they feared Congress might insist under Section 5 of the amendment that privileges and immunities included political and social rights. Seen in this light, the amendment was a "[r]adical *coup d'etat*"[35] that would destroy "the last vestiges of the rights of the states."[36] The editor of the *Republican Banner* thus concluded that those who supported the amendment wanted "to convert one half of the country into an oligarchy."[37]

Though most Unionists shared the same racial attitudes as conservatives, a majority of them had reluctantly embraced the acts adopted by the 1865 legislature for two reasons. First, they were repeatedly told that Congress would not restore Tennessee if it failed to (1) guarantee its newest citizens the privileges and immunities of that status and (2) insure their equal and fair treatment. For example, the *Nashville Daily Press-Times* warned those who opposed the Negro testimony bill that "[n]othing is more certain than that no Congressional delegation will be received at Washington from any State which refuses to allow Negro testimony. On this point Congress and the president are in perfect harmony."[38] Second, the Unionists finally realized that the Republican Party could not retain control of the government without black support and, ultimately, black votes.[39]

A small group of liberal white Unionists rejected these pragmatic justifications. The smallest of the three factions, they shared the views of most black Tennesseans. They endorsed "[t]he doctrine of equal rights [as] the cornerstone of the American Union."[40] They insisted, for example, on equal punishments for blacks and whites for the same crimes.[41] Observed one editorialist wryly: "If there are idle freedmen in the South, it is equally true that there are more idle white persons who need the gentle constraint of a vagrant law and apprenticeship, quite as much as the freedman."[42] This "liberal" coalition favored a free wage labor system, calling it a "short cut to reconstruction,"[43] and a system of common schools where "the children of the rich and the poor, the high and the low, meet up on perfect equality."[44] Even among this group, some doubted whether schools should be racially integrated. In urging the legislature to pass a bill authorizing free schools, the *Nashville Daily Press-Times* pointed out that local school boards would be permitted to establish "special schools for colored children."[45] Nevertheless, this coalition urged adoption of the Fourteenth Amendment to insure "equality of all citizens," which, they argued, was "the only basis for a peaceful society."[46]

Others outside the state were also urging Tennessee to ratify the amendment. On the House floor, Congressman Bingham, who had served on the Tennessee subcommittee of the Joint Reconstruction Committee, invited Tennessee to be the first.[47] Shortly after Congress approved the amendment, forty more members of Congress endorsed Bingham's suggestion. Some Northern papers hinted that Tennessee might even be readmitted before Congress adjourned if it acted immediately.[48]

Governor Brownlow needed no prompting. On June 19, 1866, he summoned members of the legislature to "the State Capitol, on Wednesday, July 19, 1866, to ratify certain amendments to the Constitution." In his proclamation, he summarized their content "briefly":

1. Equal protection of all citizens in the enjoyment of life, liberty and property.
2. That classes who are disfranchised without crime shall not be taken into account in fixing the basis of Federal representation.
3. That certain persons who have proved themselves dangerous to the peace of the country shall not be eligible to office.
4. The validity of the National debt shall not be questioned, while all debts incurred in aid of the rebellion are illegal and void.[49]

Brownlow's summary of Section 1 emphasized equality of rights rather than any guarantee of specific rights. That emphasis is important because it implied that the legislature was free to define rights, subject only to the constraint that any such right be extended to all, rather than that the legislature was bound to conform its acts, for example, to specific substantive guarantees found in the federal Constitution.

"Brownlow has blown his horn," complained one of his many critics, "and the dogs are on their way to kennel."[50] By the time the "dogs" arrived, the governor had prepared a fuller explanation of the amendment for them. In his message to the legislature, Brownlow once again invoked equality as the core concept guaranteed by the Fourteenth Amendment; but he did so in terms that echoed conservative sentiments about the appropriate scope of the protection to which blacks were entitled:

By the first section, equal protection in the enjoyment of life, liberty, property, is guaranteed to all citizens. Practically, this affects mainly the negro, who having been emancipated by the rebellion, and having lost that protection which the interest of the master gave him, became by the very laws of nature, entitled to the civil rights of the citizen, and to the means of enforcing those rights.[51]

In this explanation the governor does recognize that Section 1 guarantees certain natural rights as well. The governor did not even hint, however, that Section 1 incorporated the Bill of Rights. Presumably, the natural rights he had in mind were those set out in the Declaration of Independence. His further explanation also reflects the view that the section "constitutionalized" the Civil Rights Bill.

Although the governor proceeded to analyze Sections 2, 3, and 4, he did not mention Section 5 specifically. He had said, however, in discussing Section 1, that the freedmen deserved to have the rights which it guaranteed protected; and he left no doubt from whom they would have to be protected: "To deny this to him, would be to place his life, property and labor in the power of every unfriendly local authority, or evil disposed person, and would be an instance of barbarism unworthy of the age."[52]

The "barbarism" of the Memphis riots was doubtless still fresh in the governor's mind. Between April 30 and May 3, white mobs rampaged through that city's "nigger town," destroying four black churches and twelve black schools, wounding more than seventy blacks and killing forty-six.[53] Though Memphis police knew the identity of many of the white rioters, they made no arrests; and a local judge later admitted to a congressional investigating committee that no Memphis jury would have convicted white men of crimes committed against blacks during the riots.[54]

While proponents of the amendment consistently downplayed the significance of Section 5, they nevertheless understood its potential importance, particularly in light of the Memphis riots. As Governor Brownlow told a group of black school children at the "Colored High School" in Nashville in late January: "If General Thomas [the local military commander] were to withdraw his bayonets from this city, this colored school could not exist one week; nay, more, if the Federal bayonets were all withdrawn from this State, a rebel mob would drive me and this Legislature out of Nashville in one week."[55]

The proposed amendment was referred to committee; but no report was issued, and little substantive debate occurred. Members of the legislature were nevertheless familiar with the amendment. After all, it had been discussed in Tennessee long before Brownlow convened the legislature in early July. Like other Southerners, Tennesseans had followed its progress through Congress closely. As early as January 1866, local newspapers were predicting the fate of its forerunners.[56] Early in February the press speculated that the radical program would include a provision requiring that all national and state laws "apply equitably without regard to color."[57] By the end of April, it was predicting that the Reconstruction Committee would "approve an amendment forbidding all discrimination on the basis of color" with respect to "civil rights and suffrage."[58] The text of the Fourteenth Amendment and the companion Report of the Reconstruction Committee were, of course, both widely published.[59]

Conservative legislators sought to defer ratification through a variety of stratagems, but the majority simply voted to table each in turn. The conservatives protested, and their protest constitutes a kind of minority report on the amendment. After complaining that "the majority in the Senate have manifested a striking disregard for the opinions of the minority" and "laid [every amendment] upon the table, without affording its friends an opportunity of discussing its merits, or fully explaining its object," the minority set out the following specific objections:

- The proposed amendment to the constitution is couched in language ambiguous, uncertain and liable to various constructions, concealing a purpose to strike down and overthrow the legitimate rights of the States, and consolidate all power in the hands of a great centralized Government. Entertaining these views in regard to the whole proposition, the undersigned were unwilling to see it ratified and become a part of the Constitution without more qualifying conditions. We accordingly proposed a proviso to the resolution adopting the amendment, by which it was provided that said constitutional amendment should not be construed so as to confer upon negroes or free persons of color the right to exercise the elective franchise, to hold office, sit upon juries, or intermarry with white persons, or be so construed so as to abridge or diminish the rights of the States under the present Constitution. This amendment was rejected by the Senate.

- as the Congress of the United States, had refused to permit the State of Tennessee to have any participation in the administration of the general government, or any part in the passage of the amendment, that the Legislature had no power, with its present recognized relations to the government, as defined by the present Congress, to take any action upon said amendment.

- admitting that the amendment had been duly passed by Congress, and that the Legislature had the power to ratify the same, still, as the State had no representation in Congress, and the present Legislature had no direct instructions from the people, that it would be a palpable violation of every principle of free government, to force upon the people of Tennessee such an amendment to the Constitution, without first having by some means, obtained their consent and approbation. It was therefore proposed by the undersigned, to submit said amendment to the people for their ratification or rejection, as instructive to the Legislature, to be acted upon at the regular adjourned meeting in November next. This was also rejected by the Senate.

- that the proposed amendment was not passed by Congress in pursuance of the requirement of the seventh section and first article of the Constitution of the United States, which requires all laws, resolutions and orders, to be submitted to the President for his approbation or rejection, giving him a qualified veto of the passage of all acts of Congress and all concurrent resolutions. And it being an undisputed fact, that the resolution of Congress proposing the said amendment, has never been submitted to the President in the form above prescribed, we therefore believe that the Legislature of Tennessee has no right to act upon said amendment, until it has full assurance that such amendment has been properly passed by Congress, under all the forms prescribed by the Constitution.

- that, although the Legislature might wholly ignore all right of the people to instruct them, and their consent and approbation to said amendment; and, although they might force upon the people an amendment to the constitution, materially changing their rights, privileges and immunities as a people, still that a decent respect for the opinions of mankind demands that there should be a full Legislature. That there should be members from every county and district, as provided by the constitution and laws of the State, when in fact it is well known, not only to the undersigned, but to the honorable Senate, that there is at least one fourth of the Legislative districts of the State unrepresented in the present Assembly.[60]

Putting to one side their various federal and state constitutional arguments, the conservatives had only *one* substantive objection: the amendment would give Congress the power to grant Negroes political and social rights.

Outside the legislative chambers, opponents echoed these same concerns. They raised two specters. First, Section 1 might confer political rights such as the right to vote and to hold office on blacks because such rights could be considered privileges and immunities of citizenship. Opponents conceded that Section 1 did not explicitly confer political equality on blacks. Rather, they asserted that the concept of privileges and immunities was "ambiguous."[61] These critics never suggested, however, that that ambiguity might permit arguments that the amendment guaranteed all the provisions of the Bill of Rights. They did speculate that it might embrace the right to vote, to hold office, and to sit on juries.[62] Its purported ambiguity was one of the chief reasons Senator Frazier, an implacable opponent, pleaded as justification for refraining from early approval.[63] Not once, moreover, did an opponent suggest that the due process clause might prove to be an "ambiguous" source of unarticulated rights, much less that it incorporated the Bill of Rights, though—with some prescience—critics did worry that the amendment left to corrupt officeholders the right to interpret its provisions as they wished.[64]

Sophisticated opponents understood that the real danger lurked in subsequent congressional definition of privileges and immunities. A former state legislator, for example, urged rejection, arguing that Section 1 had to be read in connection with Section 5, which would permit Congress to confer voting rights on "colored citizens."[65] The second specter—consolidation—was thus the core complaint against Section 1. As a mass meeting in Montgomery County declared, the amendment "arrogated" to the "general government control of matters purely local" which "heretofore [have] been recognized as subject alone to State authority."[66] Similarly, citizens at another mass meeting at the courthouse in Greenville on July 2, "instructed" their legislator to vote against the "said amendments, and especially the first section" because it "obliterates all political distinctions between the races" and "would interfere with the reserved rights of the States."[67]

Supporters of the amendment dismissed these fears as exaggerated. The most enthusiastic and widely read Republican newspaper in the state certainly made no extravagant claims about the scope of Section 1: "The first section is so clear, and so fair on its face that it needs no argument to establish its wisdom and excellence. It is essentially a part of the Constitution already."[68] There is no reason to suppose that the newspaper, when it said that Section 1 was already part of the Constitution, was referring to the Bill of Rights. The newspaper was simply acknowledging that the Constitution already contained a privileges and immunities clause and a due process clause. This interpretation was certainly consistent with the views of Judge Houk, who spoke at an Independence Day rally in Nashville. He said: "The first section simply declares who are citizens of the United States. [It settles that] all persons born within our jurisdiction of the United States . . . are entitled to equal rights before the law and the protection of the Government against all oppressors."[69]

In the end, Unionist legislators "out-stratagemed" their conservative opponents. After the Senate approved the amendment fourteen to six on July 11, conservative representatives refused to attend the House sessions, depriving it of a quorum. On July 19, Brownlow had some of the "no-shows" rounded up and forcibly taken to the House, where the clerk recorded the resulting vote as forty-three to eleven in favor of the amendment.[70] The next day Brownlow informed Secretary of War Stanton and the clerk of the Senate that Tennessee had ratified the amendment.[71] Congress promptly admitted the Tennessee delegation to their seats. Tennessee was restored to the Union.

A month later Brownlow addressed the Southern Loyalist Convention in Philadelphia:

We have but one more law to pass, and that is, a law enfranchising the Negro, and will do it next winter. We have two reasons for doing this: The first is a selfish one; it is necessary for sixty or seventy thousand votes to kick the beam, to weigh the balance against rebelism. The second is because it is proper and just, and we will simply be returning to where we were in 1833.[72]

True to his word, Governor Brownlow urged the legislature that met that fall to enfranchise all male citizens, regardless of color.[73] Although he had once denounced Negro suffrage,[74] he now praised the Negro for his general intelligence and aptitude to learn.[75] Moreover, he reminded the legislature that under Section 2 of the Fourteenth Amendment, Tennessee would have nine representatives rather than six if it extended the right of suffrage to its black citizens.[76]

Shortly before Brownlow left for Philadelphia, black Tennesseans once again assembled in convention in Nashville. They resolved to thank Governor Brownlow and the General Assembly for ratifying the Fourteenth Amendment and petitioned both for the right to vote and serve on juries.[77] Apparently, they did not assume the Fourteenth Amendment guaranteed the latter. In the same vein, they rejected an amendment that would have included a claim to hold political office with their request to serve on juries.[78] This reticence to demand equal rights presumably pleased General Clinton B. Fisk, who counseled the convention that the legislature had made them equal before the law "as regards crime." He believed that that was sufficient "for the present."[79] While the general was not construing the Fourteenth Amendment, his remarks are consistent with the understanding that it would permit reasonable legislative classifications, including some racial ones.

The legislature acquiesced in the governor's suggestion and the pleas of its black citizens for voting rights in late February 1867. As always, the legislature insisted on adding a cautionary note: Section 16 provided that the suffrage bill should not be construed so as to allow Negro men to hold office or to sit on juries.[80] Before it adjourned on March 10, 1867, the legislature also adopted a common schools law. While it required equal access to an education, it did not require integration. The committee that drafted the law "envisioned separate schools for blacks and whites."[81] Tennessee thus completed its self-imposed reconstruction just as Congress fixed its more punitive reconstruction on the other ten Southern states. All of them had defiantly rejected the Fourteenth Amendment, ignoring the advice that Tennessee so assiduously followed.

Brownlow won reelection in 1867. Black votes provided much of his margin of victory.[82] Obviously, blacks had not deserted the Republican Party for its failure to guarantee them the right to hold office and sit on juries—as some observers had predicted.[83] Still, black leaders were disappointed; and they vowed to continue the good fight until they enjoyed full equality before the law.[84] In the wake of the Republicans' sweeping election victory in 1867, blacks did demand full political equality, adequate funding for public education, aid for the aged and infirm, and equal access to public education.[85]

The legislature finally, albeit still reluctantly, removed the statutory strictures against blacks serving on juries and holding office.[86] For a short season, blacks did serve on a few juries; for an even briefer season, a small number of blacks held public office, though the offices were invariably local and minor.[87] The legislature also passed a public accommodations law barring discrimination on common carriers, and it repealed laws that (1) prevented railroads from hiring black engineers and (2) prohibited blacks from becoming lawyers.[88]

The Brownlow Republicans, who were never passionately committed to black rights, were loath to share political power with blacks, however. After Brownlow accepted appointment to the Senate in 1869, his more conservative successor did not enforce disfranchisement, the Klan discouraged blacks from going to the polls, and conservatives regained control of the state government in 1869 and immediately began to dismantle much of the legislation enacted during Brownlow's administration.[89] Conservatives dominated the 1870 constitutional convention that drafted Tennessee's new constitution. While it maintained the formal guarantees of equal rights, it added two sections that were a harbinger of

Jim Crow. One required segregated schools, and the other prohibited mixed marriages.[90] Only four years after ratifying an amendment that embodied the philosophy of the Declaration of Independence, Tennessee enthusiastically embraced racial apartheid. Doubtless most of its white citizens considered the state redeemed.

In the wake of these decisions, Congress was asked to consider imposing a "new" reconstruction on Tennessee, like it had on Georgia. A black delegation from the state called on President Grant to explain their perilous condition, and they testified before the Reconstruction Committee.[91] There were rumors that Brownlow's successor, Governor DeWitt Senter, might resign to protest the actions of the legislature and the constitutional convention, or that he planned to request federal troops.[92] Congress declined to intervene, and the governor took no action to help those black Tennesseans whose votes had put him in office. Thus did their congressional protectors and state allies abandon black Tennesseans to the tender mercies of those who despised them.

NOTES

1. The subcommittee report is quoted in Alrutheus A. Taylor, *The Negro in Tennessee, 1865–1880* (Spartanburg, S.C.: Associated Publishers, 1941), 11.

2. Unlike the loyal government of Virginia, Tennessee's government controlled a substantial portion of the state, and its legislature had representatives from most areas of the state. It was nevertheless wholly dependent for its survival on the presence of Union troops, who had overrun much of the state in 1862. See generally Stanley J. Folmsbee, *Tennessee: A Short History* (Knoxville: University of Tennessee Press, 1969), 329–49.

3. See generally Thomas B. Alexander, *Political Reconstruction in Tennessee* (New York: Russell & Russell, 1968), 45–48.

4. Thomas B. Alexander, "Whiggery and Reconstruction in Tennessee," *Journal of Southern History* 16 (1950): 291, 294.

5. Brownlow's vitriolic condemnations of rebels were savage. Cooper, "Parson Brownlow: A Study of Reconstruction in Tennessee," *Southwestern Bulletin* 19 (1908): 3, 6 ("He could express more vituperativeness and scorching hate than any half a dozen men that ever appeared in American politics."). See also Eugene G. Feistman, "Radical Disfranchisement and the Restoration of Tennessee, 1865–1866," *Tennessee Historical Quarterly* 12 (1953): 135, 151 (Brownlow was "The first great vindictive of this era"). An example of the Brownlow style is his description of former Governor Harris, on whose head Brownlow had placed a bounty soon after assuming office:

> His complexion is sallow, his eyes are dark and penetrating—a perfect index to the heart of a traitor—with the scowl and frown of a demon resting upon his brow. The study of mischief and the practice of crime have brought upon him premature baldness and a gray beard. With brazen faced impudence, he talks loudly and boastingly about the overthrow of the Yankee army and entertains no doubt but that the South will achieve her independence. He chews tobacco rapidly and is inordinately fond of liquor. In his moral structure he is an unscrupulous man, steeped to the chin in personal and political profligacy—now about lost to all sense of shame, honor, with a heart reckless of social duty and fatally bent

upon mischief. If captured he will be found lurking in the rebel strongholds of Alabama, Mississippi, or Georgia, and in female society, alleging with the sheep-faced modesty of a virtuous man that it is not a wholesome state of public senti-ment, or of taste, that forbids the indiscriminate mixing together of married men and women. (*Proclamation Book* 2–3 [Tennessee State Archives])

Brownlow later recommended the repeal of the bounty on the ground that "the state is likely to be called upon, at any day, for this reward, and in return she would have noth-ing to show for the outlay." James W. Patton, *Unionism and Reconstruction in Tennessee* (1934; reprinted Gloucester, Mass.: Peter Smith), 97. Not surprisingly, conservative Southern papers routinely denounced Brownlow and invariably warned their readers that events in Tennessee would be replicated wherever radicals got control of the govern-ment. See generally Ellis M. Coulter, *William G. Brownlow, Fighting Parson of the Southern Highlands* (Chapel Hill: University of North Carolina Press, 1937).

6. See, e.g., *Nashville Democrat*, 21 June 1866 (Tennessee will probably be readmitted if it ratifies the Fourteenth Amendment because the state is controlled by radicals).

7. General Fisk, the head of the Freedmen's Bureau in Tennessee, advised the Joint Committee that the loyal eastern Tennesseans were extremely hostile to Negroes. Report of the Joint Committee on Reconstruction (title page missing) (n.p., 1866), 112–13 (document held by Tennessee State Library and Archives). See also J. Walker, "The Negro in Tennessee during the Reconstruction Period" (M.A. thesis, University of Ten-nessee, 1933), 14.

Judge Shackleford, advocating the adoption of the abolition amendment to the state constitution, doubtless expressed the "liberal view" of most Tennessee Unionists when he said:

You are told by the enemies of the Government the Federal authorities . . . will make the negro your equal, giving him social and political rights. Those who make such statements know them to be false, or are so profoundly ignorant that they are unworthy to be freemen. . . .

The negro if freed will fall within the laws governing his race. He is inferior to the white man, and will be controlled and governed by him, subject to such laws as may be proposed for his government. No one wants to give him equal rights, and in a social position equality cannot be attained. The God of nature has placed His fiat upon it, and no power on earth can make him the equal of the Anglo-Saxon; but as christian men we can elevate them in the scale of human be-ings. . . . They are human beings, with immortal souls, and as such, it is our duty as the superior race, to control, govern and elevate them from the degraded situa-tion in which they are. (*Nashville Daily Union*, 11 February 1865 [quoted in Al-exander, *Political Reconstruction in Tennessee*, 47])

8. Taylor, *The Negro in Tennessee*, 21.

9. Ibid., 2.

10. W. McBride, "Blacks and the Race Issue in Tennessee Politics, 1865–1876" (Ph.D. diss., Vanderbilt University, 1989), 24. (Although local Nashville papers failed to report the results of that mock election, the *New Orleans Tribune* reported it as 3,193 for Lin-coln and one for McClellan.)

11. Ibid., 27.

12. Taylor, *The Negro in Tennessee*, 8.

13. "Petitions," Tennessee Senate (1866) (microfilmed documents held by the Tennes-see Library and Archives).

14. The Senate had adopted a resolution to "avoid legislating too much on the subject of colored persons until next session"; and the House passed a bill that would have been Tennessee's Black Code had the Senate acquiesced. The passage of the bill in the House drew sharp criticism from Northern commentators, who characterized it as an attempt to reimpose slavery. See, e.g., *Harper's Weekly*, 10 June 1865 (it will reduce freedmen to serfdom); *Washington Chronicle*, 14 June 1865 (it is an attempt to reestablish slavery).

15. Taylor, *The Negro in Tennessee*, 9.

16. After Johnson vetoed the Freedmen's Bureau Bill, blacks rallied in Nashville to support Congress. Recalling the president's promise to be a Moses to the black community, one speaker declared that "Moses had betrayed the people's trust" and that they must now turn to "Joshua, Governor Brownlow, to lead them to the promised land of equality." Many white Tennesseans also supported the Bureau's activities in Tennessee. See, e.g., *Memphis Argus*, 9 August 1865:

> We regard the organization of the Freedmen's Bureau as one of the best measures that has been applied to the South since the close of the rebellion. It has already accomplished much in this end of the State through the efficiency of the agents employed to carry out the design. The chaotic condition of the labor system is being rapidly reduced to order. It gives the employer the means of compelling the fulfillment of engagements on the part of employees. It gives the employee the means of exacting justice from the employer. It organizes, and reduces to system the heterogeneous mass that before, was rolling and vibrating around the country. It prevents the collection of swarms of idlers and vagrants around military posts. It measures out justice with an equal hand. . . . The Superintendent of the Bureau and his subordinates in this district, leave no opportunity unimproved to impress upon the Freedmen the duties and responsibilities devolving upon them if they do not do their duty fully and justly, promising them at the same time protection in their just rights.

17. Acts, 34th Tenn. Gen. Ass., Adj. Sess. 1865–66, Chap. 59, p. 82.

18. Ibid., Chap. 40, p. 65.

19. Ibid., Chap. 58, pp. 22–23.

20. *Nashville Daily Union*, 2 December 1865. Brownlow himself had also suggested "providing [blacks] a separate and appropriate amount of territory, and settling them down permanently as a nation of freedmen." McBride, "Blacks and the Race Issue," 39.

21. See generally Paul D. Phillips, "White Reaction to the Freedmen's Bureau in Tennessee," *Tennessee Historical Quarterly* 25 (1966): 50.

22. *Paris Post-Intelligencer*, 20 April 1866. Tennesseans insisted, as did other Southerners, that "[t]his antipathy to practical Negro equality is as common to the masses of the North as to those of the South." *Nashville Dispatch*, 4 May 1866.

23. *Cleveland Banner*, 7 April 1866.

24. *Cleveland Banner*, 31 March 1866.

25. Cf. *Republican Banner*, 9 June 1866 (amendment contains nothing new).

26. *Fayetteville Observer*, 1 March 1866.

27. Ibid.

28. Ibid.

29. *Nashville Union*, 13 February 1866. These views were by no means universal, however. The editor of the *Republican Banner* (1 June 1866) recommended that "negroes . . . [be compelled] to engage in coarse common labor [and punished for] dere-

liction of duty . . . with sufficient severity to make . . . them productive laborers." *Nashville Republican Banner*.

30. See generally Taylor, *The Negro in Tennessee*, 21–22.

31. *Nashville Union and American*, 27 June 1866.

32. *Cleveland Banner*, 30 June 1866.

33. *Nashville Dispatch*, 4 July 1866.

34. Cf. the remarks of Congressman-elect John Leftwich, quoted in Taylor, *The Negro in Tennessee*, 22 ("We do not object to seeing the Negro, if he is able, come up to a perfect equality with our race, but we will not consent to seeing our race degraded to an equality with him.").

35. *Nashville Daily Gazette*, 11 June 1866.

36. *Republican Banner*, 20 June 1866.

37. *Republican Banner*, 11 July 1866.

38. *Nashville Daily Press-Times*, 22 November 1865. Cf. *Nashville Daily Union*, 22 October 1865 ("Negro testimony [will not] place blacks upon equality with whites but that the former [are not] so ignorant and debased that their exercise of this privilege would endanger the peace and security of society. . . . [A]s free men, [Negroes] need and deserve the same protection as other men before the courts").

39. See, e.g., *Nashville Daily Press-Times*, 22 November 1866 ("the one thing needed to secure our retention of the State Government is the enfranchisement of our colored citizens"); *Knoxville Whig*, 19 December 1866 ("the only mode by which the government of the state can be preserved in loyal hands . . . is to give the ballot to ALL loyal men"). Shortly before black Tennesseans were enfranchised, white Union Clubs and Leagues began to admit black members. McBride, "Blacks and the Race Issue," 186–87.

40. *Nashville Daily Press-Times*, 12 January 1866.

41. *Nashville Daily Press-Times*, 5 January 1866.

42. But see *Nashville Republican Banner*, 1 June 1866 ("We should be satisfied to compel them to engage in coarse common manual labor, and to punish them for dereliction of duty or nonfulfillment of their contracts with sufficient severity to make the great majority of them useful productive laborers. We would take care of those unable to provide and take care of themselves, but they should be no charge or burden on the whites.").

43. *Nashville Daily Press-Times*, 22 January 1866. The same paper reported several months later (16 March 1866) that freedmen were working well.

44. See generally McBride, "Blacks and the Race Issue," 146–47. Cf. *Columbia Herald*, 2 May 1866 (legislature should establish schools for Negroes, taught by local whites, so they can be "saved" from "foreign" teachers).

45. *Nashville Daily Press-Times*, 24 May 1866.

46. Ibid., 7 July 1866.

47. *Congressional Globe*, 39th Cong., 1st sess., 2544.

48. *Cincinnati Commercial*, 15 June 1866; *Washington Chronicle*, 15 June 1866.

49. *Senate Journal of the General Assembly of the State of Tennessee* (Nashville: S. C. Mercer, Printer to the State, 1866), 3–4.

50. *Bolivar Bulletin*, 30 June 1866. Black Tennesseans took a different view of the governor's call. During the two-week interval between the governor's call and the legislature's return, blacks held meetings and parades, many on July 4. They urged ratification of the Fourteenth Amendment and enfranchisement of blacks. McBride, "Blacks and the Race Issue," 118.

51. *Senate Journal*, 7–10. Two thousand copies of the governor's message were printed for distribution throughout the state, and many papers carried it in full. See, e.g., *Nashville Daily Press-Times*, 22 June 1866.

52. *Senate Journal*, 8.

53. See generally Joe M. Richardson, "Memphis Riots: White Reaction to Blacks in Memphis, May 1865–June 1866," *Tennessee Historical Quarterly* 24 (1964): 63; and Bobby L. Lovett, "The Memphis Race Riot and Its Aftermath," *Tennessee Historical Quarterly* 38 (1979): 9.

54. McBride, "Blacks and the Race Issue," 105.

55. In his inaugural address in 1865, Brownlow "denounced state sovereignty and denied he was 'one of those men who are alarmed at the powers assumed by the Federal Government at this time.'" Patton, *Unionism and Reconstruction*, 87–88.

56. See, e.g., *Nashville Dispatch*, 30 June 1866 (Stevens's constitutional amendment on representation "is in trouble" and will be recommitted to committee).

57. *Pulaski Citizen*, 27 April 1866; *Cleveland Banner*, 10 February 1866. One editorial writer lamented that the pending radical bills had only one purpose: to force Negro equality on the South. *Bolivar Bulletin*, 28 April 1866.

58. *Pulaski Citizen*, 27 April 1866.

59. See, e.g., *Nashville Daily Press-Times*, 2 May 1866 (Report of the Reconstruction Committee with text of proposed amendment); *Fayetteville Observer*, 24 May 1866 (House passing of amendment reported); *Clarksville Weekly Chronicle*, 15 June 1866 (text of amendment run); *Knoxville Whig*, 20 June 1866 (text of amendment run); *Pulaski Citizen*, 22 June 1866 (text of amendment run); *Fayetteville Observer*, 28 June 1866 (Senate passing of amendment reported). Conservative papers often carried President Johnson's message or praised the minority report. See, e.g., *Republican Banner*, 23 June 1866; *Pulaski Citizen*, 22 June 1866; *Paris Post-Intelligencer*, 29 June 1866.

60. *Senate Journal*, 41–43.

61. *Cleveland Banner*, 14 July 1866.

62. Ibid.

63. *Nashville Daily Press-Times*, 12 July 1866.

64. *Republican Banner*, 14 July 1866.

65. *Cleveland Banner*, 14 July 1866.

66. *Clarksville Weekly Chronicle*, 6 July 1866.

67. *The New Era*, 7 July 1866.

68. *Nashville Daily Press-Times*, 10 July 1866.

69. *Nashville Republican Banner*, 6 July 1867.

70. The story of the "arrest" of the recalcitrant legislators and the subsequent ratification of the amendment is told in James W. Fertig, *Secession and Reconstruction in Tennessee* (New York: A.M.S. Press, 1972), 77–79. The conservative press denounced the procedures and insisted that the amendment had not been ratified. See, e.g., *Nashville Dispatch*, 20 July 1866; *Republican Banner*, 20 July 1866.

71. The text of the telegram read: "My compliments to the President. We have carried the Constitutional Amendment in the House. Vote 43 to 11; two of his tools refusing to vote.—W. G. Brownlow." The governor's wire to Senate Clerk John Torney read slightly differently: "We have fought the battle and won it. We have ratified the Constitutional Amendment in the House—43 to 11 against it, two of Andrew Johnson's tools not voting. Give my respects to the dead dog of the White House."

72. *Nashville Daily Union and American*, 16 September 1866. The *Nashville Daily Press-Times* endorsed the Governor's proposal. 14 November 1866. The *Daily Union and American* flatly opposed it, 14 September 1866.

73. *House Journal of the Second Adjourned Session of the Thirty-fourth General Assembly of the State of Tennessee for the Years 1866–67* (Nashville: S. C. Mercer, Printer to the State, 1867), 15–17.

74. Debating an abolitionist minister in 1858, Brownlow endorsed slavery and favored colonizing America's free blacks. S. Atkinson, "Emerson Etheridge as a Candidate in the Tennessee Gubernatorial Election of 1867" (M.A. thesis, University of Tennessee, 1969), 45. Later, in his Knoxville paper, Brownlow declared: "To stand by the slavery is to stand by rebellion. The nigger is the rebellion and the rebellion is the nigger, and to put down the one we have to get rid of the other." *Knoxville Whig*, 11 January 1865. See also *Daily Advance*, 22 June 1867, and *Cleveland Banner*, 20 April 1867.

75. *House Journal*, 15–17.

76. Ibid.

77. McBride, "Blacks and the Race Issue," 144.

78. Ibid., 145.

79. Ibid., 148. Presumably the general believed that Negroes needed to elevate themselves morally and intellectually before they could be permitted to exercise political rights. To that end, he challenged the convention delegates to build 150 schools before the first frost and promised to pay the last hundred dollars needed to complete their construction. He also offered a $200 reward for anyone giving information that led to the conviction of a defendant charged with burning a school. Though many of the new schools were burned, the general never had to pay because the arsonists were not apprehended, charged, or convicted. Ibid., 149–50.

80. Taylor, *The Negro in Tennessee*, 24.

81. McBride, "Blacks and the Race Issue," 177.

82. Brownlow received 74,484 votes to Etheridge's 22,548. Of the roughly forty thousand to fifty thousand blacks who voted, 80 to 95 percent probably voted for Brownlow. See McBride, "Blacks and the Race Issue," 218 ("Black voters may have provided Governor Brownlow and the Republicans with their decisive margins of victory, but the vote totals suggest that Brownlow would have won even if blacks had not been enfranchised.").

83. *Nashville Union and Dispatch*, 7 February 1867.

84. *Memphis Daily Post*, 27 February 1867.

85. McBride, "Blacks and the Race Issue," 229.

86. Taylor, *The Negro in Tennessee*, 42–43.

87. Ibid.

88. Ibid., 256.

89. Folmsbee, *Tennessee*, 371.

90. *Journal of the Proceedings of the Convention of Delegates Elected by the People of Tennessee to Amend, Revise, or Form and Make a New Constitution for the State* (Nashville: Jones, Purvis and Co., 1870), 437–38, Archives and Special Collections, University of Tennessee Library, Knoxville, Tennessee. Article 11, Section 12 required segregated schools; Article 11, Section 14 prohibited mixed marriages.

91. McBride, "Blacks and the Race Issue," 332–33.

92. Ibid., 335–36.

3

Ratification in Mississippi

*[These laws] might seem rigid and stringent to sickly
modern humanitarians.*

—Mississippi Committee Report describing
the Black Code adopted in 1865

Hopes for presidential Reconstruction may have been dashed—and the seeds
that bore the Fourteenth Amendment may have been sown—in Mississippi in
the late summer of 1865. The first state convention to meet under President
Johnson's restoration program convened in Jackson that August. Its actions
were closely studied in the North for clues about the South's attitude toward the
Union and the newly freed blacks. "If," said an influential New York paper,
"Mississippi moves into her place in the Union with a constitution that will meet
the approval of the government, we shall be able to dismiss all further apprehen-
sion concerning the action of any other Southern state."[1] The president himself
sent a message to the convention, advising the delegates:

I hope that without delay your convention will amend your state constitution abolishing
slavery and denying to all future legislatures the power to legislate that there is property
in man; also that they will adopt the amendment to the Constitution of the United States
abolishing slavery. If you could extend the elective franchise to all persons of color who
can read the Constitution of the United States in English, and write their names, and to
all persons of color who own real estate valued at not less than $250, and pay taxes
thereon, you would completely disarm the adversary and set an example the other states
will follow. This you can do with perfect safety, and you thus place the Southern states,
in reference to free persons of color, upon the same basis with the free states.[2]

Had the Mississippi convention heeded the president's advice, other Southern
states might have followed its example; and the Fourteenth Amendment and

congressional Reconstruction might never have materialized. Mississippi, however, ignored the president on two key points. It refused to ratify the Thirteenth Amendment, and it declined to extend even qualified suffrage to blacks. Thus did white Mississippians hand their radical nemeses in Congress the very weapon they needed—Southern intransigence—to attack the president's program.

The convention's thinking on these two points is relevant to Mississippi's later understanding of the Fourteenth Amendment. Though the convention did abolish slavery, it refused to approve the Thirteenth Amendment for reasons the state legislature articulated a few months later when it too refused to ratify the Thirteenth Amendment.[3] Its Joint Committee on State and Federal Relations objected chiefly to Section 2, which gave Congress the power to enforce Section 1:

The second section is subject to more grave objections. It confers on Congress the power to enforce the Article by "appropriate legislation." Slavery having been already abolished, there is really no necessity for this section, nor can the committee anticipate any possible good that can result from its adoption. On the contrary, it seems to be fraught with evils which this Legislature and the people of the State of Mississippi are most anxious to guard against. . . .

The committee cannot anticipate what construction future Congresses may put on this section. It may be claimed that it would be "appropriate" for Congress to legislate in respect to freedmen in this State. This committee can hardly conceive of a more dangerous grant of power than one which, by construction, might admit Federal legislation in respect to persons denizens and inhabitants of the State. If there be no danger now, the committee fear that the time may come that the public mind might be influenced on this subject, to the degree of endangering the reserved rights of the States. The committee are also of opinion that the present is not a propitious time to enlarge the powers of the Federal Government; the tendency is already too strong in the direction of consolidation. The liberties of the people, and the preservation of the complex Federative system would be better ensured by confining the Federative and State Governments in the respective spheres already defined for them. . . .

The tendency of the section is to absorb in the Federal Government the reserved rights of the State and people, to unsettle the equilibrium of the States in the Union, and to break down the efficient authority and sovereignty of the State over its internal and domestic affairs.[4]

Mississippians would object to Section 5 of the Fourteenth Amendment, which gave Congress the same power to enforce its first section, for that same reason. This position doubtless reflected the view generally held by the white population of the state and captured in a letter to the editor of the *Clarion* in the fall of 1865. The writer asserted that Section 2 of the Amendment would "open the door for congressional legislation concerning our domestic affairs," including, of course, treatment of the freedmen.[5]

White Mississippians also adamantly opposed granting blacks any political rights. After all, the free Negro had had no such rights before the Civil War; and his status became the model for determining what rights need be accorded the freedmen. In the October 1865 session of the legislature, several senators introduced a resolution that the body refuse to elect anyone to the United States Senate "who is or shall be in favor of giving to the slaves thus manumitted any rights, civil, political, or social, further than was vouchsafed unto the same person and property of the domiciliated free negro by the statutes of the State prior to the late revolution."[6] In other words, "[t]he freedmen and the free Negro must stand on the same footing."[7]

Whites thus rejected the idea that the rights of a white citizen might be an index to those which the freedman should also enjoy. Whites considered Negroes an inferior race. Consequently, class legislation was necessary if the Negro was to be kept "in the position which God almighty intended him to occupy; *a position inferior to the white man.*"[8] Indeed, whites insisted that the preservation of the Republic depended upon "*subordinating* the inferior to the superior race, under wise and just regulations, imposed by the great fountain of justice—the State."[9]

Whites demonstrated how strongly they clung to this view in the fall elections in 1865 for governor and legislature. The only divisive issue in that campaign was whether the freedmen should be permitted to testify in the courts. From the beginning, the Freedmen's Bureau had insisted that all legal controversies between blacks and whites be tried in Bureau courts so long as the state's civil courts refused to hear black witnesses.[10] Moreover, many members of the bar and a majority of the state's newspapers recommended that Negroes be permitted to testify.[11]

The opposition to the idea was nevertheless strong: "Negroes as a class must be excluded from the witness stand. If the privilege is ever granted, it will lead to greater demands, and at last end in the admission of the negro to the jury box and ballot box."[12] This opposition reflected three views that decisively influenced the initial reaction of most white Mississippians to the Fourteenth Amendment. First, blacks were inferior to whites and thus should be treated differently. (In this particular instance, blacks were considered congenital liars whose testimony could not be trusted.) Second, any extension of equal rights to the freedmen would inevitably require the extension of more rights to them. Third, this process of piecemeal equalization would necessarily end in social equality; that is, the amalgamation and mongrelization of the two races.

Benjamin Humphreys, the newly elected governor, echoed these views in his address to the legislature, declaring that "caste" should be preserved "for the progress and purity of the races." He admonished the legislature:

The highest degree of elevation in the scale of civilization to which they [blacks] are capable morally and intellectually must be secured to them by education and religious training; but they cannot be admitted to political or social equality with the white race. It is due to ourselves and to the white immigrants invited to our shores, and it should never be forgotten to maintain the fact, that ours is and it shall ever be, a government of white men.[13]

The legislature lent a receptive ear to the governor. Though dominated by pre-war Whigs who, like Humphreys, had opposed secession, the legislature was prepared only to "adopt such laws as will protect the Negro in his rights of person and property."[14] Its decisions naturally reinforced the emerging view in the North that the South was determined to maintain the slave system.

The most important of those decisions involved the "labor question," which most white Mississippians then thought could be answered only through laws that would "compel negroes to work on plantations."[15] The problem was as stark as it was frightening. Mississippi's economy depended on cotton, and it had to be picked. The slaves had always picked it. If the freedmen refused, the crop would rot in the fields. Yet they were fleeing those fields, congregating in the cities, and perhaps plotting a race war.[16] Humphreys vividly described the problem as he saw it in his autobiography:

[The freedmen] readily became the victims of the corrupting teachings of the carpet baggers and scallawags and allured by the treacherous and seductive promise of "forty acres and a mule" soon gave evidence of turbulence and disorder.

Thousands of freedmen—both men and women—thus indoctrinated and fully intoxicated by the joys of freedom and mean whiskey, abandoned all pursuits of industry, and prowled at large, both day and night, over fields and forest, subsisting on game and plunder. Stock was utterly insecure; locks afforded no protection to stables, cribs, smoke houses or poultry yards.[17]

The legislature responded to this unprecedented circumstance by enacting what came to be known as the Black Codes.[18] These laws defined the rights and obligations of the freedmen. Under the new vagrancy law, which applied only to blacks, Negroes unable to pay fines could be "hired out" to masters, who were "empowered to inflict moderate chastisement for misbehavior." Negro minors who were orphans and unable to support themselves were to be similarly apprenticed, preferably to their former "masters." Negroes were not allowed to move about the state freely, and they were subjected to the same penal and criminal laws that had governed them during slavery.[19] The committee recommending these laws recognized that some of them "might seem rigid and stringent to sickly modern humanitarians," but it insisted the legislation "could never disturb or retard the good or true of either race."[20]

However beneficent and wise the Mississippi legislature thought these laws, many Northerners regarded them as further evidence of Southern intransigence. A Boston journalist traveling through Mississippi in 1865, for example, reported that "the recent State laws . . . show plainly enough what ideas prevail in the late Slave States on the subject of free labor. The design of all such enactments is simply to place both the labor and laborer in the power of the employer, and to reorganize slavery under a new name."[21] The Thirty-ninth Congress therefore turned its attention to the "Southern problem" as soon as it reassembled. In the first few months of 1866, more than ninety "reconstruction" proposals were submitted.

Mississippi newspapers followed the ensuing congressional debates on these proposals throughout the winter and spring of 1866. They discerned a pattern in the various plans which the radicals brought forward. "All their measures tend to centralize power," declared the *Oxford Falcon*.[22] Thus the Civil Rights Bill, which Congress passed that April, was condemned as "injurious to what remains of the authority of the States over their most domestic affairs."[23]

Additionally, the newspapers insisted that the substance of these radical proposals was shaped by a "mad passion" for "racial equality." One paper doubtless shocked its readers with an example of this policy: the Senate and House galleries were now filled, it reported, with "big negro wenches . . . who exhale their *sweet perfume* to the delight of all abolitionum."[24] The *Vicksburg Journal* concluded that the Civil Rights Act, "taken in conjunction with the second clause of the [thirteenth] amendment . . . means universal equality, without distinction of color."[25] A sister paper had reported earlier in the year that the Reconstruction Committee was considering an amendment that would "make National and State laws apply to all men, without regard to color" and predicted that no Southern state would be readmitted until it had "abolished all distinctions of color and race in respect of all civil and religious rights."[26]

Many Mississippi newspapers dismissed the Fourteenth Amendment without any detailed analysis because they saw it, too, as reflecting this pattern. For that reason the *Vicksburg Journal* pronounced the report of the Reconstruction Committee a "farce" and concluded that "it is useless to discuss it."[27] The simple fact was that "centralized power" and "negro equality" were unacceptable and repugnant. And for that reason, "the amendments . . . stink in the nostrils of honest men," declared the editor of one of the state's leading newspapers.[28] The *Vicksburg Daily Times* thought that it captured the essence of the Fourteenth Amendment when it declared that "the radical platform" was that "the nigger must be [the white man's] equal."[29]

Less pejorative characterizations of the amendment also emphasized, as its "primary aim," the "equalization of the races."[30] For example, the amendment was said to confer upon the Negro all "the privileges and immunities heretofore enjoyed only by free-born white citizens."[31] Other papers, however, emphasized that the amendment would "dissolve 36 States into one State"[32] by giving "all power to an oligarch in Congress."[33] These general descriptions of the Fourteenth Amendment were clearly consistent with the terms that white Mississippians had understood the radicals would impose and reflected the concerns they had repeatedly voiced during the preceding year.

White Mississippians who did examine the Fourteenth Amendment closely made three points. First, it tended to force Negro suffrage upon the state. Some mistakenly asserted that Section 2 by its own terms required Mississippi "to clothe our former slaves with the right of suffrage."[34] Still others argued—again, mistakenly—that voting was a privilege and immunity of citizenship.[35] Others worried that Congress might decree that voting was a privilege of citizenship.[36] Those who read the text of Section 2 carefully, however, understood that it offered Mississippi a Hobson's choice: enfranchise blacks or lose representation in the Congress. Astute observers pointed out that this provision was "an indirect way of keeping the power of the government in the hands of the Radicals,"[37] whatever the South's choice.

Second, white Mississippians fumed over the exclusion of "the only class of persons who possess the required intelligence, virtue, and capacity to advert from the State the worst form of anarchy."[38] They thus denounced Section 3. Its terms were so humiliating that the "true and gallant Southern man feels his cheeks mantle with shame to think of it."[39] In those circumstances, ratification of Section 3 would be "a gross act of perfidy,"[40] which "no honorable people would voluntarily sanction."[41]

Third, they objected to Section 5 because, when read in conjunction with Section 1, it gave Congress plenary authority to legislate on matters previously within the sole discretion of the state government. Commenting on the fact that Congress would have the power under Section 5 to define the privileges and immunities guaranteed in Section 1, the *Natchez Daily Courier* exclaimed: "States hereafter are but provinces."[42] In mid-October, the *Vicksburg Daily Times* quoted Governor Humphreys's concise summary of the amendment's impact: "The radical Congress has . . . proposed . . . amendments to the Constitution which if adopted will destroy the rights of the States and the people, and centralize all the powers of government in the Federal Head."[43] Earlier the paper had reasoned: "If the Federal Government can interfere to change the relations of the inhabitants of a State in one respect, it can in all. If it can abolish the laws which regulate the inferiority of the negro, it can certainly define what position, legally or civilly, he may occupy."[44]

In September, William Sharkey, who had served as provisional governor, wrote Governor Humphreys and urged rejection of the amendment for the same reasons. Of Section 1, he observed that its failure to define privileges and immunities necessarily left to Congress that power under Section 5, which he castigated as a "Trojan horse abounding in mischief." He reminded Governor Humphreys that the same section in the Thirteenth Amendment had produced the Civil Rights Bill, and he expressed the hope that Mississippians had learned from that unhappy experience. He also objected to the method of promulgation because the amendment was not proposed by two-thirds of the Congress, the Southern states having been excluded. He criticized Section 2 because it forced "negro suffrage upon [the state]" and denounced Section 3 because it oppressed "a very large class of the South."[45]

Governor Humphreys repeated these same objections in summary form when he recommended that the legislature refuse to ratify the Fourteenth Amendment:

This amendment, adopted by a Congress of less than three-fourths of the States of the Union, in palpable violation of the rights of more than one-fourth of the States, is such an insulting outrage and denial of the equal rights of so many of our worthiest citizens who have shed lustre and glory upon our section and our race, both in the forum and in the field, such a gross usurpation of the rights of the States, and such a centralization of power in the Federal Government, that I presume a mere reading of it, will cause its rejection by you.[46]

The legislature did read the amendment, and they did reject it. The report of the Joint Standing Committee on State and Federal Relations saw "nothing in the intrinsic merit of the proposed amendment, in the manner of its adoption by Congress, or in the circumstances that environ the State of Mississippi that commend its ratification."[47]

It nevertheless proceeded to examine seriatim the intrinsic merits of the amendment. Of Sections 1 and 5, it observed:

This amendment would disturb to a degree which no one can foresee, the established relations between the Federal and State Courts. It would transfer to the former a supervisory and appellate control over the latter, in a very large class of subjects that now belong to the exclusive cognizance of the State tribunals. It confers in Congress large and undefined power, at the expense of the reserved rights of the State. It transfers to the United States a criminal and police regulation over the inhabitants of the States, touching matters purely domestic. It intervenes between the State Government and its inhabitants on the assumption that there is an alienation of interest and sentiment between certain portions of the population. And that such intervention is for the benefit of one class against the other. It tends to create distrust and jealousy between the white and black races, and perpetually to disturb and keep alive these evil passions. It invites appeal from the domestic to the Federal judiciary on questions arising in local law, on the predicate that the State courts will not deal between the parties with fairness or impartiality. It inculcates in the colored population a distrust of State law and authority for the protection of person and property . . . constantly to require the legislative and judicial corrective of the Federal power.[48]

Thus did Judge Horatio Simrall, the chair of the Joint Committee, explain the meaning of Section 1. He underscored the obvious: Congress could legislate on matters previously confined exclusively to the states. He also emphasized the possibility that federal courts might exercise greatly expanded powers under this amendment, though it apparently never occurred to him that the Bill of Rights would define the substantive scope of that expanded power. Rather, he feared that federal courts would strike down state laws on the ground that they discriminated against blacks, an impolitic intervention that would breed racial hostility within the state.

Senator-elect Alcorn was one of the few Mississippians who favored ratification. On January 25, 1867, he spoke to the legislature for two hours, analyzing the amendment's provisions and explaining why political expediency required its ratification. Unfortunately, no text of the senator-elect's remarks has survived. What has survived is a letter to a newspaper editor in which Alcorn summarizes his remarks because he believes that they have been misrepresented. In his letter, Alcorn does not set out his understanding of any of the particular sections of the amendment. He simply emphasizes that though he opposed the amendment as a matter of principle, he would nevertheless "adopt at once the first, second, fourth and fifth sections" in order to secure Mississippi's restoration; and to that end he admitted he was also ready "to debate the justice and propriety of the third [section]."

Alcorn also included in his letter one other observation that suggests the basis upon which he probably tried to calm fears that, under Section 5, Congress might invade the reserved powers of the state. Of Section 2, he reminded the legislature that Mississippi could hardly expect to return to Congress with more power than it had before the war.[49] His was the course of the pragmatic and realistic politician. Such a politician would also have pointed out that the mere fact that Congress had the power to regulate "domestic matters" did not mean that Congress would use it. If Mississippi and the other Southern states were restored, they could, he might have argued, use their clout to block any Congressional intermeddling in their domestic affairs.

The legislature was unconvinced and unswayed. The Joint Committee conceded that it would have given "the most careful deliberation" to the "several propositions contained" in the amendment *if* "they came before the legislature in the shape of a final disposition of the subject [i.e., restoration] and thereby bring stability and repose." But that was not the case:

Congress has proposed to the States two amendments of the Constitution bearing directly on the internal affairs of the Southern people, one of which has been and the other may yet be ratified.

And . . . these propositions have been characterized, each in its turn, by some parties in the loose and general language of political debate . . . as containing terms of reconciliation. Yet . . . it is manifest that they were not offered by Congress . . . as the conditions of restoration.[50]

The legislature rejected the amendment overwhelmingly and stoically awaited the storm about to break upon the state.[51] That storm—in the form of the Reconstruction Acts—temporarily revolutionized politics in Mississippi. Mississippi was one of three states where blacks outnumbered whites, and it also had a large number of white Unionists who resented the planters' political domination of the state. Early in this revolution three political groups emerged. Conservatives, who had dominated the "great debate" over the Fourteenth Amendment during the six-month interim between the elections in the fall of 1866 and the passage of the first Reconstruction Act in the spring of 1867,[52] reorganized themselves as the Constitutional Union Party. They declared:

The nefarious design of the Republican party to place the white men of the Southern states under governmental control of their late slaves, and degrade the Caucasian race as the inferiors of the African race, is a crime against the civilization of the age which needs only to be mentioned to be scorned by all intelligent minds, and we, therefore, call upon the people of Mississippi to vindicate alike the superiority of their race over the negro, and their political power to maintain constitutional liberty.[53]

In their platform, they nevertheless declared themselves in favor of "[s]ecurity and equal protection to every citizen of every State, in all his rights of person and property, and especially his rights to the blessings of civil government, trial by jury, and due administration of law in the civil courts: and the same equal protection to the freedmen by just laws impartially administered to all classes of our population."[54] In short, they now accepted Section 1 of the Fourteenth Amendment, as its commands were then understood.

A second group of whites, known as cooperationists, sought to accommodate Congress and co-opt blacks. They would "make the best" of Reconstruction, "meet[ing] Congress on its own platform and shak[ing] hands." They hoped to "acquire ascendancy over blacks by becoming their teachers and controllers instead of allowing the Republicans to do so."[55] Senator-elect Alcorn epitomized this group. He said he would "vote with the negro, discuss politics with him, sit, if need be, in council with him, and form a platform acceptable to both, and pluck our common liberty and prosperity from the jaws of inevitable ruin."[56] Judge James Robb, in a letter sent to many conservative papers in June 1867, outlined such a platform. It included a guarantee of "all the privileges and rights of freedom," including, presumably, the right to vote; access to "public schools for [black] children; and a remedy against delinquent employers for past wages."[57] This platform, which promised the freedmen civil and political equality, grew out of a series of biracial mass meetings that were held in communities throughout the state during the spring and summer of 1867.

The Republicans were the third group, and their views on equality and other relevant issues are critically important because they were the strongest proponents of the Fourteenth Amendment. At their first state convention, held in July 1867, they adopted resolutions endorsing an impartial and economical administration of the government, full and unrestricted right of speech to all men at all times and places, unrestrained freedom of the ballot, and a system of free schools. They also declared that all men were equal before the law without regard to race, color, or previous condition of servitude.[58]

Mississippi's blacks naturally gravitated toward this third group. Blacks had held their own statewide convention in Jackson just prior to the July meeting of Republicans. At that May meeting they asserted: "[I]t is our undeniable right to hold office, sit on juries, to ride on all public conveyances, to sit at public table, and sit at public places of amusement."[59] A black speaker at a Vicksburg rally in late 1867 declared: "We are here tonight to tell the world that after being enfranchised, we are wise enough to know our rights and we are going to claim those rights."[60] As examples of such rights, he listed sitting on juries and equal access to public conveyances. Blacks clearly considered equal access to public accommodations a specific example of the more general civil and political equality that their white allies endorsed.

The Mississippi Constitutional Convention, which began on January 7, 1868, drafted a constitution that reflected these Republican principles—the very principles embodied in Section 1 of the Fourteenth Amendment.[61] Conservatives had predicted that the "bogus negro convention" would adopt a constitution "received from the North" and "adjusted to the views of New England Radicalism."[62] Radicals did not dominate the convention, however. Only eighteen of the ninety-seven delegates were black, and one of those was a conservative. Another seventeen white delegates were conservatives. The forty-one Southern white Republicans were the largest single bloc in the convention, and they generally espoused moderate views. Indeed, only thirteen of the seventy-nine Republican delegates could be classified as "true radicals."[63]

In the convention, outnumbered conservative delegates urged a program that they hoped the cooperationists would endorse. It guaranteed blacks equal civil rights and the equal protection of the laws but excluded them from voting or sitting on juries. The convention, however, rejected these suggestions. It extended suffrage to blacks and guaranteed them other rights. Indeed, the convention insisted on including in the new constitution a requirement that no one could vote until he swore to "the political and civil equality of all men." It also proscribed everyone who had supported secession or the rebellion from ever holding office and permanently denied the right to vote to those proscribed by the Reconstruction Acts of 1867.

Though these three voting provisions bespoke radicalism, the convention otherwise acted with considerable moderation.[64] The convention debate on public schools illustrates how delegates modified the most radical demands. Additionally, the convention discussion of public schools illustrates that equality—and, more specifically, the equal protection guarantee—was understood to permit at least some segregated facilities. When the convention rejected an amendment that would have required separate schools, the conservative press in Mississippi howled about the radical "scheme of plunder and miscegenation, designed . . . to supersede the laws of our civilization with the horrible creed of the Black and Tan socialists, in the name of 'Public Education.'"[65] The seventeen black Republican delegates to the convention realized, however, that a constitutional provision requiring integrated schools would "undermine the public school system at its inception."[66] While they strongly objected to a proposed provision that would have mandated segregated schools, they were willing to leave the matter to subsequent legislative decisions. Moreover, James Lynch, the leading black delegate, assured the convention that he did not intend to press immediately for integrated schools if Republicans gained control of the state government.[67] Consequently, Republicans agreed that the constitution would not require mixed schools either. The question was thus left to subsequent legislative decision.

More generally, the bill of rights of the new constitution reflected a natural law commitment to the inalienable rights of man. Section 32 declared: "The enumeration of rights in this constitution shall not be construed to deny or impair others retained by and inherent in the people." More specifically, it guaranteed the basic liberties all Americans had come to consider their birthright: freedom of speech and press, the right to assemble and petition, and freedom of religion.[68] Other specific guarantees embodied a populist, rather than absolute, equality principle. Thus several sections forbade property qualifications for jury service (Section 13), for office (Section 17), and for voting (Section 18). Additionally, Sections 28 and 30 promised that the courts would always be open to all. In short, the framers of the Mississippi bill of rights desired to guarantee liberty and equality without depriving the government of the legislative authority necessary to protect the public welfare.

The latter caveat is explicit in several "provided" clauses. The section guaranteeing religious freedom, for example, provided that "[t]he rights hereby secured shall not be construed to justify acts of licentiousness injurious to morals or dangerous to the peace and safety of the State." The caveat is implicit in Section 24, which stated that "[t]he right of all citizens to travel upon all public conveyances shall not be infringed upon nor in any manner abridged." The narrow ambit of this guarantee obviously permitted the state to tolerate, protect, or prohibit racial exclusion from other public accommodations.

Provisions like these betray no suspicion that the language of the Fourteenth Amendment dictated answers to public policy questions of this kind. Since those answers were to be left to the political process, Mississippi Republicans sought to forge an alliance between blacks and poor whites. They argued:

A white man's party, indeed! What cared these men for a man's color if he only worked? The real issue is not over a 'white-man's party,' but the poor man's party, and of equal rights to all. It is to secure the same rights before the law to the poorest as to the richest. This harms nobody. It is true Democracy. But only with the black man's help can the poor white man ever gain his just political influence in Mississippi.[69]

In his inaugural address, Governor Alcorn also reached out to poor whites, pledging to be more responsive to their interests.[70] In an interview with the *Cincinnati Commercial*, Mr. Lynch said that without white support, peace and economic security could not be assured except by a standing army.[71] These Republicans—black and white alike—thus realized that they would survive and thrive only in a biracial society.

For a brief period such a society seemed possible. Initially, Union Leagues had flourished among white Mississippians, especially in the flatwood and hill country of the state. By late 1865, 30 percent of the white population in the area had joined.[72] Resenting planter domination of the state, these whites initially responded very positively to Republican appeals; and at least some realized that poor blacks were their natural allies.

Had the Republicans not endorsed extreme disfranchisement, they thus might have succeeded in building that biracial society. Unfortunately, the convention's failure to write a document free of proscriptive features greatly diminished Republican chances for a strong biracial party by driving most whites into the Democratic Party.[73] Indeed, those whites and their Democratic allies successfully blocked adoption of the proposed constitution, a feat accomplished elsewhere in the South only in Alabama. Told that the constitution was the work of "carpetbag scoundrels," white Mississippians turned out in droves to vote "no" and effectively forced a reconsideration of the disfranchisement issues.[74]

Republicans regrouped, substituting a policy of universal amnesty and universal suffrage for the broad proscription they had previously supported. The party's new platform did reaffirm its prior commitments to free schools, free speech, and legal and political equality. When the constitution was resubmitted to the people—without the three proscriptive features to which most whites had objected—it was approved 113,755 to 955.[75]

Reconstruction nevertheless wrought a sea change in Mississippi politics. That was nowhere better illustrated than in A. R. Johnston's address to black voters in Sardis on October 13, 1869. He denounced the radicals and all their Reconstruction plans. But he was now prepared "to embrace the Congressional plan of reconstruction—not as a matter of choice—but from stern necessity." He then promised the black members of the audience speedy ratification of the Fourteenth and Fifteenth Amendments. He pledged that blacks would "be the equal before the law with the white race, the right to vote, serve on juries, give evidence in court, sue for and get all property rights. He assured them: "[Y]ou will be safe in your cabins as the rich white man is in his great house, and you may hold any office you may be elected to." Finally, Johnston told his black listeners: "[M]y party is for common schools here and all over the state, not only for our children but for yours; and we want to be taxed to put those schools everywhere, with a fair division of the money between the races." He added, however: "We think it best that the schools should not be mixed, that the white and black children should be taught separately."[76]

The editor of the *Hinds County Gazette*, the leading Whig paper in Mississippi, also acquiesced in the "new order." In June 1871 the paper ran its platform, endorsing "protection of all, whites and blacks, in the quiet enjoyment of their civil and political rights" and supporting "the Constitutional Amendments." In an editorial explaining the platform, the editor conceded that it did "not accord . . . with our views in the past." Only the "stern logic of events" dictated the choice. The paper nevertheless embraced the choice enthusiastically.[77]

The first legislature to meet under the new constitution opened on January 11, 1870, and promptly ratified the Fourteenth and Fifteenth Amendments.[78] One month later, Congress restored Mississippi to the Union. When the Republican-dominated legislature resumed business in early March, it addressed several issues that shed light on its understanding of the principles embodied in Section 1 of the Fourteenth Amendment. Public education was again a controversial issue. Governor Alcorn and the Republicans favored—and established—a state-funded system of public schools.[79] Though many conservatives criticized the public school law, they could not attack it on the ground that schools were integrated, as in neighboring New Orleans. Indeed, Alcorn clashed with Robert Flournoy, editor of the radical *Equal Rights*, who insisted that the state university be integrated. Instead, the governor persuaded the legislature to establish a separate college for Negroes;[80] and throughout Reconstruction, public schools in Mississippi were racially segregated. Apparently, the equal protection clause was not seen as a bar to that policy.

While the governor and his legislative comrades agreed on the desirability of segregated public schools, they disagreed over the desirability of integrated public transportation. In June 1870 Mr. Alcorn vetoed a railroad bill that prohibited segregation in the cars.[81] Although his veto message is phrased ambiguously on this point, he was accused of waffling on the civil rights issue. In fact, the governor had urged the Senate to amend the bill by requiring only that the railroad companies "furnish equal accommodations for the two races, the white race to be assigned to the one and the colored race to the other." In his lobbying efforts, he invited the presidents of the railroads in Mississippi and black members of the legislature to a meeting at the governor's mansion, where he extracted a promise from the former to provide separate but equal facilities.[82]

His efforts failed; the bill passed. It was not enforced, however, for fear of provoking bloodshed. In practice, Negroes continued to use segregated facilities.[83] The practice nevertheless angered them, and they deserted Alcorn three years later when he ran for reelection. Divisive and hotly debated as the issue was, neither the governor nor his opponents within the party appear to have believed that the Fourteenth Amendment either dictated or prohibited the practice. The issue was one of public policy, and either policy passed constitutional muster under the amendment. In short, the conduct of the legislature from 1870 to 1876 demonstrates that Mississippi, like every other Southern state, assumed that the Fourteenth Amendment did not by its terms proscribe segregation of the races in public places but left that issue to the legislature's discretion.

One specific social problem illustrated that Governor Alcorn, at least, was also unfamiliar with incorporation doctrine. Crime rates soared. The governor pinpointed the cause: the "barbarous practice" of carrying guns and knives, "which was almost universal among both races in the South."[84] He therefore asked the legislature to adopt laws that restricted the right to carry arms. It never occurred to the governor to explain why the Fourteenth Amendment did not prevent such laws, as it arguably might have, had the Second Amendment been incorporated in Section 1. After all, the Second Amendment guarantees the right to bear arms. Opponents of the proposed laws never relied on the Fourteenth Amendment's "incorporated" right to bear arms either. All seemed blissfully ignorant of an argument that certainly would be made by incorporationists today.

For a brief period of time it seemed as if the "bottom rail were on the top" in Mississippi. The widespread refusal of whites to participate in the 1867 election campaign resulted in a more liberal constitutional convention than otherwise would have been the case. In the 1869 election for state offices, many Negroes came into public office. Their power increased significantly in 1873 as a result of a split between white Republicans. Exploiting that split, blacks demanded and got more offices. As the "backbone of the Republican party,"[85] blacks held the balance of power in the state legislature between 1874 and 1876. They also controlled some local and county governments.[86]

Reaction to these developments among conservative whites was swift. Convinced "that the color line [had to be] drawn to prevent complete Negro domination . . . conservative Mississippians of divergent political backgrounds" organized a massive political campaign, supported by paramilitary forces, to redeem the state.[87] This campaign became known as the "Mississippi Plan." The secretary of the Democratic campaign committee in Jackson outlined its elements:

- organize a solidly Democratic front;
- intimidate Negroes if persuasion fails;
- stuff the ballot box with Democratic tickets;
- destroy Republican tickets;
- substitute Democratic for Republican tickets for illiterate Negroes;
- if these plans do not work, count the Republicans out and count the Democrats in.[88]

Racial tensions rose. Major riots broke out in Vicksburg in 1874 and in Clinton in 1875 that left white and black alike dead. Parties on both sides feared a race war.

Events came to a head in October 1876 when Governor Adelbert Ames reluctantly called out the largely black state militia because President Grant had refused his request to send in federal troops. The Democratic campaign manager, General James Z. George, pleaded with the governor to rescind his call, promising him that the Democrats would not resort to further violence. President Grant "heartily endorsed" the "peace agreement," and Ames acquiesced.[89] The *Clarion* praised the governor for refraining from "revolutionary measures" which would have "wrapped the state in the flames of civil war."[90] Though that was narrowly averted, episodic violence continued to permeate the 1875 electoral campaign.

Those October discussions in the governor's mansion foreshadowed the end of Reconstruction. The national government had lost its will to preserve freedom for the freedmen because those efforts had become a political liability in the North. South Carolina's Democrats, confident they would escape retaliation, adopted the "Mississippi Plan" a year later and successfully ended Reconstruction there.[91] Reconstruction had already died in Mississippi on the day Democrats there swept the 1875 election. One scholar has succinctly summarized the watershed consequences of that election: "The scalawags, by abandoning the Republican party in Mississippi at a time when the national commitment to reconstructing the South had all but dissolved, undermined whatever chance remained for the successful fulfillment of the equalitarian aims of the party."[92] For the next three generations, the clear commands of the Fourteenth Amendment were ignored in the state.

In one of history's ironic twists, events in Mississippi triggered a second Reconstruction. The state once again became the subject of intense Northern scrutiny when three civil rights workers were murdered there in the summer of 1964. In the wake of that widely publicized "Mississippi summer," Congress passed the Voting Rights Act and sent federal marshals into Mississippi and other Southern states to register black voters. In the decades that followed, Mississippi and her sister Southern states at last began to redeem the promises the "redeemers" had broken a century earlier. And in early 1995, Mississippi finally ratified the Thirteenth Amendment—unanimously.

NOTES

1. James W. Garner, *Reconstruction in Mississippi* (New York: Macmillan, 1901), 84.

2. James Alcorn, one of the wealthiest men in the state and the future leader of the state's Republican Party, also counseled acquiescence to the president's requests. Writing from Washington, D.C., in August 1865, he predicted that Congress would deny the Southern states readmission until they enfranchised Negroes.

> I think it would be politic for the Southern States to meet this issue with an acceptance at once. We must make the negro our friend, and we can do this if we will. Should we make him our enemy under the promptings of the Yankee, whose aim is to force us to recognize an equality, then our path lies through a way red with blood, and damp with tears. To let the negro approach the witness stand and the ballot box by no means implies his social equality. (James Alcorn to Amelia Alcorn, 26 August 1865, Alcorn Papers, Mississippi Department of Archives and History, Jackson, Mississippi)

3. For the second time in as many months, Mississippi thus ignored the counsel of the president, who had telegraphed the governor: "The action of the Mississippi legislature is looked forward to with great interest at this time, and a failure to act will create the belief that the act of your convention abolishing slavery will hereafter be revoked. The argument is, If the convention abolished slavery in good faith, why then should the legislature hesitate to make it a part of the Constitution of the United States?" Garner, *Reconstruction in Mississippi*, 112.

4. See *Laws of Mississippi*, 1865, 272–74.

5. *Jackson Clarion*, 8 November 1865. Cf. *Vicksburg Daily Herald*, 1 November 1865 (recommends that Mississippi not ratify Thirteenth Amendment because Section 2 would give Congress the power to legislate on behalf of the freedmen, thus depriving the state of power to control the Negro).

6. *Meridian Clarion*, 22 October 1865.

7. *Jackson News*, 14 November 1865. The status of the free Negro in antebellum Mississippi is described fully in Charles S. Sydnor, "The Free Negro in Mississippi before the Civil War," *American Historical Review* 32 (1927): 769.

8. *Jackson News*, 14 November 1865.

9. *The Mississippian*, 18 August 1865. Cf. *Weekly Panola Star*, 2 November 1867 (Negroes "have never developed capacity enough to administer any government than that of savage ferocity").

10. Garner, *Reconstruction in Mississippi*, 263.

11. See, e.g., *Jackson Clarion*, 19 November 1865.

12. Garner, *Reconstruction in Mississippi*, 94.

13. *Weekly Panola Star*, 28 October 1865. That this was the attitude of moderate whites is evidenced by the contemporaneous remarks of a minister at a memorial service: "We are the only true friends that this ignorant, feeble, dependent people have in all the world. And while their elevation to a social and political equality we will ever oppose, never consenting to our own degradation, yet to instruct, to counsel, to help, and to save them is a high and sacred mission." *Liberty Advocate*, 22 December 1866.

14. Speech of Judge Evans, a candidate for the legislature, reported in the *Vicksburg Journal*, 21 September 1865. See also *The Mississippian*, 18 August 1865 ("whilst the people of the South are willing to . . . [grant the Negro] all the civil rights incident to his new situation," they will not grant him the right to vote).

15. *American Citizen*, 29 October 1865. Cf. *The Coahomian*, 3 November 1865 (the "absorbing question" for the South is not suffrage but the "labor system").

16. Rumors of black plots periodically circulated through the state. In 1867 Governor Humphreys issued a proclamation, saying: "[C]ombinations and conspiracies are being formed among the blacks to seize the lands and establish farms, expecting and hoping that Congress will arrange a plan of division and distribution, but unless this is done by January next they will proceed to help themselves, and are determined to go to war and are confident that they will be victors in any conflict with the whites." The governor then admonished blacks to abandon the false hopes and violent plans. Stanley F. Horn, *Invisible Empire: The Story of the Ku Klux Klan, 1865–1871* (Boston: Houghton Mifflin Company, 1939), 148. Cf. *The American Citizen*, 5 January 1865 (Negroes allegedly threaten to use the cartridge box if they are denied the ballot box).

17. P. L. Rainwater, ed., "The Autobiography of Benjamin Grubb Humphreys," *Mississippi Valley Historical Review* 21 (September 1934): 231, 247.

18. See generally William C. Harris, "Formulation of the First Mississippi Plan: The Black Code of 1865," *Journal of Mississippi History* 29 (August 1967): 181.

19. Ibid.

20. Garner, *Reconstruction in Mississippi*, 113.

21. John J. Trowbridge, *The South: A Tour of Its Battlefields and Ruined Cities, A Journey through the Desolated States* (New York: Arno Press and the New York Times, 1969), 372–73.

22. *Oxford Falcon*, 3 May 1866. See also *American Citizen*, 14 April 1866 ("revolutionary designs" of radicals include "changing form of government").

23. *American Citizen*, 28 April 1866. See also *Weekly Standard*, 7 April 1866 (Civil Rights Bill legislates states out of existence).

24. *American Citizen*, 10 February 1866; 16 February 1866.

25. *Vicksburg Journal*, 22 April 1866.

26. *Vicksburg Daily Herald*, 2 February 1866.

27. *Vicksburg Journal*, 19 May 1866. See also *Vicksburg Daily Times*, 20 June 1866 (Fourteenth Amendment is "the most stupendous piece of folly ever perpetrated by men who profess to be, and are considered, sane").

28. *Natchez Daily Courier*, 14 June 1866.

29. *Vicksburg Daily Times*, 1 July 1866.

30. *Southern Herald*, 25 August 1866.

31. Ibid.

32. *Hinds County Gazette*, 22 June 1866.

33. *Vicksburg Daily Herald*, 1 June 1866.

34. *Oxford Falcon*, 11 November 1866. See also *Vicksburg Daily Herald*, 24 July 1868 (since "[o]ne of the dearest privileges of citizenship is the right of suffrage," ratification of the Fourteenth Amendment "has secured to [blacks] the boon of suffrage").

35. *People's Press*, 11 October 1866.

36. *Southern Herald*, 10 October 1866 ("What these privileges or immunities are is left for Congress to declare.").

37. *People's Press*, 28 June 1866. See also *Southern Herald*, 25 August 1866 (radicals want to impose universal suffrage "only to increase the strength of their party").

38. *Hinds County Gazette*, 23 August 1869. See also *Southern Herald*, 25 August 1866 (under Section 3, Mississippi must "utterly ignore the existence of the brave men who spilled their blood in her defense").

39. *Oxford Falcon*, 11 November 1866.

40. *People's Press*, 28 June 1866.

41. *Jackson Weekly Clarion*, 10 October 1866.

42. *Natchez Daily Courier*, 14 June 1866.

43. *Vicksburg Daily Times*, 17 October 1866.

44. *Vicksburg Daily Times*, 21 September 1866.

45. *Jackson Clarion*, 28 September 1866. See also *Weekly Standard*, 3 April 1866 (Civil Rights Bill "legislates states out of existence"); *American Citizen*, 14 April 1866 ("revolutionary designs" of radicals include "changing form of government").

46. *Journal of the House of Representatives of the State of Mississippi at a Called Session, October 1866* (Jackson: J. J. Shannon & Co., 1866), 8.

47. Ibid., Appendix, 78.

48. Ibid., 78–79.

49. *Hinds County Gazette*, 31 January 1867. After the passage of the Reconstruction Acts, Mr. Alcorn insisted in a letter dated 26 April 1867 that "had this const. amendment been promptly accepted by the Southern people, the Union would have long since been restored." He went on to say that this mistake was fatal because the Fourteenth Amendment did not impose Negro suffrage on the states or deprive whites of the ballot; those were subsequently imposed through the Reconstruction Acts. *Vicksburg Daily Herald*, 2 May 1867.

50. *Weekly Panola Star*, 23 February 1867.

51. In fairness to the Mississippi legislature, it did take some steps to placate Congress. At the onset of the legislative session, Humphreys had urged the legislature "to relax the rigidity of our law" by removing its discriminatory features. When the legislature reconvened in January, it acted on the governor's advice and removed most of the laws that singled blacks out for differential treatment. The willingness, first, of the governor, and, second, of the legislature, to eliminate the discriminatory features of Mississippi law illustrates how they understood Section 1 of the Fourteenth Amendment. They interpreted it essentially to require equal treatment before the law; and they hoped, as did the drafters of the Southern Compromise Amendment, to forestall any grant of power to Congress to accomplish that goal by securing it themselves.

52. William C. Harris, *Presidential Reconstruction in Mississippi* (Baton Rouge: Louisiana State University Press, 1967), 234.

53. Garner, *Reconstruction in Mississippi*, 209. In 1868 this party, now calling itself the Democratic Party, adopted a resolution that repeated the accusation that radicals were engaged "in the work of Africanizing the Southern States, establishing Negro rule and Negro supremacy, and elevating the black race, politically, over the free-born white citizens of the South, and in violation of the Constitution giving to negroes the elective

franchise." And they reasserted their belief that "[black] ignorance and incapacity to exercise the privilege of suffrage, and to discharge the responsibilities of making laws and holding office, forbid that we consent to invest them with these privileges, or to consent to any legislation designed to establish the political or social equality of the white and black races—much less the subordination of the former to the latter, as advocated by the Radical party." *Vicksburg Daily Herald*, 22 February 1868.

Later the same paper reiterated the point: "Duty of Democratic party is to save 'African negroes' from 'political suicide'—they must be saved from 'this fearful crime against themselves and the superior race on which they depend for all that is valuable in life.' The fearful crime is 'the substitution of the African negro for the white race as the source of political power' in the new constitution." Ibid., 7 April 1868.

54. *Natchez Tri-Weekly Democrat*, 1 October 1867.

55. Garner, *Reconstruction in Mississippi*, 178–79.

56. James Alcorn, *Views on the Political Situation* (1867), 2. Quoted in Garner, *Reconstruction in Mississippi*, 180.

57. William C. Harris, *The Day of the Carpetbagger: Republican Reconstruction in Mississippi* (Baton Rouge: Louisiana State University Press, 1979), 78.

58. Garner, *Reconstruction in Mississippi*, 238. The Republicans' emphasis on the importance of free speech as an independent right sheds illuminating light on the incorporation thesis. Freedom of speech was often listed, as in these resolutions, along with the rights included in Section 1 of the Fourteenth Amendment. The clear implication is that these rights were viewed as independent of each other rather than as rights subsumed one in the other, as incorporation would have had it. Moreover, the fact that First Amendment rights were generally the only ones listed from the Bill of Rights suggests that all those rights were not thought of "as a group" as, again, would have been the case if it were generally understood that Section 1 incorporated the Bill of Rights.

59. D. Smith, "Black Reconstruction in Mississippi, 1862–1870" (Ph.D. diss., University of Kansas, 1985), 240.

60. Ibid., 239.

61. See generally P. Pittman, "The Mississippi Constitutional Convention of 1868" (M.A. thesis, University of Mississippi, 1949).

62. *Hinds County Gazette*, 10 January 1868. See also *Vicksburg Daily Herald*, 8 April 1868 (proposed institution is a "mongrel political abortion").

63. Harris, *The Day of the Carpetbagger*, 115.

64. William C. Harris, "The Reconstruction of the Commonwealth," in *A History of Mississippi*, ed. Richard A. McLemore, (Jackson: University and College Press of Mississippi, 1973), 563.

65. Harris, *The Day of the Carpetbagger*, 149.

66. Ibid., 150.

67. Ibid., 230.

68. The conservatives themselves could appropriate the language of the Declaration of Independence, as in this general indictment of radical policy:

> We quote the following enumeration of grievance from the Declaration of Independence, and so far as the South is concerned, they are as true to-day, as against Congress, as they were ninety years ago as against George the Third:
>
> "He has refused to pass other laws for the accommodation of large districts of people, unless those people would relinquish the right of representation in the Legislature; a right inestimable to them, and formidable to tyrants only. (See proposed amendment to the Constitution.)

"He has created a multitude of new offices, and sent hither swarms of officers to harrass our people and eat their substance. (Congress attempts to do so under the Freedmen's Bureau bill.)

"He has kept among us in time of peace, standing armies, without the consent of the Legislature. (The Congressional policy.)

"He has affected to render the military independent of and superior to the civil power. (Congress has done so, under the Civil Rights and Freedmen's Bureau bills.)

"For imposing taxes upon us without our consent. (The South has no voice or vote in Congress.)

"For taking away our charters, abolishing our most valuable laws, and altering, fundamentally, the powers of our Governments. (The Congressional policy.)

"For suspending our own Legislatures, and declaring themselves invested with power for us in all cases whatsoever. (Congress makes claim to this power.)"
(*Weekly Panola Star*, 21 July 1866)

69. See generally Warren A. Ellem, "Who Were the Mississippi Scalawags?" *Journal of Southern History* 38 (May 1972): 217.

70. Harris, *The Reconstruction of the Commonwealth*, 573. See generally J. Alcorn, *Inaugural Address of Gov. J. L. Alcorn, Delivered at Jackson on Thursday, March 10, 1870, to the Legislature of Mississippi* (1870).

71. Ibid., 187.

72. Smith, "Black Reconstruction," 235.

73. See *Weekly Panola Star*, 2 November 1867 ("It is clear and undeniable that only ruin can come of the domination of States by negroes").

74. *Hinds County Gazette*, 14 October 1868. The constitution was defeated by 7,629 votes.

75. Harris, *The Reconstruction of the Commonwealth*, 570.

76. *Forest Register Weekly*, 17 November 1869.

77. *Hinds County Gazette*, June 28, 1871. See generally Thomas B. Alexander, "Persistent Whiggery in Mississippi Reconstruction," *Journal of Mississippi History* 23 (April 1961): 71.

78. The Senate ratified the amendments twenty-four to two and twenty-eight to zero, respectively; and the House ratified eighty-seven to six and ninety-three to one, respectively. *Senate Journal* (1870), 19; *House Journal* (1870), 20.

79. William Sansing, "Congressional Reconstruction," in *A History of Mississippi*, ed. McLemore, 578. Opposition to the new system of public education was also fueled by anger at the tax imposed to finance it. The Klan often burned schools and flogged teachers. One hapless victim was A. P. Huggins, whose blood-soaked nightshirt was taken to Washington and given to Senator Butler. In a sensational and much reported speech, the senator waved it above his head as he denounced Southern cruelty. This bit of theater produced the "bloody shirt" expression that became part of the country's political vernacular. Horn, *Invisible Empire*, 150–51.

80. William C. Harris, *A Reconsideration of the Mississippi Scalawag*, 12.

81. Sansing, "Congressional Reconstruction," 581.

82. Lillian A. Pereyra, *James Lusk Alcorn: Persistent Whig* (Baton Rouge: Louisiana State University Press, 1966), 116.

83. Vernon L. Wharton, *The Negro in Mississippi, 1865–1890* (Chapel Hill: University of North Carolina Press, 1947), 231.

84. Garner, *Reconstruction in Mississippi*, 288.

85. Smith, "Black Reconstruction," 229.

86. Cf. J. McLaughlin, "John R. Lynch: The Reconstruction Politician" (Ph.D. diss., Ball State University, 1981), 185–86.

87. David Donald has explained this reaction: "In this crisis Mississippi Whigs had to choose between open support of color line policies and a program which they firmly believed would lead to racial amalgamation. . . . For the southern planter who had never been able to accept ideas of racial equality . . . opposition to the Republicans [became] inescapable." David Donald, "The Scalawag in Mississippi Reconstruction," *Journal of Southern History* 10 (November 1944): 447, 455. Cf. Harris, "A Reconsideration of the Mississippi Scalawag."

88. Harris, "The Reconstruction of the Commonwealth," 586.

89. See generally Frank Johnston, "Conference between General George and Governor Ames," *Publications of the Mississippi Historical Society, vol. 6* (Jackson: 1902), 65.

90. Quoted in Harris, "The Reconstruction of the Commonwealth," 588.

91. Donald, "The Scalawag in Mississippi Reconstruction," 447–48 ("The . . . Mississippi Plan received much attention in other Southern states, where Democratic leaders imitated the Mississippi tactics").

92. Ellem, "Who Were the Mississippi Scalawags?" 240.

4

Ratification in North Carolina

[The radicals] propose to make us drink our own piss
and eat our own dung.

—A North Carolinian, writing to Governor Worth in the fall of 1866

The debate on the Fourteenth Amendment in North Carolina can best be understood if it is followed chronologically because the history of the Fourteenth Amendment in North Carolina cannot be understood apart from the history of the state.[1] The two-year debate over the amendment both reflected and shaped that history. The successive political crises in which the amendment became entangled both illuminated and obscured its meaning. The story of the Fourteenth Amendment in North Carolina thus begins not with its submission to the states in June 1866, but a year earlier, with Lee's surrender at Appomattox.

Following the collapse of the Confederacy, North Carolina, like other Southern states, acquiesced in what it understood to be the demands of the national government. It adopted an antisecession ordinance. The 1865 state convention organized at President Johnson's direction by William Holden, the provisional governor, promulgated the ordinance, which voters approved on November 9, 1865 by a vote of 20,870 to 1,983. The convention also ratified the antislavery amendment. During the legislative debate over ratification in late November 1865, the House defeated a resolution that would have stated the legislature's understanding that the enforcement clause did not give Congress any power to legislate on behalf of the civil or political rights of freedmen.[2] It passed laws that guaranteed the former slaves certain civil rights. It retained many class, race-based distinctions, however. For example, blacks were given the privilege of suing in court; but they could not testify in altercations between two white men unless both agreed to accept the testimony. Another example of this double standard was the punishment for rape, which carried a mandatory death penalty only for blacks.[3] By early 1866 these actions had nevertheless convinced President Johnson that North Carolina should be readmitted to the Union.[4]

Most white North Carolinians agreed, and in public they heaped praise on the president. Privately, however, the state's conservative leaders expressed grave reservations about the validity and wisdom of presidential Reconstruction. While they had submitted to its terms because they saw no other alternative, they considered their submission "a moral sacrifice justified only by overriding practical considerations."[5]

Moreover, they were unremittingly hostile to equal rights for blacks; and they remained suspicious of national authority. For example, the editor of the most influential conservative paper in the state denounced the Civil Rights Bill as the product of "a mad and foolish policy of negro equality."[6] Although the editor insisted that the bill conferred on blacks only those civil rights already guaranteed them under the laws of North Carolina,[7] he feared that blacks and their supporters would demand social and political equality under its provisions.[8] The fact that federal courts would have jurisdiction to decide those claims made recognition of these rights all the more likely. One North Carolinian thus concluded: "The Southern people can regard the bill in no other light than a direct impeachment of their declarations that they will do justice to the freedmen, and of the fidelity of our Judiciary and Courts."[9]

Discussions of the bill in the state's conservative press revealed how "the Southern people" would "do justice to the freedmen." First, they would construe the privileges and immunities of citizenship narrowly. Only those privileges and immunities peculiar to United States citizenship and necessary to civil freedom would be guaranteed blacks.[10] The privileges and immunities of citizenship did not include social or political rights. Second, conservative leaders revealed that they would view narrowly any obligation to treat blacks equally. They expressed horror that blacks "had presumed to walk into churches and occupy seats usually . . . occupied by whites"[11] or that officials might have to perform mixed marriages.

At the same time, a minority of white North Carolinians, many of whom had opposed the war or had quickly lost enthusiasm for it, refused to follow the conservative white majority. Aligning themselves with the newly freed blacks, they hoped to create a new liberal majority.[12] This coalition was prepared to recognize far broader rights for blacks than were the conservatives. Although these minority whites initially waffled on the question of Negro suffrage, they ultimately came to realize that their electoral success depended upon enfranchising blacks. The leaders of what ultimately became the Union or Republican Party worked closely with the radical leadership in Congress.[13] They plied the radicals with stories of conservative intransigence on race questions and conservative persecution of Union sympathizers. They privately urged a stringent Reconstruction that would, not surprisingly, bring them into power.

Leaders of the state's nascent Republican Party thus advised North Carolinians to accept the Fourteenth Amendment. They warned that if North Carolina refused to ratify the amendment, the state would be subjected to even harsher terms.[14] William Holden the former provisional governor who now led the radicals, speculated, for example, that Congress might confiscate land and give everyone forty acres and a mule.[15]

Conservative leaders, echoing President Johnson's plea, advised North Carolina to reject the amendment. These conservatives watched and waited, hoping that a resurgent Democratic Party under the president's leadership would snuff out Republican radicalism in the North.[16] At the same time, they fought to prevent its emergence in North Carolina.

During the late summer and fall of 1866, the people thus debated the wisdom of ratifying the Fourteenth Amendment. It was the fundamental issue in the gubernatorial election between Worth, the conservative candidate, and Dockery, Holden's stand-in,[17] and in most legislative districts. By the end of the campaign, all observers agreed that "[n]o subject has been more fully discussed in North Carolina, and none upon which the great body of our people have made up a more deliberate judgment, than that."[18]

Those who opposed ratification relentlessly savaged the amendment. They objected to it on broad constitutional grounds. Congress had no right to promulgate the amendment because the Southern states had been excluded from the deliberative process.[19] They objected to its form: the amendment combined four unrelated provisions, each one a separate amendment.[20] They objected to it because it imposed dishonorable terms. "Humiliating" and "degrading" were the adjectives most frequently used to describe its provisions.[21] One unhappy gentleman captured this sentiment graphically in a private letter: the radicals, he wrote, propose to make us "drink our own piss and eat our own dung."[22]

The disqualification provisions of Section 3 particularly incensed a majority of white North Carolinians.[23] As soon as the Reconstruction Committee made its proposal public, the most widely read conservative paper in the state labeled the third section an "insult."[24] Section 3 would "bar out all citizens who, in the estimation of the people, are fit to fill their places."[25] Most white North Carolinians refused to turn their backs on those who had led them through the war. In election after election, they returned secession leaders to public office; those elected promptly filled appointive offices with men who had been sympathetic to secession.

These leaders saw no reason why they should be disqualified. Indeed, they railed against the injustice of being excluded from office. Governor Worth, writing a friend, exclaimed: "This Howard amendment [the Fourteenth Amendment], if adopted, declares me so contaminated that I am unworthy to be elected to any office in the State—even that of Constable."[26] As the campaign drew to a close, the governor repeated the point. "Come what may I will not ratify an amendment of the Constitution by which I would declare myself ineligible as a constable."[27] At the end of the campaign, the editor of the *Wilmington*

Daily Dispatch still found that North Carolinians objected to the amendment primarily because "it excluded a class of their people."[28]

Disgust at the disqualification provision hardly exhausted the specific objections to ratification. Opponents also objected to Section 2, which forced the state to choose between granting blacks the right to vote and losing representation in Congress. Most white North Carolinians recoiled at the prospect of black voters, and diatribes against it filled the press. As the editor of the *Sentinel* declared, "Giving to the colored people generally the right of suffrage would lead to the worst consequences."[29] Most white North Carolinians believed that blacks could not vote intelligently because they had neither brains nor morals.[30] This intense fear of Negro suffrage generated enormous opposition to the amendment, which was designed, conservative leaders asserted, to force Negro suffrage on the South.[31]

Opponents did not overlook Section 1, even though the general constitutional objections to the drafting of the amendment and the more specific objections to the disqualification and representation provisions dominated the discussion.[32] In discussing Section 1, opponents concentrated their fire on three points, repeating the same arguments they had made against the Civil Rights Bill. Their rhetorical strategy thus belied their contention that Section 1 extended new rights to blacks. Instead, their arguments implicitly confirmed the view that Section 1 merely transformed the statutory provisions of the Civil Rights Bill into constitutional law. Similarly, conservatives impliedly conceded the narrow scope of Section 1 when they dismissed the argument that ratification would assure readmission, insisting that Congress would still demand political rights for blacks.[33]

The ambiguity of the privileges and immunities clause was, of course, their first objection. A radical Congress or meddlesome federal judges might construe it to include all sorts of political rights, including the right to vote. Radicals would argue that suffrage is a privilege and immunity of citizenship, and under Section 5 Congress might pass statutes guaranteeing suffrage for blacks.[34] In this way opponents raised once again the bugaboo of the black voter.

The ambiguity of the equal protection clause was a second objection. A radical Congress or meddlesome federal judges might construe it to include all sorts of rights, including the right of blacks to associate with whites. Many whites loathed any personal contact with blacks other than as their masters or employers. Going to school or church together was anathema.[35] Serving under blacks in the militia or being judged by them in court was inconceivable.[36] Intermarriage was unthinkable.[37] Whites feared mongrelization, and opponents of the amendment played on their fears.

Third and finally, opponents objected to the national government's assumption of authority in these areas. They repeatedly raised the specter that Congress would usurp traditional state authority under the guise of enforcing the Section 1 guarantees.[38] Opponents quoted the dire prediction of the governor of Mississippi: "We may find Congress assuming absolute control over all the people of a state and their domestic concerns and this virtually abolishes the State."[39] The ever vigilant editor of the *Sentinel* warned: "The first and fifth sections . . . contain the germ of consolidation and destruction of the . . . state governments."[40]

Even if Congress chose not to exercise its Section 5 powers, opponents feared that federal judges might seize upon the Section 1 guarantees as a "pretext for extending the jurisdiction of the Federal Courts into the most minute and trivial occurrences, between native white citizens and blacks, and between the former and immigrants from other states."[41] Since the only federal court in the state sat in Raleigh, black plaintiffs could force those against whom they complained to travel far from their homes. "What is this," asked one critic, "but consolidation and the destruction of the great principle of Republican liberty that the municipal government of every State shall dispense justice in the neighborhood of the parties litigant?"[42] These critics thus understood that Section 1 constituted "a radical departure from the organic character of the government."[43]

Proponents of the amendment downplayed these fears. They insisted that the privileges and immunities of citizenship included only those rights enumerated in the Civil Rights Bill: the rights to contract, sue, and hold property.[44] These were civil rights, and proponents sharply distinguished these from political and social rights. They repeatedly assured voters, for example, that the Fourteenth Amendment did not enfranchise blacks.[45] They emphasized that the equal protection clause simply insured blacks equal treatment before the law. Under this interpretation, they pointed out, for example, the criminal law could not impose stiffer penalties on blacks than on whites.[46]

Holden advocated ratification from the beginning, and his views are entitled to great weight because he was the principal spokesman for the amendment in North Carolina. Through his Raleigh newspaper, he insistently urged ratification. On the hustings, he whipped up support for the amendment. Holden dominated the debate so thoroughly that opponents invariably cited his statements whenever they summarized the argument for ratification.

Holden himself restated and summarized that argument in a sixteen-page pamphlet published in Raleigh on September 20, 1866. Holden concentrated on the general proposition that approval was essential to restoration and that only those loyal to the Union could effect restoration. He did, however, analyze "the Congressional plan," which he characterized as "generous and merciful" and "similar in principle and nearly the same in detail" as the president's plan.[47] He devoted but one paragraph to the first section:

This plan, after recognizing, as the President's plan does, the existence of the States as States, proposes, first, that a colored man from Massachusetts shall have the same liberty in North Carolina that he possesses in his own State, and that a colored man from North Carolina shall have the same liberty in Massachusetts which he possesses at home. It provides that no State shall abridge the privileges or immunities of a citizen of the United States, or deny to any person life, liberty, or property or the equal protection of the law. Who objects to that? I am sure President Johnson does not; for the civil rights bill, now in existence as a law, and which will in no event be repealed, makes the same provision for the colored race, and the objection of the President was not to this feature of that law, but to that part of it which, as he thought, improperly subordinated the State Courts to the Courts of the United States. If it be said that there is some concealed purpose in this provision hereafter to force negro suffrage on the States as the only means of securing to colored people the "privileges or immunities" referred to, the answer is that this cannot be so, for the reason that a subsequent section in the amendment leaves the question of suffrage, wholly and solely with the States.[48]

   Like most proponents of the amendment, Holden interpreted Section 1 as "constitutionalizing" the Civil Rights Bill. Recent events in North Carolina had demonstrated the need to put such guarantees beyond the reach of legislative majorities. In the same pamphlet, for example, Holden lamented the fact that "any future convention" could abrogate the recent ordinance permitting blacks to testify.[49] He rejected the contention that the privileges and immunities guarantee included the right to vote.[50] His rejection reinforced the argument that the first section simply protected *civil* rights because the right to vote had always been considered a *political* rather than a civil right. Moreover, he argued that the second section explicitly left the question of Negro suffrage to the states.

   Holden's analysis is as interesting in what it omitted as in what it included. He ignored the argument that the national government could assert its authority under Section 5 to define the privileges and immunities of citizenship and thereby supplant state powers. He glided elliptically over the argument that federal courts might entertain claims that whites had denied blacks their civil rights. Holden naturally downplayed those interpretations that aroused concern and yet, unlike the Negro suffrage argument, could not be dismissed as erroneous. That explanation cannot, however, explain his failure to discuss the due process guarantee. Holden could easily have rebutted any argument that the due process guarantee contained "some concealed purpose" to incorporate the Bill of Rights by repeating the standard interpretation of the draftsmen's intent. He did not, for one reason: no one had even hinted that the due process clause might be read as a shorthand statement of those rights or any other substantive rights.

   As the campaign wound down, the conservatives sensed victory. Although freed, blacks still could not vote. Consequently, the decision was left to propertied white North Carolinians. Encouraged by President Johnson to believe that Northerners would repudiate the radical platform (i.e., the Fourteenth Amendment) in the fall elections above the Mason-Dixon line, most Southern whites saw no reason to accept it themselves. The *Sentinel* boasted that "less than twenty 'Howard men'" would disgrace the new legislature.[51] The legislature's vote on December 13, 1866, confirmed that boast. Only eleven delegates voted to ratify. The House rejected the amendment by a vote of ninety-three to ten; the Senate rejected it by a vote of forty-five to one.[52] Conservatives gloated: "By an almost unanimous rejection of the Howard amendment . . . in the face of terrible uncertainties and threats North Carolina has spurned an offer to purchase amnesty and restoration at the expense of honor."[53]

The Report of the Joint Select Committee, upon whose recommendations the legislature had acted, reiterated the now standard conservative objection to the privileges and immunities guarantee:

Whether reference is had only to such privileges and immunities as may be supposed now to exist, or to all others which the Federal Government may hereafter declare to belong to it, or may choose to grant to citizens, is left in doubt, though the latter construction seems the more natural, and is one which that Government could at any time insist upon as correct and entirely consistent with the language used. With this construction placed upon it, what limit would remain to the power of that Government to interfere in the internal affairs of the States?[54]

The committee answered its question with an example almost too awful to contemplate. The national government might declare the right to marry a privilege and immunity of citizenship. In that event, the North Carolina law forbidding interracial marriage would abridge a citizen's privileges and immunities. The national government would therefore forbid enforcement of the law. Miscegenation would be lawful. Apparently, the "bare possibility" of such an interpretation was sufficiently horrifying that the committee saw no need to discuss the possible impact of the due process or equal protection clauses.

The legislature's rejection of the Fourteenth Amendment scarcely settled the matter. Congress, reacting to the South's defiant refusal to ratify it, imposed military Reconstruction. Under the military supervision of Generals Daniel Sickles and Edward Canby, blacks were enrolled to vote and disloyal whites were struck from the voter rolls. In the ensuing election for delegates to the constitutional convention, the Unionists, who had organized themselves into a state Republican Party, triumphed. These delegates drafted a constitution acceptable to both military authorities and the now greatly broadened electorate. This electorate also sent an overwhelming majority of Republicans to the first session of the state legislature that met under the new constitution. It immediately and enthusiastically ratified the Fourteenth Amendment.

As these events unfolded in the year and a half between January 1867 and July 1868, the Fourteenth Amendment receded in importance as a topic of public debate. Because it no longer stated all the terms of restoration, the public turned its attention to the Reconstruction Acts and the military decisions that implemented them. The amendment never disappeared entirely from discussion, however. Whatever else Congress might demand, it still demanded compliance with the terms of the amendment. Since the reconstructed South was to mirror the society envisaged by the drafters of Section 1, many decisions made during this period revealed how the concepts embodied in that section of the amendment were understood.

The organization of a Republican Party in the state—a major political development during this period—revealed much about the contemporary understanding of the equal protection concept. Meeting in Raleigh in March 1867 to establish the party, these Unionists-turned-Republicans declared themselves "in favor of complete equality for the blacks."[55] Six months later, when the party convened again, it published a formal address "to the people of North Carolina" in which it reaffirmed its commitment to equal rights:

The principles sought to be established upon the sound basis of popular sentiment, as preliminary to reconstruction, may be fully summed up in two propositions, viz: . . .
    2. Civil and political equality among all citizens, irrespective of race or color, and the protection of white and colored alike in all the rights, privileges and immunities of citizenship.[56]

What was the equality that these Republicans endorsed? Daniel Goodloe, a moderate Unionist, answered that question this way:

The enemies of freedom, for a century past, have labored to confound the ideas of equality before the law, and equality of moral, intellectual, and social conditions. Seizing upon the phrase in the Declaration of Independence, "that all men are created equal," which is explained by the context to mean only that all men have equal rights, these sophists affect to understand the proposition to be, that all men are born with equal endowments of intellect, beauty, strength, fortune and aptitude for virtue; and they then proceed elaborately to prove the contrary, and to jump to the conclusion that because men are not thus equally blessed by nature and by circumstances, therefore they should not have equal rights before human tribunals.[57]

Equality meant equality of opportunity under the law, not equality of condition, circumstance, or capacity.[58] Holden clarified this point for those who persistently misstated the concept of equality espoused by Republicans:

The *Sentinel* assails the colored people because they evince a natural and laudable disposition to acquire property. It says they think they can not be the "equals" of the white man until they possess property too: and that they reason thus: "If I am the equal of the white man, I ought of course to own houses and lands, and horses and cattle, like the white man." Well, do they now own such things? Did not the colored people before the rebellion own such things? It is not true that colored people "reason" as the *Sentinel* says they do. They insist upon the right to own property of all kinds, just like the white man, or the red man, or the tawny man, but they expect to get this property honestly. That is all.—No two men can be exactly alike in the amount of property they own, but they can be alike in the right to own property.[59]

Admittedly, Republicans had also come to understand that blacks needed the vote to protect themselves: "The right of suffrage is the shield and buckler of poverty. It commands respect from those who make the laws, and from all those who aspire to a leading post in society. Without the ballot there is no real freedom and safety to the poor. Even with it, they are often victimized by the cunning ambition of the wealthy and the powerful."[60] Republicans never suggested, however, that the pending Fourteenth Amendment contained that guarantee.[61]

Rather, they included it in their new, broader demand for political equality in addition to the civil equality previously demanded.[62]

Republicans did limit their demands to civil and political equality. They never demanded social equality. Indeed, they emphasized that equality did not and could not extend to social relationships: "It does not follow, because any man is free, and entitled to all the civil and political rights that others enjoy, that he is thereby made the equal of any other man socially; and no portion of our people understand this better, or observe it with more propriety than our colored friends."[63] Black leaders themselves reassured whites that blacks did not wish to socialize with them.[64]

While Republicans generally agreed that the state could not enforce social equality, they disagreed among themselves about whether the state could encourage or discourage social interaction. The debate over the right of blacks to use public carriers dramatized these differences. This problem was before the public constantly because General Sickles had issued an order that required that blacks be permitted to sit on juries and that forbade discrimination in public facilities. The order "aroused strong resentment."[65] In an extended discussion of "the social problem," one newspaper editor argued that blacks and whites need not "be forced into social contact" even though publicly owned or licensed businesses had "no right to exclude any class of citizens from equal accommodations and equal privileges."[66] Separate but equal facilities were the answer to the social problem. At the same time, another newspaper editor insisted that blacks had a right to ride in the same cars. He poked fun at those whites who thought such contact might contaminate them: "The Chief Justice of the United States, foreign Ministers, and members of Congress ride in the same public coach in Washington City with colored people, and with all kinds of people; and we have yet to learn that the *Sentinel* and its followers are better than the distinguished persons referred to."[67]

Although such jibes angered conservatives,[68] the 1867 election campaign was less rancorous than either the preceding or succeeding election, largely because the conservatives were disorganized, divided, and dispirited.[69] Under the Reconstruction Acts, Southern states were obliged to revise their electoral rolls and then hold elections for constitutional conventions. A group of conservatives did meet in Raleigh in late September 1867, but the group did not adopt a platform. Although conservatives stood for election in almost every county, "their canvass was listless."[70] In November the voters approved the convention call by a three-to-one margin, and Republican candidates swamped their conservative opponents.[71]

Deliberations at the constitutional convention, which met in Raleigh on January 14, 1868, shed further light on the contemporary understanding of the equality principle.[72] The Declaration of Rights sounded the general theme by incorporating the grand principles of the Declaration of Independence and the first section of the Fourteenth Amendment.[73] More specifically, the delegates decided that Negroes could vote, hold office, sit on juries, and serve in the militia.[74] The latter two decisions distressed conservative whites, who raged against the humiliating spectacle of a black juror sitting in judgment of a white defendant or a black officer commanding a white militiaman.[75] These decisions convinced the conservatives that the convention intended to go beyond the Fourteenth Amendment and the Reconstruction Acts and impose social equality.[76]

At the convention itself, conservative delegates maneuvered to smoke out the Republican majority on the issue of social equality. When the convention took up the report on the militia, Mr. Graham of Orange County moved to add the following language: "But white and colored persons shall be organized into separate commands, and no white man shall ever be required to obey a negro officer."[77] When Mr. Jones, a Republican delegate, sought to sidestep the question by suggesting that it was for the legislature rather than the convention to decide, Mr. Durham said it was a test question:

The reconstruction acts do not prevent the passage of this resolution, declaring the superiority of the white man. We claim that the white man has some rights left him, even under the reconstruction acts. But it is the evident intention of this Convention to go beyond the reconstruction acts, and thereby not only give civil and political equality, but to force upon the people of the State social equality. I want the people to know who are the men that are endeavoring to perpetrate such an outrage upon them.[78]

While some Republicans agreed with Mr. Jones that the question was best left to the legislature, other Republicans accepted the conservative dare and declared themselves in favor of social equality. And one black delegate tweaked the conservative nose by proposing that any white man who had mulatto children should be placed in the same company as his children.[79] In the end, the convention overwhelmingly rejected the Graham Amendment.

Similarly, the convention refused to require separation of the races in public schools.[80] It refused to include a prohibition against interracial marriage in the Declaration of Rights.[81] Yet at the same time it passed a resolution recommending separate schools and condemning interracial marriage.[82] The convention rejected its own committee suggestions that the constitution bar any person of African descent from ever holding executive office.[83] It also rejected a suggestion that the constitution forever bar a Negro from having a white apprentice or ward.[84] These decisions are perhaps best understood as a moderate resolution of socially divisive disputes that left their more particular decision to subsequent legislatures, which presumably would be free to react to evolving social attitudes.

The campaign in the spring of 1868 necessarily focused on the new constitution.[85] During this bitter and ugly campaign, conservative whites, who had recovered from their doldrums of the previous year,[86] denied that they wanted to build a white man's party.[87] Nevertheless, they appealed to the basest racism:

If you would save your State from Negro rule, the DAUGHTERS of our poor white people from being forced into social equality with negro BOYS at school, and yourselves from being forced into the ranks of the Militia with negroes and under negro officers, who will be empowered to hold Court Martials over and punish you for what they might call delinquency. . . , attend the Mass Meet.[88]

Repeatedly, conservative candidates asked three questions: Do you want Negro or white rule? Do you want school integration? Do you want interracial marriage?[89] On election eve, the conservative press exhorted whites: "If you would not be placed beneath the heel of negro domination, VOTE. If you would not be placed on a level with the negro in the schools and the militia, VOTE. If you would not have the marriage relation degraded, VOTE!"[90] As the campaign degenerated into demagoguery, rational discussion of the new constitution, whose Declaration of Rights, particularly Section 17, tracked the pending Fourteenth Amendment, disappeared. Even though everyone realized that a Republican legislature would ratify the Fourteenth Amendment, neither candidates nor newsmen talked about its specific provisions.

The Republicans won. The voters approved the constitution, elected Holden governor, and returned overwhelming Republican majorities in both the House and Senate.[91] The conservatives complained: "Take away the negro Radical vote, and Conservatives would have swept the whole election."[92] Regardless, the triumphant Republicans poured into Raleigh to organize themselves and the new legislature.[93] They saw no need to study the still-pending Fourteenth Amendment any further. Long committed to its adoption, they made its ratification the first order of business.

On the Senate floor, the conservatives spoke against it one last time.[94] Senator Robbins rose and in a lengthy talk rehashed the already standard objections. Congress lacked the authority to promulgate the amendment because it had excluded the Southern states. The amendment unfairly disqualified thousands of the state's "best sons." It unwisely changed the basis of congressional representation. It conferred unprecedented power on the national government. In this litany of complaints, Senator Robbins did not recite any specific objections to Section 1. He did reiterate his opposition to Negro suffrage, which he recognized was commanded by the new constitution. Although he mouthed a desire to promote the "real welfare" of blacks, he feared for any society which extended them equal rights. Presumably, he objected to Section 1 because it promoted that end.

After Senator Robbins sat down, the question was called; and the Senate joined the House in approving the amendment. North Carolina thus fittingly observed Independence Day two days early by ratifying an amendment that embodied the fundamental principle upon which America had been founded: "that all men are created equal; that they are endowed with certain inalienable rights; that among these are life, liberty, and the pursuit of happiness."

In his inaugural address, Governor Holden praised the triumph of these "free principles" and called for "absolute civil and political equality" between the races.[95] His specific recommendations showed how he understood that command. He urged creation of a militia, but added:

It is not proposed, nor is it required by the Constitution, that the two races should be mustered and drilled in the same companies and regiments. Following the example of the government of the United States, they may be divided into separate companies and regiments; but it is due to the colored race that they should have, whenever they desire it, officers of their own color for their own companies and regiments.[96]

He favored general education for all, but added: "It is believed to be better for both, and most satisfactory to both, that the schools for the two, thus separate and apart, should enjoy equally the fostering care of the State."[97] Thus did the staunchest defender of the Fourteenth Amendment in North Carolina and the leading spokesman for radicalism in the state explain his understanding of the equality principle.

The legislature's actions in the short July term and the succeeding November term indicate that a majority of its members interpreted the Fourteenth Amendment as did their governor. Committed to its principles, which they had so recently enshrined in their own state constitution, the Republican legislators tried to reform the state according to its commands. Delegates introduced numerous bills about black rights, and on nine separate occasions the legislature voted on bills involving those rights.[98] These bills ranged from measures that reaffirmed the legal equality of blacks[99] to a resolution that upheld the House speaker's ejection of a journalist for stigmatizing blacks.[100] They included measures allowing blacks to testify as witnesses,[101] to ride on public conveyances,[102] and to attend public schools.[103]

The Republican Party almost unanimously favored bills intended to insure the legal equality of blacks.[104] The legislature's failure to enact some bills that guaranteed blacks legal rights did not necessarily prove that the majority thought blacks unentitled to those rights. For example, Representative Leary questioned the wisdom of passing any law about color.[105] He argued that the new constitution nullified all existing statutes that discriminated on the basis of race. If the legislature began repealing these old laws, he warned, it would cast doubt on the validity of the constitutional proscription and presumably would validate any unrepealed statutes.[106]

Republican unanimity dissipated, however, when the legislature voted on bills intended to promote desegregation, which might lead to social equality. Whatever implications may be drawn, for example, from the legislature's failure to repeal Chapter 107 of the 1854 Revised Code, which referred to slaves, free Negroes, and persons of color,[107] one fact is clear. Only a small minority of the Republicans favored an egalitarian society in which the government enforced social as well as civil and political equality. Senator Eppes introduced a bill in March 1869 to protect the rights of all citizens traveling on public conveyances. Representative Sykes introduced a similar bill in the House in February 1870.

Representative Robbins introduced a bill in December 1869 to prevent discrimination on steamboats. None of the bills passed.[108] The debates on school legislation revealed a sense that the Fourteenth Amendment did not necessarily command integration. Even the black delegates generally took the view that "social mixing should be allowed but not forced."[109] Thus Senator Galloway answered a proposal that the galleries be segregated by suggesting instead that each race should have a side with a middle section kept open for both.[110]

The debate on the militia bills confirmed the apparently widespread belief that separate but equal treatment would insure blacks the equal protection of the laws. In August 1868, legislation for the reorganization of the state militia was introduced.[111] It passed, despite the fact that Representative Leary opposed the bill because Section 3 called for racially separate militia and because Section 13 of a substitute bill promised that white and black members would not have to serve together.[112] Indeed, seven of the ten black representatives voted for it; and all three black senators voted for the bill.[113] Some black delegates doubtless compromised their insistence on equal treatment in order to secure protection against the reign of terror that the Klan had already begun to inflict upon blacks and their friends.[114] Indeed, the conservative Democratic leadership considered the Klan "a god-send" because it "reduced the number of Negro voters through intimidation" and "[drew] out a larger and more unified white vote."[115] That blacks had to make that concession in order to obtain police protection from a legislature sympathetic to their needs only dramatized how narrowly those who favored equal protection viewed its scope.

Even that commitment vanished within a few years. The much-maligned Albion Tourgee had seen the bleak future the newly freed slaves faced in North Carolina even as the Reconstruction Acts were being passed in the spring of 1867. In fact, he had opposed those acts precisely because "they lacked effective federal implementation and were dependent upon southern Republican strength." He predicted that "the mass of poor, uneducated, and inexperienced Negro and white Republicans would not long succeed against the wealth, ability, and power which opposed them."[116]

NOTES

1. The standard history for the period is Joseph G. Hamilton, *Reconstruction in North Carolina* (New York: Columbia University, 1914). Hamilton's work is thorough but biased. At points, it reads like an apologia for the Democratic Party and its aristocratic and racist policies.

2. *Journal of the House of Commons of the General Assembly of the State of North Carolina at the Sessions of 1864–1865* (Raleigh, N.C.: Wm. E. Pell, Printer to the State, 1866), 26. These debates over Congress's enforcement powers foreshadowed the debate over Section 5 of the Fourteenth Amendment.

3. See generally Hamilton, *Reconstruction in North Carolina*, 154.

4. By the summer of 1866, most of the Southern states had reorganized their governments under the terms of presidential Reconstruction. They had complied with all the

president's demands and had elected officials who felt that their states were thus entitled to be readmitted.

5. E. McGee, "North Carolina Conservatives and Reconstruction" (Ph.D. diss., University of North Carolina, 1972), 358.

6. *Raleigh Sentinel*, 11 April 1866.

7. *Raleigh Sentinel*, 14 April 1866. Later, the conservatives conceded that freedmen possessed "certain rights . . . agreed upon and sanctioned by the universal consent of mankind, called *natural rights*. These are the rights of protection to life, to liberty, or to property, and to the pursuit of happiness, or what has been more commonly designated, of late, '*equality before the law*.'" Ibid., 5 November 1867. Freedmen in North Carolina were legally recognized as citizens.

8. *Raleigh Sentinel*, 4 April 1866.

9. *Wilmington Daily Dispatch*, 11 April 1866.

10. *Raleigh Sentinel*, 12 April 1866.

11. *Raleigh Sentinel*, 4 May 1866.

12. "In one word, conservatism means simply this: none but the educated and the property-holders should be allowed to take any part in the government. The vast majority of the people, both white and colored, not being blessed with wealth or education, are thus placed at the mercy of the governing few, and all history shows that a limited governing class or oligarchy, have invariably oppressed the masses to advance themselves. The same line of argument that takes suffrage from the black man, takes it away from the humble white man; and conservative politicians have no hesitation in saying privately, that if their views were carried out, there should be a property qualification for white and black alike. If the poor uneducated white man would guard his own rights, let him see to it that the colored citizens are not deprived of theirs." *Raleigh Standard*, 16 May 1868. According to the *Asheville Pioneer:*

> [T]here can be no doubt that the sixty thousand colored men of this State will, with perhaps a rare exception, cast their lot with the Republican party. Out of the eighty thousand white votes of this State we may safely put thirty or forty thousand as the number of loyal votes, and with these and the sixty thousand colored votes we shall have such a triumph for the Republican party. (*Asheville Pioneer*, 26 September 1867)

Conservatives may have feared this populism as much as they feared civil rights for blacks. The editor of the *Sentinel* criticized the "new [1868] constitution" for the following reason: "It will totally discard that essential republican principle that property has a claim to representation or a right to protection or guarantee in the property holder qualifications of the representative or public officer." *Raleigh Sentinel*, 18 February 1868. See also Jonathan Worth to A. M. Tomlinson and Sons, 11 April 1868:

> I regard the proposed new [1868] constitution as virtual confiscation. No government, based on the will of mere numbers, irrespective of intelligence or virtue, can last long. Providence has so ordered it that a majority of mankind are improvident. Self interest is a ruling principle of our frail nature and hence the non-property holder will be antagonistic to the property holder. Civilization consists in the possession and protection of property. If we cannot defeat the adoption of the proposed Constitution the principle will be triumphant that those who have no interest in the protection of property and the preservation of order, will be the ruling power. (Reprinted in *Correspondence of Jonathan Worth*, vol. 2, ed. Joseph G. Hamilton, [Raleigh, N.C.: Edwards & Broughton, 1909], 1185)

13. For example, Holden went to Washington in December 1866 and January 1867 to confer with congressional radicals. H. Raper, "William Woods Holden: A Political Biography" (Ph.D. diss., University of North Carolina, 1951), 204. Those who could not travel to Washington "flooded the mails with letters of advice to radicals in Congress." William A. Russ, "Radical Disfranchisement in North Carolina 1867–1868," *North Carolina Historical Review* 11 (1934): 271, 275–76.

Governor Worth was apprised of Holden's efforts by B. S. Hedrick, his "eyes" in Washington:

> I have it on good authority that Dr. Powell and Holden have a scheme, approved by certain members of Congress to go to work and organize a *new* so-called loyal State Govt. They will begin by invitations to the people to assemble in their sovereign capacity and elect delegates to a Convention at which all *loyal men*, white and black will be allowed to vote. This Convention will form a constitution and such as will be accepted by Congress. (B. S. Hedrick to Governor Worth, 26 February 1867, reprinted in *Correspondence of Jonathan Worth, vol. 2,* 300)

14. A few conservatives recommended ratification for that reason as well. See, e.g., *Western Democrat*, 9 October 1866 ("We do not like the amendment, but if we can do no better, we would advise its adoption"). See also *Western Democrat*, 26 March 1867; 5 March 1867; 19 February 1867; 4 December 1866.

15. *Raleigh Standard*, 4 April 1866. Although both the white and black leaders of the Republican Party opposed confiscation, they used it as a threat. See *Raleigh Register*, 6 September 1867 ("How can it be expected that men will cooperate with a party which threatens them with confiscation . . . ?"). One student has concluded that confiscation was one of the two most discussed issues in the summer of 1867. Raper, "William Woods Holden," 212.

16. *Wilmington Journal*, 27 September 1866 ("So long as the President stands by them, the South will refuse to ratify these amendments"). Even after the Democratic election debacle in the North, Governor Worth reassured his conservative supporters that "the great body of [the Northern people] do not entertain towards us the destroying malevolence, which we would infer from the speeches of many of their intemperate partisan leaders and a portion of the press." *Executive and Legislative Documents of North Carolina* (1866–67), Exec. Doc. No. 25, p. 4.

17. General Dockery declined to accept the nomination, given by a small group of Unionists under Holden's leadership. The general nevertheless declared in favor of the Fourteenth Amendment, and the Unionists actively campaigned for him. Worth sniffed:

> It is understood here this evening that Gen. Dockery declines to accept the nomination, on the grounds that the nominating meeting was not large enough—and on the further ground that the election is too near at hand to give him time to canvass the State,—but approving the Howard amendment.—The purpose is through secret organizations, to vote for him without subjecting him to the mortification of defeat as a Candidate. You will probably find his printed tickets at every precinct. (Worth to C. C. Clark, 1 October 1866, reprinted in *Correspondence of Jonathan Worth*, vol. 2, 806)

18. *Raleigh Sentinel*, 6 December 1866.

19. The following excerpt from a speech by Governor Worth typifies the argument made on this point:

> The Constitution provides that "the House of Representatives shall be composed of members, chosen every second year by the people of the several States," and that "the Senate of the United States shall be composed of two Senators from each State." This proposition is not made to us by a Congress so composed; this State, with eleven others, being denied representation in the body which proposed thus to amend the fundamental law. It was the clear intention of the Constitution that every State should have a right to representation in a Congress proposing alterations in the original articles of compact; and on this account alone, no State, pretending to have rights under the Constitution can, with proper scrupulousness or dignity, ratify an amendment thus proposed. (*Greensboro Patriot*, 23 November 1866)

20. The *Greensboro Patriot* (ibid.) noted: "It is remarkable that this proposed amendment contemplates, under one article, to change the Constitution in eight particulars; some of them altogether incongruous to be ratified as a whole. We are not allowed to ratify such of them as we approve and reject those we disapprove.—This is the first attempt to introduce the vice of omnibus legislation into the grave matter of changing the fundamental law."

21. See, e.g., *Raleigh Sentinel*, 7 July 1866 (amendment "designed to degrade and humiliate the South"); *Wilmington Journal*, 28 June 1866 (approval of amendment would require "surrender of honor and manhood"); *Old North State*, 26 June 1866 (amendment is a "degrading" proposition); *Wadesboro Argus*, 16 May 1866 (amendment is a "plan to heap indignity on the South"); *Fayetteville News*, 8 May 1866 (amendment is "dishonorable"); *Western Democrat*, 8 May 1866 (amendment contains "degrading" provisions).

22. D. F. Caldwell to Worth, 30 September 1866, *Correspondence of Jonathan Worth*, vol. 2, 802.

23. *Old North State*, 29 September 1866.

24. *Raleigh Sentinel*, 3 May 1866.

25. *Greensboro Patriot*, 13 July 1866.

26. Worth to D. H. Starbuck, 29 September 1866, *Correspondence of Jonathan Worth*, vol. 2, 796.

27. Worth to B. S. Hedrick, 1 October 1866, ibid., 805.

28. *Wilmington Daily Dispatch*, 31 October 1866.

29. *Raleigh Sentinel*, 16 June 1866.

30. The following description captures how most conservatives viewed the black: "He is careless, credulous and dependent; easily excited, easily duped, easily frightened; always the ready victim of the stronger will. He is material for the hands of anybody who wishes to make use of him. Invested with full political rights, the race must be a magazine of mischief." *Wadesboro Argus*, 22 November 1866.

Although the public statements of many whites about blacks shock the reader today, they were temperate in comparison to the private comments many uttered. Governor Worth wrote that "the negro is a drone—he cannot (because nature has forbidden it) be made a good and useful citizen. . . . [T]he normal condition of the African is that of a savage. . . . [P]rovidence, for inscrutable reasons, has made him incapable of permanent civilization and useful citizenship." Worth to William Clark, 16 February 1868, *Correspondence of Jonathan Worth*, vol. 2, 1155.

31. *Raleigh Sentinel*, 14 August 1866.

32. That these were the major objections is evidenced by the following summary, which the *Sentinel* (6 March 1867) later offered:

We could not give [the Fourteenth Amendment] our approval: first, because it proposed, as we thought, a radical change in the government itself, conferring powers upon the Congress over the internal police and regulations of the States, at war with the whole spirit and tone of the Constitution; at least that that was its tendency and would result from its adoption. This, we repeatedly stated, was our strongest objection to it. Secondly, because we regarded the new principle of representation embraced in it, as necessarily forcing upon the Southern States and, designed to force upon them, negro suffrage. . . .

Thirdly, we opposed it, because the disfranchising clause forced upon Southern men, no more worthy—no more loyal than the disfranchised, the dishonorable act, of fixing upon their neighbors and friends the stigma of treason.

Another recurrent criticism was that the radicals sought to insure their political supremacy through the Fourteenth Amendment (and, later, through the Reconstruction Acts). See, e.g., *Raleigh Sentinel,* 15 February 1867 ("The fixed and unalterable purpose of the Republican party, to hold on to the control of the government at all hazards, and to maintain that position, whatever may be consequences, has been apparent for some time to all attentive observers"); *Carolina Watchman,* 1 October 1866 (real point of constitutional amendment is to deprive the South of all representation for the Negro); *Wilmington Daily Dispatch,* 4 May 1866 (intent of amendment is to deprive the South of opportunity to participate in next presidential election).

33. See *Wilmington Daily Dispatch,* 10 October 1866.

34. See, e.g., *Fayetteville News,* 12 February 1867 ("universal and impartial suffrage" is a substantial feature of the Howard Amendment); *Raleigh Sentinel,* 29 September 1866; *Wilmington Daily Dispatch,* 16 May 1866 (Congress has power to declare the right to vote a privilege of citizenship and impose Negro suffrage).

35. *Raleigh Sentinel,* 19 June 1866. In an editorial on "Colored Schools" (ibid.) the editor remarked: "We have a proper sympathy for the welfare of the colored race, but we do not prefer its welfare to the ruin of the Southern whites."

36. *Raleigh Sentinel,* 7 October 1867. "We will guarantee that no intelligent lawyer of . . . the city of Boston could contemplate the spectacle, daily presented in our Courts, of negroes fresh from the corn field and the hovel filling our jury-boxes, and sitting in judgment upon the most complicated issues of fact and the most vexed problems of law, without shuddering" (ibid.)

37. *Wilmington Daily Dispatch,* 11 April 1866 (denouncing Civil Rights Bill because it will require mixed marriages to be performed on pain of penalty). Even those generally sympathetic to black rights disapproved of interracial marriages. The special committee that Provisional Governor Holden had appointed recommended, for example, that marriage between whites and blacks be forbidden and that any person issuing a license or performing a ceremony be punished.

38. See, e.g., *Raleigh Sentinel,* 15 November 1867 (the Fourteenth Amendment "changes the entire form of government"); *Greensboro Patriot,* 23 November 1866 (states will cease to be self-governing communities); *Old North State,* 11 October 1866 (amendment "is consolidation in its worst form"); *Wilmington Daily Dispatch,* 13 September 1866 (amendment would "revolutionize the whole character of the government").

39. *Wilmington Daily Dispatch,* 16 October 1866.

40. *Raleigh Sentinel,* 2 May 1866.

41. *Wadesboro Argus,* 11 October 1866. The following commentary illustrates the concern that conservatives repeatedly voiced:

> If there be any feature in the American system of freedom which gives to it prac-
> tical value, it is the fact that a municipal code is provided under the jurisdiction
> of each State, by which all controversies as to life, liberty or property, except in
> the now limited field of Federal jurisdiction, are determined by a jury of the
> county or neighborhood where the parties reside and the contest arises; but, if
> Congress is hereafter to become the protector of life, liberty and property, in the
> States and the guarantor of equal protection of the laws; and by appropriate leg-
> islation to declare a system of rights and remedies, which can be administered
> only in the Federal Courts, then the most common and familiar officers of justice
> must be transferred to the few points in the State where these courts are held, and
> to judges and other officers, deriving and holding their commissions, not from the
> authority and people of the State as heretofore, but from the President and Senate
> of the United States. (*Greensboro Patriot*, 23 November 1866)

42. *Wadesboro Argus*, 11 October 1866.

43. See *Raleigh Sentinel*, 26 April 1866; see also 2 May 1866.

44. See, e.g., *Old North State*, 6 October 1866 (Congress wants to insure freedmen in the protection of their civil rights); *Western Democrat*, 1 May 1866 (Section 1 prohibits discrimination "as to the civil rights of persons").

45. See *Raleigh Sentinel*, 14 August 1866 (no Negro suffrage in Howard Amendment). Holden did not declare himself in favor of Negro suffrage until 1 January 1867, when he spoke at the African Church in Raleigh. *Asheville Pioneer*, 26 September 1867.

46. See *Wilmington Daily Herald*, 24 January 1866 (blacks cannot be sold into servitude for an offense because laws must treat blacks and whites equally).

47. William W. Holden, *The President's Plan Considered; The Proposed Constitutional Amendment Explained, and Its Adoption Urged: The Union the Paramount Good to the People of North Carolina* (Raleigh, N.C.: F. Broadside, 1866), 10, 12.

48. Ibid., 8–9.

49. Ibid., 14–15. Cf. *Raleigh Daily Standard*, 9 February 1866.

50. Holden, *The President's Plan Considered*, 9.

51. See *Raleigh Sentinel*, 27 November 1866.

52. There may have been somewhat greater support for the amendment than the final votes indicate. Six senators had promised Senator Harris that they would vote with him in favor of ratifying the amendment. In the House, fifteen members had voted against adopting the negative Committee Report. Hamilton, *Reconstruction in North Carolina*, 187.

53. *Wilmington Journal*, 15 February 1867.

54. *Report and Resolution of the Joint Select Committee of Both Houses of the General Assembly of North Carolina on the Proposition to Adopt the Congressional Constitutional Amendment* (Raleigh, N.C.: W. E. Pell, 1866), 7–8.

55. *Raleigh Standard*, 3 April 1867. The convention was composed of 147 delegates, 101 of whom were white and 46 of whom were black. The conservative press alternately excoriated and ridiculed the group and its proceedings.

56. *Raleigh Register*, 8 November 1867.

57. Ibid., 2 July 1867.

58. *Raleigh Register*, 6 August 1867. "Now, fellow citizens, what do we want of government? We want a government that shall secure to every citizen of North Carolina equal rights before the law, and especially equal protection before the courts" (ibid.)

59. *Raleigh Standard*, 14 December 1867. At the Republican convention in Raleigh in September 1867, Holden reiterated these views. See *Asheville Pioneer*, 26 September 1867.

60. *Raleigh Register*, 2 July 1867. See also *Asheville Pioneer*, 21 May 1868 ("To abrogate or abridge the right of the people to a voice in their own government is to leave them to the same extent subject to the rule and will of the one-man power—a tyrant or a potentate").

61. In fact, Holden needled the conservatives on that very point when they complained about Reconstruction. See, e.g., *Raleigh Standard*, 8 January 1867 (if the Fourteenth Amendment had been passed, the state could have determined for itself who voted). In his inaugural address, Governor Holden specifically stated: "Instead of defining or restricting suffrage permanently, it [Congress] has left it with the respective States, to be determined and settled as they may choose; and this State, following in full measure the example of the national government, has made suffrage free to all." *Greensboro Patriot*, 9 July 1868.

62. *Greensboro Patriot*, 9 July 1868.

63. *Raleigh Standard*, 14 December 1867; see also 21 April 1868 (blacks want civil and political equality; they are not interested in mixing socially); *Raleigh Register*, 2 July 1867 ("[The doctrine of equality] has nothing whatever to do with social relations.").

64. A. DeMunro, "'We Are Men'—Black Reconstruction in North Carolina, 1865–1870" (M.A. thesis, University of North Carolina, 1979), 16. Contra Leonard Bernstein, "The Participation of Negro Delegates in the Constitutional Convention of 1868 in North Carolina," *Journal of Negro History* 34 (1949): 391, 394–406.

65. James Roy Morrill, "North Carolina and the Administration of Brevet Major General Sickles," *North Carolina Historical Review* 42 (1965): 291, 296–97.

66. See *Raleigh Register*, 14 January 1868.

67. *Raleigh Standard*, 14 December 1867.

68. Worth exploded in exasperation: "Of all the parties the Devil has ever set up to afflict good men, he has brought his work nearest to perfection in the present Republican party." Worth to J. M. Coffin, 6 November 1867, *Correspondence of Jonathan Worth*, vol. 2, 1074.

69. *Raleigh Sentinel*, 26 February 1867. Compare *New Bern Daily Journal of Commerce*, 12 February 1867 (South should pursue a policy of "masterly inactivity") with *Salisbury Tri-Weekly Banner*, 6 March 1867 (inaction by whites will give radical whites and blacks an opportunity to form "dispicable government"). In a series of letters to his wife, Senator Leander Gash, who served in the special 1866 session and the subsequent regular session in 1867, poignantly revealed the despair that immobilized conservatives. He said that "Congress seems demented" (9 December 1866), and that "the radicals are more crazy and blood-thirsty than ever" (11 December 1866). Although he spoke hopefully of compromise (7 February 1867), he finally advised his wife to "prepare for the worst" as the "political storm of fanaticism" swept over them (1 March 1867). Leander Gash to his wife, Leander Gash's Papers, North Carolina Archives, Raleigh, N.C.

70. Hamilton, *Reconstruction in North Carolina*, 251. The *Sentinel*, however, urged whites to vote for conservative delegates lest the convention be dominated by men who believed in "negro supremacy." *Raleigh Sentinel*, 15 November 1867. Throughout this period, conservatives plaintively asked themselves: "What ought the South to do?" See, e.g., *Raleigh Sentinel*, 26 February 1867.

71. In the November election, 93,006 voted for the convention, while 32,961 voted against it. Of the 120 delegates, only 13 were conservatives. The 107 Republicans in-

cluded 18 "carpetbaggers" and 15 blacks. Hamilton, *Reconstruction in North Carolina*, 253. The figures belie Hamilton's assertion that the carpetbaggers "absolutely" dominated the convention. A contemporary critic impliedly admitted that native North Carolinians were responsible for the new constitution when he urged rejection of "this damnable abortion . . . adopted by the munkey-smelling-tan-on-ring-striped and stupid scalawags of North Carolina." *Charlotte Daily Bulletin*, 23 March 1868. Of course, the paper had viewed convention prospects pessimistically from the beginning: the Southern states would be reduced to "Congressional satraps or negro provinces." *Charlotte Daily Bulletin*, 13 January 1868. Six months later, the *Greensboro Patriot* carried "[t]he radical alphabet" in which *"X"* stood for "the ten African States we must make." *Greensboro Patriot*, 23 July 1868.

72. The *Sentinel* predicted that the convention would remove "all limitations and obstacles to the free intercourse . . . of the black and white races," would admit "negro voters to the jury box and to office," and would open "the doors of the University, the common schools, and all other public institutions of learning . . . to black and white [people] alike." *Raleigh Sentinel*, 4 February 1868. The *Sentinel* and other conservative papers consistently derided the "convention so-called." Ibid., 18 February 1868. The convention did expel one reporter because it objected to his reports of the proceedings. He had filed reports like this one:

> Manager Cowles' [the Convention chairman] Museum!
> Wonderful Performances in Natural History!
> The Cowles' Museum contains Baboons, Monkeys, Mules, Tourgee [a "carpetbagger"], and other Jackasses.

Hamilton, *Reconstruction in North Carolina*, 257 note 1.

73. *Constitution of the State of North Carolina together with the Ordinances and Resolutions of the Constitutional Convention, Assembled in the City of Raleigh, January 14, 1868* (Raleigh, N.C.: Joseph W. Holden, 1868), art. 1, secs. 1, 17.

74. *Journal of the Constitutional Convention of the State of North Carolina, at Its Session 1868* (Raleigh, N.C.: Joseph W. Holden, 1868), 175.

75. *Greensboro Times*, 13 February 1868.

76. *Raleigh Sentinel*, 18 February 1868.

77. *Wadesboro Argus*, 20 February 1868.

78. Ibid.

79. Ibid.

80. *Convention Journal (1868)*, 353.

81. Ibid., 216.

82. Ibid., 473.

83. Ibid., 162.

84. Ibid., 483.

85. Raper, "William Woods Holden," 244–45.

86. One student of the period argues that conservatives "only roused themselves into political activity when it became clear that the Republican party was out to do far more than merely enfranchise Negroes. And the Conservative-Democratic party blossomed not in response to racial considerations but mainly out of a concern that if unimpeded a revolution could take place, a revolution which would leave conservative men with progressively less and less power and influence." E. McGee, "North Carolina Conservatives and Reconstruction," 375. He adds: "White supremacy was raised as *the* issue, *the* prin-

ciple because of its obvious appeal to the white electorate and because it reduced a complex set of problems to a level that penetrated the thickest skull" (ibid.).

87. Compare *Raleigh Sentinel*, 29 June 1867 (criticizes call for a white man's party), with *Greensboro Patriot*, 25 June 1868 (calls on white men to organize a party in order to defeat "negro supremacy"). Some Southerners predicted that blacks would vote for conservative candidates. See, e.g., *New Bern Daily Journal of Commerce*, 21 May 1867; *Wilmington Journal*, 25 October 1866; *Greensboro Patriot*, 15 February 1866.

88. *Asheville News*, 12 March 1868.

89. R. Hoffman, "The Republican Party in North Carolina 1867–1871" (M.A. thesis, University of North Carolina, 1960), 51.

90. *Raleigh Sentinel*, 20 April 1868. This welter of words drowned out the few moderate conservative voices. See, e.g., a letter from Chief Justice R. M. Pearson, 20 July 1868, addressed to his conservative friends, admonishing them: "[W]e must submit to the political, not the social (for that is a thing under our own control) equality of the freedmen. This is 'the situation'—the question is, shall we go on, and again make bad worse, or shall we try to make the best of it?"

91. More than 80 percent of the 196,872 persons eligible to vote voted. Across the state, 93,084 voted for the constitution; 74,015 voted against it. Since less than eighty thousand blacks were enrolled, they alone could not have accounted for the majority in favor of the constitution. The Senate had a forty-one to nine Republican majority; the House elected had an eighty-two to thirty-eight Republican majority. Hamilton, *Reconstruction in North Carolina*, 286.

92. *Raleigh Sentinel*, 4 July 1868. Whether the conservatives would have swept the elections if all of them had been allowed to vote is questionable. First, no one knows how many whites were disfranchised. Governor Worth guessed that fifteen thousand to twenty thousand had been excluded. Worth to the editors of the *New York World*, 14 May 1868, *Correspondence of Jonathan Worth*, vol. 2, 1201. General Canby reported that 11,686 had been removed from the rolls. Senate Exec. Doc. No. 53, 40th Cong., 2d sess., 1868, 5. Second, whatever the precise figure, "the number of . . . [people excluded] was too small to affect the outcome except in the closest races." Allen W. Trelease, "Republican Reconstruction in North Carolina: A Roll-Call Analysis of the State House of Representatives 1868–1870," *Journal of Southern History* 42 (1976): 319, 320. But see Hamilton, *Reconstruction in North Carolina*, 286.

93. The *Greensboro Times*, 21 May 1868, predicted that the radicals would try to impose Negro rule.

94. *Raleigh Sentinel*, 4 July 1868.

95. *Greensboro Patriot*, 9 July 1868.

96. Ibid. Holden had expressed similar views two years earlier. *Raleigh Standard*, 21 April 1866.

97. *Raleigh Standard*, 21 April 1866.

98. Trelease, "Republican Reconstruction in North Carolina," 330.

99. Ibid.

100. *Journal of the House of Representatives of the General Assembly of the State of North Carolina, at the Session of 1868* (Raleigh: N. Paige, Printer to the State, 1868), 45–47.

101. Trelease, "Republican Reconstruction in North Carolina," 330.

102. Ibid.; *Journal of the House of Representatives of the General Assembly of North Carolina, at its Session of 1869–1870* (Raleigh, N.C.: W. A. Smith & Co., Printers, "Standard" Office, 1870), 122.

103. Trelease, "Republican Reconstruction in North Carolina," 330.

104. Ibid., 323.

105. Elizabeth Balanoff, "Negro Legislators in the North Carolina General Assembly, July 1868–February 1872," *North Carolina Historical Review* 49 (1972): 22, 41; *Journal of the Senate of the General Assembly of the State of North Carolina, at its Session of 1868* (Raleigh, N.C.: N. Paige, Printer to the State, 1868), 41–42.

106. *Senate Journal* (1868), 41–42. Representative Sweat supported Leary's argument. *Raleigh Standard*, 12 February 1869.

107. The bill was referred to the Judiciary Committee, where it died. *House Journal* (1868), 42–43. See *Raleigh Standard*, 1 December 1868.

108. Balanoff, "Negro Legislators in the North Carolina General Assembly," 41.

109. Ibid., 40.

110. *Senate Journal* (1868), 41–42.

111. Earlier, in late July, Representative Laflin had introduced a resolution asking the national government to send two regiments to protect Negroes against terrorism. *Wilmington Journal*, 31 July 1868.

112. *House Journal* (1868), 142; *Senate Journal* (1868), 181. See *Raleigh Standard*, 10 August 1868.

113. Balanoff, "Negro Legislators in the North Carolina General Assembly," 44.

114. See generally Allen W. Trelease, *White Terror: The Ku Klux Klan Conspiracy and Southern Reconstruction* (New York: Harper & Row, 1971).

115. McGee, "North Carolina Conservatives and Reconstruction," 370.

116. Otto H. Olsen, "A. U. Tourgee: Carpetbagger," *North Carolina Historical Review* 40 (1963): 434, 441.

5

Ratification in Louisiana

We have no hope now but in Congress.

—A disappointed radical, reacting to the conservative capture of the state
government during presidential Reconstruction, 1865–67

For a season, "the bottom rail was on top" in Louisiana. Though there were many reasons for this brief radical triumph, a critical one was the presence in New Orleans of a relatively large group of prosperous, well-educated, and free persons of color. They constituted a black upper class unlike any other in the South or, indeed, anywhere in the country.[1] The slave population in New Orleans had also gained "a degree of education and . . . sophistication unusual in the South,"[2] in part because they mingled so freely with others in the most cosmopolitan of American cities.[3] Under the protective eye of federal troops who had occupied the city by May 1862, these blacks began to demand equal rights even before the end of the Civil War. Through the black-owned *New Orleans Tribune* (and its predecessor *L'Union*), they insistently and effectively pressed the case for absolute and complete equality long before it was voiced elsewhere.[4]

Like the society its views reflected, the *New Orleans Tribune* was a unique paper. During the early phase of Reconstruction in Louisiana, it was the only radical Republican voice in the state. From 1865 to 1868 it was the house organ of the Republican Party, and in 1867 it was designated "an official organ of the United States Government." It was edited initially by Paul Travigne, a mulatto and "a true radical," who believed in the principles of the French Revolution: "[P]low in the vast field of the future the furrow of Fraternite; plant there firmly the tree of Liberte, whose fruits, collected by future generations, will be shared by the most perfect Equalite."[5]

His successor Jean-Charles Houzeau, a Belgian-born nobleman, also believed passionately in equality and envisioned an America where "all races" would "melt together."[6] Under the guidance of these two men, the *Tribune* interpreted every law—including the Fourteenth Amendment—as liberally as its language permitted. The *Tribune*'s commentary on the Fourteenth Amendment and related issues is thus important, for it reflects the most liberal gloss given the amendment by its most thoughtful and articulate proponents in the South.

Naturally, the *Tribune* chronicled the activities of New Orleans's *gens de couleur* between the summer of 1862, when Union troops gained control of the city, and the summer of 1866, when Congress promulgated the Fourteenth Amendment. That chronicle reveals the thoughtful perspective from which they viewed the amendment. In the fall of 1862, free persons of color began attending "union meetings," sorting through ideas and developing strategies. On November 5, 1863, they gathered in Economy Hall to hear one speaker after another demand the right to vote.[7] Colonel B. S. Pinchback, who years later would become lieutenant governor, eschewed any desire for social equality. Rather, he insisted on the right to vote. "We want to be men," he thundered.[8] Those assembled, said to have "more white American than African" blood in their veins,[9] then petitioned General George Shepley, the acting mayor of New Orleans during the initial phase of the city's military occupation, for the right to vote.

In their petition they reminded the general that many of them were descended from those who had stood with Jackson at the Battle of New Orleans and been called "fellow citizens" by Old Hickory. They were thus both fit and entitled "to enjoy the privileges and immunities belonging to the condition of citizens of the United States."[10] Two months later the committee, which had been instructed to call upon General Shepley, reported at a meeting of the Union Radical Club that he had referred them to General Banks. The general, unfortunately, "had returned no definite reply."[11]

General Banks was less reticent about responding to pleas from the planter class for rules which insured that blacks would continue to labor in their fields. These rules restricted the rights of the freedmen to change jobs and negotiate wages.[12] The *Tribune* repeatedly and forcefully condemned these regulations:

The plantations were leased out by the government to the teeming swarm of avaricious adventurers . . . [T]he "tillers of the soil," till then slaves and raised by the mere presence of the National banner to the right of men and citizens were by military edict [General Order 91] handed over to the government and control of a set of men, whose sole endeavor and object was not to enlighten, improve, and elevate, but to make as much money as possible out of the labor of these unfortunate proletaries.[13]

A year later some freedmen, chafing at these restrictions, held a meeting to establish an Equal Rights League in the state. The *Tribune* described the formation of the league as "the most promising measure ever devised to promote the welfare of our people and secure the respect of our enemies."[14] Late that spring, a group of whites and blacks gathered at the old Carrollton Depot and renewed their demand for universal suffrage. The *Tribune* exulted: "It was . . . a new spectacle to see the community of feeling and sentiment between men of all races and all shades."[15]

In mid-January 1866, the *Tribune* endorsed the call of the "Colored People of Wilmington" for "the repeal of all laws and parts of laws, States and National, that make distinction on account of color." The call continued:

This is our object, in all its length and breadth. We therefore aspire to the condition and privilege of freemen. Is not this a natural aspiration? Is it not the dictate of self-respect? We ask an opportunity to be shown worthy to be free, or propose to attain the condition and privileges of freemen by becoming intelligent; by industry, by virtue, by piety. . . . We shall demand of the lawful authority protection for our property, schools, presses and churches.[16]

This call was consistent with a proposed constitutional amendment which the *Tribune* had advocated earlier in January, an amendment whose language anticipated that of Section 1 of the Fourteenth Amendment: "No state shall make any distinction in civil rights and privileges among the naturalized citizens of the United States residing within its limits, or among persons born on its soil of parents permanently resident there, on account of race, color, or descent."[17]

In that same month, the editors of the *Tribune* revealed that they also understood that the "condition and privilege" to which they aspired as freemen included the guarantees of the Bill of Rights. Tweaking a conservative editor for having characterized the Thirteenth Amendment as "the *first* ever added to the Constitution," they pointed out:

Now, were our contemporary a "negro boy," he would be sent to a "negro school," and there he would learn that TWELVE amendments to the United States Constitution have already been agreed by the requisite number of states. Moreover these amendments are not the less important part of the fundamental law of America. One guarantees to the people freedom of religion, of speech and of the press, as well as the rights they have peaceably to assemble and to petition the government—a right which we made use of at the voluntary election. One guarantees to Americans the right of keeping and bearing arms—without discrimination of color. One enacts that the people—still without distinction of color—shall be secure in their persons, houses, papers and effects, against unreasonable searches and seizures. One is intended to guarantee to every accused, in criminal prosecution, a speedy and public trial, "by an impartial jury." It gives the accused—without discriminating on account of origin or race—a right to be confronted with the witnesses against him. One provides that excessive bail shall not be required, nor excessive fines imposed, "nor cruel and unusual punishment inflicted." We readily understand that slaveholders utterly ignore the twelve constitutional amendments. But it is not to be wondered at the fact that colored schoolboys know something of the United States Constitution. It is in that immortal instrument that the colored man finds those exalted principles of equality and security, of freedom and liberty he has thought worth fighting for.[18]

Louisiana's free blacks had thus indicated months before the Fourteenth Amendment was even drafted that they expected to exercise all the fundamental rights guaranteed in the Bill of Rights by virtue of their status as citizens of the United States.

They also remained citizens of Louisiana, however; and they understood that the states retained broad police powers under the Constitution. Consequently, black Louisianans demanded that the state recognize all of its citizens as equals before the law. This equality principle was rooted, not in the Bill of Rights, but in the Declaration of Independence; and even before the Fourteenth Amendment was passed, the *Tribune* argued that Congress had the power to make the states observe its animating principle. They insisted, for example, that the Republican Guaranty Clause and the enforcement section of the Thirteenth Amendment gave Congress all the power it needed "to carry out the principles of the Declaration of Independence": "The two clauses fully meet the case and give power to Congress to pass, simply by legislative enactment, all laws which will be deemed necessary to secure substantial freedom and all the rights and immunities pertaining to full citizenship, to all the citizens in the land."[19]

Naturally, they embraced the Civil Rights Act enthusiastically. The "spirit" of that law, whatever its "letter," was "universal equality before the law." It effectively struck "the word 'white' . . . out of the statute books of the States." The *Tribune* concluded: "From this day forward no legal inquiry has any longer to be made in regard to the race or the parentage of an American citizen."[20] It demanded that the Civil Rights Act be enforced, and it later detailed what that would mean for black citizens:

We present in a condensed form the rights which, we consider, flow from the Civil Rights Law. We will discuss each of them, in particular, at an early day. We confine ourselves today to briefly mention said rights. . . .

We claim:

1st. Under the right to make contracts:—

Certificates of marriage, when husband and wife belong to different races.

2nd. Under the right to inherit:—

Full inheritance for children born from married parents belonging to different races, that is to say, complete assimilation of children of mixed blood (even those born before the Civil Rights Law was passed) to white legitimate children. Marriages contracted between persons of different races, although not lawful under the State law, are in fact legitimated by the Civil Rights Bill, and must bear all the consequences of lawful marriages as to the rights of children.

3rd. Under the right to enjoy full and equal benefit of all laws and proceedings for the security of persons and property:

The right to bear arms, guarantied [*sic*] by Amendment 2 to the Constitution of the United States.

The right to belong to the militia and practically to be embodied into its organization.

The right to vote, without which there is no true security for the unfranchised class, either to persons or to property. Class taxation may become oppressive.

The right to sit in the jury box, a right without which a colored accused has not the same security for protecting his innocence or his interests as a white accused has. The enabling act of Congress, of February 11, 1811, authorizing the territory of Orleans to form a Constitution preparatory to the admission of Louisiana as a State, made a Constitution that every accused, in criminal pursuits, would be tried before a jury of his peers.

The right for colored children to the admittance in the public schools. Without education no individual is able to adequately protect himself. The State furnishes today to the white young men means of protection (by schooling) which is denied to the colored young men. This right entails the admittance to high schools, colleges and universities, as far as supported by the State.

The right to use public conveyances, cars, railroads, steamers, etc. This right could even be claimed under the very tenor of the charters of the companies, said charters making no discrimination on account of color.

The right to be appointed or elected to any office in the State, and to be licensed for any profession or trade; and after appointment or election to office, the right to exercise the duties of said office.[21]

In short, the Civil Rights Bill conferred virtually every right, including suffrage—not because it embodied all the guarantees of the Bill of Rights (suffrage, after all, was not such a right), but because it prohibited the state from discriminating among its citizens on the basis of color.

While few would have read the substantive scope of the Civil Rights Act so broadly,[22] many would have agreed that the key provision of the Civil Rights Bill was its authorizing appeals to federal courts "to remove such discriminations." In discussing the right of blacks to serve in the militia, the *Tribune* made this point emphatically:

We agree that, in Louisiana, the colored man is admitted into the militia, according to the letter of the Constitution of 1804. But our learned opponent will agree, in turn, that this provision is a dead letter, and that not a single colored man has been put on the rolls already made—made with the avowed purpose of "keeping down the nigger." About three thousand men divided into companies, are on these rolls for the city of New Orleans, all of rebel propensities and of white skin. What has become of the Constitutional provision? What State court will enforce it? But the Civil Rights law gives us the power to have it enforced in the United States courts, and thereby to make it efficient. It is not enough that these rights be acknowledged by local laws and constitutions. We want to-day to have them put into practical operation, and it will never be done but through the interference of the United States courts and the provisions of the Civil Rights law. Is not that practical result an aim worthy of contending for?[23]

The point is that the *Tribune* expected the federal courts to enforce "universal equality before law," not by enforcing the provisions of the Bill of Rights against the states, but rather by requiring the states to apply their own laws without regard to color. Indeed, whenever the *Tribune* editors discussed the civil or political rights of blacks, such as jury service, they invariably talked about such rights as they were guaranteed by state law or constitution.[24] Even in the case of suffrage, they acknowledged the power of the state to set general, non-discriminatory qualifications.[25]

Most Louisiana whites feared what Louisiana blacks welcomed. The *Picayune* stated the point succinctly: "The [civil rights] bill is one to establish entire civil equality for the negro with the white citizen of all the States of the Union, by the direct authority of the General Government, through its own courts, and by its own military power, when disputed, acting directly to the exclusion of State jurisdiction and State agency."[26] Asked by Negro defendants to transfer their cases to the federal district court under the provisions of the Civil Rights Act, a New Orleans municipal judge refused. Declaring the Civil Rights Act unconstitutional, Judge Abell said:

In reviewing the "civil rights bill," I have discharged what I believe to be my duty to the State, by withholding the judicial sanction of this court to a bill that appears to aim at striking down the independence of the States, to sap the foundation of republican government, override the laws of the State, and to obliterate every trace of independence of State Judiciary, by disgraceful and servile ends.[27]

Distressed whites who shared that view of the Civil Rights Act hoped that President Johnson would stay or frustrate its enforcement.[28]

The activities of New Orleans's free people of color between the summers of 1862 and 1866 thus demonstrated their clear understanding of the federal structure of the American government, a fervent commitment to natural law principles, and a thorough knowledge of political philosophy. They naturally evaluated the Fourteenth Amendment on the basis of that understanding, commitment, and knowledge. They endorsed the Fourteenth Amendment because they saw it as consistent with all three of those bases. Moreover, it reinforced their political demands, including their continuing demand for the right to vote.

Explaining Section 1 of the Fourteenth Amendment to its readers, the *Tribune* argued that it had the same scope and guaranteed the same rights as did the Civil Rights Act:

Let us only consider the first section: "All persons born in the United States, and subject to the jurisdiction thereof, are citizens of the United States, and of the States wherein they reside." This is the reiteration of the declaration in the Civil Rights Bill that every person born in the United States and not subject of a foreign power, is an American citizen. This same provision is here engrafted on the Constitution; moreover, the Amendment provides that the character of American citizen is inseparable of that of citizen of the State wherein the person resides, so that in future a State cannot deny the rights, privileges and immunities of a citizen to persons who are citizens of the United States. This doctrine is the correct one. It was absurd to tell a man "you are a citizen of the Republic at large, but you have no rights in your own State: you are not even a citizen there." The populations of the States are evidently composed of citizens of the United States, and local organizations have to be made by and for these citizens, not against them. No subordinate authority has a right to practically annul what the supreme power in the land has done. When once a citizen at large, the same quality subsists a fortiori in the locality where such a citizen resides.

But this is not all. The amendment provides that "no State shall make or enforce any law which shall abridge the privileges or immunities of citizens." Every man of African descent is not only declared to be a citizen of the State wherein he resides, but he will be entitled, in future, to the same privileges and immunities as any other citizen. In other words, all classification among citizens must fall. The word "white," wherever it exists in State Constitutions and State laws, will become unconstitutional, and will have to be disregarded; for all citizens, without discrimination, will have to be admitted to the enjoyment of all privileges and immunities. The State Legislatures may, of course, fix qualifications for voters, define crimes, determine penalties, impose conditions upon those who aspire to hold public offices. But the whole legislation must consider all classes of citizens as forming one single mass, for which all laws must be equal. No discrimination can be made in future either on account of color or on account of naturalization and origin. When once a citizen, a man is a citizen in full, and no exception can be taken against him by reason of the way in which he has become an American citizen. Every title of citizenship is declared to be of like value, and to confer the same rights.[29]

In this analysis of Section 1, the *Tribune* emphasized what other proponents of the Fourteenth Amendment emphasized. It "constitutionalized" the Civil Rights Act, and it prohibited class legislation. The latter prohibition made the Fourteenth Amendment "second in importance" only to the antislavery amendment because it went "beyond the limit that the Civil Rights Bill could reach."[30] But in emphasizing that the guarantees of the Civil Rights Act were now rooted in the Constitution, the *Tribune* simultaneously recognized that the amendment did not preclude state legislation so long as that legislation did not discriminate among its citizens on the basis of race.

Louisiana blacks thus clearly understood the significance of the Fourteenth Amendment. They had a broad view of the privileges and immunities of citizenship, as they had made clear in discussing the Civil Rights Bill. Yet it is equally clear from that discussion that the basic privilege and immunity of citizenship was "universal equality before the law" rather than any set of enumerated rights. In particular, the privileges and immunities of citizenship protected by Section 1 did not necessarily include all the rights enumerated in the national Bill of Rights. Neither was its scope limited to those rights. More to the point, they understood that they enjoyed dual citizenship as citizens of both the United States and the state wherein they resided.

That Louisiana blacks were familiar with their rights as citizens of both the United States and their state of residence and demanded them is clear. There is, however, no evidence that they ever understood that Section 1 of the Fourteenth Amendment guaranteed both sets of rights, much less dissolved them into a single mass of rights. After all, Louisiana blacks did not fear a national government that had fought a war to free them. They assumed that a friendly national government would respect their rights of national citizenship, embodied in the Bill of Rights. They did fear a hostile state government that had fought a war to keep them in chains. They wanted some assurance that an unfriendly state government would respect their rights under state law. Sections 1 and 5 of the Four-teenth Amendment gave them that assurance. The *Tribune* pointedly reminded its readers that "were the Southern States to endeavor to evade their constitutional obligations under the Amendment, Congress would have, by virtue of the last section of the Amendment itself, 'the power of enforcing by appropriate legislation the provisions of these articles.'"[31]

That they had reason to fear a hostile state government is clear from the history of the Louisiana state government from 1864 to 1867. During that period, two gubernatorial elections were held, a constitutional convention met, the legislature convened twice, and the infamous New Orleans Riot unhinged the city. Race issues dominated each of these events, and their history thus dramatizes the attitudes which shaped how the white and black citizens of Louisiana viewed the Fourteenth Amendment.

The first of the gubernatorial elections was held in February 1864. Since the election was confined to the territory controlled by Union forces, it devolved into a contest between moderate and radical Unionists and their respective sympathizers. While the two factions represented different interests in Louisiana and were tied to different Republican leaders in Washington,[32] they differed substantively only on the future of the freedman in Louisiana. Consequently, "[r]ace was the only issue in a thoroughly scurrilous campaign."[33] Michael Hahn, the moderate Free-State candidate endorsed by General N. P. Banks and President Lincoln, won. Sympathetic to the concerns of the planter class, he was unalterably opposed to Negro suffrage.[34]

Moderates also controlled the constitutional convention that met in April 1864. Though the convention was thoroughly Unionist, it was also negrophobic. It did abolish slavery, though only after five days discussion. Even then, it adopted a resolution demanding federal compensation for both loyal and disloyal slaveholders.[35] The convention decisively rejected Negro suffrage, initially defying President Lincoln's private suggestion to Hahn that "some of the colored people [be given the vote], as, for instance, the intelligent, and especially those who have fought gallantly in our ranks."[36] That very proposal, when finally offered, was derided as a "nigger resolution" and was voted down fifty-two to twenty-three.[37] On May 10 the delegates voted sixty-eight to fifteen to adopt an article prohibiting the legislature from ever passing "any act authorizing free Negroes to vote, or to immigrate into this state."[38] The few friends of the freedmen in the convention despaired. This constitutional proposal, one of them pointed out, placed the freedmen "in an infinitely worse position than they were under [in] any of the antecedent pro-slavery constitutions."[39] Outside the convention, *L'Union* expressed disappointment but no surprise. Describing the convention as dominated by men who held "a miserable prejudice against a certain class of native born Americans," it condemned them for refusing "to recognize ... universal equality before the law."[40] Only after General Banks intervened did the convention relent on the suffrage question. It finally resurrected the "nigger resolution" and adopted the following article: "The Legislature shall have the power to pass laws extending suffrage to such other persons, citizens of the United States, as by military service, by taxation to support the Government, or by intellectual fitness may be deemed entitled thereto."[41]

The convention showed only slightly more generosity toward the freedmen on the issue of education, bowing once again to Banks' pressure. Most of the ninety-eight delegates not only opposed integrated schools; they flatly opposed any public education at all for blacks unless it was funded exclusively by a head tax on blacks. In the end, however, the delegates reluctantly agreed to a provision that guaranteed public schools for all children from six to eighteen.[42] The *Tribune*, concluding that the new constitution was drafted "by men who had no higher principle than hatred of their fellows of African descent," urged its rejection.[43] Two days earlier, the paper had lamented "the deep-rooted prejudice" against blacks and predicted that that prejudice would persist "till public opinion shall be brought up to a higher standard and recognizes the true principle of politics that *before the law all men are equal*."[44]

The conduct of the new legislature and Governor J. Madison Wells, who succeeded Hahn when he was elected to the United States Senate, confirmed the worst fears of the city's free persons of color. Through the fall of 1864 and the spring of 1865, both acted to return "the state [to] conservative planter control."[45] When elections for the legislature were held again, conservative Democrats swept to victory. In their platform they had declared that the government was "for the exclusive benefit of the white race," that blacks could never be citizens of the United States, and that "there can in no event nor under any circumstances be any equality between white and other races."[46] The legislature convened that same month and took up the "labor question" at the very moment Congress was reconvening to consider the question of reconstruction. Senator James Blaine later commented:

At the very moment when the Thirty-ninth Congress was assembling [December 1865] to consider the condition of the Southern States and the whole subject of their reconstruction, it was found that a bill was pending in the Legislature of Louisiana providing that "every adult freed man or woman *shall furnish themselves with a comfortable home and visible means of support within twenty days after the passage of this Act*," and that "any freed man or woman failing to obtain a home and support as thus provided shall be immediately arrested by any sheriff or constable in any parish, or by the police officer in any city or town in said parish where said freedman may be, and by them delivered to the Recorder of the parish, and by him hired out, by public advertisement, to some citizen, being the highest bidder, for the remainder of the year." And in case the laborer should leave his employer's service without his consent, "he shall be arrested and assigned to labor on some public works without compensation until his employer reclaims him." The laborers were not to be allowed to keep any live-stock, and all time spent from home without leave was to be charged against them at the rate of two dollars per day, and worked out at that rate.

By a previous law . . . Louisiana had provided that all agricultural laborers should be compelled to "make contracts for labor during the first ten days of January for the entire year." With a demonstrative show of justice it was provided that "wages due shall be a lien on the crop, one half to be paid at times agreed by the parties, the other half to be retained until the completion of the contract; but in case of sickness of the laborer, wages for the time shall be deducted, and where the sickness is supposed to be feigned for the purpose of idleness, double the amount shall be deducted; and should the refusal to work extend beyond three days, the negro shall be forced to labor on roads, levees, and public works without pay."[47]

Blaine and others obviously believed that these bills violated both the spirit and the letter of the Thirteenth Amendment. Though neither of these bills passed, the legislature did adopt a vagrant law.

In addition to these actions at the state level, local communities at the same time enacted ordinances that Henry Warmouth, the first radical governor of Louisiana, later castigated as an attempt to reestablish slavery by "municipal regulation."[48] The *Tribune* analyzed one such code, which contained the following provisions:

- Blacks were not allowed within the city limits without a pass.
- Blacks could not live within the city except as servants.
- Blacks could not in any case be on the streets after 10:00 P.M.
- Blacks could not hold meetings or preach without the major's permission.
- Blacks could not carry guns; drink liquor; sell, barter, or exchange goods without written permission from an employer or the mayor.[49]

The *Tribune* sarcastically praised the city for its enlightened policy of allowing blacks to remain on the streets one more hour than they had been permitted during slavery: "This additional hour is the fruit of our victories in the field."[50]

Objectionable as were these laws, they reflected a genuine belief among most whites that the community should treat the freedmen differently because they were deficient in intelligence, judgment, and morality. The *Baton Rouge Tri-Weekly* explained this view succinctly:

We have, in this free republican government, deprived females, minors, criminals, aliens, Indians, etc., of the ballot-box, and why? Because we think the best interests of society require this exclusion. The individuals included in the class enumerated are not, on account of education, habits and morality, qualified to cast a judicious vote, and hence have been very properly excluded from any participation in the affairs of government. And if the interests of the community should require, the ballot may be still farther restricted. Moreover, society has the perfect right to pass such laws and adopt such regulations as experience may have taught to be necessary to enforce order, promote industry and lessen crime. And if required it has the right to make any distinctions in these laws and regulations as may be found necessary.[51]

In other words, these perceived differences between blacks and whites made what the *Tribune* considered nothing more than biased and prohibited class legislation wise and legitimate police regulation.

Throughout this period, the *Tribune* "carried on a relentless war against the legislature," ridiculing the legislature for enacting laws that the local Freedmen's Bureau routinely and promptly nullified.[52] By sending the paper to every member of Congress, its editors also insured that its copy shaped attitudes in Washington. Ingenious as ever in "spinning" political events in its favor, the *Tribune* argued that the Black Codes proved that Negroes sought liberty and therefore could be trusted to preserve it, if only they were given the franchise.[53]

Conservative whites obviously had a different view. They considered blacks unfit to exercise the franchise. Indeed, blacks were thought so inferior to whites that the legislature could—and should—treat the freedmen as a separate class. Whatever the *Tribune* might think about the desirability of two sets of laws, one for whites and the other for blacks, conservative whites in Louisiana demanded them. Citizens of the Empire Parish resolved, for example:

[W]e are sincerely disposed to accord to [the freedmen] all their civil rights, and to qualify them for useful citizenship, by providing for their education and encouraging in them habits of temperance, frugality and industry; but that in their present uninformed condition, we think they are unprepared for self-government, and should be regulated by laws framed for their advancement and protection by a superior race.[54]

The clash between these two different worldviews spawned the infamous New Orleans Riot in the summer of 1866. It grew out of a confrontation between radical activists, who insisted on reconvening the convention of 1864, and government officials, who considered the effort illegal if not treasonous. The riot obviously did not affect the drafting of the Fourteenth Amendment, which by then had already been submitted to the states. The riot did impact the fall elections in the North, however. During that campaign, Republicans invariably cited it as evidence that the Fourteenth Amendment was needed to protect blacks and Unionists in the South.[55]

What actually happened at the Mechanics Institute on July 30, 1866, was widely disputed. Eyewitness accounts and subsequent investigations differed sharply over who started the riot. Most whites regarded the meeting itself as a deliberate effort "to disfranchise the white population and to place all political power in the hands of the blacks." Many were convinced that blacks and their radical sympathizers instigated the fray, perhaps, they hinted, with the conspiratorial blessings of "Stevens and company."[56] General Philip Sheridan, however, characterized the riot as a deliberate massacre of the blacks and their white supporters, orchestrated perhaps by local officials.[57] Northern Republicans accepted the latter view, and consequently Louisiana conservatives fumed at the way in which the riot was "misrepresented" in the radical press "up North."[58]

What is clear is that the call for a meeting on July 30 came from Unionists and radicals, now allied against the conservatives who controlled the legislature. The call, issued on June 23, 1866, took the form of reconvening the 1864 convention, which, before it adjourned, had adopted a resolution authorizing its president to call it back into session. That the convention would demand civil and political equality, including universal suffrage, was clear. Judge Herstand was quoted as saying: "The people of the State of Louisiana are nearly equally divided—one half wants to do the voting for the whole, and wants the other half to do the work for them. This demand will not succeed, for no demand founded in injustice ever yet succeeded."[59] These and similar incendiary declarations aroused the ire of conservatives, and tensions in the city ran high. Although the meeting opened without incident at noon, fighting broke out about one o'clock among those gathered outside and quickly escalated into a gun battle. Before the guns fell silent, seventeen whites and 117 black Unionists had been wounded and three white and thirty-four black Unionists lay dead. Many Louisiana radicals fled north in fear for their very lives. Conservative whites were unrepentant:

We are in a queer condition. Our social and civil laws are outraged and if we had not resisted there is no telling the extent to which dirt would have been crammed down our throats. We chose another course and our civil authorities arrest, after a riotous resistance, the offenders, and lo! the *innocent* blacks, armed to the teeth, and the cowardly throng of white men who marshalled them are the sufferers from every conceivable outrage from the hands of insolent rebels and traitors.[60]

Against this backdrop of racial warfare, Louisiana took up the Fourteenth Amendment. The conservative press was filled with the usual jeremiads against the "negro equalization amendment" and the "negro suffrage amendment."[61] Statements like these prompted one observer to lament that "[t]he issues have been mentioned but to be denounced; perverted to be misunderstood."[62] There were also the standard generic objections. First, the amendment had been promulgated unconstitutionally because the Southern states had been excluded from Congress.[63] Second, the amendment was denounced as "a plan to prevent reconstruction ... [because it imposes] such conditions as it is well-known will be rejected with scorn and indignation."[64]

Press analysis of the specific provisions of the amendment in Louisiana was nevertheless generally straightforward. For example, the *Picayune* in an article on the amendment argued:

It does not deprive any southern man, now, entitled or who before the war was entitled to vote, of that privilege. It confers no right to vote on any one, either white or negro. It declares all persons born or naturalized in the United States citizens of them and of the State wherein they reside, but the qualification to vote is not given to or taken from such citizens, whether male or female, black or white.

The second section, indeed, impliedly admits that we may deny the negro or any other citizen the right to vote while it so far diminishes our ration of representation in congress, unless he be so inhibited for "participation in rebellion or other crime."

Nor does the third proposed amendment disfranchise so many as has been supposed. It is quite a question, for future judicial determination, whether it will disqualify any man for the past, or if it does what is to be regarded as an "executive or judicial officer of any State," or what is, in a judicial sense, engaging in insurrection or rebellion or giving aid and comfort to the enemies of the United States.[65]

The principal objections were to disfranchisement and consolidation. Disfranchisement would result in the "Africani[zation of our] political institutions."[66] Consolidation would bring "the end of American constitutional liberty."[67] Another paper commented:

[What] we most object to in the Constitutional amendments is the Second Section [sic] which excludes from Federal and State offices the best talent of the South. If such an article should be incorporated in the Constitution it would be impossible to fill the offices with men of capacity, for the reason that nearly every man of intellect and distinction in the South would be excluded by it. The Southern States would have to submit for an indefinite period to a representation in Congress derived from the scum of her people, in place of a former representation by men of transcendent ability, and the State offices would be filled by those whose only recommendation is their hostility to the States in the time of trial and danger.[68]

Speaking of earlier, proposed amendments that were the antecedent of the Fourteenth Amendment, the *New Orleans Bee* remarked: "Politically, indeed, the States would cease to exist. Geographically, they might remain for the convenience of electoral regulation and local administration."[69] Of these same amendments, another critic had said they would so alter the Constitution that its framers would no longer recognize it in "its new patch-work garb."[70] When Section 1 was mentioned, it was said only to make blacks citizens, entitled to the privileges and immunities of that status. This was thought objectionable only in light of Section 5, which, it was argued, gave Congress the power to define those privileges and immunities and thereby supplant state authority. No one discussed, much less objected to, the guarantees of equal protection or due process contained in Section 1.

The Louisiana legislature voted on the Fourteenth Amendment in January 1867 without first referring it to committee for review and report. By that time, several other Southern states had already refused to ratify the amendment. The Louisiana press had followed its consideration in those states and reported those votes, so the legislators were doubtless aware of the major issues raised in those debates. Of course, they would have been familiar with the analysis of the amendment in the local press. They also had before them Governor Wells' message, recommending its ratification. The same man who had allied himself with the state's planters was now accused of taking "strong radical grounds in the matter of federal relations."[71] And his endorsement of equal suffrage drew the scorn of those who recalled that one of his "earliest Executive acts was to write a letter giving his reasons for refusing to register negro voters, and deprecating the attempt to force negro suffrage upon the people of the State."[72]

The legislature also scorned the governor's advice. It unanimously rejected the amendment. The *Louisiana Democrat* remarked: "We cannot recall a single other instance of the Executive of a State being without a single supporter in the legislative branch of the government."[73] It was even suggested that he be impeached.[74]

Neither the vote nor the abuse surprised Wells. He expected the former and was accustomed to the latter. Unlike the legislators and the critics, he foresaw the future, at least the immediate future; and he had been positioning himself, in the characterization of his enemies, to get some of "the crumbs which are supposed to fall from the loyal table."[75]

The future which Wells foresaw was the same one that unfolded in all the Southern states. Military rule was imposed. Blacks were enfranchised. A convention was convened to draft a new state constitution. The constitution was approved, and a new legislature was elected. Dominated by radical Republicans, it tried to transform Louisiana from a planter's barony into an everyman's democracy.

Although that new legislature ratified the Fourteenth Amendment as its first official act, the Fourteenth Amendment was no longer an important topic of public discussion. During military reconstruction and immediately thereafter, the focus of public discussion shifted simultaneously to broader issues of public policy and to narrower legislative questions of economic development. At a general level the question became a political one: who would control the government? Most whites dreaded the prospect of "state governments in the hands of negro majorities":

Do you realize the meaning of that? A negro Governor and Lieutenant Governor; a negro Supreme Bench; a negro legislature; negro Sheriffs, clerks, police jurors, magistrates, mayors—all negroes. Negroes to fill the Governor's Mansion; negroes to make our laws; negroes to interpret them and give them the weight of judicial sanction, and negroes to enforce them. Negroes to propose amendments to the Constitution, and negro ballots to ratify them, (the more they discriminate against the whites, the surer of ratification) negroes to levy taxes, white men to pay them and negroes to enjoy the benefit; negroes to rule, and white men to wear the collar! That is what "negro majorities" mean. That is what the Radicals and the Southern allies are proposing to do for us![76]

What Louisiana got was a government distinguished less by its blackness than by its corruption. Unfortunately, its reform efforts sank beneath the sea of dollars that floated through the legislative chambers and the governor's mansion.

The period nevertheless illuminates the contemporary understanding of concepts such as privileges and immunities, equal protection, and due process. Four events in particular are illuminating: (1) the integration of street cars in New Orleans; (2) the drafting of a new state constitution, especially its Bill of Rights; (3) the continuing fight over access to public accommodations; and (4) the controversy over integrated schools in New Orleans.

Equal access to public facilities had long been a concern for black Louisi-anans, especially in New Orleans where some streetcars were reserved for blacks only. These cars were identified by a large black star, and "star" became a general symbol for segregated facilities or practices, as in "star" schools or "star" juries. No sooner had Union forces occupied the city than a delegation of prominent free blacks entreated General Butler to desegregate the streetcars. He obliged, but a local court set his order aside. Two years later black soldiers complained about being confined to "star" cars. General Banks, though gener-ally less sympathetic than his predecessor to claims of black equality, persuaded the car companies to allow the soldiers to ride on all cars. Other blacks were still confined to the "star" cars, however; and this double standard only fueled fur-ther but ultimately futile protests.[77] Thus matters stood until the spring of 1867 when blacks simply refused to wait for a "star" car and forcibly entered any available car. When the companies asked General Sheridan to intervene and enforce segregation in the cars, he refused; and the companies, having no re-course to civil courts, had no choice but to capitulate.[78]

The capitulation of the streetcar companies emboldened blacks, who next de-manded admission to white theaters, restaurants, and businesses. Relying on an opinion of the city attorney, the mayor issued a proclamation prohibiting "all persons whatever from intruding into any store, shop or other place of business conducted by private individuals, against the consent and wishes of the owners, proprietors, or keepers of the same."[79] Although the *Tribune* condemned the mayor's decision, the city's blacks apparently acquiesced. They thereafter de-clined to cross the color line.

Public accommodation was thus naturally an issue of particular importance to the black delegates to the 1868 constitutional convention, and they succeeded in securing the only equal access provision found in the Reconstruction constitu-tions of the eleven Southern states. The Bill of Rights in the new constitution guaranteed equal access to all public accommodations:

All persons shall enjoy equal rights and privileges upon any conveyance of a public character; and all places of business, or of public resort, or for which a license is required by either State, Parish, or Municipal authority, shall be deemed places of public character and shall be opened to patronage of all persons, without distinction or discrimination on account of race or color.[80]

Blacks were initially jubilant. "We want," said the *Tribune*, "to ride in any con-veyance, to travel on steamboats, eat in any steamboat, dine at any restaurant, or educate our children at any school."[81] Its principal advocate, B. S. Pinchback, was less sanguine. He had initially opposed inserting this guarantee into the new constitution, arguing that "[s]ocial equality, like water, must be left to find its own level, and no legislation can affect it. Any attempt to legislate on it will be the death blow of our people."[82]

The prospect of such enforced "social equality" certainly horrified most whites, who reminded "Sambo" that if he tried to "force" himself into such facilities, he would suffer the "fate" of the red man.[83] When the new legislature passed an implementing act, the *Carroll Reader* called its passage a declaration of war.[84] Blacks, apparently recognizing how vehemently most whites opposed integration, never attempted to avail themselves of the act's provisions. White outrage thus rendered it a dead letter.[85]

The issue of public accommodations was but one of many issues that arose in the drafting of the new constitution. The constitutional convention, which sat from November 23, 1867, to March 9, 1868, was overwhelmingly radical. Half of its delegates were black, many of whom were well-educated businessmen and landowners.[86] The conservative press described "the personnel of the convention" somewhat differently. It was "thoroughly and emphatically *nigger*," said the *Louisiana Democrat*, particularly if one counted all the "*white niggers*."[87] Whatever their characterization, the philosophy that inspired these delegates was the philosophy of the Declaration of Independence: the concept of equality was invoked far more frequently than was the language of the Fourteenth Amendment.

The draftsmen of the new constitution did invoke the Fourteenth Amendment in the framing of its Bill of Rights. They borrowed from the language of Section 1 when they declared that all persons born or naturalized in the United States who were residents of Louisiana were citizens of Louisiana. The draftsmen were thus intimately familiar with the language of the Fourteenth Amendment. Had they understood its language to incorporate the Bill of Rights, they would not have needed to include in their own Bill of Rights provisions guaranteeing peaceful assembly and petition, freedom of speech and press, freedom of religion, trial by jury, the right to bail, and the right of private property. Yet they did just that. The enumeration of these rights sparked no controversy.

The commitment to equality, however, did anger critics of the new constitution: "The most conspicuous feature of the whole instrument is, of course, its entire adaptation to the new philosophy of a social and political equality, which it is its chief design to establish."[88] Critics saw evidence of it everywhere, including in Article 132, which provided that "[a]ll lands sold in pursuance of decrees of courts shall be divided into tracts of ten to fifty acres."[89] In truth, radicals did want to encourage the redistribution of property so that blacks could become landowners.

The convention nevertheless repeatedly rejected the most extreme interpretations of the equality principle. When one delegate, for example, proposed that all minor convention offices be divided equally between the races, he was charged with elevating color above merit.[90] Quotas were thus anathema to a majority of the delegates, who defeated the motion forty-seven to thirty-eight. Typically, what blacks demanded was equal protection; and they understood that it was the equality of the protection that mattered, as the following newspaper column illustrates:

Give us Equal Protection.

"WILL BE STOPPED.—The Police report that the negro soldiers who are quartered near the corner of Palmyra and Glavez streets are acting in a most outrageous manner generally and particularly by entering private residences and threatening those who wish to stop such proceedings. If the allegations be true, we are quite sure the military authorities will at once correct the conduct of these men, and in a way they won't like very particularly. [*N.O. Crescent*, Feb. 13]

If the *Crescent*'s reporter would take the trouble to visit the Mission Church of the A.M.E. Zion connection, at 95 Palmyra street, Rev. J. Allen, Pastor, some Sunday evening, he would be satisfied of the necessity of having colored troops stationed in that locality. One of our editors happened to be there last Wednesday evening, when a crowd of white boys commenced brick-batting the house, breaking windows, and otherwise disturbing the congregation. The Minister applied to two policemen on the beat, and pointed out the boys; but the policemen wanted an "affidavit" made out before they could arrest the boys. Last Sunday night by the advice of some white persons, who complimented the Rev. Allen for his forbearance toward these boys, he applied to a squad of colored troops to disperse them. On the appearance of the soldiers the boys ran away, the soldiers then went into a house hard by to await their return. This, we suppose, is the cause of dissatisfaction on the part of the police. Had they discharged their duty, there would have been no need of the soldiers.[91]

To be treated the same as whites was all most blacks demanded.

Part of that demand was an insistence on public schools open to all, regardless of race. From the beginning, blacks in Louisiana had demanded integrated public schools:

We hold this opinion that the question of schools will only be settled when all children, without discrimination on account of race or color, will be admitted to sit together on the same benches and receive from the same teachers the light of knowledge. At that time there will only be one set of schools and all the energies of the State, all the talent of the teachers, will be directed to one end and one aim—the promotion of public education for the greatest good of all. Being one nation we want to see the young generation raised as one people, and we want the State to take care of educating all her children.[92]

The *Tribune* objected to the practice of educating children in separate schools in New Orleans, as well as the "suppression of the educational service outside of the city . . . so as to get rid of . . . colored schools in the country parishes."[93] During the election campaign in 1867, a radical speaker echoed these themes, asking his New Orleans audience: "If my colored brother and I touch elbows at the polls, why should not his child and mine stand side by side in the school room?"[94] This rhetorical question reflected the Republican platform, which promised to "enforce the opening of all schools, from the highest to the lowest . . . to all children."[95]

At the same time the *Tribune* was making these complaints and issuing these demands, conservative newspapers were questioning the value and purpose of public education. Condemning public education as "an exotic of Yankee vegetation [that] has never flourished in this climate and never will," the *Louisiana*

Democrat charged that public schools bred immorality and had caused a five-fold increase in crime. But that was not all, or even the worst:

We suppose that under the humane and philanthropic reign of "New England Ideas," a portion of the Public School moneys is to be appropriated to the Education of "little African piccaninnies," and that negro children and white children are to be drawn, by a levelling process, into a grand Democratic equality in the Republic of letters, through the medium of the Public Schools. Under the benign influence of enlightened School marms sent by Gov. Andrew fresh from Massachusetts, the sons and daughters of "rebel soldiers," on the floor of the Public Schools, are to be regaled with such delightful symphonies as "hang Jeff Davis on a sour apple tree," "John Brown's body lies a mouldering in the grave," and other approved Black Republican melodies, chanted in full chorus by the little darkies fresh from the sugar house and the cotton gin. Public Education will then have reached its acme, and have brought forth its legitimate fruits.[96]

More moderate whites recognized both the importance and necessity of educating blacks.[97] They insisted, however, that the schools be separate and "taught by southern people" rather than by Freedmen's Bureau "hirelings."[98]

The 1868 constitutional convention agreed that a common school system was needed and insisted that it be integrated. Article 135 provided for universal, desegregated education. Indeed, it specifically forbade "separate schools . . . established exclusively for any race." For a time, the experiment worked, at least in New Orleans, as one historian has noted:

For a period of nearly seven years, at a time when school integration was virtually non-existent in other southern communities and quite uncommon north of the Ohio, sizeable numbers of white and black children attended the same public schools in New Orleans. This unusual achievement was the high-water mark of the struggle to bring about a new social order in post-Civil War Louisiana.[99]

Outside New Orleans, however, the public schools remained segregated. The state's superintendent of public education explained why in this annual report to the legislature in 1869: "The removal of prejudices, however irrational, is rarely the work of a day. . . . In all great changes . . . time is needed for the public mind to adjust itself to the change. . . . At such times a too precipitate attempt to force desirable reforms might delay their secure establishment."[100] Those prejudices were never overcome during Reconstruction, and Article 135 was conveniently ignored outside New Orleans throughout the period.[101]

Though the debate over public education was a lively one, no one who participated in that debate appears to have argued that integrated schools would be required by the equal protection clause of the Fourteenth Amendment, even though its ratification was a foregone conclusion when the constitutional convention adopted Article 135. Rather, all the participants in the debate viewed the question as one of public policy, which the legislature was free to frame as it saw fit. Indeed, the history of the educational issue in Louisiana illustrated the wisdom of that view, for pragmatic concerns about the welfare of the children had required those committed to integrated schools to stay that demand.[102]

For all the rhetoric about liberty, equality, and the rights of man, pragmatic accommodation characterized Reconstruction in Louisiana. The "Unification Movement" that flowered briefly in 1873 sought to preserve the fruits of that policy. Savage violence had engulfed the state during the preceding fall elections. The governor's race had ended in a dead heat, and the Republican candidate had been installed largely because Union troops still occupied the state. Worried that the now endemic violence would destroy the city's prosperity, the leading white citizens of New Orleans invited black leaders to join them in a party that would promote "union . . . on terms of broadest liberality. Let there be an end of prejudice and proscription, and for the future let there be no differences of opinion dividing our people except upon questions of governmental polity."[103] Blacks accepted: "Let your people come out fairly and squarely and guarantee [our rights], and a party can be formed that will sweep the state like wildfire."[104]

A Committee of One Hundred—fifty whites and fifty blacks—set to work. On June 16 the committee submitted its recommendations to a public meeting that unanimously approved it. The resolution adopted that evening read:

FIRST—That henceforward we dedicate ourselves to the unification of our people.

SECOND—That by "our people," we mean all men, of whatever race, color or religion, who are citizens of Louisiana, and who are willing to work for her prosperity.

THIRD—That we shall advocate, by speech, and pen, and deed, the equal and impartial exercise by every citizen of Louisiana of every civil and political right guaranteed, by the constitution and laws of the United States, and by the laws of honor, brotherhood and fair dealing.

FOURTH—That we shall maintain and advocate the right of every citizen of Louisiana, and of every citizen of the United States, to frequent at will all places of public resort, and to travel at will on all vehicles of public conveyance, upon terms of perfect equality with any and every other citizen; and we pledge ourselves, so far as our influence, counsel and example may go, to make this right a live and practical right, and that there may be no misunderstanding of our views on this point:

1. We shall recommend to the proprietors of all places of licensed public resort in the State of Louisiana, the opening of said places to the patronage of both races inhabiting our State.

2. And we shall further recommend that all railroads, steamboats, steamships, and other public conveyances pursue the same policy.

3. We shall further recommend that our banks, insurance offices, and other public corporations recognize and concede to our colored fellow-citizens, where they are stockholders in such institutions, the right of being represented in the direction thereof.

4. We shall further recommend that hereafter no distinction shall exist among citizens of Louisiana in any of our public schools or State institutions of education, or in any other public institutions supported by the State, city or parishes.

5. We shall also recommend that the proprietors of all foundries, factories, and other industrial establishments, in employing mechanics or workmen, make no distinction between the two races.

6. We shall encourage, by every means in our power, our colored citizens in the rural districts to become the proprietors of the soil, thus enhancing the value of lands and adding to the productiveness of the State, while it will create a political conservatism which is the offspring of proprietorship: and we furthermore recommend to all landed proprietors in our State the policy of considering the question of breaking up the same into small farms, in order that the [our] colored citizens and white emigrants may become practical farmers and cultivators of the soil.

FIFTH—That we pledge our honor and good faith to exercise our moral influence, both through personal advice and personal example, to bring about the rapid removal of all prejudices heretofore existing against the colored citizens of Louisiana, in order that they may hereafter enjoy all the rights belonging to citizens of the United States.

Be it further resolved, That we earnestly appeal to the press of this State to join and cooperate with us in erecting this monument to unity, concord and justice, and like ourselves forever to bury beneath it all party prejudices.

Resolved, also, That we deprecate and thoroughly condemn all acts of violence, from whatever source, and appeal to our people of both races to abide by the law in all their differences as the surest way to preserve to all the blessings of life, liberty and property.

Resolved, That we pledge ourselves to the cultivation of a broad sentiment of nationality, which shall embrace the whole country, and uphold the flag of the Union.

Resolved, That as an earnest of our holy purpose, we hereby offer upon the altar of the common good, all party ties, and all prejudices of education which may tend to hinder the political unity of our people.

Resolved, That in view of numerical equality between the white and colored elements of our population, we shall advocate an equal distribution of the offices of trust and emolument in our State, demanding, as the only conditions of our suffrage, honesty, diligence and ability; and we advocate this not because of the offices themselves, but simply as another earnest and proof upon our part, that the union we desire is an equal union and not an illusive conjunction brought about for the sole benefit of one or the other of the parties to the union.[105]

The resolution thus endorsed every key black demand: equal and impartial administration of the laws; equal access to places of public accommodation; integrated schools; agrarian, business, and employment reform to enhance economic opportunities for blacks; and "an equal distribution of the offices of trust and emolument in our State." These promises were not cast in terms of legal obligations, however. To state the obvious, there was no assertion that the Fourteenth Amendment commanded any of them. Rather, the promises constituted a political commitment to fight for their achievement. This resolution thus dramatized how little the Fourteenth Amendment was thought to cabin the discretion of local political bodies, apart from whatever legislation Congress might think necessary to insure compliance with its principles.

Although a majority of New Orleans citizens endorsed the Unification Movement enthusiastically, the rest of white Louisiana rejected it. Its critics thought the movement promoted amalgamation and socialism. Both were anathema, as the following editorial comments demonstrated:

- Unification on the basis of perfect equality of whites and blacks. We abhor it in every fibre of our being.[106]
- The battle between the races for supremacy . . . must be fought out here . . . boldly and squarely; the issue cannot be satisfactorily adjusted by a repulsive commingling of antagonistic races, and the promulgation of platforms enunciating as the political tenets of the people of Louisiana the vilest Socialist doctrines.[107]

By the end of the summer, the movement was dead.[108] There were no formal rites, as there was none for the Jubilee. It too was fading, and no one would publicly mourn its silent passing a few years later. By then, blacks and their erstwhile white allies had lost the decade-long guerrilla struggle with negrophobic whites. One of the casualties of that struggle was the Fourteenth Amendment. It, too, proved to be "an exotic" unsuited to racist climes. "By 1880," comments Joe G. Taylor, "black Louisianans were back almost to where they had been in 1860."[109]

NOTES

1. Joe G. Taylor, *Louisiana Reconstructed 1863–1877* (Baton Rouge: Louisiana State University Press, 1974), 94. The 1860 census listed 10,689 free persons of color in Orleans Parish. This number "included . . . substantial merchants, cotton factors, caterers, doctors and lawyers, even newspaper editors and poets." Harlan, "Desegregation in New Orleans Public Schools," *American Historical Review* 67 (April 1962): 663, 674. See generally Annie Lee West Stahl, "The Free Negro in Ante-Bellum Louisiana," *Louisiana Historical Quarterly* 25 (April 1942): 301.

2. Joe G. Taylor, "Louisiana: An Impossible Task," in *Reconstruction and Redemption in the South*, ed. Otto H. Olsen (Baton Rouge: Louisiana State University Press, 1980), 203.

3. R. Fischer, *The Segregation Struggle in Louisiana, 1862–1877* (Champaign: University of Illinois Press, 1974), 11. New Orleans, with a population of two hundred thousand, was linked to both continental Europe and Latin America by its cultural heritage and trading relationships. Colored residents lived throughout the city; and many of them worshiped alongside whites in the city's Catholic churches, which held desegregated services. Visitors to the city frequently commented on the relaxed racial attitudes that set New Orleans apart from other Southern cities. See, e.g., *New Orleans Times*, 1 July 1877 (letter to editor from "A Frenchman").

4. Vincent Harding, *There Is a River: The Black Struggle for Freedom in America* (San Antonio: Harcourt Brace Jovanovich, 1981), 256–57 (*Tribune* sought to redefine the Civil War by tying it "to the best egalitarian traditions of the unfinished American Revolution"). See also F. Leavens, "*L'Union* and the *New Orleans Tribune* and Louisiana Reconstruction" (M.A. thesis, Louisiana State University, 1966), 17 ("From the beginning, *L'Union* advocated . . . civil and political equality").

5. *L'Union*, 6 December 1862, quoted in L. Rouzan, "A Rhetorical Analysis of Editorials in *L'Union* and the *New Orleans Tribune*" (Ph.D. diss., Florida State University, 1989), 45.

6. Jean-Charles Houzeau, *My Passage at the New Orleans Tribune: A Memoir of the Civil War Era*, ed. D. Rankin (Baton Rouge: Louisiana State University Press, 1984), 96. See generally C. Nero, "'To Develop Our Manhood': Free Black Leadership and the Rhetoric of the *New Orleans Tribune*" (Ph.D. diss., Indiana University, 1991), 202–21.

7. Donald E. Everett, "Demands of the New Orleans Free Colored Population for Political Equality, 1862–1865," *Louisiana Historical Quarterly* 38 (April 1955): 41, 45.

8. *New Orleans Times*, 6 November 1863.

9. Ibid.

10. Everett, "Demands of the New Orleans Free Colored Population," 46.

11. Ibid., 47. Dissatisfied and disappointed, the club decided to appeal its case to President Lincoln. The petition which the delegates carried to Washington listed the names of a thousand colored persons who owned property and emphasized their services and loyalty to the Union. Although the president acknowledged their moral claim, he told them he could not intervene on their behalf (ibid., 50–51).

12. Ted Tunnell argues that the free-labor "program that emerged in 1863 was so oppressive that, by comparison, the notorious black codes adopted after the war appear merely as extensions of Federal policy." Ted Tunnell, *Crucible of Reconstruction: War, Radicalism and Race in Louisiana, 1862–1877* (Baton Rouge: Louisiana State University Press, 1984), 84.

13. *New Orleans Tribune*, 22 September 1864.

14. Ibid., 4 January 1865.

15. Quoted in Taylor, *Louisiana Reconstructed*, 74.

16. *New Orleans Tribune*, 14 January 1866.

17. Ibid., 9 January 1866.

18. Ibid., 23 January 1866.

19. Ibid., 18 March 1866. Consequently, they feigned unconcern that Congress might not submit additional amendments, for none was "necessary to secure all the benefits and full effect of freedom and Republican liberties."

20. Ibid., 2 May 1866.

21. Ibid., 27 May 1866.

22. Cf. Taylor, *Louisiana Reconstructed*, 122.

23. *New Orleans Tribune*, 8 May 1866.

24. Ibid., 24 May 1866.

25. Ibid., 26 April 1866.

26. *New Orleans Picayune*, 29 May 1866.

27. *Weekly Advocate*, 12 May 1866.

28. See, e.g., *Louisiana Democrat*, 18 April 1866; *Sugar Planter*, 14 April 1866. See also *Bossier Banner*, 4 April 1868 ("We must escape equality with the negroes in our churches, our hotels, our public conveyances, our places of amusement, our schools and colleges.").

29. *New Orleans Tribune*, 16 June 1866.

30. Ibid.

31. Ibid.

32. C. Peter Ripley, *Slaves and Freedmen in Civil War Louisiana* (Baton Rouge: Louisiana State University Press, 1976), 167. One faction was allied with General Banks and the planters and supported Lincoln. The other, which supported Treasury Secretary Chase, represented the prewar Unionists and the free blacks.

33. Fischer, *The Segregation Struggle in Louisiana*, 24.

34. See generally Baker, "Michael Hahn: Steady Patriot," *Louisiana History* 13 (1972): 229.

35. Ripley, *Slaves and Freedmen in Civil War Louisiana*, 171.

36. Lincoln to Hahn, 13 March 1864, in *The Collected Works of Abraham Lincoln*, vol. 7, ed. Roy P. Basler (New Brunswick, N.J.: Rutgers University Press, 1953), 243.

37. *Debates in the Convention for the Revision and Amendment of the Constitution of the State of Louisiana, Assembled at Liberty Hall, New Orleans, April 6, 1864* (New Orleans: W. R. Fish, Printer to the Convention, 1864), 250.

38. *Journal of the Convention for the Revision and Amendment of the Constitution of Louisiana* (title page missing, n.p., 1864), 71 (Louisiana State Archives, Baton Rouge, Louisiana).

39. *Debates*, 216.

40. *L'Union*, 9 April 1864.

41. *Journal*, 175.

42. Fischer, *The Segregation Struggle in Louisiana*, 24–26.

43. *New Orleans Tribune*, 13 August 1864.

44. Ibid., 11 August 1864.

45. Ripley, *Slaves and Freedmen in Civil War Louisiana*, 183.

46. John R. Ficklen, *A History of Reconstruction in Louisiana, through 1868* (1910; reprinted Gloucester, Mass.: Peter Smith), 109. See also Taylor, *Louisiana Reconstructed*, 71–72.

47. James G. Blaine, *Twenty Years of Congress: From Lincoln to Garfield, vol. 2* (Norwich, Conn.: Henry Hill Publishing Company, 1884–86), 101–2.

48. Henry C. Warmouth, *War, Politics and Reconstruction: Stormy Days in Louisiana* (New York: Macmillan, 1930). See also Taylor, *Louisiana Reconstructed*, 98 ("municipalities adopted ordinances which ... were reenactments of the "municipal regulations" in force for slaves in 1860").

49. Ripley, *Slaves and Freedmen in Civil War Louisiana*, 183. Commenting on the cumulative impact of laws like these, a parish agent of the Freedmen's Bureau observed: "Slavery is reestablished" (ibid., 191).

50. *New Orleans Tribune*, 15 July 1865.

51. *Baton Rouge Tri-Weekly*, 9 January 1866. Cf. *Weekly Gazette and Comet*, 27 April 1867 ("Experience has demonstrated and wisdom sanctioned it, that the only safe expedient to adopt in the matter of suffrage is to be found in that conservative principle of restricting the right of franchise to a standard of intelligence, in other words, to withhold the free exercise of that right from any individual not possessing the virtuous education and intelligence rightly to understand the true nature and importance of such right"); *Opelousas Courier*, 21 December 1867 ("Colored men" are not fit jurors and their use "degrades" juries to such an extent that the system should be abolished).

52. Ficklen, *History of Reconstruction in Louisiana*, 142; see, e.g., *New Orleans Tribune*, 20 December 1865.

53. *New Orleans Tribune*, 15 June 1866.

54. *Opelousas Courier*, 29 February 1868.

55. See James E. Bond, "Ratification of the 14th Amendment in North Carolina," *Wake Forest Law Review* 20 (Spring 1984): 89; see also *Louisiana Democrat*, 26 September 1866 (commenting on the importance to the South of the fall elections in the North).

56. See *Quanchita Telegraph*, 23 August 1866; *Sugar Planter*, 4 August 1866; *Iberville South*, 11 August 1866.

57. Sheridan to Grant, 2 August 1866, quoted in Howard K. Beale, *The Critical Years: A Study of Andrew Johnson and Reconstruction* (New York: F. Unger Publishing Company, 1958), 352.

58. See, e.g., *Weekly Gazette and Comet*, 28 August (11 September) 1866; *Sugar Planter*, 8 September 1866. For a contemporary assessment of the evidence that suggests that neither of the conspiracy theories is correct, see Ficklen, *History of Reconstruction in Louisiana*, 176.

59. *South Western*, 8 August 1866.

60. *Baton Rouge Weekly Advocate*, 4 August 1866.

61. *South Western*, 10 October 1866.

62. *Semi-Weekly Times*, 14 November 1866. Cf. *South Western*, 17 October 1866 ("the terms of the proposed amendment seem to be generally misunderstood by the people").

63. See, e.g., *Bossier Banner*, 16 February 1867; *Iberville South*, 20 October 1866. See also *New Orleans Bee*, 8 February 1866.

64. *Louisiana Democrat*, 16 May 1866.

65. *New Orleans Picayune*, 29 May 1866.

66. *South Western*, 14 February 1866 (commenting on an earlier proposed representation amendment whose provisions paralleled Section 3).

67. *New Orleans Picayune*, 26 June 1866.

68. *Louisiana Democrat*, 10 October 1866.

69. *New Orleans Bee*, 26 January 1866.

70. *Semi-Weekly Times*, 7 February 1866.

71. *Weekly Gazette and Comet*, 2 February 1867.

72. *Louisiana Democrat*, 6 February 1867.

73. Ibid., 13 February 1867.

74. Taylor, *Louisiana Reconstructed*, 126.

75. *Louisiana Democrat*, 6 February 1866. See also Ripley, *Slaves and Freedmen in Civil War Louisiana*, 182 ("One of the more overt political opportunists in a state full of the species, Wells was willing to flow with the source of power as long as it was blue not gray.").

76. Cf. *Quanchita Telegraph*, 15 February 1868 ("Such is the prospect under negro domination. It offers no prosperity, gives not a scintilla of hope, promises nothing but the gloomiest of fates.").

77. Fischer, *The Segregation Struggle in Louisiana*, 30–31.

78. Taylor, *Louisiana Reconstructed*, 51.

79. Fischer, *The Segregation Struggle in Louisiana*, 40.

80. *Constitution Adopted by the State Constitutional Convention of the State of Louisiana, March 7, 1868* (New Orleans: Printed by the *New Orleans Republican*, in accordance with a resolution of the Constitutional Convention, 1868).

81. Ficklen, *History of Reconstruction in Louisiana*, 187–88.

82. Ibid., 208.

83. *Quanchita Telegraph*, 9 January 1868.

84. *Carroll Reader*, 19 July 1868. Earlier, the same paper had condemned Article 13 as a violation of private property rights, "abhorrent to all our traditions and repugnant to the law of nature" (4 April 1868).

85. Warmouth, *War, Politics and Reconstruction*, 92. See generally Fischer, *The Segregation Struggle in Louisiana*, 61–87.

86. Fischer describes the convention as "composed of three factions": the negro members and a few white allies, committed to the equality principle; approximately thirty

white radicals, many of whom were "carpetbaggers" and took a more "pragmatic" view of race issues; and sixteen rural white Unionists, unalterably opposed to "social equality." Fischer, *The Segregation Struggle in Louisiana*, 49–50.

87. *Louisiana Democrat*, 4 December 1867. Cf. *Bossier Banner*, 25 March 1868 (denounces the "convention of Mongrels").

88. *South Western*, 25 March 1868.

89. Ibid., 8 April 1868.

90. Fischer, *The Segregation Struggle in Louisiana*, 50. See also Ficklen, *History of Reconstruction in Louisiana*, 194. The Republicans had encouraged local parties to elect an equal number of black and white convention delegates, however. Ella Lonn, *Reconstruction in Louisiana after 1868* (1918; reprinted Gloucester, Mass.: Peter Smith), 5–6. See, e.g., *South Western*, 1 May 1867 (attacking letter from the Central Committee of the Republican Party advising that one-half of delegates selected be colored).

91. *Carroll Reader*, 18 July 1868.

92. *New Orleans Tribune*, 30 January 1866.

93. Ibid., 26 June 1866.

94. Fischer, *The Segregation Struggle in Louisiana*, 43.

95. Ibid.

96. *Louisiana Democrat*, 21 February 1866.

97. *New Orleans Bee*, 5 March 1866:

> Viewed in the light of a useful laborer, the freedman is as much an object of solicitude for his material welfare and preservation, to the community at large, as he was to the master who formerly owned him. Viewed in the light of a free person, removed from under the personal authority attending slavery, and therefore valuable as a social element only as he is disposed and knows how to make good use of his freedom, he is an object of not less solicitude for his moral and intellectual elevation.

See also *Semi-Weekly Times*, 13 April 1867 ("It is to our own immediate advantage to encourage the improvement and elevation of the colored race"); *Bossier Banner*, 23 May 1868 ("[I]t is our duty to humanize and civilize [the Negro], as much as [is] in our power"); *Weekly Gazette and Comet*, 2 May 1868 ("We owe it to the freedmen . . . to teach them.").

98. *Weekly Gazette and Comet*, 15 December 1866. Little more than a year later, the same paper repeated its plea for a system of common schools. (11 January 1868).

99. Fischer, *The Segregation Struggle in Louisiana*, 110. See generally Louis R. Harlan, "Desegregation in New Orleans Public Schools during Reconstruction," 67 *American Historical Review* (April 1962): 663.

100. *Report of the State Superintendent of Education, 1869*, 12–13 (contained in the State Board of Education Records, 1863–1869, Louisiana State Archives, Baton Rouge, Louisiana).

101. Taylor, "Louisiana: An Impossible Task," 211.

102. Fischer, *The Segregation Struggle in Louisiana*, 46 ("[A] Negro principal pointed out that black students fought continually with the lighter-skinned children of mixed ancestry in her school and predicted that disciplinary problems would be insurmountable if black and white children were placed together").

103. *New Orleans Picayune*, 6 June 1873.

104. *New Orleans Times*, 29 May 1873.

105. T. Williams, "The Louisiana Unification Movement of 1873," *Journal of Southern History* 11 (August 1945): 347, 360–61.

106. *Quanchita Telegraph*, 21 June 1873.

107. *Shreveport Times*, quoted in *Quanchita Telegraph*, 19 June 1873. Rural whites had made their views clear years earlier when they voted against the Reconstruction constitution:

> If you don't want negro equality forced upon you, go to the polls and vote against the proposed Constitution, framed by the social banditi, domestic bastards, catamites, scallawags, slubberdegullions, cow thieves and jay-hawkers of Louisiana.
>
> If you don't want your State, District, Parish and Ward offices filled with negroes and white vagabonds, vote down the black vomit spewed up by the scrofulous vermin, late of the Mechanic's Institute.
>
> If you don't want negro jurors, go to the polls and vote against the new constitution.
>
> If you don't want to be ground down by taxes to educate negroes, go [*sic*] the polls and vote against the new constitution.
>
> If you don't want your wives and daughters to be insulted by insolent and depraved negro vagabonds, go to the polls and vote against the new constitution.
>
> If you don't want negroes and Yankee thieves to be your masters and rulers, go to the polls and vote against the new constitution.
>
> If you are opposed to amalgamation and miscegenation, vote against the new constitution.
>
> If you wish the respect of all honest white men, go to the polls and vote against the new constitution.
>
> If you prefer the Southern white man to the Northern thief as an office holder, go to the polls and vote down the infamous libel proposed as a constitution.
>
> If you feel like stealing something, and wish to associate with negroes and white jayhawkers the balance of your life, go to the polls and vote FOR the new constitution.
>
> If you want your children to go to the same school, eat at the same table, and sit in the same church pews with negro children, and wish to turn negro and jay-hawker yourself, go to the polls and vote FOR the cow thieves' constitution. (*Bossier Banner*, 28 March 1868)

108. Williams, "The Louisiana Unification Movement of 1873," 367.

109. Taylor, "Louisiana: An Impossible Task," 230.

6

Ratification in Alabama

*The great truths of the Declaration of Independence are for the first time
to be made the governing principles of the land.*

—A black newspaper editor from Mobile, inspired by Reconstruction
developments in Alabama, 1867–68

The bloom had faded from the rose of secession in Alabama months before
Lee's surrender. As early as 1862, north Alabamians had begun to join the Union army; and enlistments accelerated as the Confederacy's fortunes waned.[1] In
the same year, former Whig "cooperationists" who had opposed secession
formed a secret Peace Society. By the winter of 1865, William Smith, one of the
society's founders, was planning to run for governor on a platform which called
for Alabama to leave the Confederacy and return to the Union.[2] The "Dunning
chronicler" of Alabama's Reconstruction conceded that the state might have
chosen that course had the war not ended before the summer elections of 1865.[3]

In any case, prewar Whigs rather than unrepentant secessionists dominated the
provisional government,[4] the 1865 constitutional convention,[5] and the 1865–66
session of the state legislature.[6] Thoroughly Unionist in their sentiments and
ardently desirous of restoration, these persons and bodies were more likely to
give the Fourteenth Amendment a fair hearing than were most of their counterparts in the other Southern states. Though Alabama came closer to ratifying the
amendment than did any of the other nine Southern states that initially refused,
it too rejected it.[7]

Governor Robert M. Patton's conduct reflected an ambivalence toward the
amendment which many white Alabamians may have shared. Initially he advised the legislature to reject the amendment.[8] A month later he implored them
to ratify it.[9] In his initial message, Governor Patton subjected the amendment,
including Section 1, to a thorough analysis. Like most of its critics, he lambasted

Section 1 because it would transfer power from the state government to the national government. Unlike most of its other critics, however, the governor did not emphasize the danger of transferring such power to the Congress. Rather, he emphasized the danger of giving federal courts a warrant to review every decision of a state court:

[Section 1] would enlarge the judicial powers of the General Government to such gigantic dimensions as would not only overshadow and weaken the authority and influence of the State courts, but might possibly reduce them to a complete nullity. It would give to the United States courts complete and unlimited jurisdiction over every conceivable case, however important or however trivial, which could arise under State laws. Every individual dissatisfied with the decision of a State court, might apply to a Federal tribunal for redress. It matters not what might be the character of his case. . . . Upon a simple complaint that his rights, either of person or property, had been infringed, it would be the bounden duty of the tribunal to which he made his application to hear and determine his case. The granting of such an immense power as this over the State tribunals would, at the very best, subordinate them to a condition of comparative unimportance and significance.[10]

Though the governor's analysis is superficially consistent with the view that the due process clause embodied substantive standards by which a federal court might police state court judgments, that was probably not what concerned him. He certainly never even hinted that the Bill of Rights would be the source of such substantive standards—though that would have been the case had it been incorporated into Section 1.

Rather, his major concern appears to have been grounded in the perennial Southern obsession with states' rights, an obsession that permeated the general public discussion of Section 1. After all, the major objections to the Civil Rights Bill in Alabama had been its invasion of "state prerogatives"[11] and its "centralization of power in the national government."[12] Section 1 was generally understood to reaffirm the provisions of the Civil Rights Bill and incorporate them into the Constitution;[13] and in discussing the Civil Rights Act, white Alabamians had not objected to its grant of civil rights to the freedmen. They had, however, protested strenuously against the expanded enforcement powers which the act gave the national government and more particularly federal courts.[14] In other words, they feared federal judicial review of legal classifications that commended themselves to the state legislature.

Governor Patton's conduct in the winter of 1866 confirms this understanding of what was "due" the freedmen, and that understanding doubtless shaped his interpretation of Section 1 of the Fourteenth Amendment. Like most of the other Southern legislatures, Alabama's had adopted various laws in late 1865 to deal with the "problems" that the emancipation of the slaves appeared to have created.[15] Although Governor Patton approved two vagrancy laws, he vetoed all the other bills, including one that would have extended to the freedmen the antebellum laws governing free persons of color.[16] In explaining his vetoes to the legislature, the governor said:

The negroes always had their natural rights. While they were in slavery those rights were protected and maintained by their masters; but now they are free, they can look to the law alone for the protection of their persons and property. For this protection I do not think that discriminating laws are necessary.

In deliberating upon a subject of this character, we may very properly take into consideration facts and events now actually occurring. Information from various parts of the State shows that the negroes are everywhere making contracts for the present year upon terms that are entirely satisfactory to the employers. They are also entering faithfully upon the discharge of the obligations contracted. There is every prospect that the engagements formed will be observed with perfect good faith. I, therefore, think that special laws for regulating contracts between whites and freedmen would accomplish no good, and might result in much harm.[17]

The governor also vetoed an apprentice bill because he considered it class legislation.[18] He pointed out that Alabama already provided for the disposition of indigent children.

In light of this record, Governor Patton's principal objection to Section 1 could not have been that it constitutionalized the guarantees of the Civil Rights Act. He obviously believed that natural law and sound public policy required that the freedmen be given the same civil rights which whites enjoyed, absent some strong factual basis for believing that differential treatment was needed. He had warned the legislature that "[n]o good to the country can result from having one code of laws for whites and another for blacks, in their new relations, and so far as concerns the rights of persons and property."[19] But he also believed that judgments of this kind were reserved to the states. Consequently, he considered the amendment as "a violation of the rights of one quarter of the states, . . . a gross usurpation of the rights of the states, . . . a centralization of power in the national government."[20] In other words, the mere possibility that Congress or the federal courts might review state judgments was offensive. It would infringe the retained sovereignty of the state.

Within a month of recommending rejection of the amendment, Governor Patton had changed his mind. On December 7 he sent a special message to the legislature, urging them to ratify the Fourteenth Amendment. The Governor was still concerned about the loss of states' rights, and he found Sections 2 and 3 insulting. He nevertheless decided to set aside those concerns and swallow his pride, probably in part because Section 1 had so narrow an ambit. In any case, he was now prepared to bow to reality. Objectionable as Sections 2 and 3 of the Fourteenth Amendment might be, he had come to believe that terms even more objectionable would be imposed if Alabama failed to ratify.[21] He at least understood the implications of the stunning radical triumph in the Northern congressional campaigns that fall.

During the Christmas holidays, the governor canvassed north Alabama. Admitting that he remained opposed "in principle" to the Fourteenth Amendment, he repeatedly asked his audiences to "look the situation squarely in the face." Congress was determined to impose it; and if Alabama refused to accept it, worse might follow.[22] He was reported to have sought and received assurances that Alabama would be readmitted if it ratified the Amendment,[23] and he therefore recommended its ratification. Pilloried for his pragmatic decision,[24] the governor still tried one more time in late January 1867 to persuade the legislature to ratify the amendment. It refused. Like all the other Southern legislatures except Tennessee's, it thought the settlement terms embodied in the Fourteenth Amendment humiliating. They could not believe that they would be forced to accept them.

Former Provisional Governor Parsons played a key role in insuring the defeat of the amendment. During the fall congressional campaigns in the North, he had spoken in favor of presidential Reconstruction. He now twice effectively blunted his successor's pleas for ratification. On the first occasion, he advised the legislature that the Northern people would support the president on Reconstruction. On the second occasion, he got the president himself to say that no good could come of ratification and that the legislature should stand firm against those who would "change the whole character of the government."[25]

Since the Joint Committee on State and Federal Relations did not submit a report on the Fourteenth Amendment and the legislature did not keep an official record of its debate on the issue, the legislature's understanding of the Fourteenth Amendment must be inferred from the understanding of the constituents whom it represented. The principal concern that white Alabamians expressed about Section 1 was Congress's power under Section 5 to define the privileges and immunities of citizenship. Specifically, they feared that voting and other political privileges such as holding public office might be denominated privileges and immunities of citizenship.[26]

Since the major immediate fear of those who opposed ratification was the prospect of "political domination by blacks,"[27] white Alabamians would have been especially alert to any possibility that an incorporated Bill of Rights might be invoked to secure political rights for blacks. At that time, for example, jury service was considered a political right. Most white Alabamians were so opposed to Negro jurors that they urged arbitration rather than jury trials with "ignorant and incompetent blacks" in the jury box.[28] The Sixth Amendment, of course, guarantees all persons the right to a jury trial of their peers. Had white Alabamians suspected that the Fourteenth Amendment vouchsafed that right to blacks, they would have denounced it on that ground alone. They did not. The possibility that the Fourteenth Amendment incorporated the Bill of Rights seems never to have dawned on them.

Only once did anyone even mention the possibility that the due process clause of Section 1 might be invoked as a source of substantive rights. In November 1866, one of the state's major newspapers asked why the due process clause had been inserted into Section 1. It correctly answered that the "present provision" [i.e., the Fifth Amendment] was "a restraint only on the general government."[29] It then added the startling surmise that voting might be construed to be a liberty protected by the Fourteenth Amendment due process clause!

The surmise was, of course, well calculated to fan the anxieties of white Alabamians about the possibility of blacks being given the right to vote. It was not, however, well founded. That liberty which was protected in the Fifth Amendment from deprivation without due process of law had never been construed to include the right to vote. More to the point, Section 2 of the Fourteenth Amendment explicitly conceded control over voting rights to the states and therefore precluded any inference that the national government could supplant that control under the more general grant of authority in Section 5 to protect citizens from state deprivations of due process.[30]

Interestingly, the author of the surmise, imaginative as he was to raise the point, apparently never thought to suggest that that liberty protected from deprivation without due process of law might also embrace all the rights guaranteed in the Bill of Rights, including the right to bear arms—a right which most white Alabamians thought blacks should never exercise.[31]

In Alabama, as elsewhere, the general populace appeared to hold the conventional view of Section 1: it merely "legitimated" the "bastard" Civil Rights Bill.[32] White Alabamians were prepared to grant blacks the civil rights to buy and sell, contract, and use the courts. Because blacks were now free, they deserved governmental protection. But that was all: "I want the negro to have his legal and civil rights and nothing more," declared one Unionist.[33] So long as the state retained the authority to legislate on matters relating to the freedmen, white Alabamians were reasonably confident that the freedmen would get "nothing more."[34] White Alabamians, like most white Southerners, were after all profoundly negrophobic: "No negro ever comprehended or grasped any purely abstract idea; no negro ever distinguished himself in art, or service, or literature; no negro ever administered a stable post; no negro ever found happiness in intellectual pursuits, nor ever will. The enjoyments of the whole black race are purely sensual."[35] They genuinely feared and loathed the very idea of Negro equality, in all its manifestations. They feared that political equality would lead first to a Negro legislature and a Negro governor, thence to Negro supremacy, and finally to that dreaded "social equality."

Few Alabama blacks participated in the debate over the Fourteenth Amendment. Most of the freedmen were illiterate,[36] and many may have been unaware of its existence. In any case, they were excluded from the political process. The freedmen nevertheless had an intuitive sense of what freedom meant. Slavery had subjected them to innumerable restraints, and they naturally equated freedom with the absence of those restraints. Moreover, they had all seen how white men and women acted; their conduct was necessarily another guide to the incidents of individual liberty.

One such incident was the freedom to meet in public, a right which had been denied slaves. Mass meetings of blacks were common in Alabama throughout the summer and fall of 1865.[37] Cautious in tone, these well-attended meetings produced resolutions that eschewed any claim to political rights and stressed instead the importance of hard work and obedience to civil law.[38]

There were a few well-educated persons of color in Alabama at the time; they did know about the Fourteenth Amendment; and their attitude toward it was not cautious. Most of these blacks lived in Mobile, and most of them had been free persons of color before the Civil War.[39] Late in 1865 they established a paper, the *Nationalist*, which they intended to be "the grand political and commercial organ of the colored people of the South."[40]

The paper's philosophy was clear. Its editors insisted that "all men are born free and have the same inalienable rights."[41] They also insisted on universal suffrage because "justice" could be "secured to all" only when "all are allowed a voice in making the law."[42] Thus they endorsed "[t]he theory . . . that the sovereign power belongs to the people, not a portion of the people, not to the learned, not to the ignorant, not to the rich, not to the poor, not to the great, not to the weak, but to all the people."[43]

Consequently, they were unenthusiastic about the Fourteenth Amendment. It was "a mere political expedient" that did not "meet the present difficulties squarely in the face."[44] In other words, the amendment did not guarantee universal suffrage. In particular, Section 1 did not go far enough; like the Civil Rights Act, it only guaranteed the equality "to acquire property, to sue and be sued, and to be protected from outlaws."[45] While those were important rights, they could not prevent the state legislature from "[using] its ingenuity to devise some additional scheme whereby the condition of the freedmen might more nearly be assimilated to what it was before the abolition of slavery."[46] According to the *Nationalist*, blacks could protect themselves against such schemes more effectively through the ballot box than by appeals to federal tribunals. They nevertheless welcomed the latter opportunity[47] because "[e]very man should be allowed equal opportunities, as far as the law is concerned."[48]

Thus the *Nationalist* understood the Fourteenth Amendment just as did its critics. Those critics thought it went too far, of course; the *Nationalist* thought it did not go far enough. The paper, consequently, concluded that the state's failure to ratify it would be "no great misfortune."[49]

The debate over ratification in Alabama did not turn, then, on different and strongly disputed interpretations of the Fourteenth Amendment among those who participated in the debate. The few who favored and the many who opposed generally agreed on its meaning. None embraced it enthusiastically. Most whites were offended by the disfranchisement provision, resented the voting provision, and feared that Congress or the federal courts might usurp state authority over domestic affairs. Those whites who favored ratification were willing to endure the affront to their sensibilities and risk the danger of consolidation in order to secure an early restoration and thereby forestall a more stringent reconstruction.[50]

On these questions, otherwise like-minded persons could differ. Those who favored ratification may have assumed too naively that that act alone would insure Alabama's restoration, and they may have exaggerated the extent to which a restored South could prevent Congress from exercising the powers which lay dormant in Section 5 of the amendment. Those who opposed ratification may have assumed too naively that the president could prevent congressional radicals from seizing control of reconstruction policy, and they may have exaggerated the extent to which Congress would have crammed Negro equality down their throats.

Congressional Reconstruction mooted these differences and polarized Alabama politics. Many Unionists, particularly those from south Alabama, recoiled in horror at the prospect of black participation in the government. Allying themselves with the conservative ex-Confederates, they ultimately sought to salvage a white man's government from the wreckage which radicalism wrought. Initially, however, they were dispirited, disorganized, and divided over how best to proceed. When some of the conservatives assembled in September 1867 in Montgomery, they sought Negro participation, adopted a vague program,[51] and attacked the Republicans for favoring Negro supremacy.[52] Dissenting, die-hard conservatives derided the "Montgomery Political Picnic" for its limited representation and its inclusion of Negroes.[53]

Other Unionists, predominantly from north Alabama, embraced blacks. Political necessity dictated that they swallow this "bitter pill,"[54] and Negroes became "the backbone of the Republican party."[55] Blacks had first convened in Alabama in 1865 in Mobile. At that time they concentrated on education, which they regarded as "vital to the preservation of their liberties."[56] Their other resolutions stressed the need to cultivate "all the virtues of good citizenship" and good relations with whites "among whom our lot is cast."[57] By the time they reconvened in Mobile eighteen months later, they had other and broader concerns. They asserted they had an "undeniable right to hold office, sit on juries, to ride on all public conveyances, to sit at public tables, and in public places of amusement."[58] In its address to the people of Alabama, the convention asked "for blacks the same legal rights as whites."[59]

A month later, on June 4, 1867, the Union Republican Convention met in Montgomery with the Union League Convention and endorsed these demands.[60] Judge Smith, the convention chairman, opened the meeting by urging all to work for Reconstruction "without distinction of race, color, or condition."[61] On the second day of the convention, the delegates adopted resolutions calling for amendments to insure the equality of all men and for the enjoyment of the rights of citizenship without distinction of color.[62] Resolution 10 specifically called for political equality.[63] These resolutions constituted the platform of the Republican Party, and the state's leading Republican paper carried them daily on page two throughout the summer and fall of 1867.[64]

Throughout the same period, the *Daily State Sentinel* ran resolutions from various local Republican meetings. Though the wording of these resolutions differed one from the other, the August resolution of a meeting in Cherokee is representative. It called for "according to the black man ... every right, civil and political, under the law."[65] The overarching demand was, thus, simply a call for equality of rights: "The essence of Republicanism is that every man has exactly the same rights, immunities, and privileges as every other man."[66] Republicans grounded their demand, not in the specific guarantees of the Bill of Rights, but in the general principles of the Declaration of Independence. When they did demand particular rights, they never used the Bill of Rights as an index of those rights. Rather, they often demanded very specific rights that were relevant to day-to-day living, such as "riding with whites in public conveyances."[67]

This philosophy permeated the work of the constitutional convention. The first of the conventions convened under the Reconstruction Acts[68] met in Montgomery from November 5 to December 6, 1867.[69] The dispirited conservatives had sought to prevent the convention by registering to vote and then staying at home, since the Reconstruction Acts authorized a convention only if a majority of those registered approved the call. This bit of "masterly inactivity" did not succeed in preventing the convention;[70] it did insure a Republican-dominated convention.

That fact scarcely insured a conflict-free convention, however. Some of the delegates were more interested in drafting a constitution that freed the capitalist to develop Alabama's economy than they were in drafting one that finally freed the freedmen.[71] The reconciliation of those two aims demonstrated that there were practical limits both to the philosophy of the Declaration and to the principles embodied in Section 1 of the Fourteenth Amendment. As a result, the tone of the convention was moderate rather than radical; and "the Convention did little for Alabama blacks."[72]

That evaluation is borne out by an analysis of specific convention issues that might have been thought to raise questions about the scope of the Fourteenth Amendment. From the beginning, Alabama blacks wanted land. They detested the plantation labor system, which they equated with slavery. In late 1865 the *Nationalist* prophesied: "These large plantations ... are destined soon to be cut up into small farms, to be controlled by the owners and their sons. Hired labor will become more and more difficult to procure, yet a laboring, self reliant, and intelligent population will multiply all over the country."[73] That never came to pass, in part because the national government refused to confiscate rebel lands, in part because most blacks lacked the money to buy or rent land, and in part because landowners generally refused to sell or rent to Negroes.[74] Although radicals in Alabama occasionally talked about confiscation and redistribution,[75] they never "walked the talk." By the time of the constitutional convention, the Republican Party had repudiated confiscation (though an occasional radical might still brandish the possibility as a threat).[76] Consequently, that issue did not even arise in the convention.

Three other issues did arise: public schools, miscegenation, and equal access to public accommodations. In each case, the convention rejected the solutions offered by both radicals and conservatives. Blacks wanted schools almost as much as they wanted land, and the Republican Party did endorse that demand. It was thus a foregone conclusion that the constitution would provide for public schools. Whether those schools would be integrated or segregated was not a foregone conclusion, however. The convention tabled a motion that would have required segregated schools,[77] thus leaving that decision to the new Board of Education. Since an overwhelming majority of the delegates in fact favored segregated schools, they assumed that there would be separate schools for each race. They were right.[78]

Twice conservatives demanded that the constitution prohibit interracial marriages. The convention refused.[79] Mulatto delegates from Mobile, where a majority of Alabama's mulattos lived, importuned the convention to protect interracial marriages. It also refused that demand. In exasperation, one of the black delegates proposed that "any white man intermarrying or cohabiting with colored women shall be imprisoned for life."[80] That, too, was rejected; and the constitution remained silent on the subject.

The debate on public accommodations "produced the most excited and inflammatory discussions in the convention."[81] No sooner had the motion to ban discrimination "between citizens of this State traveling on public conveyances" been made than the following exchange occurred, as summarized in the local press:

Mr. McLeod (black negro) said he hoped the Convention would give this matter their best consideration. Suppose one of the gentlemen wanted a colored man in the same car with him, the conductor would not allow it. He thought this ought to be changed.

Mr. Jim Green (black negro) said he had done a great deal of traveling, and he felt interested in this question. It was a common thing for colored people to be put into a smoking car with drunkards and low white men. He thought they ought to be allowed to go among decent white people.

Major Semple said he thought the Convention had better meet this question fairly. He asked was it unreasonable, considering the history of this country, and the attitude in which the two races stood to each other, that the steamboat captain should have the right to say to the colored people—"you shall not sit at the same table with white men and mix up with them as you please?" It had been recently decided in some of the States that this was a justifiable exercise of authority. After having inserted in the Constitution various provisions which were intended to secure to all races civil rights, he thought the question of what said rights were ought to be left to the courts.

Mr. Gregory (mulatto negro) asked how could the delegates go home to their constituents, nineteen-twentieths of whom were colored men, after having voted against their enjoying the same rights in all respects as white people. Did the gentleman from Montgomery (Semple) feel polluted by sitting alongside of Finley, his colored colleague? And if not, why should he feel polluted by sitting by his side in a car? For himself, he thought Napoleon on his throne was not a better man than he (Gregory) was.

Mr. Carraway (mulatto negro) said at present the colored man could not send his wife from one part of the State to another, because she would be placed in a smoking car and exposed to the insults of low and obscene white men. He did not see how any friend of the colored man could vote against breaking down this monopoly.

Mr. Griffin ("incarnate fiend") said he was sorry this question had come up, but he should meet the question squarely and vote for the proposed amendment.

Mr. Rapier (mulatto negro) said the manner in which colored gentlemen and colored ladies were treated was past his comprehension. He wanted the gentleman from Montgomery to understand that he did not consider himself honored by sitting in a car beside him, because he was a white man simply, but only because of his intelligence. He (Rapier) had dined with lords in England in his lifetime. Out of respect for their constituents the delegates ought to vote for the amendment.

Mr. Saffold (white) said he regretted such a firebrand had been thrown unnecessarily in their midst. But he hoped they would meet the issue like men who know what was right and dared to do it. While they were protecting the rights of one section of the people of Alabama, they ought not to neglect the rights of another section. Did not the Convention know what had recently been the issue in the Northern States, and what the decision had been? As a friend of the colored man, as a friend of philanthropy, he protested against a war of races. They know their opponents sought to force that issue upon them, and he hoped they would not be so unwise as to allow them to do so. He should vote against the proposition.

Mr. Morgan said the question had been already legally decided in the North. A colored man ought to be content with getting the same value for his money as a white man, and ought not to seek to force himself into the same car with white people.[82]

Following a weekend respite, Mr. Keffer, who had introduced the motion, withdrew it, allegedly because "several members of the convention had threatened to withdraw . . . if that 'odious feature' were incorporated into the constitution."[83] Mr. Semple then taunted the motion's supporters:

Mr. President: On Saturday Mr. Keffer, of Montgomery, offered the following as a section of the Bill of Rights:

> That common carriers shall make no distinctions between citizens of
> this State traveling on public conveyance.

It was offered us by the champion of the colored race, and was done as upon a calculation of the cowardice of the white race, and that they would quail and submit.

Terrified by the formidable opposition which it aroused, it was tremblingly withdrawn. Its author and abettors found that they were mistaken, that the white natives and old residents of the South, and many of the most honorable of the newcomers among us, were unwilling to prove recreant to the pride of the race, and ignobly surrender.

The delegate feels the shoe pinch. I was gagged yesterday when discussing this subject, but I can probe it to the bottom in ten minutes and I intend to do it. They feel that it is necessary to stifle the voice of the white people in Alabama to accomplish their purposes; but, if they will follow their blind guides, it will not be for lack of timely warning.

Yes, the question has been made and it must be decided. The proud, heroic race, descended from the great European stocks, from the English, the Irish, the French, the German, and the Italians, will never prove recreant to their noble ancestry. Treasuring jealously, the rich heritage of their achievements in literature, poetry, arts and arms, they will and do demand that the established usages of society should be so respected. When habits have become so imbedded in the social system as to become a part of the very life of a race, they cannot safely be disregarded by governments. You may call them prejudices if you will, they have no foundation in reason, but if trampled upon ruthlessly, no power on earth can control the storm which will be raised.

Men are made up not of reason only, but of imagination and sentiment also, and nothing can be more ruinous than to disregard and violate every usage which is founded in sentiment only, because not supported by that reason.[84]

The debate illustrates once again how little the language of the Fourteenth Amendment was involved in these debates. Proponents of equal access to public accommodations relied on the equality of rights principle. Opponents cited the police power of the state. Mr. Semple, for example, insisted that "[e]quality of rights is not invaded by the adoption of . . . reasonable regulations."[85] He argued that society owed certain duties to itself, the first of which was self-preservation. Therefore, when the exercise of any natural right became dangerous to the country, society had a right to circumscribe it.

The constitution which the convention recommended to the people nevertheless rang with the language of the Declaration. Indeed, Section 1 of Article I repeated its very language: "That all men are created equal; they are endowed by their Creator with certain inalienable rights; that among these are life, liberty, and the pursuit of happiness." Section 2 guaranteed all the citizens of Alabama equal civil and political rights and public privileges; and other sections protected freedom of speech and assembly, freedom of religion and conscience, and a panoply of procedural rights. While a few of these guarantees were cast in language identical to that of the national Bill of Rights,[86] most were not. Moreover, Section 10 explicitly empowered the legislature to "dispense with a grand jury" and provide alternative processes in "cases of petit larceny, assault, assault and battery, affray, unlawful assemblies, vagrancies, and other misdemeanors."

Some of the language of the Alabama Declaration of Rights is thus derived—word for word—from either the Declaration of Independence or the national Constitution. It therefore follows that the Alabama drafters were quite familiar with the language of both documents. Had they been equally familiar with the incorporation thesis, they presumably would have used the language of the Bill of Rights more frequently. Clearly, they would not have authorized alternative prosecutorial procedures flatly prohibited by the Sixth Amendment.

And while the constitution did incorporate the equality of rights principle, no one understood it to require equality of condition. It required only equality before the law. The triumphant Republican Party in Alabama was thus described as wanting "a Union wherein all men may have an equal chance before the laws; where all have the opportunity of bettering their condition, without means of degrading any."[87] The latter point illuminates their understanding of the equal protection clause as a guarantee of opportunity unfettered by governmental favoritism but reinforced, if necessary, by neutral enforcement of the laws.

Even this moderate constitution aroused the antipathy of conservatives, who asked, "Shall the white man be subordinate to the negro? Shall the property classes be robbed by the no property herd?"[88] Their specific objections to the document were numerous, but at the root of them all were racial and economic attitudes. The conservatives believed the constitution would make the blacks the ruling class in Alabama through disfranchisement of whites and enfranchisement of blacks. Convinced that blacks were racially inferior, white conservatives were outraged that "ignorant, propertyless, half vagabonds, incompetent to comprehend politics," would be allowed to tax, humiliate, and subordinate whites. Frankly, they said, "We cannot live here in Alabama under a negro government," for such black rule would quickly return some counties of the state to its "original jungle."[89] They denounced the convention as a "farce" and labeled its product "the menagerie constitution."[90]

Consequently, conservatives set out to defeat the constitution by insuring that less than a majority of registered voters voted. At a series of conservative mass meetings around the state, conservatives were urged to "abstain from voting at all" in the February referendum on the constitution. Conservatives were implored "touch not, taste not, handle not the unclean thing [the constitution]."[91] Though the constitution was approved 70,812 to 1,005, less than half the 170,631 registered voters had gone to the polls during the five-day election period; and the Reconstruction Act required that at least half the registered voters approve a constitution before it could take effect.[92] The *Montgomery Daily Mail* ran the following headstone for deceased Radicalism:

> In Memory of
> RADICALISM IN ALABAMA
> Who died in attempting to give birth to a
> BOGUS CONSTITUTION
> After a painful illness of five days.

The *Mail* added that "she leaves a family of carpet-baggers and scalawags to mourn her loss."[93]

Conservative exultation was premature. Congress rewrote the rules and declared that the constitution was valid because it had been approved by an overwhelming majority of those who voted. Alabama was thus readmitted to the Union along with Georgia, Louisiana, North Carolina, and South Carolina.

When the new legislature convened in July 1868, Governor Smith once again invoked as a measure of progress, not the national Bill of Rights, but the principles of the Declaration:

It is especially gratifying that [Alabama] will resume her place in the nation with a constitution embodying the fullest assertion of the just principle set forth in the Declaration of Independence—"That all men are created equal; that they are endowed by their creator with certain inalienable rights; that among these are life, liberty and the pursuit of happiness"—the principle which underlies the whole fabric of our National Government, and by which, in her short history, our country has achieved results hitherto unexampled in the world's annals. This principle has heretofore been applied to but a portion of our people. We now enter upon a new era, in which it is to be made applicable to all classes; and as its partial operation has resulted so beneficially in the past, it is no violent presumption to suppose that its more extended application in the future will secure to us correspondingly greater blessings.[94]

And he added, "It will be for you gentlemen of the General Assembly to frame the laws necessary to give effect to this principle." He expected those laws to reflect the principle of equality before the law:

Our Constitution affords to every man the same opportunity enjoyed by other men, upon the single condition that he will not seek to deprive his fellows of that which he esteems to be good for himself. Let our laws, made in pursuance of the Constitution, conform in like manner and justice and even-handed dealing, so that the humble or the ignorant shall have the same opportunity for the development of himself and his children with his more fortunate neighbor. Give every one encouragement to work out his own elevation, and from the efforts of individuals to advance themselves, we shall have the highest possible aggregate development of the State.[95]

That development was the overriding concern of Alabama's Reconstruction legislatures.[96] The first of those legislatures promptly ratified the Fourteenth Amendment, of course; but it and its successors did little else to help the freedmen. Indeed, in the same month that it ratified the Fourteenth Amendment, it refused to prohibit discrimination in public accommodations.[97] Five years later blacks tried once again to get a public accommodations bill through the legislature. The Democratic-controlled Senate actually passed such a bill, but the Republican-controlled House did not take it up before adjournment in April 1873. The House itself had already voted down a similar bill amidst an acrimonious debate that exposed the deep fissures within the Republican Party on the race issue.[98]

Throughout Reconstruction, both political parties struggled to organize a majority unbeholden to blacks, who, it was said, "regarded their votes as the 'most valuable merchandize they possess.'"[99] Though most blacks were determined to purchase an equal accommodation bill with those votes, at least some recognized that the civil rights issue could backfire on them. A black preacher counseled patience: "Some men with strong stomachs [sic] would call for their whiskey or brandy straight; others with weaker stomachs, required much water in it. So it is with the members of our party. Some of them can take Civil Rights unmixed already; others with weaker stomachs must take them in a diluted form for [a] while longer. We must wait until their stomachs grow stronger and must do nothing that will drive them off."[100] The Republican Party adopted that counsel in 1874 and declared it wanted "no social equality enforced by law."[101]

Democrats nevertheless decided to exploit the explosive issue. Drawing a color line that fall, they invited Alabama's whites to cross over. Enough accepted the invitation to seal the fate of the Republican Party, sending it into "permanent eclipse."[102] The biggest losers were Alabama's black citizens. Prejudice, fraud,[103] and violence[104] sealed their fate; and they would not be heard from again until a tired Rosa Parks refused to move to the back of a Birmingham bus.

NOTES

1. Sarah W. Wiggins, *The Scalawag in Alabama Politics, 1865–1881* (University, Ala.: University of Alabama Press, 1977), 7.

2. Thomas B. Alexander, "Persistent Whiggery in Alabama and the Lower South, 1860–1867," *Alabama Review* 12 (1959): 35, 42. In spite of his Unionist sympathies, Smith twice represented Alabama in the Confederate Congress. From there he wrote his wife: "There is a sullen *deadness* here to the condition of the country. The men who inaugurated the war are unwilling to admit the possibility of a failure. And I really believe that the slaughter of the women and children of the entire South would not change their stubbornness." Russell Smith to his wife, 2 October 1862, William Russell Smith Papers, Library of Congress.

Smith did run that fall, finishing third.

3. Walter L. Fleming, *Civil War and Reconstruction in Alabama* (New York: Columbia University Press, 1905), 148, 342. See also Fleming, "The Peace Movement in Alabama during the Civil War," (parts 1 and 2), *South Atlantic Quarterly* (April/July 1903): 114, 246.

4. President Johnson appointed Lewis Parsons, a Whig who had opposed secession, provisional governor on 21 June 1865.

5. A majority of the delegates to the constitutional convention that met in Montgomery during September 1865 had Whig or Unionist roots. Alexander, "Persistent Whiggery in Alabama and the Lower South," 46. The *New York Times*, 25 September 1865, commented that the Alabama convention was "generally composed of old Whigs, who originally were utterly opposed to the secession movement."

6. The *New York Times*, 30 November 1866, also described the state legislature that convened on 20 November 1865, as "greatly national, not sectional" and predicted that it would rise above "party spirit and political prejudice." Both houses chose former Whigs as their presiding officers and elected Provisional Governor Lewis C. Parsons to the long-term U.S. Senate seat.

7. The vote was twenty-seven to two in the Senate and sixty-nine to eight in the House. See Fleming, *Civil War and Reconstruction in Alabama*, 396–97. (In mid-December "chances were favorable for ratification"; in mid-January "it seemed almost sure to be ratified.")

8. *Selma Daily Messenger*, 15 November 1866.

9. Wiggins, *The Scalawag in Alabama Politics*, 14.

10. *Journal of the Session of 1866–7 of the Senate of the State of Alabama, Held in the City of Montgomery, Commencing on the Second Monday in November, 1866* (Montgomery, Ala.: Reid & Screws, State Printers, 1867), 176.

11. *Montgomery Daily Mail*, 5 October 1866.

12. *Selma Morning Times*, 15 April 1866.

13. See, e.g., *Clarke County Journal*, 10 May 1866.

14. See *South Western*, 2 May 1866, quoting the *Mobile Times* as criticizing the Civil Rights Bill for that reason. The *Mobile Times* did not object to the section that guaranteed freedmen civil rights ("[t]his is nothing more than what every Southern state has voluntarily done since the close of the rebellion"). It did object to the sections that gave jurisdiction to federal courts (the act "annihilates State jurisdiction" and prefers "one particular class, to the detriment of the other").

15. Wiggins, *The Scalawag in Alabama Politics*, 15–16. ("[T]he most acute of these [economic problems] was the matter of labor relations . . . [and] the legislature acted . . . to pass discriminatory laws intended to regulate blacks.") See also George A. Wood, "The Black Codes of Alabama," *South Atlantic Quarterly* 13 (January 1916): 356.

16. M. Cook, "Restoration and Innovation: Alabamians Adjust to Defeat, 1865–1867" (Ph.D. diss., University of Alabama, 1968), 67.

17. Quoted in the *Vicksburg Herald*, 27 January 1866.

18. Ibid.

19. Cook, "Restoration and Innovation," 71.

20. *Montgomery Daily Mail*, 19 October 1866 (this characterization was taken from Mississippi Governor Humphrey's message to the Mississippi legislature).

21. General Swayne, the Union military commander with whom Patton had attended law school, may well have persuaded the governor to change his mind. Cook, "Restoration and Innovation," 199.

22. Fleming, *Civil War and Reconstruction in Alabama*, 397.

23. *Southern Advertiser*, 18 January 1867. But see *Mobile Advertiser and Register*, 10 January 1867, and *Register*, 10 January 1867 (Governor Patton did *not* seek any assurances and remains opposed to the amendment). An interested "foreign" observer, commenting on the governor's shift in views, said, "So sudden a change does not speak well of the stability of the Alabama Governor." *Savannah Daily News*, 12 December 1866.

24. See, e.g., *Mobile Advertiser and Register*, 1 January 1867. See also *Clarke County Democrat*, 13 December 1866 (mocking those who criticized the legislature for refusing to "placate the radicals," the paper snidely observed, "A good slave will obey the commands of his master").

25. Fleming, *Civil War and Reconstruction in Alabama*, 396–97.

26. See, e.g., *Montgomery Daily Mail*, 15 June 1866 (Negro made citizen and may therefore sit in legislature); *Clarke County Journal*, 28 June 1866 (same); *Montgomery Daily Mail*, 27 September 1866 (Section 1 imposes universal suffrage because voting is a privilege and immunity of citizenship); *Selma Daily Messenger*, 29 September 1866 (same).

27. *Selma Messenger*, 12 September 1867 (speech by Joseph Taylor to the Conservative Convention).

28. Cf. *Montgomery Daily Mail*, 27 February 1866 (white Alabamians opposed permitting Negro testimony because it would lead to political equality).

29. *Montgomery Daily Mail*, 7 November 1866.

30. *Montgomery Daily Mail*, 2 May 1866 (reconstruction plan leaves suffrage to the states; it distinguishes between colored civil rights and colored political rights). Of course, white Alabamians generally did not favor Section 2. They understood that the state would lose representation unless Negroes were given the vote. The *Selma Morning Times* estimated that Alabama would be entitled to seven representatives if Negro suffrage was allowed but only to four representatives if it were denied (17 February 1866); cf. *Montgomery Daily Mail*, 15 June 1866 (Alabama's congressional delegation cut in

half unless it lets Negroes vote). Section 2 thus discriminated against the South because the North did not face such a proverbial Hobson's choice (*Selma Daily Messenger*, 15 November 1866). At the same time, those in favor of the amendment insisted that Section 2 was consistent with the principles of republican government because it left the suffrage question to the states (*Elmore Standard*, 10 October 1867).

31. Cf. Peter Kolchin, *First Freedom: The Response of Alabama's Blacks to Emancipation and Reconstruction* (Westport, Conn.: Greenwood Press, 1972), 178 note 46.

32. See, e.g., *Union Springs Times*, 11 April 1866 (laments and ridicules Civil Rights Bill, saying "Sambō" will never have more than a personal dog to transmit to his heirs).

33. Wiggins, *The Scalawag in Alabama Politics*, 8. The *Huntsville Advocate* reminded its readers that legal rights and political privileges were "essentially different" and pointed out that the freedmen had been granted the one, not the other. O. Bailey, "Black Legislators during the Reconstruction of Alabama, 1867–1878" (Ph.D. diss., Kansas State University, 1984), 11. A Mobile white conceded that blacks should be given equal rights to hold property, to contract, and to testify, but "[t]here the equality must I think *cease* and *cease forever* for they are not equal." J. Brent, "No Surrender: Mobile, Alabama, during Presidential Reconstruction, 1865–1867" (M.A. thesis, University of Southern Alabama, 1988), 22.

34. Cook, "Restoration and Innovation," 61 ("Special laws had governed the free Negro during slavery, and whites expected that special laws would also govern the freedmen.").

35. *Athens Post*, 2 April 1868. See also Wiggins, *The Scalawag in Alabama Politics*, 8 ("Unionists and ex-Confederates alike . . . regarded blacks as 'socially and intellectually inferior'"). Cf. *Athens Post*, 9 June 1867 (letter from W. J. Sykes). See also *Mobile Advertiser and Register*, 18 August 1867 (Negro supremacy in most "reconstructed" states predicted).

36. Elizabeth Bethel, "The Freedman's Bureau in Alabama," *Journal of Southern History* 14 (1948): 49, 74 ("Ninety-nine of 100 negroes could not read."). A particularly poignant example of that illiteracy came to light in 1870 when a former slave, hearing that the Democrats had won the state elections, returned to his old plantation and asked his former master: "Well, massa, what house must I goes to? I understands the Democrats has succeeded, and that we are slaves again."

37. Kolchin, *First Freedom*, 162.

38. Ibid., 152–53.

39. L. Dorman, "The Free Negro in Alabama from 1819 to 1861" (M.A. thesis, University of Alabama, 1916), 23–24.

40. *Nationalist*, 6 June 1866.

41. Ibid.

42. Ibid.

43. *Nationalist*, 22 February 1869.

44. *Nationalist*, 17 May 1866; 25 October 1866.

45. *Nationalist*, 5 April 1866.

46. Ibid.

47. Ibid.

48. *Nationalist*, 6 June 1866.

49. *Nationalist*, 25 October 1866.

50. Discussion of the Fourteenth Amendment in the state's conservative newspapers was "noticeably restrained," far more so than in most of the other Southern states. Wiggins, *The Scalawag in Alabama Politics*, 19. In Alabama, as in the other Southern states,

the ratification debate did not focus primarily on Section 1. Oftentimes, Section 1 was not even mentioned, much less analyzed, in discussions of the amendment. See, e.g., *Selma Morning Times*, 15 May 1866; *Moulton Advertiser*, 9 February 1867. As one newspaper editor observed, "Most large city journals scarcely touched on the negro rights provision of the Amendment." Instead, Alabamians objected primarily to Section 3. Indeed, the *Selma Daily Messenger*, objecting to four amendments being presented as one, predicted the South would have approved Sections 1, 2, and 4.

Section 3 was, however, "degrading and humiliating" (*Southern Advertiser*, 11 May 1866; *Mobile Advertiser and Register*, 9 January 1867), and Alabama could not disgrace itself (*Union Springs Times*, 22 November 1866). Alabamians would "die at the stake before [they would] help these radical hangmen put the rope around our free necks." *Clarke County Journal*, 21 June 1866. They thanked God that the radicals could not compel them to enact measures intended for their own humiliation. *Selma Morning Times*, 12 June 1866. Essentially, they dismissed the amendment as a squalid attempt to preclude Southern participation in the next presidential election. See, e.g., *Huntsville Daily Independent*, 9 May 1866; *Selma Morning Times*, 12 May 1866; *Union Springs Times*, 16 May 1866. But see *Elmore Standard*, 20 December 1867 (disqualifying provision should frighten no one because Congress will remove disabilities once the amendment is ratified).

51. Wiggins, *The Scalawag in Alabama Politics*, 23.

52. But see *The Reconstructionist*, 6 June 1868 (Union Republican Party does *not* favor Negro supremacy).

53. See, e.g., *Union Springs Times*, 11 September 1867.

54. Wiggins, *The Scalawag in Alabama Politics*, 21.

55. Kolchin, *First Freedom*, 151.

56. Ibid., 84–85.

57. Ibid., 225.

58. Ibid., 58; ibid., 157. (As one black speaker said, "We are here tonight to tell the world that after being enfranchised we are wise enough to know our rights and we are going to claim those rights.")

59. Ibid.

60. Two-thirds of the one hundred fifty delegates were black, and the local press described the delegates as either "colored," "Yankee," or "Pale faced." Wiggins, *The Scalawag in Alabama Politics*, 21–22. And the white and black delegates sat on opposite sides of the convention hall. H. Cobb, "Negroes in Alabama during the Reconstruction Period, 1865–1875" (Ph.D. diss., Temple University, 1952), 140.

61. Wiggins, *The Scalawag in Alabama Politics*, 22.

62. Ibid.

63. Ibid.

64. See, e.g., *Daily State Sentinel*, 22 August 1867.

65. *Daily State Sentinel*, 29 August 1867.

66. *Monroe Eagle*, 27 May 1868. See also O. Bailey, "Black Legislators during the Reconstruction of Alabama, 1867–1878" (Ph.D. diss., Kansas State University, 1984), 41 (a black delegate to the constitutional convention is quoted as saying: "I have no desire to take away any rights of the white man; all I want is equal rights in the courthouse and equal rights when I go to vote").

67. *Nationalist*, 25 April 1867 (speech of L. S. Berry).

68. Like Mississippi's earlier 1865 convention, Alabama's 1867 convention was anxiously anticipated and closely observed. See, e.g., *Tuscaloosa Independent Monitor*, 30 October 1867 (a "great revolution" was under way).

69. The makeup and organization of the convention is succinctly described in Wiggins, *The Scalawag in Alabama Politics*, 25–28.

70. The vote was 90,283 to 5,583 to approve the calling of a convention; 164,800 voters had been registered. Most of the whites had "stayed at home."

71. Horace Mann Bond, "Social and Economic Forces in Alabama Reconstruction," *Journal of Negro History* 23 (1938): 290, 347 ("[A]ccumulations of capital, and the men who controlled them, were as unaffected by attitudinal prejudices as it is possible to be. Without sentiment, without emotion, those who sought profit from an exploitation of Alabama's natural resources turned other men's prejudices and attitudes to their own account, and did so with skill and a ruthless acumen."). See also Kolchin, *First Freedom*, 93–95.

72. Wiggins, *The Scalawag in Alabama Politics*, 28.

73. *Nationalist*, 31 October 1866; 22 November 1866.

74. Michael William Fitzgerald, "The Union League Movement in Alabama and Mississippi: Politics and Agricultural Change in the Deep South during Reconstruction" (Ph.D. diss., University of California at Los Angeles, 1986), 186.

75. Cf. Cobb, "Negroes in Alabama," 152 (a black delegate to the 1867 constitutional convention wanted compensation for the services that slaves performed on plantations from the date of the Emancipation Proclamation to the end of the war).

76. But see Cobb, "Negroes in Alabama," 74 (a group of Mobile blacks declared in November 1865 that they did not "desire to receive any man's property without giving him the just equivalent").

77. *Official Journal of the Constitutional Convention of the State of Alabama, Held in the City of Montgomery, Commencing on Tuesday, November 5th, A.D. 1867* (Montgomery: Barrett & Brown, 1868), 152–53.

78. *School Laws of the State of Alabama* (1870), 15 ("In no case shall it be lawful to unite in one school both colored and white children, unless it be by the unanimous consent of the parents and guardians of such children").

79. *Journal*, 188–89, 218.

80. Ibid., 189.

81. J. Thomas, "The Alabama Constitutional Convention of 1867" (M.S. thesis, Alabama Polytechnic Institute, 1947), 96.

82. This summary or report was carried in the *Montgomery Daily Advertiser*, 26 November 1867.

83. Thomas, "The Alabama Constitutional Convention of 1867," 104.

84. *Montgomery Daily Mail*, 26 November 1867.

85. *Journal*, 149; *Montgomery Daily Mail*, 26 November 1867.

86. *Clarke County Democrat*, 5 December 1867. See also Kolchin, *First Freedom*, 93–95.

87. Ibid.

88. Wiggins, *The Scalawag in Alabama Politics*, 28.

89. Ibid.

90. Cobb, "Negroes in Alabama," 148.

91. Wiggins, *The Scalawag in Alabama Politics*, 35.

92. Conservative members of the convention petitioned the Congress to continue military rule. They preferred "the rule of [Congress's] sword" to being subjected "to the

blighting, brutalizing, and unnatural dominion of an alien and inferior race, a race which has never exhibited sufficient administrative ability for the good government of even the tribes into which it is broken up in its native seats; and which in all ages has itself furnished slaves for all the other races of the earth." Thomas, "The Alabama Constitutional Convention of 1867," 128.

93. Wiggins, *The Scalawag in Alabama Politics*, 37.

94. Governor's Message (14 July 1868), *Journal of the Senate of the State of Alabama during the Session Commencing in July, September, and November, 1868* (Montgomery, Alabama: J. G. Stoxes and Company, State Printers, 1868), 13.

95. Ibid.

96. See generally Bond, "Social and Economic Forces in Alabama Reconstruction."

97. Kolchin, *First Freedom*, 318. Cf. *Montgomery Daily Advertiser*, 31 July 1868 (a black legislator is quoted as saying: "The colored man certainly had as much right in a first class car as the dirty Irishmen who were allowed this privilege").

98. Wiggins, *The Scalawag in Alabama Politics*, 85.

99. Ibid., 101.

100. *Montgomery Daily Advertiser*, 30 June 1874.

101. Wiggins, *The Scalawag in Alabama Politics*, 94.

102. Ibid., 104.

103. See Sarah W. Wiggins, "Alabama: Democratic Bulldozing and Republican Folly," in *Reconstruction and Redemption in the South*, ed. Otto Olsen (Baton Rouge: Louisiana State University Press, 1980), 47. She cites the following incidents: "In Opelika in Lee County, Democrats voted at box one, Republicans at box two. When the Democratic board of supervisors counted the votes, they threw out box two, which one Republican manager claimed contained 1,252 Republican votes. Election supervisors in Bullock County threw out 732 ballots, predominately Republican, because the poll lists were uncertified" (ibid., 63).

104. Violence was endemic in Reconstruction Alabama, and most of it was directed at blacks and their white supporters. See generally Stanley F. Horn, *Invisible Empire: The Story of the Ku Klux Klan, 1865–1871* (Boston: Houghton Mifflin Company, 1939), 115–44. The single most egregious incident occurred in Eutaw in October 1870. Governor Smith and Congressman Hays were speaking to a large crowd of freedmen when Democratic spectators precipitated a riot that left fifty-four blacks wounded and four dead. Michael William Fitzgerald, "Union League Movement," 316. Though Smith had viewed the violence firsthand and was repeatedly and regularly informed of similar efforts to intimidate Republican voters, he refused to call out the militia. The only reliable militia would have been black or largely so, and the governor feared that a black militia would only exacerbate the violence. He did ask Washington to send additional federal troops, but the government declined; and the federal troops stationed in Alabama were inadequate and occasionally unsympathetic.

7

Ratification in South Carolina

We will never have true freedom until we abolish the system of
agriculture. . . . If we pass this resolution, the large landowners will keep
the land in their hands. If they are obliged to sell their lands,
the poor man will have a chance to buy.

—A black delegate to South Carolina's 1868
constitutional convention, urging his fellow delegates
to defeat a resolution offering relief to indebted planters

South Carolina, viewed from the battlements of the North, was the archetypal Southern state. From the days of Calhoun and nullification on, its "fire-eaters" had defiantly seethed the doctrine of states' rights. South Carolina had been the first state to secede from the Union, and the Civil War began when its militia fired on Fort Sumter. For these reasons, General Sherman laid waste the state. He wanted to destroy the symbolic citadel of the Confederacy.[1]

In fact, South Carolina was atypical.[2] It was more prosperous, had fewer Unionist sympathizers, and had far more blacks and many more free educated blacks than did most other Southern states. Precisely because of these differences, South Carolina had led the Southern resistance; for the same reasons, it initially rejected the Fourteenth Amendment.

Although the legislature did not have before it any committee report on the amendment, members were thoroughly familiar with its provisions when they voted it down in December 1866 with but one dissenting vote in the House.[3] The amendment, after all, had been widely discussed. Contemporary accounts in leading South Carolina newspapers reflect the nature of that discussion and, presumably, the legislature's understanding of the amendment.

As might be expected from those who had schooled themselves in constitutional debate for more than a generation, white South Carolinians marshaled many constitutional arguments against the Fourteenth Amendment. The mildest charge was that its proposal was impolitic and unstatesmanlike.[4] The most significant procedural objection to it was that it consolidated four different provisions, each dealing with a separate subject, into a single omnibus amendment, which had to be voted up or down as a whole.[5] South Carolinians also bitterly resented what they believed to be the substitution of new peace terms, and they insisted that "there [was] no warrant in the Constitution" for the new terms.[6] In November 1866 the *Charleston Mercury* introduced a series of lengthy articles in which it "proposed" to "discuss and expose" the "unconstitutionality of the proposed amendments." It stated: "The amendments to the Constitution proposed by Congress, have not been in conformity to the Constitution in two particulars: 1. They were not submitted to the President for his approval; 2. The Southern States were not present in Congress, and did not participate in proposing the amendments."[7]

The argument on the second point had been anticipated by the *Marion Star* when it commented acerbically:

[Congress] has no right to propose either the amendment in question, or any other conditions to the Southern States, as the terms on which they will restore to those States their representation in the Senate, because that representation has not only never been lawfully taken away, but cannot be taken away, the Constitution having placed this privilege of the States, by express exception, in the amendatory clause; beyond even the power of the amendment. It follows that what even a regularly proposed and adopted amendment could not do, the act of Mr. McPherson did not accomplish; and that hence the offer of the Rump Congress to restore to the South what they have not taken, and cannot constitutionally take from the South, is simply an offer to restore stolen property to the rightful owner, upon conditions prescribed by the thief, and are only an aggravation of the outrage committed.[8]

Several other constitutional objections were raised. The disfranchisement provision would result in the imposition of taxation without representation.[9] The disfranchisement provision obviously had a differential impact on Southern and Northern states, as Southerners never tired of pointing out. Since Northern states had few blacks, they would lose no representation in Congress if they denied their black citizens the right to vote. This objection also stung because it reflected the political machinations of the Republican Party. The disfranchisement provision had been framed deliberately to disadvantage the South and, in its view, secure "the unjust supremacy of the North."[10] Moreover, the amendment violated the equality of states principle.[11] South Carolinians also decried the politicizing of the amendment process: "The moment any party succeeds in incorporating into the written charter of right, and common compact of protection, and privilege, its platform based upon the temporary passions of the hour, the fall of free government is sealed."[12] Though these constitutional objections were repeated throughout the South, they had little practical significance. Although occasionally cited as grounds for rejecting the amendment, they were generally conceded to be beside the point, even by those opposed to it.[13]

More persuasive were substantive objections, especially to Sections 2 and 3, the representation and disfranchisement provisions. Section 2 was seen as dictating a Hobson's choice: give blacks the vote (an unthinkable choice) or lose representation in the Congress (an unacceptable choice). On the latter choice, white South Carolinians pointed out that the North already enjoyed a majority in the House of Representatives,[14] conveniently ignoring, of course, Republican concerns that the majority was insufficient to prevent Northern and Southern Democrats from combining to regain control of at least the House and perhaps the Senate and presidency as well.[15]

The mere suggestion that the freedmen might vote shocked most white South Carolinians. Almost universally, they viewed blacks as incompetents.[16] A sympathetic chronicler of this reaction summarized conservative outrage when blacks did get the vote: "One of the most ignorant and undeveloped of races was to be placed by mere legislative fiat in absolute power over a large portion of a race notable for centuries for the highest success in self-government, to whom the independence and self-direction now to be destroyed were almost as dear as life."[17]

A year later the state's Democratic "senator-elect" James B. Campbell bluntly advised the newly enfranchised that some day the right to vote would be taken from them. He pointed out that he and his fellow whites had been deprived of the vote by "bayonet and ball and powder" and warned "they will do the same for you when law . . . or the voice of the white people bids them do it." He confidently predicted: "You will not be permitted to participate permanently and *substantially* in the political power of the government."[18]

In contrast to their contempt for the freedmen, most white South Carolinians revered their Civil War leaders. The prospect that such men would be excluded not only from office, but later even from voting, shocked and galled.[19] It was humiliating and insulting.[20] Thus critics of these provisions in South Carolina decried the "amendments" as "bills of pains and penalties,"[21] intended, once again, simply to consolidate the power of the radicals.[22]

Although Sections 2 and 3 drew the most comment, Section 1 was scrutinized as well. Standing alone, it excited few fears:

The first section of this amendment declares the equality in their civil rights of all persons of all colors, born or naturalized in the United States and subject to their jurisdiction. It strikes me that as the Institution of African slavery and all its collateral securities have been wiped out of the Constitution by the amendment abolishing slavery, the new amendment, in its first section, is only a re-affirmation of the instrument as it now stands; for in taking out slavery no distinction in relation to the African race remains in the Constitution—none whatever.[23]

This analysis was certainly consistent with the common view that Section 1 was intended solely to reverse *Dred Scott* and to constitutionalize the Civil Rights Bill.[24] The following analysis from the *Daily Courier* confirms that view:

The proposed amendment consists of a single article divided into different sections. The first section defines citizenship of the United States.

Before the late emancipation of the slaves there were in this country many free persons of color. These were not recognized, under the Constitution, as citizens of the United States. The Supreme Court, in the famous Dred Scott case, decided that free persons of African descent were not citizens within the contemplation of the founders of the Government, or according to the articles of the Constitution.

The object of the first section is, by an amendment to the Constitution, to reverse the Dred Scott decision, and to incorporate into the organic law that all persons born or naturalized in this country, without distinction of race or color, are henceforth citizens of the United States, and shall enjoy all the rights of citizens evermore, and that no State shall have the power to deny or impair this conferred right.[25]

The *Daily Courier* conceded that the incorporation "into the organic law of the citizenship of all inhabitants, irrespective of race or color, may be accepted."[26] South Carolina had itself in the fall of 1866 passed a "civil rights bill," making "all the citizens of the state, black and white, equal before the law."[27] Two years later the convention of South Carolina's "conservative party" recognized that "the colored population of the State . . . [were] entitled in person and property to a full and equal protection [of] the State Constitution and laws."[28]

Opponents of the Fourteenth Amendment in the state thus never disputed the right of blacks to "equality of civil rights."[29] That was, after all, the core meaning of privileges and immunities, as the "White People of South Carolina" conceded in their *Remonstrance* to Congress in 1868:

When South Carolina assented to the act of Federal emancipation, we held that the freed people became members of the body politic, and, as such, entitled to all the civil rights that are enjoyed alike by all classes of the people. They became entitled to "life, liberty and the pursuit of happiness"—to all that the Declaration of American Independence and the English *Magna Charta* claim for man as his inalienable rights.[30]

Indeed, Section 1 was apparently so unobjectionable that one early, detailed analysis of the Amendment omitted any comment on it.[31]

The discussion, even of the privileges and immunities clause, was thus limited. White South Carolinians necessarily studied that clause closely, however. After all, they viewed voting as a privilege, albeit a political privilege; and they knew that under Section 5 of the Fourteenth Amendment Congress had the power to prevent any abridgment of the privileges and immunities guaranteed by Section 1. The consequences of universal suffrage in South Carolina were clear to its conservative white citizens, and they abhorred them:

We already see, by their open declarations, that the negro-party of the South must be a party of confiscation and agrarianism. The property holders of the country, consisting of the white race, are to be proscribed from political power: and the non-property holders— the negroes, are to be clothed with all the political power of the country, and to make its constitution and impose its laws. What must be the natural result? Of course confiscation and agrarianism, in one form or another. The form suggested by the negro-party at their late meeting at Columbia, for South Carolina was: 1. To educate all their children by the property of the white race, taken by taxes; and 2. To confiscate and distribute the lands owned by the white race, by putting such taxes on them, and then by selling the lands to pay the taxes, either to sacrifice them to negro purchasers, or to buy them in for distribution.[32]

Virtually all white South Carolinians initially opposed even qualified suffrage for blacks. For example, ex-Governor Perry, a staunch Unionist, recoiled at the prospect of black South Carolinians voting. He said: "It is against nature and reason to suppose that an ignorant and debased majority will not . . . carry out their wicked purposes . . . the negro . . . will use . . . the political power of the state . . . [to] oppress and plunder the white man."[33]

Conservative white South Carolinians insisted that voting was a political privilege which a state could limit as prudence appeared to require:

If, in the opinion of the majority of a community, the officers or agents of the government should be created by elections,—elections, will be rightfully held. If they shall deem it better that one man—like a Governor or a President—should choose and nominate an individual for office to a body of men, like a Senate, who may approve of the nomination or reject it,—this mode of obtaining good agents will be proper. If they determine, that at elections to be held, only a certain class of the population—those only who have a certain degree of education, or intelligence, or property, or sex, or age, shall vote,—they have a perfect right to do so. It is an affair merely of administration; in which the best way to carry on or perpetuate the government, is sought to be obtained. There is no human abstract right in the matter. Voting is simply a political privilege; and no one can justly complain that he has not a privilege bestowed upon him to rule others, which they think, that it will be inexpedient or dangerous to them, that he should possess. [34]

The right of controlling suffrage was thus "the most important of the powers expressly reserved" to the states.[35] The right of a state to control suffrage was beyond cavil (as, indeed, Section 2 of the Fourteenth Amendment impliedly conceded it was):

To be deprived of this power would be to lose all the conservatism—so necessary to the good government of society—which springs from having the governing class, at the same time, the class most deeply interested, by property and interest, in the wisdom and stability of law, and would in fact place the state at the mercy of an ignorant rabble. The best governments are those where the sense of the nation is spoken by the few; who are more enlightened, and who are the representatives not only of the intelligence, but of the conservatism of the people. Such legislators will always legislate to secure a sufficient amount of liberty, and at the same time secure property on a firm basis—and their legislation will conduce to the prosperity of those who own no property—for where wealth is protected there labor is well paid.[36]

Moreover, voting was simply not a privilege of citizenship. Women and children, for example, were citizens; but they could not vote. As one observer pointed out: "[P]rotection of a citizen is not afforded, by the ballot, but by the laws. Protection to person and property may exist just as completely without it as with it."[37] Whatever the validity of that assertion, most white South Carolinians believed that the states should determine the incidents of citizenship.

At bottom, then, South Carolinians were concerned primarily about Congress's power under Section 5 to enforce Section 1 because the latter section gave Congress the power to police and supplant state authority in matters traditionally reserved to the states. Throughout the fall of 1866, the *Charleston Daily Courier* ran a series of articles in which leading public figures made that point. On October 5, it endorsed the comments of Mississippi Governor Sharkey when he said:

Another objection to the [Fourteenth] Amendment is, that while it prohibits the States from abridging the privileges or immunities of citizens, it does not specify what those privileges are, that being left to Congress, which is empowered to enforce the article by appropriate legislation. Congress may confer privileges on one class to the exclusion of another; or it may assume absolute control over the people and their domestic concerns and thus virtually abolish the State.[38]

Early in November the Honorable O. H. Browning was similarly praised for warning that the Fourteenth Amendment would "revolutionize the whole structure of the Government, by conferring upon Congress new, enormous and almost sovereign powers."[39] Later that same month, the *Courier* approvingly summarized remarks by Governor Charles Jenkins of Georgia:

To the first article declaring all persons born in the United States citizens, irrespective of color, he objects, because it centralizes power into the hands of the Legislative departments of the Government by affirming in Congress the right to settle definitely the question of citizenship in the several States as political communities, thereby depriving these in the future of all discretionary power over the subject within their respective limits.[40]

Consolidation was thus the principal—indeed, the only—objection to Section 1 voiced in South Carolina prior to the legislature's rejection of the amendment: "The great controlling policy of the Northern Radicals, is to destroy the limitations of the Constitution, and make the United States Government omnipotent, under the caucus control of a party majority, in Congress."[41] The same sentiment had been expressed even before the Fourteenth Amendment had been promulgated. Commenting on the evolving discussion of Reconstruction in Congress in the early winter of 1866, one observer reported:

It has settled that the States are little more than corporations, possessing no inherent sovereignty of their own, but dependent for their very existence upon the central national government. . . .

It has settled that the Government of the United States may act directly upon the people, without needing to refer to any of the usual media of State agency. [42]

The Civil Rights Bill[43] and the Freedmen's Bureau Bill[44] were cited as proof.

No one, however, voiced any fear that Section 1, standing alone, conferred specific rights on state citizens, as would have been the case had it been understood to incorporate the Bill of Rights. The fear, to repeat, was of *unspecified* rights which Congress might later legislatively impose (as it had already shown a willingness to do when it adopted the Civil Rights Bill). Indeed, that fear was the major reason why Governor James Orr, as close a friend to the Union as then could be found among whites in South Carolina, urged the legislature to reject the amendment. He argued that Sections 1 and 5 transformed the national government from one of limited powers into a centralized one that would have the power to determine all the incidents of citizenship.[45]

Certainly no one suggested that privileges and immunities was a shorthand expression for the Bill of Rights. Of course, South Carolinians prized the rights enumerated in the Bill of Rights. Most were guaranteed in their state constitution and had been guaranteed in the Constitution of the Confederacy. The press periodically rhapsodized, for example, about the "liberty of the press," calling it "the greatest of all the rights of a free people."[46] At the same time, they recognized that the right was not absolute:

The liberty of the press, like the liberty of the citizen and the freedom of speech, under all free governments, ought to be inviolable; but what is the liberty of the press, or of speech, or of the person? Do they authorize a man, to speak, write, or act towards others as he pleases? The law answers, no! A man who speaks or writes falsely or unjustly against another, is amenable to an action for damages; and if he aggresses upon the person of another, he is indictable for misdemeanor or felony. The liberty of the press, is the liberty to write the truth and maintain justice. That is all.[47]

Concern about license or excess was common because the contemporary press was often scurrilous. Moreover, many Southern states had prohibited some "incendiary" publications in the antebellum era and during the Civil War. South Carolinians would have been alarmed if they had thought that they might lose their right to control that license or excess, as might have been the case if the First Amendment had been incorporated in Section 1, for many in South Carolina attributed riots and crime perpetrated by blacks to the "incendiary teachings" of the Freedmen's Bureau.[48] The authority to control the incidents of such rights must therefore be retained by the states: "Human or natural rights, doubtless exist. They are described generally in the American Declaration of Independence as being the right to 'life, liberty and the pursuit of happiness,' but how and by what means these natural rights shall be enjoyed or preserved, is under the absolute discretion and will of all, established for their common benefit, by their common government."[49]

To transfer to the national government control of the civil incidents of those natural rights was simply unacceptable: "The first section, confers the rights of citizenship upon all native born or naturalized citizens, and restrains the States from abridging their rights and immunities, whilst the last section bestows upon Congress the 'power to enforce by appropriate legislation the provisions of this article'—a dangerous and undefined power, which is subversive of all State rights."[50] This objection resonated powerfully among white South Carolinians, steeped as they were in the states' rights philosophy that permeated South Carolina's antebellum political culture. This philosophy was succinctly stated even as the Reconstruction Committee was issuing its report:

The protection of the civil and political rights of the inhabitants of every State within its own bounds were [sic] amply cared for by its people in their State Constitution. The Federal Government was looked to or depended upon for no such purpose, except in the solitary and specified instance where a rightful State Government might chance to be overthrown by some power above the control of its people, as evinced in the clause guaranteeing to each State a republican form of government. With that single exception, the people felt themselves amply competent to protect their liberty and all civil or political rights within the bounds of their respective States, and would have indignantly spurned anything which even looked like a leaning upon the Federal Government.[51]

The author of these remarks would have been astounded, one surmises, at any suggestion that the Bill of Rights guarantees should be embossed upon state law. The states themselves could and did protect such rights, and white South Carolinians believed that the Constitution reserved that power to them.[52]

South Carolina's freedmen did not share this states' rights philosophy, and they exalted the Declaration of Independence rather than the Constitution. Because of these differences, they not only embraced the Fourteenth Amendment; they came to demand far more than the natural and civil rights guaranteed in its first section. No sooner had Union troops occupied Charleston in March 1865 than four thousand of its black residents staged a celebratory parade. Among the marchers were schoolchildren, who proudly waved banners that said: "We Know No Cast [sic] or Color."[53] Though black demands would become more detailed in succeeding months and years, they would remain rooted in that single, simple color-blind principle of nondiscrimination.

Charleston, like New Orleans, had a large population of freeborn, relatively affluent blacks, most of whom were tradesmen.[54] In the fall of 1865 they organized a Colored People's Convention in the city. Using the Declaration as a model, they wrote a "Declaration of Rights and Wrongs" that echoed the rhetoric of the American Revolution. They demanded their natural, inalienable rights to life, liberty, and the pursuit of happiness; denounced taxation without representation; and complained that they had been "deprived of the free exercise of political rights."[55]

At the close of the convention, the delegates issued an "Address to the People of the State of South Carolina" in which they conceded their "poverty and weakness" and acknowledged the "wealth and greatness" of whites. They then gently reminded their white brethren that the freedmen, as "descendants of a race feeble and long oppressed," might ask "for special favors and encouragement on the principle that the strong should aid the weak, the learned should teach the unlearned."[56] But in the end they asked "for no special privileges or peculiar favors." Instead, they asked "only for even-handed Justice." In that week of Thanksgiving, they looked forward to the day when all South Carolinians would realize "the truth that 'all men are endowed by their Creator with inalienable rights,' and that on the American continent this is the right of all, whether he come from east, west, north or south; and, although complexions may differ, 'a man's a man for a' that.'"[57]

The Charleston meeting was but the most prominent of a number of such meetings that had blossomed across South Carolina in that Jubilee year.[58] Even before the Charleston Convention, a smaller group of black Charlestonians had met and "declared that their interests were 'identical' with those of the whites, as long as the latter stood on the 'common ground' of 'perfect equality of all men *before the law.*'"[59] Understanding that such equality dictated impartial suffrage, the freedmen from the island of St. Helena had demanded the right of suffrage for "every man of the age of twenty-one years, without other qualifications than that required for the white citizens of this State."[60] From the beginning, blacks in South Carolina insisted that the principles of Republican government required that they be given the vote.[61]

Although these meetings—especially the Charleston convention—prompted a new Charleston paper to declare "Reconstruction Begun,"[62] the state legislature turned a deaf ear to the pleas of its newest citizens. Instead of acknowledging their equality, it adopted a Black Code that would have consigned them to a permanent, inferior status.[63] General Sickles, the Union commander in South Carolina, promptly issued an order prohibiting its enforcement. Anticipating the equal protection clause of the yet unpromulgated Fourteenth Amendment, the order decreed: "All laws shall be applicable alike to all inhabitants."[64]

Unfortunately, the general's order did not end discrimination against black South Carolinians. On the very eve of congressional Reconstruction, the "Colored Citizens of South Carolina" petitioned the Congress. They demanded equal protection, due process, and "every privilege secured by law to any other class of American citizens." Most of all, they demanded the vote because only then would "Republican liberty be safe" and they "protected from outrage and wrong." The outrageous wrongs which they detailed in their petition shed light on their understanding of equal protection and due process, for they complained about disparate treatment before the law (e.g., whites go unindicted for murder, while blacks are punished for trivial offenses) and unfairness (justice in civil courts is a mockery because judges are prejudiced).[65]

Less than a month later, Congress adopted the Reconstruction Acts, answering at last the prayers which Charleston's free blacks had first offered at Zion Church eighteen months earlier. Thomas Holt described their reaction to these acts:

They poured into mass meetings in Charleston and Columbia to celebrate, to organize, and to prepare for their new responsibilities. It was the middle of March; spring in the Palmetto State. This season of regeneration, of new beginnings, seemed appropriate to the freedmen's excitement as they looked forward to the dawn of a new era. The times seemed pregnant with hope, and summer lay just ahead. Yet, on March 13, like a portent of the winters of discontent still to come, a light snow fell on Charleston.[66]

In South Carolina, as elsewhere in the South, the Reconstruction Acts transformed the debate over the Fourteenth Amendment and the fundamental issues its provisions raised. The tenor of the pre-Reconstruction debate, however, was different in South Carolina from that in most other Southern states. While negrophobia ran as deep in South Carolina as it did anywhere else, it did not skew the public debate in South Carolina. Only infrequently did opponents of the Fourteenth Amendment trot out dire predictions of—horror of horrors—social equality.[67] For the most part, they confined their objections to legitimate, substantive concerns. Thus one political observer could plead as the Reconstruction Acts took effect: "What we want is a Constitution and a system of laws that shall acknowledge and protect the rights of all classes, white and black, and that shall give security of person and property to every citizen of the State."[68]

To that end, the freedmen and a few white allies began to organize the Republican Party.[69] At a series of meetings in Charleston during March 1867, they hammered out eleven points "which . . . [became] the major tenants [sic] of South Carolina Republicanism."[70] The platform was decidedly populist. It demanded free, universal education; internal improvements, to be undertaken by "all our citizens" on a "fair" and "equal" basis; the dissolution of large land-holdings and their sale to the poor; protection against eviction; and governmental programs for the aged, the infirm, and the needy. The platform also demanded changes in the law, including no more imprisonment for debt and no more corporal punishment. Finally, it demanded a general reorganization of the court system and the legal code in order to preserve "their newly won rights . . . in perpetuity."[71]

While the Republicans energetically prepared for the coming campaigns, conservative whites were perplexed. They could not agree on whether to register to vote; whether, if they registered, to vote for or against a convention; or whether, if a convention was held, to vote or refrain from voting on the new constitution which the convention had prepared.[72] "What is to be done?" they fretted. In the end, their indecision made no difference. Given the "rules of the game" which the military commander of the region propounded and the numerical superiority which blacks enjoyed, conservative whites could not have controlled the process, whatever the decisions they made.

Black registrants outnumbered white registrants two to one; and on November 19–20, 1867, they voted overwhelmingly for a constitutional convention.[73] The conservative press denounced the convention, which sat in Charleston from January 14, 1868, to March 14, 1868, as "ring streaked and striped"[74] because three-fifths of the delegates were black.[75] These delegates nevertheless produced a constitution that later scholars have praised as "progressive" and "democratic."[76] Conservative critics of the day dismissed the constitution as based "on a triangular foundation of ignorance, repudiation, and miscegenation."[77]

In a convention completely dominated by black Republicans,[78] four issues arose that might have been thought to raise questions about the meaning of the equal protection clause of the Fourteenth Amendment. All four issues involved questions of "social equality," as that term was then understood: would blacks and whites be permitted to, or prohibited from, "intermingling" in the state militia, in public accommodations, in the schools, or in marriage? The delegates answered that the schools and militia should be open to all without regard to color, though they declined to require integration. Anticipating arguments made in *Brown v. Board of Education*, one black delegate argued that requiring black and white children to go to schools together might prevent the development of prejudice. Yet even he refused to support a prohibition of segregated schools, and he conceded that such schools would probably flourish in the cities.[79]

There was greater support for an amendment that would have prohibited discrimination in public accommodations. In the end, however, it too failed. Despite pleas to put guarantees into the constitution that no "cunning lawyer" could "misinterpret,"[80] the convention refused to approve the amendment. The constitution would remain color-blind, as one black delegate demanded when he insisted that "race and color" should not appear in the document.[81] Consistent with that view, the delegates also declined to include any prohibition against interracial marriages.

Though the delegates who supported these decisions doubtless saw them as consistent with the equality principle embedded in the Fourteenth Amendment, there is scant evidence they thought that that principle dictated any of the particular decisions. Rather, the debates reflect a subtle and pragmatic sense of the relevant, competing public policies.[82] Moreover, the subsequent radical government acted as if it retained the discretion to reevaluate those policies in deciding when and how to enforce the convention decisions. While it did enforce integration at the state college, for example, it declined to require integration in the lower public schools.[83]

When conservatives attacked these decisions, they denounced them not as mad interpretations of the equal protection clause, but as bad public policies:

All the public schools, colleges and universities in the State are, by section 10, to be free and open to all the children, without regard to race or color. There seems to be a studied desire throughout all the provisions of this most infamous Constitution, to degrade the white race and elevate the black race, to force upon us social as well as political equality, and bring about an amalgamation of races.[84]

The provisions of the new constitution also shed light on what the staunchest supporters of the Fourteenth Amendment in South Carolina understood it to command. South Carolina's Declaration of Rights, like so many of those contained in the other constitutions of 1868, reaffirms the ringing claims of the Declaration of Independence as the doctrinal foundation of its citizens' rights. It then proceeds to define those rights in apparent ignorance of any notion that the Fourteenth Amendment might fasten upon the state all the guarantees contained in the Bill of Rights, particularly as defined by the Supreme Court of the United States. For example, the South Carolina Declaration permitted justices of the peace to try all misdemeanor offenses where the punishment did not exceed a one hundred dollar fine or thirty days' imprisonment. The white citizens who filed a Remonstrance with Congress castigated this provision as "a gross invasion of that bulwark of Anglo-Saxon liberty, the trial by jury."[85] They did not condemn it as a violation of the Bill of Rights, though that would have been a persuasive rhetorical ploy had they any understanding that the Congress had intended the Fourteenth Amendment to bind the states to observe those guarantees.

Moreover, the state repeatedly reserved the power to circumscribe the exercise of certain rights in order to preserve the health and safety of the community. Specifically, it provided that:

- the liberty of conscience hereby declared shall not justify practices inconsistent with the peace and moral safety of society [Section 9]
- that laws may be made securing to persons or corporations the right of way over the lands of either persons or corporations, and, for works of internal improvement, the right to establish depots, stations, and turnouts [Section 23]

Radical Republicans in South Carolina were thus as interested as conservative Democrats in preserving state autonomy in matters of public policy.

The 1868 constitution nevertheless reflected an understanding that the principle of equality before the law required significant changes in the way the government conducted its business. Section 39 of the Declaration of Rights prohibited "[d]istinction, on account of race or color, in any case whatever" and guaranteed that "all classes of citizens shall enjoy, equally, all common, public, legal, and political privileges." Other sections echo this general guarantee. Section 12, for instance, states: "No person shall be disqualified as a witness, or be prevented from acquiring, holding, and transmitting property, or be hindered in acquiring education or be liable to any other punishment for any offence, or be subjected in law to any other restraints or disqualifications in regard to any personal rights than such as are laid upon others under like circumstances." And Section 36 makes clear that burdens must be shared equally: "All property subject to taxation shall be taxed in proportion to its value. Each individual of society has a right to be protected in the enjoyment of life, liberty, and property, according to standing laws. He should, therefore, contribute his share to the expense of his protection, and give his personal service, when necessary."

Finally, the South Carolina Declaration is filled with specific procedural guarantees that illuminate the contemporary understanding of the general right to due process. Although a few are stated in the same language found in the federal Bill of Rights, most are stated in slightly different and often far fuller terms. Section 13 is illustrative. It guarantees several trial rights. It also specifies that "[n]o person shall be held to answer for any crime or offense until the same is fully, fairly, plainly, substantially, and formally explained to him."

The Declaration of Rights thus refutes any suggestion that the equal protection and due process clauses were viewed as a source of substantive rights. Rather, they were understood to be procedural guarantees. The one insured that persons would be protected equally in the exercise of their rights, and the other promised that those who exercised their rights would be treated fairly. In one sense the two concepts tended to merge together, for equal treatment constituted one aspect of fairness.

The conduct of military authorities in South Carolina during the same period confirms this understanding of equal protection and due process. On May 30, 1867, General Canby issued General Orders #32. The Orders touched many subjects. Among others, they made all citizens who had been assessed and had paid their taxes eligible for jury service. The *Marion Star* asked: "Would any man, the wildest asserter of human rights be willing to trust his life in a trial for murder, his character in a case for libel, his property in a case of civil litigation to such juries as might be drawn at any court from the plantation laborers, the common field hands of any District."[86] The *Charleston Mercury* answered: "Of course such courts must be the greatest curses. We do not suppose that they are to exist as tribunals of justice. They will work to be instruments of oppression, by which the white man is to be put under the negro."[87] Viewed in another, "radical" light, these courts assured blacks an equal voice in the administration of justice and maximized the prospect that blacks would be treated fairly in the courts.

The Orders made all citizens eligible to follow any licensed calling, employment, or vocation, subject only to impartial regulation.[88] The Orders also declared that all persons had a common right to equal accommodations and transportation in all railroads, streetcars, sailing vessels, steamers, or other public conveyances. Finally, the Orders abolished distress for rent as a remedy. A renter who failed to pay could be ejected, of course, under a suit for breach of contract. The *Charleston Mercury* predicted:

This clause will probably lead to a change in the form of all contracts hereafter made for the renting or hire of property. Two courses can be adopted—1st. To provide in the contract that the rent shall be paid in advance, or 2d. To make an express stipulation that failure to pay rent at the time agreed on shall cancel the contract and make the rentee liable to summary ejectment.[89]

These various Orders did not, properly understood, create new rights. Rather, they provided for equal treatment and created fair procedures or, perhaps more neutrally stated, procedures that were thought to be fair. They conferred no preferences. Indeed, their language was color-blind. Though the Fourteenth Amendment was not explicitly invoked as a justification for any of these specific orders, the Orders were all consistent with what was generally understood to be its core meaning.

The irony is that conservative whites, though they viewed the facts quite differently, shared the same understanding of those concepts. Thus, for example, one complained:

Our civil officers have a right to enforce impartially every civil law or military order; they have no right to allow the negro to go scot-free when, for the same offense, a white man would be tried, condemned and punished. Let a Southern white man pass through the Districts of this State, and urge the people to disobey and set at naught the laws of the United States, and he will be immediately arrested and tried as a disturber of the public peace. But the white politician who inflames the passions of the negro, who prates of confiscation and taking by force, while he is equally inciting to disobedience of the law and to a disturbance of the general tranquillity, is, in nine cases out of ten, allowed to pass unscathed. The negro who goes about in open day with arms in hand, in defiance of municipal law and military order, is generally allowed by our civil officers to escape unchidden. This must not be! There is no law in favor of the black as against the white, and as much diligence should be used in tracing, apprehending and correcting black offenders, as is used against the white. This is the only way in which the community can now have justice; the only way in which justice will not be unjust.[90]

Once the new constitution was adopted and a new legislature and governor elected, state officials—not military commanders—had to give consent to the concepts of privileges and immunities, equal protection, and due process. These Republican governors embraced their black allies socially[91] but moderated their demands for social legislation. In 1870 David Chamberlain, who would become the last of the Reconstruction Republican governors, reiterated the party's commitment to color-blind public policies:

I do not come to speak in the interest of any class or complexion of my fellow-citizens, but to present to you such political truths and policies as are intended to secure the welfare of all men alike. I put the foot of my utmost contempt alike upon that doctrine which proclaims this "a white man's Government," and that which seeks to make a black skin the passport to popular favor and position. No doctrine, no practice is worthy of an American which does not forget all these trivial distinctions, and look only to the perpetuation of a Republic whose laws shall know no race, no color, no outward distinction whatever, but shall gather beneath its impartial and generous protection all races and colors.[92]

In a seventeen-page campaign document, however, he devoted only a few paragraphs to public schools, never once mentioning the desirability of their being integrated; and he buried his reference "to the law which supplements and applies to our domestic affairs the great principle embodied in the Civil Rights [Bill]" in a long list of acts "which benefit the working people." Chamberlain's treatment of these issues was consistent, of course, with the party's color-blind standard. But his treatment also reflected a desire to deemphasize the "social equality" issues which might inflame whites and derail the "fusion" with other whites which white Republicans sought.[93]

Black Republicans in South Carolina were in a better position to press their demands than were their counterparts in most other Southern states because they outnumbered whites. Despite their numerical superiority, blacks nevertheless initially deferred to white leadership of the party. Over time, however, they demanded responsibility and offices commensurate with their numbers. As early as 1867, Martin Delany had observed that "no people [had] become a great people who had not their own leaders."[94] By 1870 he was advocating an equitable distribution of offices based on population ratios: one senator, two congressmen, and the lieutenant governorship.[95] Another prominent black politician ridiculed the concern of some white party members that "you [blacks] want too much; you want everything." He replied: "We placed them in position; we elected them and by our votes we made them our masters. We now propose to change this thing a little, and let them vote for us. It is no more than reasonable they should do so."[96] These demands were never couched in terms of any constitutional rights, however. Rather, public office was considered the just deserts of political power.

And black voters did vote for black leaders. In 1870, blacks were elected lieutenant governor, secretary of state, treasurer, and adjutant general; and another was elected to the Supreme Court. Three blacks were sent to Congress, and by 1872, four of South Carolina's five representatives in Washington were black. By then the leaders of both state houses were black, and blacks chaired a majority of legislative committees through 1876.[97]

Despite these majorities, the most radical blacks were unable to secure adoption of a strong public accommodations law. The first attempt was made in the special 1868 session of the legislature. The bill, introduced in the House, prohibited racial discrimination in public services or facilities. It carried severe penalties. Anyone who violated it lost his business charter or license, had to pay a $500 fine, and went to jail for a year. Black members were angry about the issue because some of their colleagues had been turned out into the rain by a Greenville hotelkeeper. Defying counsels of prudence from their white colleagues, they pushed the bill through the lower house. Tabled in the Senate, it died there.[98]

The following fall, when another black house member was removed from the first-class car on the Richmond–Danville Railroad in Virginia, blacks introduced a bill to revoke the charter of its South Carolina subsidiary. The move failed.

Apparently, the more conservative black members of the House thought the remedy too extreme. Consequently, they joined their white colleagues to defeat the bill fifty-three to forty-two.[99]

Still later, black members failed in their efforts to beef up the state militia, whose protection they considered essential to the preservation of black voting rights. During the 1870 elections, Klansmen had fought a kind of guerrilla war with the state militia in the up-country and border counties. A Luerans County grand jury recommended that the all-black militia in that county be disarmed. A sympathetic judge then ordered the confiscation of their arms, which were stored at the home of State Representative Joseph Crews. He promptly introduced a bill to impeach the judge.

Simultaneously, another radical black legislator introduced a bill, giving the militia expanded martial law powers and instructing the governor to deploy it in several counties. Governor Scott demurred. Indeed, he himself advocated disarmament. His attorney general, David Chamberlain, suggested a moderate substitute that was eventually adopted.[100] Again, conservative blacks deserted their more radical brethren. Five of them issued a statement explaining that any declaration of martial law would "depress the credit of the state."[101]

Similar concerns about fiscal responsibility sapped the black drive to establish a system of public schools for children of both races. The Freedmen's Bureau had failed to establish a successful system of schools in the state, and whites were generally opposed to spending public monies to educate black children.[102] As a consequence, the school system envisioned in the constitution "remained largely on paper."[103]

While these legislative debates reveal sharp differences over the desirability of particular public policies, they do not reflect any dispute about the meaning of the Fourteenth Amendment. So far as one can tell from the public records, it was never invoked in these debates. Presumably, legislators—black and white alike—thought its commands largely irrelevant to their exercise of legislative authority.

Their decisions thus reflected the same understanding that had emerged from the earlier debates. Privileges and immunities was a somewhat ambiguous concept because it included both natural rights and civil rights, both of whose incidents were necessarily defined legislatively; and the legislature thus retained an undefined authority to determine those incidents. On the other hand, the equality of rights principle did constrain the legislature's authority to create special statutory privileges and immunities. Due process was understood in the abstract as a guarantee of procedural fairness. While there was general agreement about what fairness required in many circumstances, the legislature was still thought to have considerable discretion to determine the particular process due in specific circumstances. Equal protection, an important component of the equality of rights principle, both affirmed the fundamental duty of the government to protect all persons in the exercise of their rights and recognized that preservation of equality before the law generally discharged that obligation.

Moreover, the national government in general and Congress in particular retained the authority to enforce the Fourteenth Amendment if, in their judgment, a state violated its commands. In the spring of 1877, the national government abdicated that responsibility in South Carolina. Violence had suffused the preceding fall election in South Carolina, and the election results were disputed. Two rival legislatures and governors claimed to be the legitimate government, and for a time both occupied the capitol. Chamberlain, who thought he had been reelected and who still retained power because he had the support of federal troops stationed in South Carolina, appealed to President Hayes.

The new President turned Chamberlain's appeal aside. The presidential election had also been disputed, and the national Republican Party agreed to withdraw troops from the South in exchange for Southern acquiescence in Hayes's election. Pursuant to that agreement, federal troops marched out of Columbia at noon on April 10, 1877, and Chamberlain vacated his office.[104] The *News and Courier* exulted: "Republican rule was dead, never to be reborn."[105] Like a rope of sand, South Carolina's Republican Party did dissolve; and its black supporters drowned in a sea of white supremacy. Martin Delany had written their epitaph two years earlier: "[I]t is useless and doing injustice to both races to conceal the fact, that in giving liberty and equality of rights to blacks, whites had no desire to see [blacks] rule over [the white] race. . . . [T]here is no scheme that can be laid, no measure that may be entered into, [no] expense . . . they will not incur, to change such a relation between blacks and whites in this country."[106]

The Jubilee was over.

NOTES

1. See generally John G. Barrett, *Sherman's March through the Carolinas* (Chapel Hill: University of North Carolina Press, 1956).

2. Among the standard texts on Reconstruction in South Carolina are Thomas C. Holt, *Black over White: Negro Political Leadership in South Carolina during Reconstruction* (Champaign: University of Illinois Press, 1977); James S. Pike, *The Prostrate State: South Carolina under Negro Government* (New York: D. Appleton, 1874); Francis B. Simkins and Robert-Hilliard Woody, *South Carolina during Reconstruction* (1966; reprinted Gloucester, Mass.: Peter Smith); Alrutheus A. Taylor, *The Negro in South Carolina during the Reconstruction* (Washington, D.C.: Association for the Study of Negro Life and History, 1924); David D. Wallace, *The History of South Carolina, vol. 3* (New York: American Historical Society, Inc., 1934), 222–321; David D. Wallace, *South Carolina; A Short History, 1520–1948* (Columbia: University of South Carolina Press, 1961), 556–606; Joel Williamson, *After Slavery: the Negro in South Carolina during Reconstruction, 1861–1877* (Hanover, N.H.: University Press of New England, 1965).

3. Wallace, *South Carolina*, 568.

4. *Charleston Daily Courier*, 27 November 1866 ("It [the amendment] cannot bring repose. Its elements are those of agitation, discord, and penalties.").

5. Ibid., 26 September 1866.

6. Ibid., 18 October 1866.

7. *Charleston Mercury*, 23 November 1866; 24 November 1866.

8. *Marion Star*, 21 November 1866. Like the other Southern states, South Carolina's then existing government felt that it had complied with all the president's terms for restoration and was therefore entitled to be readmitted into the Union.

9. *Charleston Daily Courier*, 7 November 1866. (This particular claim was seldom emphasized for obvious reasons: free blacks could make the same claim with respect to state voting laws.)

10. See, e.g., *Charleston Daily Courier*, 27 September 1866; 19 October 1866.

11. *Charleston Daily Courier*, 18 October 1866; 23 January 1866. See also *The Crescent*, 28 November 1866 ("our rights [should be] restored under a constitution which shall bear equally on all states").

12. *Charleston Daily Courier*, 19 October 1866.

13. *Lancaster Ledger*, 31 October 1866 ("It [the amendment] is going to be a part of the supreme law of the land, all our tastes to the contrary notwithstanding.").

14. *Charleston Daily Courier*, 27 September 1866.

15. *Anderson Intelligencer*, 8 February 1866 (radicals want constitutional amendment to consolidate their power).

16. Benjamin Perry, the state's provisional governor, declared: "The African has been, in all ages, a savage or a slave. God created him inferior to the white man in form, color, and intellect, and no legislation or culture can make him his equal. You might as well expect to make the fox the equal of the lion in courage and strength, or the ass the equal of the horse in symmetry and fleetness." *Charleston Daily Courier*, 1 October 1866. Former Congressman James Brooks insisted that "[t]he Negro is not the equal of the white man" because he was "a different creature, with a different brain, and different structural organization . . . in every respect inferior to the white." *Charleston Mercury*, 8 January 1868. Later that year, the *Mercury* adduced the "scientific evidence" that supported this "common wisdom": "[The Negro] differs from him in the structure of his body, in not less than one hundred and twenty-four particulars. His blood—his bones—his flesh, his head, legs, arms, as well as skin, are all different." *Charleston Mercury*, 30 June 1868. On this point the South Carolina press also cited the account of the Englishman Samuel White Baker, who had observed the race in Africa and pronounced him a "wild savage." *Abbeville Press*, 28 February 1868.

History was also thought to prove the Negroes' inferiority as well as his unfitness for any civic responsibility:

> It is simply the affirmation of *a matter of fact*, which the history of the world from the flood, lays open, for confirmation or refutation. Every one must admit, who knows anything of the history of governments in the world, that of all governments, a free government is the most difficult to carry on. In the long lapse of ages, only now and then, have free governments arisen—lived for a brief time—and then sunk down into the general blackness of despotism. And during all these ages, not only has the negro, not been able to frame and administer a free government, but he has been unable, to administer any government of laws at all. He has been unable to produce a written language—any literature of any kind—any government of laws of any kind. (*Charleston Mercury*, 30 June 1866)

17. Wallace, *South Carolina*, 569.

18. *Two Letters from the Hon. James B. Campbell, U.S. Senator Elect from South Carolina, on Public Affairs and our Duties to the Colored Race* (Charleston: Walker, Evans & Cogswell, Stationers and Printers, 1868), 10–11.

19. *Charleston Daily Courier*, 19 October 1866; 1 November 1866.

20. Ibid., 4 October 1866 ("The South ought not to be asked . . . to place around her sons the fetters and badges of abject servitude").

21. Ibid., 19 October 1866.

22. *Anderson Intelligencer*, 8 February 1866.

23. *Lancaster Ledger*, 31 October 1866.

24. Cf. *Charleston Daily Courier*, 2 April 1866.

25. Ibid., 27 September 1866.

26. *Charleston Daily Courier*, 4 October 1866; accord, 19 October 1866.

27. *The New South*, 29 September 1866. The South Carolina legislature had enacted the law in response to the angry criticism of the Black Code it had adopted during the preceding session and to General Sickles's order suspending enforcement of the laws. Implementation of this "equality policy" produced mixed results:

> Though not specifically applied to Negroes, many parts of the Code (such as the vagrancy laws) were left intact and actually operated primarily against Negroes. Thus, the district courts, retaining jurisdiction over the least important cases, became pre-eminently the tribunal for the Negro. "The principle business," wrote one reporter, after observing the district court of Anderson in session in January, 1867, "seemed to consist in indictments against freedpeople for larceny, malicious trespass & c." Nevertheless, the informant noted, the court commanded "dignity." Both district courts and the higher tribunals of the state generally evinced a laudable fairness in dealing with Negroes. And occasionally, in their desire to be perfectly fair, these passed beyond true justice and exhibited exceptional leniency to individual Negro offenders. Such partiality was excused by the Negroes' "disadvantages in the war of ignorance and social inferiority." (Williamson, *After Slavery*, 328)

28. *Remonstrance* (1868), 14 (held in the Fitz William McMaster Collection, the South Caroliniana Library, University of South Carolina, Columbia, South Carolina).

29. See, e.g., *Charleston Daily Courier*, 15 February 1866.

30. *Remonstrance*, 13.

31. *Abbeville Press*, 4 May 1866.

32. *Charleston Mercury*, 15 August 1867.

33. *Lancaster Ledger*, 15 May 1867. Interestingly, Perry, as provisional governor, had initially planned to recommend qualified suffrage (presumably at President Johnson's urging). And he later said that granting blacks a qualified right to vote then (in 1865) "might have checked the Republicans' demand for unlimited Negro voting privileges in 1868." Ernest M. Lander, *A History of South Carolina, 1865–1900* (Chapel Hill, University of North Carolina Press, 1960), 7.

34. *Charleston Mercury*, 18 April 1867.

35. *Anderson Intelligencer*, 25 January 1866.

36. Ibid.

37. *Charleston Mercury*, 1 October 1867.

38. *Charleston Daily Courier*, 5 October 1866.

39. Ibid., 1 November 1866.

40. Ibid., 7 November 1866.

41. *Charleston Mercury*, 4 December 1866.

42. *Daily South Carolinian*, 23 March 1866.

43. *Abbeville Press*, 30 March 1866 ("The great objection to the measures, is that it encroaches upon the reserved powers of the States, and is part and parcel of a great scheme to consolidate the government"). See also *Charleston Daily Courier*, 2 April 1866.

44. South Carolina papers generally endorsed President Johnson's veto of the Freedmen's Bureau Bill, which he denounced for invading the reserved powers of the states. See, e.g., *Lancaster Ledger*, 7 March 1866; *Abbeville Press*, 2 March 1866. See also *Charleston Mercury*, 17 December 1867.

45. *Journal of the House of Representatives of the State of South Carolina, Being the Regular Session of 1866* (Columbia: F. G. DeFontaine, State Printer, 1866), 34.

46. *Daily South Carolinian*, 7 March 1866.

47. *Charleston Mercury*, 8 June 1868.

48. Ibid., 17 December 1867. Cf. Martin Abbott, *The Freedman's Bureau in South Carolina, 1865–1872* (Chapel Hill: University of North Carolina Press, 1967), 95 ("Whites came increasingly to believe that Northern teachers were using their classrooms to indoctrinate, less to instruct than to propagandize in behalf of the Republican party.").

49. *Charleston Mercury*, 18 April 1867.

50. *Abbeville Press*, 19 October 1866.

51. *Charleston Daily Courier*, 24 May 1866.

52. See, e.g., *Charleston Mercury*, 9 April 1867 (Southern states are not "conquered territories," quoting a July 1861 Resolution of the Congress of the United States: *"Resolved,* The war is not waged on our part, in any spirit of oppression, or for any *purpose of conquest,* or for *interfering with the rights* or the *established institutions* of these States; but, to defend and maintain the supremacy of the Constitution of the United States, and to preserve the Union with *all the dignity and rights of the several States unimpaired.").*

53. *Charleston Daily Courier*, 22 March 1865.

54. Holt, *Black over White*, 15–16. See also E. Horace Fitchett, "The Tradition of the Free Negro in Charleston, South Carolina," *Journal of Negro History* 25 (1940): 139; and I. Wikramanajake, "The Free Negro in Antebellum South Carolina" (Ph.D. diss., Wisconsin, 1966).

55. *Proceedings of the Colored People's Convention of South Carolina, Held in Zion Church, Charleston, November 1865* (Charleston: South Carolina Leader Office, 1865), 27.

56. Ibid., 24.

57. Ibid., 26.

58. See generally Herbert Aptheker, "South Carolina Negro Conventions, 1865," *Journal of Negro History* 31 (1946): 91.

59. Holt, *Black over White*, 21.

60. Ibid.

61. Ibid., 29 ("We would ask your Honorable body [the state legislature of South Carolina] for the right of suffrage and the right of testifying in courts of law. These two things we deem necessary to our welfare and elevation. They are the rights of every freeman, and are inherent and essential to every republican form of government.").

62. *South Carolina Leader*, 15 November 1865.

63. These laws prohibited blacks from engaging in any work other than farming or domestic work without a special license, established procedures by which blacks could be contracted out to whites as servants, curtailed their freedom of movement, permitted blacks to be punished for a wider range of crimes than whites, and imposed harsher punishments on blacks. Lander, *A History of South Carolina*, 8.

64. Ibid., 9.

65. *The Crescent*, 20 February 1867.

66. Holt, *Black over White*, 26. One black South Carolinian, sitting in the House gallery when the first Reconstruction Act was passed, said he felt as if "the clock of civilization had been put forward a hundred years." Williamson, *After Slavery*, 33. Twelve days later, that observer was back in South Carolina, leading a meeting of blacks in Richland County. They offered up a prayer to Providence, thanking it for causing "this great nation to release them from the disadvantages and deprivations that they labored under as a people, and to acknowledge their manhood, and return to those great principles of the Declaration of Independence, which declares all men to be equal." *New York Times*, 21 March 1867.

67. The argument was occasionally made, of course. Commenting on the 1868 constitution, one paper remarked:

> With ignorant, dishonest, degraded negroes in the Legislature, in the Courts, and as Conservators of the Peace and on Juries, how can educated, refined Christian men and their wives and their daughters live in peace and safety? Where will be the protection for life, for woman's honor—more precious than all property, than every life? These are questions for every honorable, reasonable man to ask himself and ponder upon. Let him ask his own heart and conscience, calmly, earnestly, prayerfully. (*Marion Star*, 22 November 1868)

See also *The Crescent*, 5 February 1868; *Marion Star*, 14 March 1868.

68. *The Crescent*, 10 April 1867.

69. The Republican Party in South Carolina never attracted more than three thousand to four thousand whites. Except for prewar Unionists in Charleston, Lexington County, and the mountains, few whites joined the party. Williamson, *After Slavery*, 349. Whites were disproportionately represented in the leadership ranks of the party—though they were not nearly so dominant in party councils as they were in most other Southern states.

70. Williamson, *After Slavery*, 340.

71. Ibid. These planks reflected many of the same demands that the delegates to the Charleston convention had made in November 1865. See Holt, *Black over White*, 27.

72. See, e.g., *Lancaster Ledger*, 29 May 1867; 10 July 1867; and *Charleston Mercury*, 1 August 1867.

73. Sixty-nine thousand (or 85 percent) of a possible eighty-one thousand black voters cast ballots; and according to one government report, "not a single Negro voted against the convention." Williamson, *After Slavery*, 343.

74. This epithet was commonly used to describe the constitutional convention that met during 1867–68. The *Charleston Mercury* simply referred to it as the "negro convention." See, e.g., 31 January 1868.

75. Seventy-six delegates were black; forty-eight were white. Wallace, *South Carolina*, 573.

76. Lander, *A History of South Carolina*, 11.

77. Cf. *Charleston Courier*, 9 April 1868 ("Sixty odd Negroes, many of them ignorant and depraved, together with fifty white men, 'outcasts of Northern society and Southern renegades, betrayers of their race and country, have assembled in Convention and framed a Constitution for the government of South Carolina.'"). See also *Charleston Mercury*, 21 March 1868 (constitution referred to as "negro constitution").

78. For a subtle analysis of voting patterns in the convention, see Holt, *Black over White*, 125–34.

79. *Proceedings of the Constitutional Convention of South Carolina, Held at Charleston, S.C., beginning January 14th and ending March 17th, 1868. Including the Debates and Proceedings* (Charleston: Denny & Perry, 1868), 901.

80. Ibid., 354.

81. Ibid.

82. See generally Taylor, *The Negro in South Carolina*, 125–52.

83. Wallace, *South Carolina*, 573.

84. *Remonstrance*, 8.

85. Ibid., 4.

86. *Marion Star*, 15 May 1867.

87. *Charleston Mercury*, 4 October 1867.

88. Ibid., 5 June 1867.

89. Ibid., 15 June 1867.

90. Ibid., 14 June 1867.

91. Wallace, *South Carolina*, 576. Many white South Carolinians objected to these activities, of course. Historians who shared that revulsion described one such an occasion, a dinner at the governor's mansion: "The colored band was playing 'Rally 'Round the Flag.' . . . There was a mixture of white and black, male and female. Supper was announced, and you ought to have seen the scrambling for the table. Social equality was at its highest pitch. It was amusing to see Cuffy reaching across the table and swallowing grapes by the bunch, champagne by the bottle, and turkey, ham and pound cake by the bushel. Simkins and Woody, *South Carolina during Reconstruction*, 369–70.

92. Daniel H. Chamberlain, "The Facts and Figures: The Practical and Truthful Record of the Republican Party of South Carolina" (Columbia: n.p., 1870), 2 (available at the South Caroliniana Library, University of South Carolina, Columbia, South Carolina).

93. The "fusion movement" is described in Williamson, *After Slavery*, 354–56.

94. Victor Ullman, *Martin R. Delany: The Beginning of Black Nationalism* (Boston: Beacon Press, 1971), 414.

95. *Charleston Daily Republican*, 24 June 1870.

96. Ibid.

97. Holt, *Black over White*, 108–9. Williamson concluded that "[b]y 1876 no white Republican politician could expect long to survive who was not willing to grant Negroes access to all offices." Williamson, *After Slavery*, 361.

98. Holt, *Black over White*, 143–44.

99. Ibid., 144.

100. Ibid., 142–43. See generally Herbert Shapiro, "Ku Klux Klan during Reconstruction: The South Carolina Episode," *Journal of Negro History* 49 (1964): 34.

101. *Journal of the House of Representatives of the State of South Carolina, Being the Regular Session of 1870–71* (Columbia: Republican Printing Company, 1871), 288.

102. See generally Abbott, *The Freedmen's Bureau in South Carolina*.

103. Lander, *A History of South Carolina*, 12. See also Wallace, *South Carolina*, 589 ("The schools at times had to close, and Jillson [the superintendent] feared the collapse of the system for lack of money, despite the large nominal, but often unpaid, appropriations.").

104. See generally Francis Butler Simkins, "Election of 1876 in South Carolina," *South Atlantic Quarterly* 21 (1922): 225, 335.

105. *News and Courier*, 11 April 1877.

106. *Beaufort Republican*, 19 February 1874.

8

Ratification in Virginia

Americans are the only race in America.

—A Republican delegate to Virginia's 1867 constitutional
convention arguing, for a color-blind constitution

Once proud Virginia lay prostrate and wasted in the spring of 1865, its factories reduced to rubble, its bridges destroyed, its livestock slaughtered, its fields scorched.[1] Amidst this ruin, only its newest citizens—the freedmen—were jubilant. They imagined a future that most of Virginia's older, white citizens dreaded. These new citizens imagined a free economy in which they could rise according to their talents; a legal regime that treated all persons fairly and equally; and a political community indifferent to the color of its citizens. Thomas Bayne, a black delegate to the state's 1867 constitutional convention, evoked this dream with the following plea: "And so shall the colored people and the loyal white men of Virginia say, in one chorus. Sink or swim, live or die, survive or perish, we are together, one and indivisible and inseparable, for the procuring and perpetuation of civil and political rights to all men, of whatever shade or color of skin."[2]

Blacks like Bayne also understood two other things. The Fourteenth Amendment was intended to insure the first two dreams, and its natural rights philosophy was wholly consistent with the third. Precisely because white Virginians shared that same understanding, most opposed ratification of the amendment. When they finally lost that battle, they fought to limit the amendment's practical impact. That battle they won. When Virginia was finally readmitted to the Union in 1870, its conservative white citizens had already "redeemed" its government.

The story of this five-year internecine political war is far more than a tale of the Fourteenth Amendment rejected, ratified, repudiated. But that tale is an important part of the war, and its telling makes clear that Virginians of both races shared a common understanding of the meaning and potential scope of the Fourteenth Amendment.

By 1865 Virginia had already demonstrated a vacillating attitude on the questions which Section 1 of the Fourteenth Amendment was intended to resolve. The first of the Confederate states to be restored to civil government,[3] Virginia had a loyal government ensconced in Alexandria by August 1863. Its writ extended to only a few northern counties, however; and Thad Stevens ridiculed it as nothing more than a city council government.[4] Nevertheless, the Pierpont government called a convention in early 1864 that adopted a new state constitution which abolished slavery, limited the franchise to loyal white citizens, otherwise enlarged the franchise by reducing residency requirements, established public education in Virginia for the first time, and repudiated the Confederate debt. In May 1865, President Johnson recognized this regime as the government of Virginia; and later that same month the governor and his supporters moved their offices to Richmond and promptly began to function as the "real" government of "all" Virginia.

Pierpont summoned a special session of the legislature, which met in June, and asked them to repeal the disfranchisement article of the 1864 constitution. "It is folly," he said, "to suppose that a State can be governed under a republican form of government when in a large portion of the State, nineteen-twentieths of the people are disfranchised and cannot hold office."[5] The three senators and nine members of the House of Delegates present obliged. Speaker Downey then pronounced Virginia "safe" from "radicals and abolitionists": "Whatever they may do to other States, they cannot force a provisional governor upon [Virginia]. Whatever they may do to other States, thank God, they cannot now saddle negro suffrage upon us."[6]

Virginia radicals and abolitionists, shocked by the action of the legislature,[7] had begun to organize even before Downey spoke. On June 13, 1865, Republicans in Alexandria formed the Union Association of Alexandria and demanded a constitutional amendment that would "confer the right of suffrage upon, and restrict it to, loyal male citizens without regard to color."[8] For the first time in Virginia, Negro suffrage had been advocated publicly. Radicals also demanded disfranchisement of Confederates. For example, "the Unconditional Union Men of Frederick County" held a mass meeting in Winchester on June 28 to protest "the recent action of the Virginia legislature in extending the right of suffrage to rebels and their aiders and abettors."[9]

If the June session of the legislature had shocked the radicals, the subsequent December session infuriated them. The new senators and delegates, who had been elected in October, promptly reaffirmed the decision to reenfranchise "rebs"; rescinded the recognition of West Virginia; asked President Johnson to pardon Mr. Davis; and hinted that it would prefer Mr. Lee to Mr. Pierpont, whose modest civil rights proposal it rejected.[10] In its stead, the legislature adopted a vagrancy law that critics characterized as reinstituting slavery.[11] The military commander of Virginia, General A. H. Terry, shared that view and ordered that the law not be enforced.[12]

No one could order the legislature to ratify the Fourteenth Amendment, however. Governor Pierpont did earnestly implore his colleagues to do so in a message suffused with Realpolitik.[13] He did not bother to analyze the amendment's specific provisions, claiming "[t]here is no ambiguity in the language of the proposed amendment."[14] Instead, he noted the results of the Northern congressional elections and counseled against any hope that the South could be spared that verdict by the president or Northern Democrats. Quite to the contrary, he predicted that the dominant "congressional party" would "become stronger for many years to come." In these circumstances, "[t]he practical question for your consideration now is," the governor continued, "whether by the rejection of the proposed amendment, you are likely to place *the people* of our state in a better condition." He thought not. Predicting congressional Reconstruction if the amendment was rejected, he warned: "The conditions are not as hard as they might be." In an effort to sweeten the medicine offered, the governor rejected the argument that ratification would be dishonorable; and he minimized the practical impact of the disqualification provisions. For recommending ratification, the governor was vilified.[15] His critics, turning his prophecy on its head, predicted worse should the amendment be adopted: "The amendment is a no truth, prepared and offered by quacks, and once accepted, other amendments, more objectionable and detestable, would be submitted, and forced upon the people of the South."[16]

General Schofield, who had been assigned to command the Department of the Potomac in August 1866 and who would become Virginia's military governor in March 1867, also urged the Virginia legislature to ratify the Fourteenth Amendment. As inducements, he brandished a club and dangled a carrot. If Virginia refused to ratify, Congress would surely "impose harsher conditions." On the other hand, he predicted Congress would readmit Virginia if it ratified. On the latter point, he himself had sought and received such assurances "from leading Republicans in Congress."[17]

Privately, the general thought the amendment unwise and unjust. In a written but unpublished analysis of the amendment, he focused primarily on the disqualification section. Like Governor Pierpont, he dismissed as "folly" the disqualification of those "whose social position, intellectual attainments and known moral character entitle [them] to the confidence of the people."[18] He also questioned the wisdom and legality of Congress's trying to impose universal suffrage on the South. First, the Negro, "in his present ignorant and degraded condition," could not discharge the duty responsibly. Second, the Constitution left control of suffrage to the states.[19] He did not object to Section 1, though he might have been expected to voice some concern, given his apparent sensitivity to issues of federalism, had he understood that section to incorporate the Bill of Rights.

Most white Virginians also objected primarily to Sections 2 and 3. Commenting on the governor's endorsement of the amendment, the *Charlottesville Chronicle* remarked:

[W]e have never yet seen in a single article (and we have read a hundred) an attempt to answer the objections which lie to these two sections: *the objection*, namely, to the second that it reduces the legitimate Congressional representation of the South from sixty-eight to forty-one members—not only providing against the full representation of the freedmen, but taking away even the three-fifths representation of the original compact of Union: and *the objection* farther to the third clause, that it is so sweeping in its proscription as to reach nearly the whole of our population above thirty years of age who are fitted for even the petty offices of the counties of the Southern States.[20]

It had earlier explained why Section 2 was so objectionable:

[T]he object of representing any locality in a legislative body is to secure legislation which will protect the general interests of that locality. The South wants representation in Congress in order to develop the industrial interests of the South, for example. Now every successful effort to procure beneficent legislation for the South, will advantage every human being in the South. But if the South does not have its legitimate weight in the National Legislature, her interests will suffer, *and every human being in the South will suffer also.* If the South prospers, the negro will prosper; if the South languishes, the negro will languish.[21]

Others objected to Section 2 because they thought almost all blacks unfit to vote and therefore resented having the state's representation reduced for excluding them from the ballot box. The *Richmond Dispatch* explained:

[T]o disfranchise a man because he is ignorant, or because he is not worth property of the value of two hundred dollars, would not be to deny him the right of voting either on account of his race or his color. Such a qualification upon voting would exclude a good many white men as well as negroes; and if such exclusion can be justly held to be on account of race or color, then all persons of both the white and black races would, under such a construction of the amendment, be excluded from the basis of representation! The idea is too preposterous to call for a refutation.[22]

The *Dispatch* also strongly objected to the "sweeping" exclusions contained in Section 3: "We should not like to be the man to go before the people and ask LEE's, or LONGSTREET's, or JOHNSTON's, or HOOD's old soldiers to vote to disqualify their old commanders, or to ask the civilians to vote to disqualify our old judges and justices."[23] Virginia would never reject her "best and brightest":

The Southern people have not, in this matter, any honorable alternative. There is but one course that they can pursue without base recreancy. To secure political privileges to themselves by ratifying, with their votes, the political proscription and outlawry of all those leaders whom they have respected and trusted and follow, would be to bring upon themselves a degree of shame for which no political franchises could be regarded as even half compensation. The very idea is too disgusting and shocking to be entertained by the Southern mind. We have read of beleaguered cities in the barbarous age being required by the generals of the invading armies to send out as a condition of capitulation, all their public men with ropes around their necks; but the Southern people can hardly be expected, as a condition of forgiveness by their conquerors, to deliver up forty thousand of their chief men with the halters of outlawry around their throats. The shame of the deed, if done, would resound throughout all the ages of the world.[24]

Just as many Virginians rejected the governor's prediction of worse to come if they refused to ratify, others rejected the general's assurance of future restoration. On the eve of the legislature's formal vote on the amendment, the *Richmond Enquirer* scornfully commented:

The Amendment was contrived to exclude, not to admit [the Southern states]. But there is now a political advantage to be maneuvered for. Some party capital—a partisan cry— is to be won or lost. If the dominant party were perfectly sure that the Southern States would reject the Amendment, and adhere to the rejection, they would plainly declare that the said Amendment was offered as the sole condition of admission; and they would then go before their people and whip up their passions by declaiming about "rebel obstinacy," and "rebel sullenness" and the like. But as they do not feel sure of this, they are afraid to risk such a declaration. They prefer to content themselves with such advantage as the more unscrupulous journals and speakers may be able to make of the present status. They suffer these to declare that the offer has been made, and thus to take the profit of it without the commitment, to reap the gain without the peril of the offer. If hard pressed they will say, that the offer had been made, but not being promptly accepted, is now withdrawn. The South has no such option,—never had, and it was never intended she should have.[25]

Moreover, the amendment was dismissed as a "diabolically clever . . . party trick" to prevent "recognition of the lately Confederate States until they [the radicals] secure the next Presidential election."[26] In any case, the legislature, perhaps encouraged by President Johnson himself,[27] clung to the ideology of states' rights and white man's government and voted the amendment down with near unanimity.[28]

Praising the body for its rejection of the amendment, one newspaper commented that it cannot be alleged that the Legislature acted without due reflection or under the impulse of passion, for the subject has been before them more than a month.[29] In truth of course, the amendment had been before them much longer, for, as New York's governor had remarked in presenting the amendment to his legislature: "I need not discuss the features of this amendment; they have undergone the ordeal of public consideration . . . and they are understood."[30] Moreover, Virginians had followed that public consideration closely. In early May 1866, for example, the Richmond press was reporting the deliberations of the Reconstruction Committee on the soon-to-be unveiled constitutional amendment.[31] Even after its promulgation, the *State Line Gazette* sarcastically summarized the sense of the many amendments that had been offered that spring:

There are no less than seventy propositions before Congress to amend the Constitution, all having for their aim the elevation of the African. The following, says an exchange, would cover the ground sought to be gained by the proposed amendments:

1. Every freedman shall have a bureau for himself, with a looking glass on the top if he wants it.
2. Every freedman shall have a secretary.
3. Every freedman shall have a wardrobe.
4. Every freed child shall have whatever it cries for.
5. White people, whether free or not must behave themselves.
6. Every white male citizen of the age of twenty-one years or under, and of sound mind or otherwise, may vote, if he will take the oath that he would be a negro if he could.[32]

Earlier the citizens of the state had followed the debate over the Civil Rights Bill. It was said to "establish for the Chinese, the Indians, the Gipsies, as well as the entire race designated as blacks, people of color, negroes, mulattos and persons of African blood, 'safeguards which go indefinitely beyond any that the General Government has ever provided for the white race.'"[33] Naturally, conservative white Virginians were aghast:

If a clerk of our courts, under color of State statute, refuse to issue license to a male teacher of a freedman's school to wed a negro woman; if the conductor of a railroad train refuse to permit some presuming Sambo and Dinah to enter a car specially reserved by company regulation for exclusive use of white ladies and their escorts; or, if a hotel-keeper, influenced by time-honored custom, refuse to entertain the kinky-haired contraband who may demand a room and meals—neither statute, nor regulation, nor custom will avail as a defense. The party thus guilty of discriminating between races and depriving the negro of these rights secured to him by this bill, incurs a penalty of $1000 or 12 months imprisonment, or both, as a U.S. Judge may determine.[34]

The Fourteenth Amendment, when it was unveiled, was thus plain and clear, in part because Section 1 was understood to have established a constitutional basis for the Civil Rights Act. The *Abingdon Virginian*, which opposed the amendment, summarized it as follows:

The report is in three parts. The first is a proposed amendment to the Constitution, in the form of a new article with five sections. The first of these sections is the "Civil Rights Bill." The second is negro suffrage. The third is to secure the electoral votes of the Southern States to Stephens or Sumner at the next Presidential election. The fourth is to strangle certain honest claims. The fifth is to commit the whole subject to the absolute discretion of Congress, and makes of the whole article simply a grant of unlimited power to Congress.[35]

The more extended analysis of the *Charlottesville Chronicle* mirrored that of the *Virginian*:

The first section makes negroes citizens of the United States, and gives the express sanction of the Constitution to the "Civil Rights bill."

The second section gives the South the alternative of adopting negro suffrage or losing all Federal representation for the negro population. If the elective franchise is extended to the negroes, the South will have 68 members of Congress; if it is refused, they are to have but 41 members.

The third clause would exclude from Federal and State office our old members of the Federal Congress, all officers of the U. S. Army who sided with the South, all persons who have been in the Legislature of any Southern State, and all persons who ever held an executive or judicial office in any Southern State (our language is sufficiently accurate for practical purposes.) We call attention to the fact that the language of this third section seems to reject the idea that a member of a State legislature holds a State *office*, and therefore the persons prohibited from holding office under it, would not (if our conjecture is correct) be disabled from being members of the legislature.

The fourth section refers to the public debt of the United States, and to the repudiation of all obligations incurred in aid of the Southern cause.

The fifth section is extremely broad, and Congress might pervert it to the most tyrannical ends.[36]

The *Richmond Dispatch* similarly commented on the proposed amendment: "The first section would make a civil rights act constitutional. The present civil rights act is clearly unconstitutional. The second section concedes that the States have the right to regulate suffrage, but provides that if any State refuse to let negroes vote, it shall surrender a part of its representation, proportioned to the persons so disfranchised. The third section is very objectionable."

The *Dispatch* also objected to Section 4 and then added, doubtless with Section 5 in mind, that the "Radical Congress . . . will read the Constitution to suit themselves."[37] The *American Union*, one of the few Virginia newspapers which favored the amendment, summarized it similarly (allowing, of course, for partisan differences):

[I]t is proposed that all citizens of the United States, without regard to color, shall be alike protected in life, liberty, and property; secondly that representation shall be based on population, but that if the right of suffrage shall be denied to any on account of color, such colored persons shall not be counted; thirdly, that certain persons shall be excluded from the right to hold office, for certain assigned reasons, unless such disability shall be removed by a two-thirds vote of Congress; fourthly that the public debt, and bounties, and pensions, shall be guaranteed and rendered inviolate; and fifthly, that Congress shall have power to inforce these proposed amendments. [38]

Interestingly, no paper chose to explain Section 1 by saying it incorporated the Bill of Rights, though that would have been as rhetorically convenient as explaining that it recapitulated the Civil Rights Bill. The difference, of course, was that the latter was true; the former would not have been.

In the absence of this straightforward explanation of Section 1, one might have expected critics to assail its three great clauses—privileges and immunities, due process, and equal protection—for their ambiguity. In fact, some opponents of the amendment did worry about the purported ambiguity of these clauses; but their expressions of concern were largely rhetorical.[39] The concepts of privileges and immunities and due process were part of the original Constitution, and the concept of equal protection appeared to be widely understood. Indeed, the real concern of opponents in Virginia was not the ambiguous content of the clauses, but the clarity with which the amendment transferred power from the states to the national government to define and protect the rights which it guaranteed.[40] For example, the *Charlottesville Chronicle* reminded its readers: "The fifth clause of the proposed Amendment gives Congress the power 'to enforce by appropriate legislation the foregoing provisions' of that instrument. What 'appropriate legislation' would be construed to mean in the administration of a party which has found in the Federal Constitution authority, not only to issue Treasury Notes, but to make them *a legal tender*, we leave it to every one to conjecture."[41]

In sharp contrast, Virginia Republicans enthusiastically embraced Section 5. They recognized that the protection of basic liberties depended upon the national government. Several prominent Virginia Republicans—including their radical leaders, James Hunnicutt and Judge John C. Underwood—joined the national call for a Southern Loyal Convention to be held in Philadelphia in the fall of 1866. Echoing the language of Section 1 of the only recently promulgated Fourteenth Amendment, they demanded that protection be "made co-extensive with citizenship" and added:

We maintain that no State, either by its organic law or legislation can make transgression on the rights of the citizen legitimate. We demand, and ask you to concur in demanding, protection to every citizen of the great Republic on the basis of equality before the law and further, that no State Government should be recognized as legitimate under the Constitution in so far as it does not by its organic law make impartial protection full and complete.[42]

Interestingly, the call did not speak of any need to insure that every citizen in every state be guaranteed every right in the Bill of Rights. Rather, it demanded that the states be required to administer their respective state laws impartially.

The vast majority of white Virginians nevertheless remained committed to a doctrine of states' rights that precluded any national "check" on the "impartiality" with which they administered the laws. In the summer of 1866, conservative Virginians, meeting in Richmond, urged their state central committee to appoint delegates to the National Union Convention in Philadelphia to explain their resolution "that the States and people of the South [should] at once be restored to all the equality of right and power possessed by the other States of the Union" and to urge the convention to "revise the best and most practical means of gathering up and efficiently organizing all the elements of opposition to the violent, lawless, unconstitutional and revolutionary schemes of the radicals who now wield the powers of the Federal Congress to the oppression of the South and the overthrow of our republican government."[43] They insisted that "the states of the Union are guaranteed State Governments constituted by their own people, and they reserve the right to determine the qualification of their own governing classes."[44] Thus they recognized that the amendment's last section—Section 5—was "[i]ts most pregnant" because "[w]ho can tell what this legislation will be?"[45]

They did not object, in theory at least, to the idea that blacks, once freed, enjoyed rights which the government was obliged to protect. Virginia, like all the other Southern states, had enacted laws to protect those rights. Admittedly, the state did not define those rights generously. Moreover, the government was often unwilling in actual circumstances to protect them. Still, conservative Virginians were willing to concede, as they did in Section 3 of the Southern Compromise Amendment, that"[n]o state shall make or enforce any law which shall abridge the privileges and immunities of citizens of the United States; nor shall any state deprive any person of life, liberty, or property without due process of law, nor deny to any person within its jurisdiction the equal protection of the laws."[46] What they would not concede was the power of Congress, first, to define the privileges and immunities of state citizenship and, second, to protect by "appropriate legislation" those privileges and immunities and the guarantees of due process and equal protection from infringement by the states. In December 1867, Virginia conservatives thus declared:

This Convention, for the people of Virginia, both declare that they disclaim all hostility to the black population; that they sincerely desire to see them advance in intelligence and national prosperity, and are willing to extend to them a liberal and generous protection. But that while, in the opinion of this Convention, any Constitution of Virginia ought to make all men equal before the law, and should protect the liberty and property of all, yet this Convention doth distinctly declare that the government of the States of the Union were formed by white men to be subject to their control; and that the suffrage should still be so regulated by the States as to continue the Federal and State systems under the control and direction of the white race.[47]

This declaration makes clear that Virginia's opposition to the Fourteenth Amendment had nothing to do with its reading of the language of Section 1 and everything to do with its fear that Congress might through that language impose "negro suffrage," "the most savory dish in [the Radical's] bill of fare."[48]

Even Virginia's repeated denunciations of the disqualification clause are best understood in light of that fear. Disqualification and disfranchisement, combined with universal Negro suffrage, would tip the electoral balance in favor of

blacks.[49] Conservative Virginia newspapers routinely described the consequences of Negro political domination with examples that presumably shocked
their readers' sensibilities. The *Charlottesville Chronicle* pointed out that in
counties with black majorities the state representatives, attorney, sheriff, constables, and tax commissioner would be black.[50] Under the new constitution, it predicted that blacks would control the state legislature and could "tax at pleasure.
Of some three millions to be raised under the Constitution by taxation, it is estimated that about $40,000 will come out of the negroes."[51] It declared: "You
will have a Constitution which will make this State too hot for any man with
straight hair and a plain complexion. It will be literally universal Negro rule."[52]

Congressional Reconstruction did bring disfranchisement and universal Negro
suffrage; and, for a brief time, it appeared as if they would result in the
"Africanization" of Virginia that conservatives prophesied.[53] Radicals were well
represented at the constitutional convention, which met for 104 days, from
late 1867 to April 1868; and they clearly intended to structure the new government in order to secure their political hegemony.[54] Consequently, the new
"mongrel Constitution" extended universal suffrage to blacks while disfranchising large numbers of whites.[55]

In the process of drafting the new constitution, Mr. Porter, a Republican delegate, advised his colleagues to rely upon the Fourteenth Amendment as a "sure
and reliable" guide, both in phraseology and ideas.[56] He made clear his understanding of its philosophy when, in the midst of debate, he declared that
"Americans [were] the only race in America." He then vowed to make "a constitution that shall not use the words 'race' or 'color' from beginning to end."[57]
This was the color-blind philosophy of the Declaration of Independence; and
delegate after delegate endorsed it, forswearing racial distinctions. Mr. Snead
said: "I came here . . . to frame a Constitution which shall make no distinction in
the rights of individuals on account of color."[58] So did Delegate White: "[I]t was
the purpose of the gentlemen of this Convention," he said, "to enact a Constitution which should not make . . . or recognize any distinction on the account of
color."[59] Mr. Norton agreed, saying: "I have always been opposed to making
distinctions between classes and colors." He explained the vice of such distinctions: "[S]uch a course breeds enmity and hostile feelings in one or both
classes."[60]

Radicals had endorsed this philosophy long before the constitutional convention convened. The *True Southerner*, established in November 1865, carried the
motto, "We hold these truths to be self-evident: that all men are created equal."[61]
In the March 22, 1866, inaugural issue of the *New Nation*, its editor—the fiery
radical Hunnicutt—announced that the paper would advocate equal rights for all
citizens and a color-blind political system.[62] In accepting the nomination of
Richmond Republicans for a seat in the constitutional convention, Hunnicutt
reiterated and particularized his beliefs:

It is proper that I should give my platform, and it is the same one I had in 1866, when I first came to Richmond. It is "Unconditional preservation of the Union—Republican principles—equal rights for white and black, and free education." . . . I shall advocate in the Convention the broad platform of "universal manhood suffrage." Free education I shall also urge. Free schools and money to start them we must have.[63]

Subscribing to the philosophy of the Declaration, convention delegates accepted the doctrine of natural rights. Responding to a demand that he enumerate "natural and inherent rights," Snead unhesitatingly answered: "The right to life, to liberty, to the pursuit of happiness, to acquire and possess property, to obtain happiness and safety."[64] Some radical delegates thought that voting and other "political rights" like jury service were also natural rights. One delegate declared, for example, that suffrage "is an inherent and God-given right . . . not obtain[ed] through any set of men"; another insisted that jury service was such a right.[65] These rights fell outside the categories which Snead recognized; and the judge replied: "You might as well say that a man has a right to pay taxes." He added: "Political rights are not the gift of God."[66] The minority report would later add that "no republican government could succeed unless the electors possessed intelligence, moral culture and a property stake."[67] The delegates rejected these efforts to have political rights declared natural rights, perhaps because they were unwilling to extend them to women. Moreover, the Republicans adopted very proscriptive disfranchisement provisions, which were arguably inconsistent with any theory that voting was a natural right.

While the constitution which emerged from the convention was very proscriptive, it did not otherwise reflect the radicalism of the Republican Party platform, which had been adopted in April 1867 by a Richmond convention, 160 of whose 210 delegates were black. Many were "extreme radicals," and the platform had been adopted amidst demands for confiscation and social equality.[68] Yet the new constitution did not include an explicit guarantee of equal access to public accommodations, even though Richmond blacks had forcibly integrated streetcars in that city the preceding spring,[69] and black delegates to the convention had been directed to sit in the "gallery" rather than the "dress circle" of a Richmond theater. They refused, and their admission fees were returned.[70] And while the constitution provided for public schools, it did not specify that they be integrated (as some radicals demanded) or segregated (as most conservatives insisted).[71]

The proscriptive provisions of the new constitution were nevertheless sufficiently objectionable that the reenergized conservatives set about to defeat it. They explained its potential impact in their post-convention address to the citizens of Virginia:

We will attempt now very briefly, as we have proposed, to explain what will be the operation of the new constitution if it shall become the law of the State. The pivot of the system to be inaugurated is, of course, negro suffrage. The instrument submitted provides for this on the widest basis. There is universal negro suffrage, without limitation, except that the party shall be a male, of sound mind, twenty-one years of age, who has not been convicted of crime and who has resided twelve months in the State and three months in the county where he proposes to vote. We could not secure any educational or property qualification whatever, not even in the prepayment of taxes; not even the pre-payment of the one-dollar poll tax. We could not even persuade them to exclude paupers. But this universal suffrage was confined to the negroes; all whites who ever held any office whatever under the Federal Government, or any civil or military office in the State, including the large list of county and municipal officers, and who afterwards par-ticipated in the "rebellion," are excluded not only from office, but from the elective fran-chise. The object of this was to secure, as Mr. Botts expressed it in an address he made to the Radical members of the Convention, "a good working majority" in the State, and to give a decided preponderance to the negroes in the Legislature, as well as in the country organization.[72]

Conservatives also objected to the "test oath" provision of the constitution. It conditioned the right to vote on the person's swearing that he believed in the social and political equality of all men. Though conservatives clearly thought the oath violated their right of conscience, they never attacked the oath on the ground that it violated the Fourteenth Amendment, understood to incorporate the First Amendment.

These same conservatives, reversing their prior refusal to accept blacks as partners, now reached out to them. Mass meetings of freedmen were common, and conservative whites sometimes ventured forth to deliver paternalistic homi-lies:

We see it stated in the Lynchburg papers, that Maj. Garland and others were to address the freedmen at Lynchburg on the 4th inst. This is a good example, and should be adopted in every county in the State. The colored people have been greatly unsettled by their new condition, and a very large proportion of them have been misled and bewil-dered by their new friends and allies. They have been made to believe that they are the equals of whites in all respects, and as much entitled to place and power, honor and dis-tinction, as the other race.

As far as we are concerned, (and we are sure we speak the sentiments of nine-tenths of the white people,) we wish the colored people well, and want to see them prosperous and happy—but putting them in possession of either political power, or social eminence, is like giving children edge-tools or rattle snakes to play with. They are not qualified for political power, and there is not one among them so ignorant as not to know that there is not one in Washington county, (and they are as intelligent here as anywhere,) who is qualified to fill the office of judge, legislator, magistrate, clerk, or any other office. Their condition heretofore has debarred them from any such qualification, and ruin and chaos, both to their own race and ours, would follow their rule.[73]

Understandably, the efforts of the conservatives were not generally appreciated by the freedmen; and they often interrupted white speakers with "impertinent and inappropriate questions."[74]

Conservatives enjoyed greater success in siphoning more moderate Republi-cans into an alliance. These Republicans remained willing to concede civil and political equality to blacks. They had unanimously endorsed that platform in a "mass meeting of white and colored citizens" in Petersburg in late April 1867:

[W]e will therefore insist that a new Constitution shall be framed for Virginia, which shall provide that all men, white or black, without reference to previous condition of servitude, shall be perfectly equal before the laws, both in respect to political privileges and power and of civil rights, and that all laws creating distinctions or differences of any sort between persons of different races shall be unconstitutional, null and void.[75]

These moderates—almost all prewar Whigs and Unionists—were nevertheless concerned about the radicalism of the Underwood/Hunnicutt faction that had seized control of the Virginia Republican Party that spring. Some blacks had come to expect social equality, as well as civil and political equality. Some, like Lewis Lindsay, were demanding a spoils system based on quotas. They insisted that appointments to public office "be made equally between the races."[76] Others urged confiscation of "rebel" property and its redistribution to the freedmen.[77]

The latter plea especially alarmed the moderates and their Northern Republican allies, who were frankly more interested in promoting economic development than in protecting the welfare of the freedmen. In fact, the Northern Loyal League sent Senator Henry Wilson to the state in the spring of 1867 to quell the "irresponsible" demands of the radicals and urge them to work with the moderates.[78] The radicals refused to compromise. Rebuffing moderate overtures, Hunnicutt made clear to them the terms of their admission into the party:

Now, we tell the strangers that if they want to come with us they will have to swallow a bitter pill. They must swallow the Constitutional Amendments, the Civil Rights Bill, the Sherman-Shellabarger-Wilson Bill, the Supplementary Bills, every Reconstruction Act, the Iron-clad Oath, the 17th of April platform, Wardwell, Hunnicutt, and the nigger; yes, the nigger, his head, his feet, his hide, his hair, his tallow, his bones, and suet? Nay, his body and soul! Yes, all these they must swallow, and then, perhaps, they can be called Republicans.[79]

The radicals' victory proved Pyrrhic. While they won control of the constitutional convention in the fall of 1867, they subsequently failed to secure adoption of the most proscriptive provisions of the new constitution and the test oath General Schofield, who of course disapproved of the proscriptive provisions, refused to authorize expenditure of the funds needed to hold an immediate election. Congress also declined to appropriate them. These decisions left the various political factions time to maneuver, and they divided it between organizing their Virginia supporters and seeking congressional allies and the backing of President Grant in Washington. Congress finally gave the president the discretion to submit the constitution and particular provisions to the people separately, and Grant directed that the disfranchisement and test oath provisions be voted on separately from the constitution itself. They were then defeated, though the constitution was overwhelmingly approved.[80]

In the meantime, the uncompromising radicalism of Hunnicutt and Underwood had driven many moderates into the welcoming embrace of conservative whites. During the 1869 campaign, conservatives junked their public chatter about a white man's party[81] and persuaded their gubernatorial candidate to withdraw. They then campaigned on behalf of the moderate Republican candidate Gilbert Walker.[82] He won, and Virginia thus became the only Southern state to be "redeemed" by a "carpetbagger."[83]

Walker, declaring himself in favor of "the civil and political equality of all men before the law,"[84] became governor on September 21, 1869. On October 8, the Virginia Senate and House ratified the Fourteenth and Fifteenth Amendments with very little discussion. Among those voting against the Fourteenth Amendment was James Lyons, a radical black. Presumably he shared the view of the *New Nation* that the amendment did not go "far enough." Analyzing the amendment in the fall of 1866, the paper had declared that "rebels should be disfranchised forever."[85] Three years later, the Fourteenth Amendment had ceased to be the focus of public discussion, and its passage was merely one last requirement that had to be satisfied before Virginia could be restored.

The Fourteenth Amendment had become a theoretical irrelevance in one sense because Virginia had guaranteed blacks far broader rights in its state constitution. In another, more practical sense, the Fourteenth Amendment became irrelevant because enforcement of its commands now depended upon the good faith of the state government and the political will of the national government.

The issue of jury service illustrates how the absence of that good faith and political will precluded effective enforcement of the Fourteenth Amendment. During Reconstruction, blacks in Virginia served on juries in Freedmen's Bureau courts and federal courts.[86] After Virginia was restored to the Union, federal courts in Virginia tried to prevent their systematic exclusion from jury duty in the state courts. They especially sought to assure the presence of some Negro members on all juries trying Negro defendants. These decisions were grounded, first, on the judgment that the deliberate exclusion of Negroes from jury duty violated the Fourteenth Amendment, and, second, on the belief that Negroes could not be guaranteed the protection of the laws before an all-white jury. Unfortunately, these efforts by the federal courts "availed little."[87]

State efforts to assure the Negro an equal chance of selection for jury duty were equally ineffective. In 1872 the House Committee for Courts of Justice had referred to it a motion which would have guaranteed to all Negro defendants a trial before juries, one-half of whose membership would be black. The committee declined to endorse the motion. Instead, it reported that "the law at present makes provision for the qualification of jurors, and it is inexpedient to amend it as proposed."[88]

No action was taken to insure integrated access to public accommodations either. Although some black legislators insisted on the integration of railroads and streetcars,[89] most objected primarily to the railroad's practice of assigning blacks to smoking cars (which, incidentally, were integrated). These delegates accepted the provision of "Jim Crow" cars for blacks only.[90] Whatever the law might say, blacks in Virginia did not enjoy equal treatment. One historian has observed:

[Blacks] were nowhere admitted to the public inns and hotels of the whites in accordance with their legal rights. Proprietors prepared to charge the Negroes exorbitant prices for drinks and cigars, while they stood ready to sell such articles to "regular customers" at a discount. The public press suggested that hotels and inns surrender their licenses and become private boarding houses, if necessary, in order to prevent Negroes from dining in such places with whites. Referring to the efforts of Negroes to abolish such distinction, the editor of the *Dispatch* said on January 11, 1871:

> It is idle for the Negro to suppose that there is to be any so-
> cial equality between the black and the white races here.
> When they demand it they not only demand what it is impos-
> sible to obtain, but they disgrace themselves by lowering
> their own race since they aspire to association with another
> which they thus confess to be superior to theirs.[91]

Of course, separate schools were established in Virginia even though the new state constitution would have permitted integrated schools. As previously indicated, the controversial question of education had arisen in the constitutional convention where some delegates had advocated integrated public schools, derided as "salt and pepper" schools in the conservative press.[92] Indeed, black delegates had threatened to vote against any constitution that did not provide for mixed schools.[93] Despite the threat, "white Republicans clearly saw that the people of Virginia would not endure such a measure, and refused to insert a provision for mixed schools in the constitution."[94] Virginia's first superintendent of public instruction, Henry Ruffner, was appointed because he had "grasp enough to master a new subject—yet [had] caution and prudence enough to avoid all rash or ill considered experiments in the body politic."[95] When Sumner's Civil Rights Bill was pending in 1874, Ruffner showed that "prudence." He wrote in *Scribner's Magazine* that although history seemed to foreshadow a gradual diminution of race friction, for the present the common school education in fifteen states would be a failure unless there was due recognition of caste in public education at the South.[96]

For nearly another hundred years, Virginia paid "due recognition to caste" in all phases of its life; and the state thus enjoyed what its leading white citizens had demanded on the eve of Reconstruction: a white man's government in a states' rights world. Hamilton Eckenrode accurately summarized the dawn of that sad day when Virginia's "first Redeemer legislature" met:

The reconstruction of Virginia had come to an end after well-nigh five years of weary waiting. Nearly nine years had passed since the State had withdrawn her representation from the Federal Congress. After this long period of war and of political subjection, the white people of Virginia now regained control of affairs. The reconstruction had for its ultimate purposes proven a failure. For it was the desire of Congress and the aim of the radical politicians in Virginia to place the two races on an equality of rights and privileges—to abolish the belief of the white man in the essential inferiority of the black. . . . It was impossible that any such attempt should succeed.[97]

Black Virginians offered another verdict: "For the Virginia Negro there was truly no hiding place and no refuge from the long arm of white supremacy. Even the scales of justice could not be made to balance when Negro rights and equal treatment were concerned. For many, in their bitterness, the Emancipation Proclamation and the Thirteenth Amendment seemed to be hollow victories, while the Fourteenth and Fifteenth Amendments were a mockery."[98]

NOTES

1. Virginius Dabney, *Virginia: The New Dominion* (Charlottesville: University Press of Virginia, 1971), 353 ("Virginia had been the chief battleground of the war, and the physical devastation there was greater than in any other southern state"). Testifying before the Joint Committee on Reconstruction, Reverend Robert McCurdy said: "It is impossible to make [Virginia's] physical humiliation more complete than it is." U.S. Congress, *Report of the Joint Committee on Reconstruction*, 39th Cong., 1st Sess., Part II, 92.

2. *Journal of the Constitutional Convention of the State of Virginia, Convened in the City of Richmond December 8 by an Order of General Schofield Dated November 2, 1867, in Pursuance of the Act of Congress of March 29, 1867* (Richmond: Office of the New Nation, 1867), 545.

3. Although Arkansas, Louisiana, and Tennessee all had been "restored" under Lincoln's "10 percent plan" prior to the end of the war, they all had had military governors. There was no military governor in occupied Virginia. Francis Pierpont, the loyalist who had presided over the birth of West Virginia, subsequently moved his Virginia government to Alexandria, where it had survived under the protection of federal troops.

4. Cf. R. Lowe, "Republicans, Rebellion, and Reconstruction: The Republican Party in Virginia, 1856–1870" (Ph.D. diss., University of Virginia, 1968), 133 (the "midget" size of "restored Virginia" was almost "farcical").

5. *Fredericksburg New Era*, 27 June 1865.

6. Hamilton J. Eckenrode, *The Political History of Virginia during Reconstruction* (Baltimore: Johns Hopkins University Press, 1904), 30.

7. Lewis McKenzie said in his testimony before the Reconstruction Committee: "When that legislature went to Richmond, they altered the constitutional provisions in such a manner that I found that the loyal men of the State were to be totally sacrificed and turned over to the power of the secessionists." U.S. Congress, *Report of the Joint Committee on Reconstruction*, 39th Cong., 1st Sess., Part II, 11.

8. *Alexandria Gazette*, 13 June 1865. Early in June 1865, Negroes in Petersburg also "met publically to advocate Negro suffrage." See also Richard L. Morton, Philip A. Bruce, and Lyon G. Tyler, *History of Virginia* vol. 3 (New York: American Historical Society, 1924), 80; and Lowe, "Republicans, Rebellion, and Reconstruction," 203–4. Cf. *True Index*, 10 February 1866 (reports that a freedmen's convention, while opposing universal Negro suffrage, "advocated the voting of colored people who could read and write well; and who possessed certain property qualifications").

9. *Alexandria Gazette*, 8 July 1865; *Fredericksburg New Era*, 18 July 1865.

10. Virginia Maddox, "The Persistence of Centrist Hegemony," in *Reconstruction and Redemption in the South*, ed. Otto H. Olsen (Baton Rouge: Louisiana State University Press, 1980), 116–17. Pierpont had asked the legislature "to make all punishments for negroes and whites the same, to repeal the law prohibiting Negro education, to allow Negroes to testify in all cases ... and to legalize all slave marriages." Lowe, "Republicans, Rebellion, and Reconstruction," 182. Pierpont hoped to create "a liberal Republican party favorable to equal rights for freedmen, free public schools for both blacks and whites, and an enlarged program for internal improvements." Charles H. Ambler, *Francis H. Pierpont, Union War Governor of Virginia and Father of West Virginia* (Chapel Hill: University of North Carolina Press, 1937), 288.

11. That "aimless, vagrant freedmen" posed a "problem" was conceded. Richard L. Morton, *The Negro in Virginia Politics, 1865–1870* (Charlottesville: University of Virginia Press, 1919), 18. In June 1865 the Union general at Lynchburg declared: "No freedman can be allowed to live in idleness when he can obtain any description of work" (ibid., 19). On the other hand, the law permitted "free" Negroes to be worked with "ball and chain" in some circumstances. Eckenrode, *The Political History of Virginia during the Reconstruction*, 42.

12. Morton, *The Negro in Virginia Politics*, 21. The Virginia legislature subsequently adopted a resolution that it hoped would negate any inference that it had attempted to reinstitute slavery: "*Resolved*, That involuntary servitude, except for crime, is abolished, and ought not to be re-established, and that the negro race among us be treated with justice, humanity, and good faith, and every means that the wisdom of the Legislature can devise should be used to make them useful and intelligent members of society." *Journal of the House of Delegates of the State of Virginia, for the Session of 1865–66* (Richmond: Allegre & Goode, Printers, 1865), 283.

13. *Journal of the House of Delegates of the State of Virginia for the Session of 1866–'67* (Richmond: Enquirer Print, 1866), 34. The governor's message was carried or noted in major papers. See, e.g., *State Line Gazette*, 12 December 1866. See also *Norfolk Virginian*, 6 December 1866.

14. But see *Abingdon Virginian*, 17 August 1866 ("It would take a Philadelphian lawyer to put [Section 2] in clear language").

15. After Pierpont's dismissal as provisional governor, the *Richmond Enquirer and Examiner*, his most uncompromising critic and bitter assailant, described him, in an editorial for 6 April 1868, as the "deceased pasha from the Pan-Handle" who had received the order for his execution with "Oriental submissiveness." Continuing, it said: "Thus has perished by the sword the official whom the sword inaugurated.... Verily as he totters beneath the weight of his carpet-bag, and creeps back to the State which he permitted to be torn from the Old Dominion, he may exclaim to his loyal aide-de-camp, as Woolsey did to Cromwell, 'Oh, Lewis, had I served my God half as faithfully as I served the Federal Government, I should not have thus been treated.'" Pierpont's speech of 27 February 1868 in the constitutional convention was described by the same organ as a belated confession of faith, and he was said to have "abjured all the heresies of Conservatism" for the "sweet odor of Hunnicuttism." Ambler, *Francis H. Pierpont*, 308.

16. *Richmond Whig*, 10 January 1867. See also *Abingdon Virginian*, 22 June 1866 (Southern states will *gain nothing* by ratifying amendment: "in fact their condition will be worse than it is now"). Cf. *Richmond Dispatch*, 10 November 1866. But see *American Union*, 17 November 1866:

> Thus with the rejection of the amendment, we shall enter upon another political struggle, more intense than that through which we are now passing, more injuri-

ous to the country, and especially to the South States—a contest of which the issue is not doubtful; for the twenty millions of the Northern States will begin to
see the unreasonableness of the Southern leaders, and will lose patience with
these men, who so stubbornly refuse the mildest forms ever offered to beaten rebels. Hitherto the country has wonderfully restrained itself; but we advise no one
to push its patience to [sic] far. It is not at all impossible, it is not even improb-
able, if the amendment should fail through the obstinacy of the Southern leaders,
that the laws which are still on the statute book may be enforced against the politicians who led their states into treason and rebellion.

17. John M. Schofield, *Forty-Six Years in the Army* (New York: Century, 1897), 394–
95.

18. James McDonough, *Schofield: Union General in the Civil War and Reconstruction*
(Tallahassee: Florida State University Press, 1972), 168.

19. Ibid. See also Schofield, *Forty-Six Years in the Army*, 373–76.

20. *Charlottesville Chronicle*, 6 December 1866.

21. *Charlottesville Chronicle*, 13 October 1866.

22. *Richmond Dispatch*, 2 February 1866 (commenting on a prior proposed amendment).

23. *Richmond Dispatch*, 19 October 1866. The *Dispatch* later offered a clever theory of
interpretation of Section 3 that would reduce its "sweeping" impact:

> The language [of Section 3], if construed strictly, would require that the
> "insurrection or rebellion" spoken of should be against the "Constitution," and
> that the "enemies" spoken of should be enemies of the Constitution, though Con-
> gress meant the word "same" to describe "the United States," and not the
> "Constitution." As the southern statesmen seceded because the Constitution was
> violated, and claimed to be its best friends to the last, they would not consider
> themselves proscribed by this language if the Federal courts should hold that it
> bears the construction we have put upon it. (Ibid., 1 November 1866)

24. *Richmond Whig*, 11 January 1867. See also *Charlottesville Chronicle*,
15 November 1866 (Section 3 "excludes . . . about nine-tenths of the men of average
intelligence and standing, above thirty years of age, in the South").

25. *Richmond Enquirer*, 1 January 1867. Cf. *Chronicle*, 9 October 1866 (Fourteenth
Amendment acceptable as "final settlement" only if accompanied by assurances that
Negro suffrage would not be imposed, the test oath would be repealed, and confiscation
would be rejected).

26. *Richmond Examiner*, 3 May 1866. See also *Norfolk Virginian*, 20 March 1866
(amendments are used for party purposes); *Richmond Whig*, 11 January 1867 (plea that
ratification will lead to restoration is a "gross and impudent falsehood"); *Roanoke Times*,
8 January 1867 (there should be no ratification without pledge of restoration); *Richmond
Dispatch*, 10 November 1866 ("were every Southern state to adopt [the 14th Amend-
ment], the South would not be admitted to equal rights under the Constitution").

27. Jack Maddex, *The Virginia Conservatives, 1867–1879* (Chapel Hill: University of
North Carolina Press, 1970), 44. See also *Abingdon Virginian*, 5 October 1866. Some
conservative Virginians never lost hope that they might be saved from the amendment.
Two years later the same paper carried a report from Washington, expressing optimism
that some Northern legislatures could be induced to repeal their ratifications. *Abingdon
Virginian*, 10 January 1868.

28. The vote was unanimous in the Senate and seventy-four to one in the House. That even one person would vote to ratify the amendment must have surprised the editor of the *Richmond Whig*:

> We cannot suppose that any member of the Virginia Legislature could so degrade himself and outrage public sentiment as to vote for the ratification of a measure which makes Pariahs of those noble men who perilled their lives and lost their property in the cause of the South. We shall not believe that there is one such man in the Legislature until he actually votes for this measure. (Ibid., 4 January 1867)

29. *Richmond Enquirer*, 8 January 1867.

30. *State of New York Messages from the Governors: Comprising Executive Communications to the Legislature and Other Papers Relating to Legislation from the Organization of the First Colonial Assembly in 1683 to and Including the Year 1906, with Notes*, ed. Charles Z. Lincoln (Albany: J. B. Lyon Co., 1909), 742–44.

31. See, e.g., *Richmond Examiner*, 3 May 1866.

32. *State Line Gazette*, 22 June 1866.

33. *Virginia Sentinel*, 12 April 1866.

34. *True Index*, 14 April 1866.

35. *Abingdon Virginian*, 4 May 1866.

36. *Charlottesville Chronicle*, 6 November 1866.

37. *Richmond Dispatch*, 31 May 1866.

38. *American Union*, 16 June 1866.

39. The *Charlottesville Chronicle*, 15 November 1866, speculated, for example, that Section 1 might be construed to guarantee blacks the right to vote.

40. *Abingdon Virginian*, 22 June 1866 ("Its most pregnant section is its last and briefest"). See also *Norfolk Virginian*, 3 December 1866. Objecting to the proposed amendment, the paper said:

> The Federal Constitution contemplates no such condition as that of conquered provinces, ruled by despotic legislation or oppressive and invidious laws. To the States of the Union are guaranteed State Governments established and constituted by their own people, and they deserve the right to determine the qualifications of their own governing classes.

In the summer of 1866, the *Lynchburg Virginian*, carried the remarks of George Pendleton, who said that the Fourteenth Amendment was intended "to break down State rights, State power, State limits, State authorities" (quoted in the *Abingdon Virginian*, 17 August 1866).

41. *Charlottesville Chronicle*, 15 November 1866.

42. *State Line Gazette*, 22 July 1866.

43. *True Index*, 28 July 1866 (report of Chairman J. M. Forbes).

44. Ibid.

45. Ibid.

46. *State Line Gazette*, 13 February 1867.

47. *Richmond Whig*, 13 December 1867; *Roanoke Times*, 21 December 1867.

48. *Roanoke Times*, 5 February 1867.

49. *True Index*, 14 September 1867 (South doomed to Negro supremacy).

50. *Charlottesville Chronicle*, 26 February 1867.

51. Ibid., 26 May 1868. Once blacks were enfranchised by the Reconstruction Acts, the *Chronicle* offered them this advice:

> By the right to vote, you have acquired an immense power to protect yourselves. If you use this power without abusing it, if you are prudent, the legislatures of the States will pass kind laws to protect you, and the courts of the country will enforce them.
>
> Remember that although you are free, and although you will vote, you are still *the laboring class of the country.* Do not abuse the freedom which God has given you by forgetting your position in society. Do not undertake to be fine gentlemen.—Do not put on airs. Attend to your business, do your daily work, do it well, deal honestly and uprightly; and you will *command* respect. Live peaceably with the whites. Make them your friends. They can do you infinite harm, if you make them enemies. They can persecute you to death in a thousand ways which no laws can reach. (*Charlottesville Chronicle*, 19 March 1867)

52. Ibid., 21 April 1868. The *Richmond Dispatch*, 31 October 1866, rejected the argument that republican government required Negro suffrage: "If a State could make slaves of black men on account of their color, and still be 'republican,' it follows inevitably that a State might deprive him of the right of suffrage and still be republican."

53. For example, the minority report on the proposed constitution invoked that image, calling it a "plan for 'the Africanization of the State.'" J. Smith, "Virginia during Reconstruction, 1865–1870" (Ph.D. diss., University of Virginia 1960), 87. A few white Unionists nevertheless welcomed Reconstruction, preferring the possibility of Negro domination to the certainty of rebel domination. Thus one Virginia Unionist wrote Thaddeus Stevens:

> The loyal people of this nation are under many obligations to you for your . . . devotion to their interests . . . you have placed us under particular obligations such as we can never forget.
>
> Occupying [a portion of Virginia] in which the [Federal] Government has more staunch friends than in any like portion of the state I consider that I can furnish you with somewhat of an intelligent public opinion [on your proposed bill]. . . . I have seen and conversed with many . . . and the almost universal opinion is that it is the best adapted in *every* respect to secure the desired object. There is some . . . squirming about the privileges extended to the recent slaves . . . but . . . there is no union man who does not infinitely more fear and dread the domination of the recent Rebels than that of the Recent Slaves. You have certainly discriminated in such a manner as to serve the rights and interests of every possible union man.
>
> The rebellious portion of the community are not disappointed [for] they know that it is not in the nature of things that the enemies of an individual or of a Government will be preferred to its friends. . . .
>
> Some of my union friends have spoken of getting up a petition endorsing your bill if you think any thing of the kind necessary [;] nearly every union man in this County can be got to sign it and I believe throughout the State.

The writer concluded with the hope that "Congress may act and that speedily for our safety and protection against the cohorts of treason." William Downey to Thaddeus Stevens, 7 January 1867, Thaddeus Stevens Papers, Library of Congress, quoted in Smith, "Virginia during Reconstruction," 35–36. Writing to Congressman Washburne in late 1867, Judge Underwood, the leading white radical in the state, plaintively asked, "Can Congress save us [Radical Republicans] from annihilation?" Underwood to E. B. Washburne, 16 December 1867, Elihu Washburne Papers, Library of Congress.

54. The draft constitution, in sharp contrast to Florida's, provided, for example, for popular election of all local offices. This would insure Radical control of the state's forty-three most populous counties. Dabney, *Virginia: The New Dominion*, 369 ("blacks

would have gained political control of the state if the entire 'Underwood Constitution' had been approved by the people and put into effect"). Conservatives expected the worst from this "mongrel convention" whose "nigger jargon, nigger impertinence and nigger stupidity are extremely . . . disgraceful." *Abingdon Virginian*, 13 March 1868. Cf. Dabney, *Virginia: The New Dominion*, 367, quoting a black delegate as saying, "Dis convention is a equal convention, and we all has equal and illegal rights here." One white radical delegate urged the Negroes to stand together because, united, they could control the state and secure to themselves political power "for all time to come." Smith, "Virginia during Reconstruction," 106.

55. *Page News-Courier*, 15 January 1869 ("They [the radicals] have already forced negro suffrage on us, and the only way by which they can retain this power is to disfranchise as many as possible of the white men of the State").

56. *Journal of the Constitutional Convention* (1867), 632.

57. Ibid., 251.

58. Ibid., 642.

59. Ibid., 567.

60. Ibid., 253.

61. Quoted in Lowe, "Republicans, Rebellion, and Reconstruction," 227.

62. Ibid., 225–26.

63. *Savannah Daily News and Herald*, 18 October 1867.

64. *Journal of the Constitutional Convention* (1867), 634.

65. Quoted in Eckenrode, *The Political History of Virginia during Reconstruction*, 96.

66. *Journal of the Constitutional Convention* (1867), 634.

67. Ibid., 97–98.

68. Eckenrode summarizes the six resolutions upon which the platform was based as follows:

> First, Congress was thanked for the reconstruction act, the beneficial effects of which were felt in the increased security of "loyal" men. Secondly, the principles of the Republican party were adopted as a platform, and the cooperation of all the classes, without distinction of race or color, was invited. The third resolution proclaimed equal protection to all men before the courts and equal political rights, including the right to hold office; free schools for all classes, and a free and equal participation therein; a more equitable system of taxation, which should be apportioned on property only; and a modification of the usury laws, to induce capital to flow into the State. The fourth resolution declared that all men are free, equal, etc., and pledged the party to a strict adherence to these sentiments. Fifth, the party was bound to support no man for office who did not openly identify himself with it and support its principles. The sixth resolution recognized the interests of all the laboring classes of the State as identical, and denied the wish to deprive any white laborer of his privileges. (Eckenrode, *The Political History of Virginia during Reconstruction*, 68)

The *New York Tribune* warned in its 12 April 1867 issue: "To organize a campaign on the Hunnicutt plan is to abandon any hope of a permanent Union party in the South. We cannot afford to array the white against the black or the black against the white."

69. *Richmond Dispatch*, 25 April 1867. See generally Morton, *The Negro in Virginia Politics*, 36.

70. Alrutheus A. Taylor, *The Negro in the Reconstruction of Virginia* (Washington, D.C.: Association for the Study of Negro Life and History, 1926), 53.

71. Morton, *The Negro in Virginia Politics*, 36.

72. *Bristol News*, 1 May 1868.

73. *Abingdon Virginian*, 8 May 1868. See also *Bristol News*, 17 April 1868:

> It is but the duty of the whites to talk with the black man—not to fall in with the idea that it's "nigger equality" to talk with them for their good. The law recognizes them as citizens, as voters, and their votes are as good as any at the polls. Convince them of their error, and show them that they have been swindled and humbugged by a class of scoundrels, for no other purpose but to get into office themselves, while at the same time they entertain for them, personally, the utmost contempt. It is our duty as citizens of this government to do it. Let them see their *natural position*—the inferior of the white man, as they were so intended to be by God himself—and they will eventually *come down* to their proper status—citizens, but not law-makers.

74. *Abingdon Virginian*, 19 April 1867. At least one black man, however, had been persuaded even before the constitutional convention to cast his lot with the conservatives:

> Having seen my name published in the *American Union*, of Harrisonburg, as a delegate to the Convention to be held in Richmond on the 1st day of August, I beg leave most respectfully to decline acting in that position. I have always been a free man, and take pleasure now in saying that I sympathised cordially with my white friends of the South in their late unfortunate struggle, so that I might be termed "a rebel colored man." My political opinions, so far as I have been capable of forming them, are in favor of the strictest conservative principles and justice. I wish the white people of the South to retain all the privileges which they ever possessed in voting and in holding of their property free from confiscation; and whilst I, of course, wish to see my own race advanced in intelligence and wealth, I do not desire this to be done unjustly at the expense of the whites who have always treated me kindly. I have been born and raised among the Virginia people, and know them to be an honorable people, and will be guilty of no act which tends to strike them down or degrade them. I am not a member of the Union League, nor can I consent to act with that party in their movements. I would advise all intelligent colored people to vote with the white conservatives. They have to live in the South, and the conservatives are their best friends. We can trust the best people in the South.—The Yankees, if they get a good chance, will do as they wish in Massachusetts. The radicals only want the votes of the colored people. They want power to prevent restoration of the Union and peace. Have not our intelligent friends, the conservatives, shown a willingness to help us? Have they not helped to build our churches and school houses in the South? Why should well-disposed colored men in the South seek to enslave and injure and oppress their white friends? Will it do them any good? Will they not, if we make ourselves their enemies, employ men and women of their own color, to the exclusion of our race?
>
> Respectfully,
>
> Joseph T. Williams

True Index, 17 August 1867.

75. *Vicksburg Daily Herald*, 1 May 1867.

76. *Charlottesville Chronicle*, 2 July 1867. See also *True Index*, 15 June 1867 (the "colored" president of a mass meeting "set out with the broad proposition that it was the duty of the whites to 'divide the spoils' with their colored brethren").

77. Morton, *The Negro in Virginia Politics*, 35 (Negro delegates to the April 1867 Republican convention in Richmond "advocated confiscation almost unanimously"). Hun-

nicutt was arrested by civil authorities in November 1867 for making the following remarks: "You colored people have no property. The white race has houses and lands. Some of you are old and feeble and cannot carry the musket, but you can apply the torch to the dwellings of your enemies. There are none too young—the boy of ten and the girl of twelve can apply the torch." Military authorities intervened, and he was released on bail until after the constitutional convention. He was never prosecuted. Jack Maddex summarized the radical position as follows:

> The Reverend James W. Hunnicutt, a Southern Unionist and editor of the Richmond *New Nation*, led the left wing. In April, 1867, his black followers, some of whom advocated land confiscation, dominated the Republican State Convention at Richmond. In its platform, the convention placed equalitarian demands for racial equality, free schools, and equitable taxation ahead of capitalist demands for a higher interest rate and encouragement to internal improvements and immigration. It committed the party to represent the interests of the laboring classes regardless of race, to restrain the arrogant and lift up the downtrodden and to promote the greatest good for the greatest number. (Maddex, *The Virginia Conservatives*, 49–50)

78. The *New York Tribune* of 12 April 1867 made this comment on the subject:

> Far be it from us to advise a campaign of bitterness. We do not propose to influence the negro by exciting in his mind a hatred of his former masters. Nor should we advise any organization antagonistic to those masters. Agitators like Mr. Hunnicutt, of Virginia, may mean well, but their zeal is bitter and offensive. To organize a campaign on the Hunnicutt plan is to abandon any hope of a permanent Union party in the South. We cannot afford to array the white against the black, or the black against the white.

See example of Wilson's "stump address" in the *Vicksburg Herald*, 27 April 1867.

79. *Richmond Dispatch*, 2 August 1867. The next day the *Dispatch* warned its readers:

> The disgusting and loathsome exhibition of the past week demonstrates to the plainest intellect that the fate of Hayti awaits Virginia if, through apathy and indifference, the Caucasian majority in this State permit the African minority to obtain the control of the government. Completely demoralized and corrupted by the infamous renegades who have affiliated with them, a large portion of the negroes are now inaccessible to reason. If there were not, fortunately, in Virginia a large majority of white men, to whose instincts of race and interests we may be permitted to look hopefully, our prospects would be no better than those of Hayti when French radicalism kindled in that unhappy land the fires of servile insurrection. . . . The recent hideous radical carnival in this city, like a fire-bell at midnight, should arouse every honest white man in Virginia to a sense of danger. (*Richmond Dispatch*, 3 August 1867)

See also *Charlottesville Chronicle*, 6 August 1867.

80. See generally R. Glass and C. Glass, *Virginia Democrats: A History of the Achievements of the Party and Its Leaders in the Mother of Commonwealths, the Old Dominion* (Springfield, Ill.: Democratic Historical Association, Inc., 1937), 179–200.

81. The turning point for conservatives was the anonymous publication of the "Senex letter" in Virginia newspapers in December 1868. Its author, H. H. Stuart, had chaired the December 1867 convention that had demanded white control of the government. One year later he urged "universal suffrage and universal amnesty." Despite initial criticism, most conservatives "came around"; and a committee of nine persons went to Washington to lobby for the policy. For Stuart's account of the "New Movement," see Alexander F.

Robertson, *Alexander Hugh Holmes Stuart, 1807–1891: A Biography* (Richmond: William Byrd Press, Inc., 1925), 406–61. See generally Maddex, *The Virginia Conservatives*, 67–73.

82. *Richmond Daily Whig*, 30 April 1869 (conservative convention votes to withdraw the state ticket). The *Whig* had explained the conservative case for supporting Walker earlier:

> The Wellsites came here ... to prey upon the substance of the people. The Walkerites ... seek their own interest by promoting the general welfare. They have something, and, by honest industry, hope to have more; they, therefore, favor wise legislation and honest administration. . . . The Wellsites are our enemies; the Walkerites are our *friends.*
>
> As to principles, we know nothing of them—we thought they were all extinct. *Measures and men*—practical expedients for the evils of the day—are all that we are privileged to consider now. (*Daily Whig*, 19 March 1869)

83. One Walker supporter wrote that a Walker victory was the only foreseeable opportunity to "emancipate" Virginia from "oppression." Maddex, *The Virginia Conservatives*, 79.

84. A. Cahill, "Gilbert Carelton Walker: Virginia's Redeemer Governor" (M.A. thesis, University of Virginia, 1956).

85. Quoted in Lowe, "Republicans, Rebellion, and Reconstruction," 242. The vote to ratify was 36 to 4 in the Senate and 126 to 6 in the House.

86. Underwood opened the United States District Court on 6 May 1867, by summoning twelve potential black jurors. The judge pointed out the significance of this act: "Another subject of thanksgiving is presented in the very constitution of your body, furnishing ocular evidence that the age of caste and class cruelty is departed, and a new era of justice and equality, breaking through the clouds of persecution and prejudice, is now dawning over us." *Richmond Dispatch*, 7 May 1867. See generally Charles E. Wynes, *Race Relations in Virginia, 1870–1962* (Totowa, N.J.: Rowman and Littlefield, 1961), 139–41.

87. See generally Wynes, *Race Relations*, 139–41. Cf. Maddox, "The Persistence of Centrist Hegemony," 134 ("blacks therefore suffered in courts in which they very rarely served on juries and in a penal system that hired convicts out to private companies and occasionally still used the whipping post").

88. *Journal of the Senate of the Commonwealth of Virginia: Begun and Held at the Capitol, in the City of Richmond, on Thursday, the First Day of January, in the Year One Thousand Eight Hundred and Seventy-Four—Being the Ninety-Eighth Year of the Commonwealth* (Richmond: H. P. Walker, Superintendent of Public Printing, 1874), 353, 355–56, 395.

89. Wynes, *Race Relations*, 69–70.

90. Ibid., 69.

91. Ibid., 141.

92. Though white Virginia strongly and almost unanimously opposed integrated schools, they otherwise had conflicting ideas on the value of educating the Negro. Some thought him incapable of learning. *Roanoke Times*, 11 November 1866 ("God has [not] given him the intelligence of the white man"). Others recommended that they be educated in order to enhance their "usefulness." *Abingdon Virginian*, 30 March 1866. They disliked Negroes being educated by radicals. *Roanoke Times*, 12 February 1867 (radical teachers "will . . . lead [Negroes] to ruin"). And they feared that the freedmen might treat them as they had treated Negroes: "In a few years it will not be a question whether there

will be schools for colored children, but it will be whether white children will be admitted to our institutions of learning." *True Index*, 28 September 1867.

93. Lewis Lindsay declared that if integrated schools were not required, he would urge all carpetbaggers to flee the state. He assured them that his race did not intend to be hobbyhorses to ride them into office, and gave notice that if a provision for mixed schools was not placed in the constitution, nine-tenths of the Negroes in Virginia would vote against its adoption. *Richmond Enquirer*, 8 April 1868.

94. Eckenrode, *The Political History of Virginia during Reconstruction*, 94.

95. Walter J. Fraser, Jr., "William Henry Ruffner and the Establishment of Virginia's Public School System," *Virginia Magazine of History and Biography* 79 (1971): 259, 261.

96. Charles Chilton Pearson, "William Henry Ruffner: Reconstruction Statesman of Virginia," *South Atlantic Quarterly* 20 (1921): 137, 146.

97. Eckenrode, *The Political History of Virginia during Reconstruction*, 127.

98. Wynes, *Race Relations*, 143.

9

Ratification in Florida

[Whites carry] the colored voters like a pack of cards to be shuffled, dealt, and played at their pleasure.

—A black congressman from "reconstructed" Florida, denouncing the manipulation of black voters

"The smallest tadpole in the dirty pool of secession," Florida's tiny population was almost evenly divided at the end of the war between whites and blacks.[1] A frontier state, Florida had attracted the interest of Northern capitalists even before the Civil War;[2] and no sooner had the war ended than more Northerners descended upon the state in search of their fortunes.[3] Though these men founded the Republican Party in Florida and allied themselves with the freedmen, they never allowed radical blacks to set the party's policies.

The political divisions that bedeviled most of the Southern states during the early years of Reconstruction thus divided Floridians only briefly. There were, of course, a wide range of competing political factions in Florida, including a radical faction.[4] The radical faction was marginalized early, however, and was never able to implement its political agenda. Instead, moderate Republicans wrested control of the 1868 constitutional convention from radicals, and they dominated the subsequent state government. Primarily interested in the economic development of the state, these moderates sought economic and political stability. That required some solution to the problem of race relations. Moreover, blacks provided most of the Republican Party's voting muscle. Consequently, it had to endorse black rights; but it sought to do so without empowering the freedmen or alienating conservative whites.[5]

This dominant Republican majority did not aggressively implement the Fourteenth Amendment. Their interest in black rights was, after all, instrumental rather than principled. They understood it to command—by its own terms—the protection of basic civil rights: the right to own and transfer property, to contract, and to sue. While they might have conceded that the Fourteenth Amendment permitted more expansive legislative protections, they insisted that it dictated nothing additional, other than that a state insure civil equality among its citizens and the fair treatment of all persons within its jurisdiction.

Ultimately, these white Republicans did come to support political rights for blacks; but there is no evidence that the dominant Republican majority ever believed that the Fourteenth Amendment required Florida to extend any of those political rights to the freedmen. Only political necessity dictated that extension, and even then the party structured the political process to preserve white hegemony. The *Tallahassee Sentinel* captured the circumstances in which Florida's freedmen thus found themselves when it said: "If he is no longer bearing the burden of slavery, he is bearing the burden of politicians, who are astride of the freedman . . . their legs twisted around his neck . . . determined to make him carry them to high places of power."[6] Josiah Walls, one of only two freedmen to rise to high office in reconstructed Florida, railed against that fact: "[Whites] talk and write as if they carried the colored voters like a pack of cards to be shuffled, dealt, and played at their pleasure."[7]

While conservative Democrats briefly flirted with playing the "colored card" themselves, their negrophobic attitudes left them implacably opposed to granting the freedmen anything more than the most basic civil rights. The actions of the state in the period between Lee's surrender and the imposition of congressional Reconstruction illustrate these attitudes, which decisively influenced how most white Floridians interpreted or at least applied the Fourteenth Amendment. A month after General Lee surrendered, federal forces entered Tallahassee unopposed. In mid-May, Major General Quincy Adams Gilmore ordered slaves freed; later that month martial law was imposed. In mid-July, President Johnson appointed William Marvin, a native Northerner who had moved to Florida in 1835, provisional governor.

Governor Marvin admonished the former slaves to conduct themselves "precisely as you formerly did" and cautioned them "against any pretensions to equality, particularly social equality."[8] In a speech to blacks at Mariana on September 18, 1865, the governor warned: "You must be contented with having your freedom and what else you will have to get by work."[9] He specifically sought to disabuse them of the belief that they would get forty acres and a mule:

There has been a story circulated in Middle Florida that on the first day of January next the land and mules will be taken from your former owners and divided among you. Such a story, I suppose, you have all heard. Have you? Speak out if you have and tell me. ("I'se hearn it! I'se hearn it!" say all.) Well, who told you so? (An answer: "The soldiers.") . . . I want you to understand me. The President will not give you one foot of land, nor a mule, nor a hog, nor a cow, nor even a knife or fork or spoon. (A voice: "Dar, ole man, you hear dat!")[10]

At the same time, Marvin reminded his fellow whites that "[a]s citizens before the law the freedmen must in all respects be our equals."[11] In his message to the state convention in October, the governor elaborated upon his understanding of that civil equality. He advised the convention that it need not give blacks the right to sit on juries, hold public office or vote. In short, they were to have no political rights. All it need do, he explained, was protect them in their person and property.[12] A committee of three former slaveholders echoed Governor Marvin's advice in their report to the convention: "Nor will it be insisted, we presume, that the emancipated slave, technically denominated a Freedman, occupies any higher position in the scale of rights and privileges than did the free Negro."[13]

The model of civil equality which white Floridians apparently had in mind was the status that free persons of color had "enjoyed" during slavery. Basically, these one thousand free persons of color had been allowed to exercise a limited set of civil rights. They could purchase, hold and convey property, and transmit it to their heirs. They could sue and be sued in the state courts. They could move from place to place in the state freely. They could invoke the writ of habeas corpus. The limitations on their freedom were substantial, however:

[T]he law required every free black to have a white "guardian" appointed by a judge of probate. He could not lawfully keep or use firearms or buy them, or powder, lead, shot or even spirituous liquor without the consent of this guardian. He was forbidden to purchase or have poisonous drugs under any circumstances. He was forbidden to use abusive or provoking language or to lift his hand in opposition to any person "not a negro or mulatto." He could be a witness in the courts only when "slaves, free negroes or mulattos" were involved. In case of an execution against him, "without payment in five days" he might be "sold as a slave." He could be lawfully "whipped" for committing offenses which entailed no such punishment for the white man. He could be apprehended for vagrancy and "sold as a slave" for a limited period. Free negroes were required to pay a small special capitation tax, and if one failed to pay this, he was liable to be sold as a slave till by labor he paid up the debt.[14]

As one scholar has observed, "The rights of the free Negro had been so restricted that, legally and socially, he was little better off than a slave."[15] Ironically, the convention committee had summarized its recommendation on rights for the freedmen by pointing out that it sought to preserve the "better aspects" of slavery.[16]

The convention heeded the governor's advice and that of its committee. It abolished slavery but adopted a constitution that kept blacks subordinated and preserved white control of the government. These actions reflected a widespread belief among white Floridians that, as one Florida newspaper declared in July 1865, whites were the dominant race and would remain so in "political power, wealth, intellect, energy, ambition, education, self-possession, and self-dependence."[17] Most white Floridians considered the Negro "but a few removes from brute creation"; and Florida newspapers approvingly quoted Dr. Josiah C.

Nott of Alabama, who said that blacks could be civilized only if kept in a subordinate position.[18]

Given their belief in the inferiority of blacks, white Floridians naturally assumed that that fact justified some differential treatment before the law.[19] Moreover, they insisted on retaining the discretion to determine those instances. Thus the legislature which met in December 1865 ratified the Thirteenth Amendment, but only upon "the understanding that it [did] not confer upon Congress the power to legislate on the status of the freedmen in this state."[20] Florida intended to preserve untrammeled its authority to define that status, and it exercised that authority early in 1866. Like many other Southern states, it enacted a series of laws that circumscribed the right of blacks to contract, imposed apprenticeship requirements, prescribed differential punishments for blacks, prohibited intermarriage between the races, taxed blacks to support schools, forbade them from carrying firearms, and subjected them to severe penalties for vagrancy.[21] As the superintendent for Florida's Negro schools said in 1866: "White citizens would resist any legislation that would appear to put freedmen on equality with whites."[22]

Florida radicals immediately denounced these Black Codes. On February 8, 1866, freedmen, meeting in the Baptist Church at Fernandina, adopted a resolution condemning the new laws and demanding "civil rights for all citizens."[23] When the freedmen demanded civil rights for themselves, they meant that the law should treat them the same as it treated whites, without regard to the color of their respective skins. This was the intent of the 1866 Civil Rights Act, as they understood it; and the provisions of the Black Codes clearly conflicted with that law. Unfortunately, it was not then vigorously enforced in Florida.[24]

In these circumstances, the radical demand fell on deaf ears, at least in Florida. The court records of the period illustrate the problem. A Hernando County court sold a freedman for his labor for eleven months because he was unable to pay a $40 debt. In Bradford County criminal court, a seventeen-year-old freedman was sold for three years' labor because he could not pay a $200 fine, which had been imposed for riding his employer's horse without permission. Later Freedmen's Bureau records indicate that the man who purchased him routinely and severely beat him.[25] The cries of these freedmen were heard in Congress, however. Section 1 of the Fourteenth Amendment was Congress's answer to the radical demand. The freedmen understood that it addressed their plight: it guaranteed them the civil equality they sought.

Initially, white Floridians dismissed the Fourteenth Amendment as a "mere electioneering document."[26] The charge was a plausible one, since the amendment did become the Republican Party platform in the fall Congressional campaign in the North. More specifically, they viewed it as an "attempt to keep the Union divided until 1870," by which time the radicals would have elected "one of their number" president.[27] In this view the amendment was "designed solely to perpetuate party ascendancy, not to subserve the public good."[28]

Section 3, which was said to disfranchise "ninety-nine hundredths of the Southern people,"[29] was the primary basis for these charges. It was thus the "most obnoxious" provision in the amendment.[30] Section 3 was especially obnoxious because it required white Floridians "to ostracise and proscribe all of our citizens deemed worthy of trust in the past."[31] This prospect galled them. They could not do it because "[w]e are required to unite in *affixing the brand* [of treason] *and imposing the punishment.*"[32] Even more galling, the disability was made "far more fatal and revolting" by the process specified for its removal:

Congress may remove it *in any individual case*. Not remove as to the whole class of proscripts, but from such individuals as shall, by servile solicitations, win the favor of two-thirds of a Congress inimical to our people. The purpose is, and the tendency would be, to demoralize our citizens,—to make them fawning crawlers after Congressional favor,—to fill Washington with some exemption-seekers, whose pardon would depend on their treachery to every virtuous and manly instinct, and on their pledges of slavish obedience and devotion to alien interests and prejudices. Could it be expected that we would both brand and punish our best citizens as perjurers, and then tempt and invite them to infamy, by making the punishment remissible through disgraceful self-abasement? Better far to make their proscription unconditional and irremovable.[33]

White Floridians also objected strongly to Section 2, which they correctly understood as intended to punish them for refusing to extend the right to vote to the freedmen. White Floridians abhorred the prospect of the newly freed blacks casting ballots. They were considered "'shiftless, improvident, idle,' and unfitted for voting."[34] Governor Walker had expressed the prevailing view on the suffrage question a year earlier when he said in his inaugural address to the legislature that "Florida could never give in to the demand for Negro suffrage. Much as I have worshipped the Union," he said, "and as much as I would rejoice to see my state once more a recognized member," it would be better, "a thousand times better, that she should remain out of the Union, even as one of her subjugated provinces" than to return "'eviscerated of her manhood,' despoiled of her honor, recreant of her duty, and without her self-respect," which would result from granting the freedmen the right to vote.[35] As in all Southern states, the chief objection to the Fourteenth Amendment was thus to Sections 2 and 3. So universal was the white opposition to the amendment that one Florida editor declared in mid-November, just four days before the legislature met: "Having seen no evidence of favor to the Constitutional Amendment from any respectable quarter in the South, we have felt no disposition to discuss its merits."[36]

The governor and the legislature did address the merits, including the merits of Section 1. David Walker had been elected governor in November 1865. An antebellum Whig who had opposed secession, he nevertheless shared the general political views of the planter class. Not surprisingly, Governor Walker urged rejection. Of Section 1, he said: "These two Sections [1 and 5] taken together, give Congress the power to legislate in all cases touching the citizenship, life, liberty or property of every individual in the Union, of whatever race or color, and leave no further use for the State governments. It is in fact a measure of consolidation entirely changing the form of the government."[37] The governor did not object to the guarantees of equal protection or due process themselves, much less wail that they would vouchsafe blacks still other rights such as the right to bear arms (which would have been the case, of course, had the due process clause or any other clause of Section 1 been understood to incorporate the Bill of Rights). He would scarcely have overlooked that fact—had it been a fact—because he had been personally involved in an ongoing dispute between the state's attorney general and the legislature over the freedman's right to own firearms.[38] Instead, Governor Walker went right to the one plausible objection to Section 1: it carried within it the seed of consolidation which Congress, under Section 5, could sow and reap.

The Senate and House Committees on Federal Relations, to whom the amendment was referred for study and report, concurred with Governor Walker. Like him, they expressed no fears that Section 1 incorporated the Bill of Rights. They did object to its consolidating effect. The Senate report stated: "From the moment of its engraftment upon the Constitution of the United States, the States would in effect cease to exist as bodies politic."[39] The House elaborated:

The first section of this Amendment, considered in connection with the fifth, is virtually an annulment of State authority in regard to rights of citizenship. It invests the Congress of the United States with extraordinary power at the expense of the States. It would so operate that under its provisions all persons, without distinction of color, would become entitled to the "privileges and immunities" of citizens of the States, and among those privileges would be embraced the elective franchise, as well as competency to discharge the duty of jurors. In addition to this, without denying to the State the power and right to legislate and to control to some extent the liberty and property of the citizen, it vests in the General Government the power to annul the laws of a State affecting the life, liberty and property of its people, if Congress should deem them subject to the objections therein specified.[40]

The language of this remonstrance betrays no suspicion that the Fourteenth Amendment itself would, for example, require that Negroes serve as jurors, as presumably would have been the case if it had incorporated the Bill of Rights. Rather, the remonstrance reflects the fear that an irresponsible Congress might impose that requirement and others. Plainly also, the House committee feared that Section 5 licensed Congress to meddle in the state's regulation of matters touching the life, liberty, or property interests of those within the state's juris-diction.

In late 1866 then, Florida's governor and legislature did not worry that Section 1 might fasten upon them all the strictures of the federal Bill of Rights, however defined by the Supreme Court. Rather, they worried that it might prove to be a source of broad, unspecified rights for black Floridians. It never dawned on the governor or the legislature that that source might be the due process clause, or that the author of those rights would be the Supreme Court of the United States. Instead, their fear was the only legitimate one in light of the amendment, as it was then generally understood: Congress could through legislation redefine the privileges and immunities of citizens and, through its enforcement of the due process and equal protection guarantees, could also dictate how the state should treat persons within its jurisdiction. The governor and legislature were simply unwilling to assent to organic changes like these, changes that would "totally destroy the nature of Government."

Within months of the legislature's unanimous rejection of the Fourteenth Amendment, white Floridians nevertheless realized that they would have to accept it. An angry and determined Congress made its ratification a condition of readmission to the Union. By that time—the spring of 1867—the three major factions in the state shared a common view of Section 1 of the amendment: the state must grant blacks "the rights of citizenship"[41] and "perfect equality before the law."[42]

Consequently, the state conservative convention, which met in Tallahassee in late September of that year, endorsed the civil and political equality of all citizens; the sanctity of life, liberty, and property; and an impartial administration of the laws.[43] In short, the state's conservatives accepted the constitutional regime embodied in Section 1. In their address to the voting public, they assured their "colored fellow citizens" that they would "accord him everything that will enure to the white citizen" and promised that "the law that protects the one will necessarily protect the other."[44]

The resolutions of the Constitutional Union Party of Leon County were more specific and in that sense illuminated the contemporary understanding: "That freedom of speech and of the press, education, equality before the law, and in political rights and privileges, are the essentials of any satisfactory reconstruction of the South."[45] The list is illuminating both for what it includes and what it excludes. For example, it includes one (but only one) provision of the Bill of Rights as "essential": freedom of speech and press. Had it been widely understood that the Bill of Rights was the concrete manifestation of the privileges and immunities of citizenship mentioned in Section 1 of the Fourteenth Amendment, all those rights would presumably have been understood to be an "essential" part of the constitutional order that had to be established. Thus one might have expected the Leon County resolution to include at a minimum some statement like "and other guarantees of the Bill of Rights" after they specified "freedom of speech." But their resolution did not. It also includes as essential what is nowhere specified in the Bill of Rights or the Fourteenth Amendment: education.[46]

In addition, conservative Floridians had by the spring of 1867 also acquiesced in Congress's demand that blacks be given the vote. Thus one of the many county conservative meetings held during the summer of 1867 "hailed with pleasure" the prospect that a state convention "honestly elected by the male citizens of the State without regard to color or race" would draft a new constitution "in all aspects in conformity with the Constitution of the United States."[47] During the convention campaign, Florida's conservatives reached out to the blacks and asked them to trust "those with whom their real interests are so closely identified" and thereby "secure their peace and prosperity."[48] The same Governor Walker who had so contemptuously dismissed black suffrage now put the point metaphorically: "The colored man and the white man are in the same boat, and the boat is in a storm . . . if she goes down, they both go down with her; if she lives to reach the shore they are both saved."[49]

Most blacks, however, did not reach out and grasp the hand which conservatives extended them. A group of freedmen, meeting on Capitol Square in Tallahassee on a Saturday in mid-April 1867, resolved:

[T]hose who have unswervingly for years looked in and watched our welfare, who have by their principles, wealth, blood and actions made us free, responsible citizens, are the people whom we can now sincerely trust, and we now unreservedly declare that their interests shall be our interests, their principles our principles: in other words, we are resolved to identify ourselves with the Republican party and sustain the principle of it in all our political actions.[50]

In fact, over the course of the year, a radical coalition of blacks and whites emerged in favor of sweeping social and political changes. This radical coalition was led by three persons: Daniel Richards, a white radical from Illinois; William Saunders, a mulatto ex-barber from Baltimore; and another mulatto, Liberty Billings, a Unitarian minister from New Hampshire who had been a chaplain in a "colored" regiment in the Union Army and who proclaimed everywhere that "Jesus Christ was a Republican."[51] The first two had been sent to Florida by the Republican National Committee to organize the party there. Billings was already in Florida, organizing the newly freed blacks into the Loyal League, which became the engine of radicalism in Florida. By November 1867, Richards boasted that the three men had "literally created the Republican Party in Florida."[52] And when they lost control of the party to the moderates at the 1868 constitutional convention, the radicals howled that the moderates had, like "hungry wolves around a carcass," torn the Republican flesh from the plan of reconstruction which the radicals had pushed.[53] That plan did not, however, reflect a different sense of what the pending Fourteenth Amendment required, at least as a matter of law.

There is no evidence, for example, that Florida radicals ever considered the first eight amendments to the Constitution the *sine qua non* of the legal or constitutional order they favored. Concededly, those amendments could have been viewed as a specification of the rights that would secure person and property. Florida radicals never made that argument, however. In fact, in their 1868 memorial to Congress, the radicals admitted that they had taken the then current Florida constitution and made only "such changes in it as the altered circumstances seemed to require."[54] Had they understood those altered circumstances to include Florida's being bound by the national Bill of Rights, they would have drafted Article I of their proposed constitution differently. Instead, that article contained provisions inconsistent with some of the guarantees found in the Bill of Rights. If asked about the relationship of the national Bill of Rights to the constitutional order they favored, Florida radicals might even have agreed that its guarantees were consistent with the order they favored. They were never asked that question, however, because the debate was not framed in those terms.

Josiah Walls, who represented Florida in Congress in the early 1870s, considered himself an exponent of Republican principles; and he emphasized the terms within which the debate did proceed: "The touchstone of the black common view of political rights and human equality rested upon the Declaration of Independence and the political traditions of the 18th century."[55] His view was that "racial inferiority rested on inferior racial opportunities, not inferior racial characteristics."[56] Walls recognized that the "protection of [one's] natural and inalienable rights required political power in government,"[57] and as a congressman he argued that the national government was "the guardian of the liberties of all its subjects."[58] This view is wholly consistent with a straightforward reading of the Fourteenth Amendment. First, it was seen as imposing an affirmative obligation upon the states (1) to protect their citizens in the exercise of their natural and inalienable rights, and otherwise (2) to insure the fair and equal treatment of all persons within the respective states. Second, it was understood to give Congress the power to enforce that obligation if, in its political judgment, a state had been derelict in its duty.

Moderate Republicans shared that view. Early in 1867 a group of local businessmen established the Union Republican Club of Jacksonville. Its conservative critics denounced it as "the head-quarters of the Florida Radicals ... vile wretches who would stir [the freedmen] to any action calculated to produce division."[59] In fact, the Union Club took a moderate position, at least relative to the position taken by Messrs. Billings, Saunders, and Richards. Its goal was to draft "a platform upon which certain Democrats would be willing to unite with them in carrying out Congressional Reconstruction."[60]

The club's Declaration of Principles said only that "[n]o distinction founded on race or color ought to abridge or in any way interfere with the civil or political rights and privileges of any citizen of the United States."[61] Later that spring, the club resolved that "the people of this State shall be protected in their civil and political rights by equal and impartial laws."[62] At a subsequent meeting, the club adopted a committee report that "there can be no adequate security for rights of person and property until 'freedom of speech' is fully acknowledged and guaranteed in [the Southern states]."[63] The club favored "early instruction of the Freedmen in respect to their rights and duties as citizens" and a "well-devised" and "impartial system of common education."[64] It also endorsed "the measures proposed by Congress" for Reconstruction.[65]

The sum and substance of the moderate agenda in Florida was captured in the Union Club's statement that "the hope of a permanent reconstruction of these states rests in the supremacy of law; freedom of speech; security of person and property and the triumph of the Republican Party in the South."[66] In other words, the moderate agenda embodied two distinct parts: one was a commitment to a particular legal or constitutional order; the other was advocacy of a specific political program. The two should not be confused. Section 1 of the Fourteenth Amendment, supplemented by the Reconstruction Act's requirement that blacks be given the right to vote, established the legal or constitutional order.

All parties accepted that legal order, though with varying degrees of enthusiasm. The legal order reflected a belief that persons should be free to rise according to their individual talent and character. Governor Reed succinctly stated this position in an open letter to the *Florida Union* in July 1868: "I believe that *all* men have equal natural *rights* and that only intellectual and moral supremacy should obtain. If the 'negro' can secure *such* supremacy over the white man, I can see no reason why legal barriers should be imposed."[67] And the governor clearly thought that the freedmen could prosper in freedom if only equality before the law were assured. He said: "Under the most unfavorable circumstances—no adequate security protections, in the midst of prejudice and demoralization consequent upon the war—the freedman has given sufficient assurance of his capacity and qualification for self-subsistence and freedom."[68] A year earlier, Governor Walker had made the same point in an impromptu speech to a gathering of freedmen in Tallahassee. He pledged that the law would protect them in their exercise of their rights and then urged them to evaluate all persons as individuals:

If one black man robs my chicken coop that is no reason why I should denounce the whole black race as robbers and thieves; and so if one white man cheats a black man that is no reason why you should denounce the entire white race as scoundrels and enemies. There are bad white men and there are bad black men. Let us punish both alike, and let the balance of us live together as friends and christians ought to do.[69]

The parties did not agree, however, on the political program that would best serve Florida. While the ensuing political struggle took place within the legal order ordained by a radical Congress, that order "left room for compromise and concession."[70] Although the meaning of the Fourteenth Amendment ceased to be a major issue in Florida, the resulting compromises and concessions do shed light on the participants' understanding of the amendment. After all, the overriding political issue was whether blacks or whites would control the Reconstruction government.[71] The answer to that question would determine whether the new government would give priority to general economic development or to the protection and advancement of its black citizens.

The constitutional convention met in Tallahassee on January 20, 1868.[72] Forty-three of the forty-six convention delegates were Republican. The Republicans were almost evenly split, however, between radicals and moderates. The eighteen black delegates and their few white allies opposed the remaining Republicans and Democrats, all of whom were white.[73] This divided convention made no progress for weeks as moderate and radical Republicans engaged in parliamentary shenanigans and plied delegates with booze and money, which, railed one critic, "was like tendering bread to a starving man."[74] Finally, the convention dissolved into two competing conventions, each claiming to be the "real" convention and each offering a draft constitution. Eventually, federal authorities approved the moderate or "Monticello" constitution.[75] It was submitted to the people, who ratified it and elected Harrison Reed, the moderate Republican candidate, governor in May 1868.[76] Conservative whites breathed a sigh of relief. Radicalism had been sent "howling from [their] midst."[77]

The differences between the two proffered constitutions illustrate both the reason for that relief and the scope of discretion which public officials thought they enjoyed in conforming their state's legal order to the commands of the Fourteenth Amendment. There were only three significant differences. First, the moderate constitution disfranchised far fewer whites than did the radical constitution. Second, the moderate constitution gave the governor the right to appoint most local officials, making it possible for whites to control local governments in predominantly black communities. Contrariwise, the radical constitution had provided for the direct election of local officials. Third and finally, the moderate constitution, by specifying that every county was entitled to one representative and that no county could have more than four, limited the number of representatives that could be elected from the more populous black belt counties. The radical constitution would have made representation proportional to population. Under that scheme, populous Leon County would have had seven representatives, for example, while four other sparsely settled counties would have shared a representative.

The latter difference is especially instructive in terms of the contemporary understanding of the equal protection clause of the Fourteenth Amendment and the government's general obligation to protect the natural and inalienable rights of its citizens. The radical constitution embodied a one-person, one-vote principle. The moderate constitution was intended to dilute the political power of black voters. Although the dispute over these competing modes of representation was critical, both sides treated it as an open question of public policy rather than one whose answer was dictated by the Fourteenth Amendment or by the government's duty to protect its citizens.

Other aspects of the constitution are equally instructive. For example, Section 28 of Article XIV stated that "[t]here shall be no civil or political distinction in this State on account of race, color or previous condition of servitude." This provision reflected the common Republican understanding of what the principles of the Declaration of Independence required in their time and place. It thus harmonized the Florida constitution with Section 1 of the Fourteenth Amendment, understood generally to require respect for the fundamental rights of citizens and the fair and equal treatment of all persons.

As in other Southern states, unreconciled conservative critics still railed against the implications they read into that guarantee:

Now, your new provision does not in terms propose social equality of the races, [but] it unquestionably undertakes to secure civil and political equality; and under it there may be negro jurors, Constables, Sheriffs, Clerks, Legislators, Judges, Governors and Congressmen. It goes further: under it, there may be negro administrators on the estates of white men and negro guardians for white children. Moreover, the word "civil," as employed in the section quoted, is, in the estimation of many, equivalent to social and includes all the rights and privileges that that phrase conveys; and if so, then the Legislature may provide for mixed schools—for intermarriage between the races—for entertainment at hotels, seats in railroad cars and in churches. If we are wrong in defining the words employed, let those better skilled in construing legal terms enlighten us; but if we are right, then reasons suggest themselves why the fate of the Constitution should be left to those who framed it, and to those who are not startled at the idea of negro equality not only at the ballot box but in the social relations.[78]

Obviously, some conservatives still clung to their old views on the equality of the races. Civil equality might be tolerable. Political equality was indefensible both because blacks were not fit to vote and because it would lead to that dreaded social equality. Give the Negro the right to vote, reasoned one editor, and he would soon win public office in areas dominated by blacks; and then the equality question "would be settled forever, and the unnatural doctrine of miscegenation would be firmly established."[79] Intemperate as these criticisms were, they hardly suggested that the conservatives suspected, much less believed, that Section 1 of the Fourteenth Amendment obliged Florida to grant blacks all the guarantees of the Bill of Rights. Rather, the concern reflected political and sociological realities. Freedmen would use the vote to advance their interests. And if blacks and whites mixed together in public places, they or at least some of them would mix together privately. After all, they already had, as the huge mulatto population demonstrated.

More generally, the persons who drafted the 1868 Florida constitution could not have understood that the Fourteenth Amendment incorporated the first eight amendments to the Constitution and applied them against the states. Both the general structure and the particular provisions of the Florida Declaration of Rights are inconsistent with the incorporation thesis. Admittedly, the 1868 constitution includes some guarantees in the same or virtually the same language as is used in the Bill of Rights. In other instances, however, it states analogous guarantees very differently from the way in which they appear in the Bill of Rights. Some guarantees in the Florida declaration appear to be broader than those in the Bill of Rights; other guarantees seem narrower. Moreover, the 1868 constitution does not include at all some guarantees found in the Bill of Rights. The structure of the Declaration of Rights thus reflects a belief that the state was substantially free to frame a set of guarantees independent of, and to some degree inconsistent with, the Bill of Rights. In other words, Florida's Declaration of Rights and the Bill of Rights created overlapping rather than identical universes.

An analysis of particular provisions supports this conclusion. Sections 7 ("excessive bail shall not be required, nor excessive fines imposed, nor cruel or unusual punishment imposed"), 14 ("no soldier shall, in time of peace, be quartered in any house, except with the consent of the owner, nor in time of war, except in manner prescribed by law"), and 20 ("the right of the people to be secure in either person, houses, papers, and effects, against unreasonable seizures and searches, shall not be violated, and no warrants issued but in probable cause, supported by oath or affirmation, particularly describing the place or places to be searched, and the person or persons, and thing or things to be seized") prove that the framers of the Florida constitution were familiar with the language of the Bill of Rights and capable of incorporating it verbatim (or nearly so). Yet the third, fourth, and eighth amendments were the only amendments they "incorporated" in that manner.

The strategy of particularizing and thereby both contracting and expanding the scope of guarantees also found in the Bill of Rights is evident in Florida's treatment of those subjects addressed in the First Amendment: freedom of speech and the press, free exercise of religion, prohibition against the establishment of religion, and the right to petition the government for redress of grievances. The Florida declaration addresses these subjects in four separate sections. Section 5 guarantees "forever" the "free exercise of religious profession and worship" but qualifies that guarantee by adding that "the liberty of conscience hereby secured shall not be so construed as to justify licentiousness, or practices subversive of the peace and safety of the State." Section 23 deals with the establishment issue in the language of neutrality rather than hostility toward religion. It says simply: "No preference can be given by law to any church, sect, or mode of worship." Such language scarcely dictates a doctrine of strict separation between church and state (though it presumably leaves that option open as a matter of public policy). Section 11 guarantees the people the right to assemble and petition for redress of grievances, but it also guarantees them the right "to instruct their representatives." Section 10 guarantees "every citizen" the right "fully [to] speak out and write his sentiments on all subjects" but cautions that citizens are "responsible for the abuse of that right." Moreover, the section makes publication "from good motives" a defense to any libel action.

Some provisions of the Florida declaration contradict analogous provisions in the Bill of Rights. Although much of Section 9 tracks the language of the Sixth Amendment, it departs from that amendment in two particulars. One, it permits the legislature to waive the requirement of indictment by grand jury in cases of petit larceny. Two, it does not limit the state's obligation to compensate for takings for "public use." Moreover, the Florida declaration contains no speedy trial guarantee. It also explicitly permits parties to waive their right to a jury trial in civil cases.

Finally, at least one guarantee in Florida's declaration is given a somewhat different, or at least more explicit, alternative justification than is found in the analogous provision in the Bill of Rights. Section 2 of the declaration declares:

"The people shall have the right to bear arms in defence of themselves and of the lawful authority of the State." The Second Amendment justifies the right to bear arms solely in terms of the need to maintain a militia for public defense. This striking difference in justificatory language suggests that the Florida provision was intended to have a different, perhaps broader, scope.

Florida's reaction to legislative proposals for the advancement of black rights in the years following ratification of the Fourteenth Amendment also illuminates the state's understanding of its commands. The moderate Republicans did not need to make any concessions to black voters in the 1868 legislative campaign; and Governor Reed, in his inaugural address, made no specific promises to his black supporters. He contented himself with a paraphrase of the Declaration of Independence, saying "all men are by their nature free and endowed with equal rights."[80] He offered no civil rights bills. Indeed, he vetoed a law which the legislature passed, assuring all citizens that they could ride together on public conveyances.[81] Apparently Governor Reed did not believe that segregation in public conveyances violated either the Fourteenth Amendment or the state constitutional guarantee against class discrimination. Besides, he felt the bill would cause a race war.[82] Similarly, Republicans resisted efforts to create a system of common schools because some blacks initially insisted that they be "open to all," and white legislators insisted on a segregation clause. They finally compromised. The 1869 law permitted but did not require separate schools.[83] Almost all were in fact separate.[84]

As more and more Democrats deserted the Reed administration, white Republicans "rediscovered" the importance of their black allies. In those circumstances, blacks were able to achieve some political goals. In 1870 the legislature required equal accommodation in railroad cars.[85] The 1873 legislature adopted a civil rights bill, extending the principle of equal treatment to all in public accommodations; but it also specifically authorized continued school segregation.[86] Presumably, Florida's Reconstruction legislators believed that the Fourteenth Amendment permitted these choices.

The lesson from this legislative record as to the meaning of Section 1 is clear. Floridians understood that the amendment commanded equality before the law, but they also believed that it permitted a state legislature broad discretion in fashioning public policy. Specifically, Florida's governor and its legislature did not insist on a color-blind standard where public resistance would have made such insistence problematic. In other words, the Fourteenth Amendment only established a principled framework within which the state remained free to decide the "who-gets-what" questions that dominate the political process. It did not supplant the political process by dictating particular policy choices.

In making these policy choices, moderate Republicans "preferred to collaborate with native state leaders who were their economic allies rather than with their own radical political associates."[87] As a result, Florida's blacks simply lacked the political power to enact their legislative agenda. They "were never able to influence policy in proportion to their voting strength."[88] Blacks never received full support from white Republicans for legislation they deemed essential to their well-being. Indeed, civil rights bills repeatedly failed to pass because Republican votes were cast against them.[89]

Within a few years blacks would also lose the protections of the legal and constitutional order ostensibly guaranteed by Section 1 of the Fourteenth Amendment and formally enshrined in Florida's Reconstruction constitution. They did not lose those protections because there was any misunderstanding about the meaning or intended scope of Section 1, however. They lost those protections for two reasons. First, the resurgent Democrats captured control of the state government in 1876 and thereafter systematically excluded blacks from the political process and successfully relegated them to economic dependency. Second, Congress failed to use its powers under Section 5 of the Fourteenth Amendment (and Section 2 of the Fifteenth Amendment) to preserve and enforce the civil and political rights of blacks.

In the century-long reign of white supremacy that followed, the more hopeful prospects that Colonel John T. Sprague, the assistant commissioner for the Florida Freedmen's Bureau, had predicted in the spring of 1867 were all but forgotten. After commenting on some injustices suffered by the freedmen, the colonel hastened to promise: "Time and prosperity will, however, regulate these evils, and as communities, families and individuals feel the necessity of the colored man, prejudices will subside, old associations will be renewed, kindly relations must prevail without the feeling of servitude, and mutual responsibilities will insure justice in the course of law, and legislatures will see the necessity of enacting judicious laws to insure the prosperity of the State."[90]

NOTES

1. Joe M. Richardson, *The Negro in the Reconstruction of Florida, 1865–1877* (Tallahassee: Florida State University, 1965), 1. The 1870 census counted 96,057 whites and 91,689 blacks.

2. George Washington Smith, "Carpetbag Imperialism in Florida 1862–1868," *Florida Historical Quarterly* 27 (July 1948): 99.

3. Jerrell H. Shofner, "Political Reconstruction of Florida," *Florida Historical Quarterly* 45 (October 1966): 145, 159 (all parties encouraged immigration from the North in order to facilitate economic development).

4. In addition to the freedmen and the Northern entrepreneurs, there were the planter class, the former Whigs who had opposed secession, and the poor whites. A Union general divided Florida whites into the following three classes: (1) the wealthy and well educated; (2) the partially educated, who were "more numerous"; and (3) poor whites, whom he described as "idle and vicious" men who "hated the freedmen." Richardson, *The Negro in the Reconstruction of Florida*, 4.

5. See generally Shofner, "Political Reconstruction of Florida."

6. *Tallahassee Sentinel*, 9 September 1867.

7. P. Klingman, "Josiah Walls: Florida's Black Congressman of Reconstruction" (Ph.D. diss., University of Florida, 1972), 99. Cf. *St. Augustine Examiner*, 31 August 1867 (the remarks of a "colored candidate for Congress" in Georgia were cited as proof

that the freedmen were mere puppets of the radicals. Mr. Fickling, the candidate, said: "[W]e are . . . menacingly instructed and impertinently commanded to . . . swallow down all the ingredients of the Radical cauldron"). A Louisiana black described the same plight when he remarked:

> As a race [we] are between the hawk of Republican demagogism and the buzzards of Democratic prejudices. The aspirants for position in our party threaten us with excommunication if we do not follow every jack o'lantern who raises his feeble light, and the Democrats invite us to annihilation if we turn away from these Republican jack o'lanterns. (Joe G. Taylor, "Louisiana: An Impossible Task," in *Reconstruction and Redemption in the South*, ed. Otto H. Olsen (Baton Rouge: Louisiana State University Press, 1980), 223)

8. Richardson, *The Negro in the Reconstruction of Florida*, 130.

9. *The Floridian*, 26 September 1865, quoted in M. Cahill, "The Negro in Florida during Reconstruction 1865–1877," (M.A. thesis, University of Florida, 1954), 27.

10. William W. Davis, *The Civil War and Reconstruction in Florida* (New York: Columbia University Press, 1913), 359.

11. Ibid., 358. Governor Marvin made these statements during an intense canvass of the state during the late summer and early fall of 1865. He "took the bull by the horns, going over the state and explaining to the people what he expected of them."

12. Governor Walker echoed that recommendation two months later when he advised the new legislature on its responsibilities. Richardson, *The Negro in the Reconstruction of Florida*, 134.

13. *A Journal of the Proceedings of the House of Representatives of the General Assembly of the State of Florida, at Its Fourteenth Session, Begun and Held at the Capitol, in the City of Tallahassee, on Monday, December 18, 1865* (Tallahassee: Office of the Floridian: Dyke & Sparhawk, 1865), 53.

14. Davis, *The Civil War and Reconstruction in Florida*, 414–15.

15. Cahill, "The Negro in Florida during Reconstruction," 10. See also Richardson, *The Negro in the Reconstruction of Florida*, 137 ("The State appeared to be attempting to give the Negro a position somewhere between slavery and full citizenship").

16. *House Journal* (1865), 58–69.

17. See also *New Era*, 8 June 1865, quoted in Joe M. Richardson, "Florida Black Codes," *Florida Historical Quarterly* 47 (1969): 365, 367 ("[T]his is a government of WHITE MEN" and "inferiority of social and political position for the Negro race, and superiority for the white race, is the natural order of American Society").

18. Ibid., 368. See also Jerrell H. Shofner, *Nor Is It Over Yet: Florida in the Era of Reconstruction, 1863–1877* (Gainesville: University Presses of Florida, 1974), 84 (difference between white and freedman was thought to be the difference "between man and beast").

19. Richardson, *The Negro in the Reconstruction of Florida*, 135:

> Since the emancipated slave occupied no higher position than did the free Negro, it logically followed . . . that the general assembly had authority to discriminate in the case of the freedman. The report recommended that when the law called for fine and imprisonment, there be superadded the alternative of standing in the pillory or thirty-nine lashes or both. The discrimination was based on the difference in the social and political status of the two races. "To *degrade* a white man by punishment," the report stated, would make a bad member of society and a dangerous political agent. To fine and imprison a freedman, on the other hand, would punish the State instead of the individual.

20. *Journal of the Proceedings of the Senate of the General Assembly of the State of Florida at the Fourteenth Session, Begun and Held at the Capitol, in the City of Talla-hassee on Monday, December 18th, 1865* (Tallahassee: Hart & Shober, 1865), 73. *House Journal* (1865), 96.

21. See Theodore B. Wilson, *The Black Codes of the South* (University, Ala.: University of Alabama Press, 1965), 143–44 (in adopting these codes, the Florida legislature proved itself the most "bigoted and shortsighted of all the southern legislatures of 1865–1866"). But see John Wallace, *Carpet-bag Rule in Florida: The Inside Workings of the Reconstruction of Civil Government in Florida after the Close of the Civil War* (Jacksonville, Fla.: Da Costa Printing and Publishing House, 1888), 35–36 ("[W]e are of the opinion that any other people, under like circumstances, would have passed the same character of laws relative to the freedmen").

22. Davis, *The Civil War and Reconstruction in Florida*, 423. Cf. *St. Augustine Examiner*, 8 September 1866 (South unanimously agrees that it is bound to give black people "perfect equality before the law").

23. Richardson, "The Negro in the Reconstruction of Florida," 226.

24. Davis, *The Civil War and Reconstruction in Florida*, 433.

25. Shofner, *Nor Is It Over Yet*, 87.

26. *Semi-Weekly Floridian*, 2 October 1866.

27. Ibid., 11 May 1866.

28. Ibid., 2 October 1866.

29. Ibid., 11 May 1866.

30. *Weekly Floridian*, 6 September 1867. See also *Semi-Weekly Floridian*, 5 October 1866 ("The features of the third section . . . are monstrous").

31. *Weekly Floridian*, 18 January 1867.

32. Ibid.

33. Ibid.

34. Jerrell H. Shofner, "A Failure of Moderate Republicanism," in *Reconstruction and Redemption in the South*, ed. Otto H. Olsen (Baton Rouge: Louisiana State University Press, 1980), 131.

35. Richardson, *The Negro in the Reconstruction of Florida*, 134. The debate over Section 2 was nevertheless somewhat muted in Florida because it would lose no representation. Florida's population was so small that it would have been entitled only to one representative even if blacks were counted for that purpose. See, e.g., *Semi-Weekly Floridian*, 29 May 1866 (Florida "will lose nothing" under Section 2 of the Fourteenth Amendment, though the "loss in our [i.e., the Southern] delegation" will be 25).

36. *St. Augustine Examiner*, 10 November 1866.

37. *Senate Journal—2d Session, 14th General Assembly, Journal of the Proceedings of the Senate of the General Assembly of the State of Florida, Begun and Held at the Capitol in the City of Tallahassee on Wednesday, November 14, 1866* (Tallahassee: J. B. Oliver, 1866), 8; *House Journal—2d Session, 14th General Assembly, A Journal of the Proceedings of the House of Representatives of the General Assembly of the State of Florida, Begun and Held at the Capitol, in the City of Tallahassee, on Wednesday, November 14, 1866* (Tallahassee: Dyke & Sparhawk, 1866), 11.

38. Richardson, "Florida's Black Codes," 372.

39. Federal Relations Committee Report, *Senate Journal–2d Session* (1866), 101–3.

40. Federal Relations Committee Report, *House Journal–2d Session* (1866), 75–80.

41. *East Florida Banner*, 12 October 1867.

42. *St. Augustine Examiner*, 8 September 1866.

43. *East Florida Banner*, 12 October 1867; *St. Augustine Examiner*, 19 October 1867.

44. *East Florida Banner*, 12 October 1867; *St. Augustine Examiner*, 19 October 1867.

45. *St. Augustine Examiner*, 7 September 1867.

46. Florida's freedmen, like freedmen throughout the South, prized education; and as they acquired political power, they demanded that the state provide "free" education. Whites in Florida seemed less ambivalent toward the education of Negroes than did most of their Southern brethren, though some "poor whites" did oppose "Negro schooling." Cahill, "The Negro in Florida during Reconstruction," 50–51.

47. *St. Augustine Examiner*, 27 July 1867.

48. *Weekly Floridian*, 26 March 1867. Once the conservatives realized that blacks would have to be given the franchise, they tried to convince themselves that their former slaves could be persuaded to support them rather than the radicals. Shofner, "Political Reconstruction of Florida," 159–60. One argument was that blacks could be pressured economically:

> From . . . his present dependent condition, we entertain no fear as to the course which he will pursue in the exercise of the elective franchise. . . . Nineteen twentieths of the black voters can be influenced and controlled by those who give them food, lodging and employment. It lies now in the power of the white employer to cast as many ballots in our future elections as he may have adult male negroes in his service. (*Weekly Floridian*, 29 March 1867)

Another argument assumed that the blacks would be influenced by the supposed ties of friendship that had bound slaves to their masters, and still another reflected the belief that blacks would come to understand that, as Southerners, their political interests coincided with those of the conservatives.

49. *Weekly Floridian*, 23 April 1867. See also Nita Katherine Pyburn, "David Selby Walker: Educational Statesman of Florida," *Florida Historical Quarterly* 34 (1955): 159, 167.

50. This rejection refueled the traditional conservative antipathy toward blacks, and anti-Negro sentiment grew over the last half of 1867. Ralph Peek, "Military Reconstruction and the Growth of Anti-Negro Sentiment in Florida, 1867," *Florida Historical Quarterly* 47 (1969): 380.

51. Joe M. Richardson, "The Freedman's Bureau in Florida" (M.A. thesis, Florida State University, 1959). 70.

52. Jerrell H. Shofner, "The Constitution of 1868," *Florida Historical Quarterly* 41 (1963): 356, 358.

53. Memorial to Congress, Misc. Doc. 109, 40th Cong., 2d Sess., 1.

54. Ibid., 2.

55. Klingman, "Josiah Walls," 118.

56. Ibid., 125.

57. Ibid., 119.

58. Ibid., 124.

59. *Weekly Floridian*, 26 March 1867.

60. Shofner, "Political Reconstruction of Florida," 147.

61. *Proceedings of the Union Republican Club of Jacksonville* (1867), 1 (manuscript held at the P. K. Yonge Library of Florida History, University of Florida, Gainesville, Florida).

62. Ibid., 17.

63. Ibid., 20.

64. Ibid., 17.

65. Ibid., 23.

66. Ibid., 19.

67. Philip D. Ackerman, "Florida Reconstruction from Walker through Reed 1865–1873" (Ph.D. diss., University of Florida, 1948), 133.

68. Cahill, "The Negro in Florida during Reconstruction," 76.

69. *St. Augustine Examiner*, 4 May 1867.

70. Shofner, "The Constitution of 1868," 372.

71. *Weekly Floridian*, 19 February, 1867 (the real question was political—who will control state and national governments).

72. Approximately 26,500 persons registered to vote. Of those, about 15,500 were black. Many—perhaps most—of the 11,000 registered whites did not vote. The convention was nevertheless approved by the required 50 percent of all registered voters—14,300 to 203. The 7 December 1867, issue of the *St. Augustine Examiner* reported slightly different figures:

Registered voters	27,521
For convention	13,882
Against convention	111

It castigated those conservative Floridians who had not registered to vote because "[h]ad 223 more voters registered there would have been no Constitutional Convention in this state."

73. The Freedmen's Bureau in Florida did not support the radical faction, as it did in most other Southern states. Thomas Osborn, the head of the Florida Bureau, tried to organize blacks for the Republican Party; but most of them deserted his Lincoln Brotherhood when he aligned himself with the moderate wing of the party. Although Florida conservatives did not like the Bureau, they were grateful "it was headed by a man like Osborn." George R. Bentley, "The Political Activity of the Freedmen's Bureau in Florida," *Florida Historical Quarterly* 28 (1949): 28, 30. During the bitter campaign for the new constitution and legislature that followed the convention, Billings and other radicals accused Bureau officials of prostituting themselves and misusing Bureau funds for "electioneering purposes" (ibid., 6).

74. Cf. Shofner, "The Constitution of 1868," 362. Persons sharing these sentiments called for the creation of "a white man's party," not only in Florida but throughout the South. *St. Augustine Examiner*, 30 November 1867.

75. The story of the constitutional convention is told in Shofner, "The Constitution of 1868." The clash between the moderate and radical factions might have degenerated into armed battle, but Governor Walker asked federal troops to preserve peace and order. They did. Eventually, General Meade ordered both factions to reassemble and subsequently accepted the "more moderate [constitution] on the ground that it was signed by a majority of the Convention" (ibid., 366). The radicals pursued their cause by submitting a "bitter memorial, denouncing the moderate [constitution]" to the Joint Committee on Reconstruction (ibid., 367). It rejected the radical plea and ordered that the moderate constitution be submitted to the people of Florida for their approval.

76. One student of the period describes the subsequent campaign to approve the constitution as "bitter." Radicals denounced it for its "enlargement of the franchise in favor of the disloyal." Richardson, "The Negro in the Reconstruction of Florida," 253–54. The constitution was nevertheless approved—14,520 to 9,491.

77. *Florida Union*, 7 March 1868. William Purham, a Bureau agent, was an influential delegate at the constitutional convention and later claimed that his parliamentary maneuvers on behalf of the moderates had saved Florida from being "niggerized." Shofner, "The Constitution of 1868," 374. That is doubtless why the conservative Edward M. L'Engle declared in a private letter: "The proposed constitution will if adopted not absolutely ruin us." 5 March 1868, E. M. L'Engle Papers, Southern Historical Collection, University of North Carolina, Chapel Hill, North Carolina.

78. *Weekly Floridian*, 24 March 1868.

79. Richardson, *The Negro in the Reconstruction of Florida*, 131.

80. *Journal of the Senate, First Session, Fifteenth Legislature, of the State of Florida, Begun and Held at the Capitol, in the City of Tallahassee, on the Eighth Day of June, and Concluded on the Sixth Day of August, in the Year of our Lord One Thousand Eight Hundred and Sixty-Eight* (Tallahassee: Printed at the Office of the Tallahassee Sentinel, 1868), 5–6.

81. *Tallahassee Sentinel*, 13 August 1868.

82. Shofner, *Nor Is It Over Yet*, 203.

83. Ibid.

84. Ibid., 150–51.

85. Ibid., 223

86. Shofner, "Political Reconstruction of Florida," 164.

87. Ibid., 152. Throughout Reconstruction, the moderate Republicans cooperated with Democrats, "southern men who had served in the Confederate Army." In fact, the "Monticello constitution" was drafted with the help of conservative Democrats. "Florida's First Reconstruction Legislature (A Letter of William H. Gleason to C. W. Holmes, Dated October 10, 1890)," ed. Robert E. Rutherford, *Florida Historical Quarterly* 32 (1953): 41, 42. Governor Reed appointed many such Democrats to his cabinet; and he and his successor "balanced" appointments to local offices:

> In the legislature, where the democrats were in a majority in the counties, or in the senatorial districts, the Governor appointed a democrat as County clerk, and a Republican as County Judge, and gave the democrats a majority of Commissioners. When a republican senator and member of legislature were elected, he then made the Clerk of Court a republican, and the County Judge a democrat. We had five judicial districts, and three out of the five judges were democrats. ("Florida's First Reconstruction Legislature," 41–42)

Though Florida "redeemers" would later claim that they were saving their state from carpetbaggers and scalawags, the claim rang hollow: "There [is] little justification for the old assertion that white Floridians were helpless under a corrupt government staffed with outsiders and supported by ignorant Negro voters. . . . Democrats bargained with more or less success at every possible point for concessions during the period." Shofner, "Political Reconstruction of Florida," 169.

88. Shofner, *Nor Is It Over Yet*, 223.

89. Shofner, "Political Reconstruction of Florida," 170.

90. *Weekly Floridian*, 29 March 1867.

10

Ratification in Arkansas

Freedmen in many places are still freedmen, *not* free men.

—An agent of the Freedmen's Bureau in Arkansas,
describing the plight of blacks there to his superior

Arkansas was one of several Southern states that had a functioning, loyal government well before General Lee's surrender. Established in 1864 under the leadership of Governor Isaac Murphy, the Arkansas government was cited by Lincoln that year as an example of restoration that negated the need for more radical Reconstruction. Whatever Lincoln—and, later, Johnson—may have thought of the Murphy government, its critics were legion in Arkansas. On the right, conservatives questioned its legitimacy, arguing that it did not have the confidence of the people. On the left, many Unionists lamented its lack of enthusiasm for the disfranchisement of "rebs" and its insensitivity to the needs of the freedmen. In the fall of 1865, an Arkansan wrote President Johnson: "The present [state] government is a failure, represents nobody, and is nothing in fact."[1]

The Murphy government might nevertheless have survived its Arkansas critics if it had had the unified support of the national government. Unfortunately, its fate became enmeshed in the bitter struggle between the radical Republicans in Congress and the more moderate Johnson in the White House. The fall 1866 election campaign in Arkansas and the subsequent legislative session sealed its demise. In that campaign, the conservatives said that blacks should be given civil rights but not political rights. In particular, conservatives bitterly opposed blacks voting, sitting on juries, or holding office.[2] Conservatives repeatedly raised the specter of black equality, which, they insisted, the "Black Republican" Party would impose on the South.[3] Conservatives in turn were charged with favoring "universal amnesty, indemnity for the state's war losses, assumption of the Confederate debt, repudiation of the national war debt, and a general curtailment of the civil rights of the negro."[4]

The conservatives swept the election that fall. Only five Unionist legislators were elected, all to the House. The legislature promptly vindicated the campaign charges leveled against it by enacting a law that provided pensions to Confederate soldiers, as well as several other bills that benefited Confederate soldiers and officials. It also considered resolutions, first, praising President Johnson for protecting the people from irresponsible radicals and, second, thanking Jefferson Davis for his "noble and patriotic" service.[5] It refused to establish a system of schools for the freedmen. While it did extend to the freedmen those civil rights "demanded by humanity [and] sound public policy," it hedged the grant with some exceptions "essential to the safety of society."[6] Freedmen thus were denied the right to testify, serve on juries, or vote.

During this turbulent period, the Fourteenth Amendment was the subject of intense scrutiny by the state's leading—and very conservative—newspaper. Throughout the spring of 1866, the *Arkansas Daily Gazette* had followed the evolution of the amendment within the Reconstruction Committee. The *Gazette* duly noted the amendment's adoption by Congress in June and later that fall carefully analyzed its language, both generally and section by section.

Earlier in the year, the *Gazette* had expressed its distaste for "the proposed mode" of promulgating constitutional amendments without the participation of the eleven Southern states. The paper approvingly quoted President Johnson, who objected to the "gross inconsistency" of treating the Southern states as "unfit to be represented in Congress" but "fit to ratify a Constitutional amendment." The *Gazette* concluded:

When the amendments come to be presented to the States for ratification, it is hoped they will adopt the same sober view and pursue the same steady course of the Executive. It will still be more favorable to early repose, if the amendment should fail to pass Congress, and thus save the country from the evils of continued agitation. But if the dominant faction persist in demanding amendments, in the name of justice, the Constitution and right, let them at once call a convention of ALL the States, when all can be fairly heard and can at least have the semblance of a voice in framing organic acts, that are to be a bond upon themselves and posterity forever![7]

Later that spring, the *Gazette* reported the "New York Plan of Reconstruction," a plan whose three sections paralleled Sections 2, 3, and 4 of the Fourteenth Amendment. The New York plan contained no provision analogous to Section 1, however; and it did not explicitly grant Congress the power to enforce its provisions "by appropriate legislation."[8] These "omitted" provisions were the very ones, of course, that subsequently became the basis for the *Gazette*'s charge that the Fourteenth Amendment, if ratified, would consolidate all power in the national government.

On July 2, 1866, the *Gazette* ran—without editorial comment—the text "of the proposed amendment to the Constitution of the United States that has passed both Houses of Congress by the Constitutional majority, and which will become a part of the Constitution [if] ratified by the Legislatures of three fourths of the States." The next day the *Gazette* provided its readers with an "abstract" of the Minority Report of the Joint Committee. The abstract emphasized the inconsistency and injustice of submitting the amendment to states that had been excluded from framing it. Thus the *Gazette*'s initial objection to the Fourteenth Amendment remained what its general objection to all constitutional amendments had been six months earlier. The Southern states were improperly—nay, unconstitutionally—being kept out of the Union; and no amendment proposed by what amounted to a rump Congress could be considered valid.

Shortly thereafter, the *Gazette* expanded its general objections to the Fourteenth Amendment, attacking its "omnibus" nature:

One of the greatest outrages committed by the revolutionary party in Congress, is the fact of their putting the various subjects of the proposed amendment to the Constitution in the form of one general amendment. In the present shape, by no possibility can any one of them be approved or rejected, without the ratification or rejection of the whole batch. Heretofore, when a Congress has proposed several amendments to the Constitution, it has always been the practice to put each subject in a separate and distinct amendment, and to submit "all or any" of them for ratification or rejection by the Legislatures. The failure to do so in this case, is a trick of political jugglery, by which the radicals hope to compel the Northern States to adopt all the objectionable features of the proposed amendments, taking advantage of the feeling which exists in the North, that the Southern States should not be permitted hastily and without *some* conditions, to resume their part in the administration of affairs, and forcing them to vote for the bad, to attain whatever of good there is in the amendment.[9]

This was a common, early objection to the Fourteenth Amendment. The objection, while plausible, ignored political realities. Embodying the conditions upon which the rebellious states would be readmitted into the Union, the amendment stated the peace terms which the victorious North intended to dictate to the defeated South. In that sense, it did address a single subject. The subject was simply very broad, and its complexity necessitated multiple provisions.

The *Gazette* predicted that the Southern states would refuse to accept these "degrading terms." Indeed, it assumed that the radicals knew "full well" that the "character" of the Southern people would not permit them to so "dishonor [themselves]." It therefore dismissed the amendment as a crass political stratagem by which "this party [aims] to keep the South in a state of vassalage."[10] These, too, were widely held objections throughout the South.

The *Gazette* had two other general objections to the amendment. One was procedural (and clearly wrong): the amendment had not been "presented" to the President. The *Gazette* mistakenly thought that that failure violated clause seven, Article 3 of the Constitution. The other general objection was substantive. The amendment, which the *Gazette* attributed to "the meddling spirit of New England," sought to accomplish "objects" outside "the purview of the General Government." Presumably, the *Gazette* had in mind "objects" like the incidents of citizenship and the qualifications of voters. As a result, the amendment would establish "a Government, which, under the form of a Republic, will be as despotic as an absolute monarchy."[11]

This latter objection was repeated when the *Gazette* turned its attention specifically to Sections 1 and 5. The *Gazette* shrank in horror at what would follow if Congress were given the power to define the privileges and immunities of citizenship:

Judging from the threats the [radical] party has made, its enunciated doctrines, and uniform course of oppression, it is easy to be perceived that the design is, if the amendment should be adopted, to pass laws by a simple majority, declaring that the "privileges and immunities of citizens of the United States," are rights to hold office, vote, act as jurors, and even to cotract [*sic*] marriage with whomsoever they please, thus giving negroes political and social equality with the whites.[12]

The *Gazette* did not condemn Section 1 for guaranteeing blacks civil, as opposed to political and social, equality. Indeed, it recognized that civil equality was a necessary incident of freedom and endorsed civil rights for blacks:

As free persons, who are dependent upon their own exertions for the means of securing a support they should be allowed to make and enforce contracts, to sue and be sued, to secure themselves against being robbed of their just dues by unprincipled men. That they may be permitted to enjoy the fruits of their labor and dispose of what they may acquire, in whatever manner they may see fit, it is no more than proper that they be allowed to inherit, purchase, sell, lease, hold, or convey all kinds of property, and dispose of the same by wills and testaments.[13]

The *Gazette* did recommend that these civil rights be specified in order to avoid any implication that they included political or social rights such as jury service, office-holding, suffrage, or the right "to intermarry with whites."[14] Given its insistence that any rights guaranteed blacks be specified, it is unlikely that the *Gazette* would have ignored the possibility that the Bill of Rights provided that very specification, had any such possibility been commonly entertained. Quite to the contrary, it was the very generality of the privileges and immunities clause that alarmed the *Gazette*—especially since Congress could, under Section 5, reduce that generality to undesirable and distasteful particulars.

Neither did the *Gazette* condemn Section 1 for guaranteeing blacks due process and equal protection. Indeed, it did not deign to discuss either, suggesting how innocuous these guarantees were to a critic ever alert to the danger that some provision might give blacks and their supporters a basis for demanding more than civil equality. One could hardly object to blacks being given due process, understood as a guarantee of procedural fairness. Indeed, for that very reason the *Gazette* favored permitting blacks to testify:

There can be but little doubt but what the ends of justice would be greatly advanced by permitting all classes to be affiants, and to give evidence in all cases. The object of all judicial investigations is to discover the truth, and we should dispose [*sic*] no means by which that end may be reached. Because of the proneness of some negroes to testify falsely, there is no good reason to reject the testimony of the whole class. The disposition of a part of any order of people to bear false witness, should not destroy the competency of all of them, to testify. The credibility of the testimony of all witnesses, under the general principles of law, is a matter left to the jury to determine.[15]

Similarly, one could not object to blacks being assured the equal protection of the laws, particularly in the context of civil transactions. The *Gazette* conceded that "as an incident to their condition, and a matter of simple justice, they should be held liable to the same punishments, pains and penalties as other classes of the community, and have equal benefits of the rights of personal liberty, personal security and private property."[16] In midsummer the *Gazette* published a letter to the editor that generally reflected the same view:

I suppose about the first thing it [the legislature] will do, is to pass a negro law, giving to freed men the right to contract, to sue and be sued, to be taxed as white men, and to do military duty, when necessity requires it; but further than that, I don't think an Arkansas Legislature will ever go, unless it will be to allow them to give testimony against one another as now, and against a white man as a circumstance, to be corroborated or rejected.[17]

The *Gazette* probably did not foresee that the equal protection clause might be given a broader construction because it assumed the blacks could be considered a legitimate class for purposes of differential treatment in political and social contexts. The *Gazette* asserted, for example, that "[o]ver what little mind his Maker has seen fit to give him hangs the pall of unqualified ignorance."[18] Negroes also had "licentious disposition and indolent natures."[19] These supposed weaknesses of character and intellect were naturally thought to justify differential treatment. Commenting on Governor Murphy's fall message to the legislature, the *Gazette* thus said:

The views of the Governor relative to the bestowal of civil rights upon all classes, appear to us rather equivocal. If he simply recommends the passage of laws, securing to all the equal enjoyment of laws for the protection of person and property . . . his suggestions will doubtless meet with approval. But if he goes to the extent of asking the Assembly to concede, that the negro is a full citizen of the State, and as such, is entitled to an equality of all rights, then in respect to this point, the Executive and the Legislative branches sustain an antipodal relation to each other.[20]

The *Gazette*, for example, consistently rejected black suffrage on the ground that blacks were, as a class, unfit to exercise the privilege. Not surprisingly, the *Gazette* railed against Section 2 of the Fourteenth Amendment because it was "designed to reduce us either to the alternative of granting suffrage to the negroes or having the number of our representatives reduced, thus adding greatly to the political preponderance of the North in Congress."[21] On this question of suffrage, the *Gazette* gleefully quoted the Great Emancipator himself: "I am not, nor ever have been, in favor of making voters . . . of negroes";[22] and it routinely carried news articles reporting opposition elsewhere to Negro suffrage.[23] Contrariwise, the *Gazette* did view the equal protection clause as a bar to "special legislation favoring a petted class." Such legislation was "repugnant to the principles of republican institutions."[24]

The *Gazette*'s analysis of the Fourteenth Amendment reflected the common understanding of the provisions throughout the state, as reflected in other newspaper commentary. The *Des Arc Citizen*, for example, echoed the charge that Congress was no Congress at all because the Southern states were excluded;[25] and the *Fort Smith Tri-Weekly Herald* ridiculed "radical logic" on the point: "If the legislatures of the Southern States should ratify the constitutional amendment, then they are states. If they do not ratify it, they are territories."[26] Endorsing the other general objection to the amendment—its omnibus nature—the *Van Buren Press* called for resistance to "all this doctrine of amendments to the Constitution."[27]

Strong as were these general objections, they paled in comparison to the furious reaction to "the infamous" Section 3, which disfranchised "patriotic heroes" who had sacrificed all for the Southern cause.[28] Denouncing Governor Murphy's endorsement of the amendment, one paper editorialized: "[The Fourteenth Amendment] destroys the honor of Arkansas, insults the memory of her noble dead, and writes infamy and disgrace on her brow."[29] Section 2 was discussed somewhat less, but regular readers of the state's papers were almost certainly familiar with the argument that it embodied a clever radical stratagem to reduce "a large portion of her [i.e., the South's] representative strength in the [national] government . . . to a cypher."[30]

Believing that "[a] vast union is compatible with free government [only] on a States' Rights principle," other newspapers condemned Section 1, as had the *Gazette*, because it would permit Congress to assume "absolute control over all the people of a State and their domestic concerns."[31] The *Van Buren Press* had objected to the Civil Rights Bill on the same ground;[32] and it saw the same danger in Section 1, when combined with Section 5.[33] After all, "[t]he tendancy [*sic*] of all of [the radicals'] late acts [had been] to centralize power in the Federal government."[34]

Several papers carried the letters of Interior Secretary O. H. Browning, Mississippi's Governor Sharkey, and former South Carolina Governor Perry, all of whom explained precisely how that calamity might come to pass.[35] First, Sections 1 and 5 gave Congress the power to determine the privileges and immunities of citizenship and thereby impose the pernicious doctrine of racial equality. Secretary Browning emphasized yet another danger. He predicted that inter-meddling federal courts would invoke the due process and equal protection clauses as a basis for reviewing and invalidating state laws. He never suggested, however, that the Bill of Rights would provide a guide to this "federal supervision" in "all things."[36]

The prospect of such "supervision" naturally alarmed conservative Arkansans because they rejected the idea of racial equality and were determined to preserve white superiority through class-based legislation. Although Colonel Forshey might testify before the Reconstruction Committee that "[w]e would probably pass but few laws relating to the late slaves that would not [also] apply to whites,"[37] the *Des Arc Citizen* spoke more candidly: "[The next legislature should] throw around him [the freedman] certain restrictions, while we give him certain rights and privileges, that he may be made most subservient to our purposes and interests."[38] Even after the Reconstruction Acts were passed, the *Pine Bluff Dispatch* insisted that "[o]ur criminal laws must be amended so as to provide some kind of penal work house system in each county for petty larceny and other crimes."[39]

For most white Arkansans, the inferiority of the Negro was a fact.[40] The Negro was "the link between brute and man"[41] and but "barely above the brute in intelligence."[42] As such, he was "free, but not equal to the Anglo-Saxon race"[43] and simply lacked "the capacity . . . for Republican citizenship."[44]

As a result, other Arkansas papers agreed with the *Gazette* that blacks should be denied political rights: "The Negro should be clothed with certain rights which naturally follow his new state of freedom; but voting and holding office and sitting on jurys is no part of [those] rights."[45] Indeed, "negro suffrage" was "the most odious and disgusting" of the radical proposals.[46] Understanding that "[t]he political force of a demand for just rights is proportionate to the numbers of the community which makes it," conservative whites advocated an "increase in the numeral superiority of the Caucasian race, . . . that it might direct the destinies and shape the policy of the commonwealth."[47] Conservative Arkansans also recoiled at the prospect of blacks in public office or the jury box.[48]

The extent to which most white Arkansans wished to retain control over these matters is illustrated by a proposal which the *Little Rock Daily Conservative* advanced in the summer of 1866. One issue then consuming the public's attention was whether blacks would be permitted to testify. Though the *Gazette* supported Negro testimony in all cases, the *Daily Conservative* advocated a more cautious course. It recommended their right to testify be limited initially to cases involving other Negroes. During the seven-year "test" period it suggested, the courts and legislature could observe the intelligence and character of Negro witnesses. The paper concluded: "[T]ime will be ample to have other legislation, by which the right [to testify] shall be subjected to still other guards and restrictions or, if approved, left free to be exercised in all cases."[49]

Persons holding such views would not want the national government to set policy on such questions. That "consolidation" was a principal objection to the Fourteenth Amendment in Arkansas is further evidenced by private correspondence. Writing to David Walker, who had been elected to the state's Supreme Court in 1866, George Watkins exclaimed: "I distain the whole thing [the Fourteenth Amendment] as a fraud and a swindle. This amendment destroys the independance [*sic*] and separate existence of the States, and changes the whole form of Government. . . . We would be no longer a Union of States but a Nation."[50]

Despite this and the other widely shared objections, Governor Murphy recommended that the legislature ratify the Fourteenth Amendment. The only delegate to the 1861 Secession Convention who voted to remain in the Union, Murphy again counseled prudence:

This [the Fourteenth Amendment] is the Congressional scheme of reconstruction, and has been made the leading issue in the late elections, and sustained by large majorities. Though not all the insurgent States could desire, it becomes a very grave question for the Legislature to decide, whether any terms more favorable are likely to be attained by opposition, or whether it is not the better policy for the State to accept the proposed terms, and thus secure the prompt reconstruction of the State in harmonious action with the governing States, and on an equality with them in the Union.

Judging from the results of the late elections, and from the decided tone of public sentiment in the States that subdued the insurrection, it is not probable that better terms will be granted. The effect of rejection on the prosperity and happiness of the people of the State, demands solemn consideration.[51]

The *Gazette* rejected the governor's counsel and urged the legislature to do likewise. The paper doubted that Congress would readmit Arkansas even if it did ratify the amendment. And in the meantime, the *Gazette* argued, Arkansas would have conceded that Congress had the authority to legislate on questions involving social and political rights within the state. Only the foolish would purchase false hope at so dear a price.[52]

The legislature also rejected Governor Murphy's counsel. The Committee on Federal Relations, to whom the amendment had been referred, submitted its brief report on December 10. Echoing the analysis of the *Gazette*, it said of Section 1: "The great and enormous power sought to be conferred on Congress . . . to enforce by appropriate legislation the provisions of [Section 1] . . . takes from the States all control over all the people in their local and their domestic concerns, and virtually abolishes the States."[53] The report proceeded to trash Section 2 because it "is but an effort to force negro suffrage upon the States" and Section 3 because it disfranchised "many of our best and wisest citizens."[54]

The report then returned to the language of Section 1, focusing on the due process clause. It remarked: "[The due process clause] is almost identical with the language contained in the fifth amendment to the Constitution. And this amendment was intended by our wise and good Congress, to operate on the

States and Congress; and, if this be not good enough already surely no additional amendment will do any good. If the one now existing be disregarded, will not this one be ignored?"[55] Whatever one makes of this curious misstatement of then-existing constitutional law, it conclusively refutes the idea that the Arkansas Committee on Federal Relations could have understood that Section 1 incorporated and made applicable against the states the provisions of the federal Bill of Rights. Had they any inkling of that understanding, the committee would not have mistakenly assumed that the due process clause of the Fifth Amendment already applied to the states. Still less would they have passed it off as meaning nothing more than its Fifth Amendment twin. On December 10, 1866, the Senate rejected the Fourteenth Amendment twenty-four to one.[56] A week later the House rejected the amendment sixty-two to two.[57]

The Arkansas legislature thus closed the first and very turbulent phase of Reconstruction. It refused to purchase restoration "at such sacrifice of principle, of dignity and of self-respect."[58] While the committee acknowledged that Arkansas might "be forced to take this amendment, and even harsher terms,"[59] it almost certainly did not anticipate how harsh those terms would be.[60]

Anticipating these actions, the defeated Unionists had already issued a call to Arkansas loyalists to meet in Fort Smith on December 13. The call explained the strategy they would pursue:

Nothing is left us but to apply to Congress for redress and help, and Congress will not be deaf to our prayer. Congress will listen to our petition for an enabling act, permitting the loyal people to form a government in accordance with justice, freedom, and the inalienable rights of man. The late rebels have scornfully rejected every proffer of settling our difficulties on terms infinitely better than they deserve. Let us go back therefore and build up the house of state on a new foundation, removing the decayed and rotten timbers and erect an edifice which can never again be shaken, because its corner stone is laid upon justice and truth eternal as the Heavens.[61]

The Unionists met, passed resolutions, and memorialized Congress. Angry conservatives denounced these efforts and, pronouncing them treasonous, demanded that Governor Murphy disband the meeting and prosecute its members.[62]

The passage of the Reconstruction Acts later that spring ushered in an equally turbulent second phase of Arkansas history. The conservative-dominated legislature naturally protested the imposition of military rule. On March 9—just two days before General E. O. C. Ord assumed command of the Fourth District—the Senate and House overwhelmingly passed a resolution that described the "existing government *republican* in form, in conformity with the constitution, laws and treaties of the United States, a member of the federal Union, and entitled to its due representation in the Congress of the United States."[63] Under the terms of the Supplementary Reconstruction Act, voters were nevertheless registered. "Rebels" were purged from the rolls; blacks were added. A date was set for the voters to approve or disapprove the call for a new constitutional convention and to elect delegates to that convention.

Once military rule became a reality, conservatives split over how best to respond. Most were paralyzed by the fear of Negro suffrage.[64] Indeed, many preferred "permanent despotism" to a "restoration" that would transform Arkansas into "a hell on earth, a hideous, horrid pandemonium filled with all the devils of vice, crime, pauperism, corruption, violence, political debauchery, social anarchy."[65] The editor of the *Gazette* predicted a similar chamber of horrors: "social degradation, amalgamation of the two races, and the generation of a race of mongrels."[66] To forestall that calamity, he recommended that white immigration be encouraged in order "to increase the numerical superiority of the Caucasian race, so that it may direct the destinies and shape the policy of the commonwealth."[67] Whatever the merits of that recommendation, it was a long-term solution.

In the short term, power passed to white Unionists and their black allies. Even before passage of the Reconstruction Acts, Unionists had been organizing to take advantage of the state's emerging situation. Within months, radicals within the Unionist forces gained control of the Republican Party and adopted a platform that affirmed equal rights for all.[68] The freedmen, like all other citizens, were entitled to equal civil and political rights.[69] In the ensuing convention campaign, the well-organized Republicans routed the despairing, dismayed, and disorganized conservatives.

These Republicans dominated discussions in the constitutional convention. Those discussions illuminated the contemporary understanding of general concepts like privileges and immunities and equal protection, as well as their particularized meaning in the Fourteenth Amendment, largely because conservative delegates raised two specific issues that generated an extended exploration of these subjects. First, Mr. Jesse N. Cypert, the conservative delegate from— appropriately enough—White County, insisted that the convention simply submit the existing 1864 constitution to the people for their ratification.[70] The reason for this insistence was clear. The 1864 constitution did not enfranchise blacks. Second, Cypert and other conservatives demanded that any new constitution contain a provision forbidding intermarriage between the races.[71]

From the discussion of these two proposals, it is clear that Republicans considered "equality before the law" to be the fundamental principle of the new constitutional order that they intended to establish. Their most articulate spokesman was a Negro delegate, Mr. William Grey of Phillips County. Repeatedly invoking the language of the Declaration of Independence, he said: "I believe the hand of an angel guided the hand that wrote those words ['all men are created equal'], and that they were recorded in heaven. God intends you shall keep the original contract." He implored the delegates to "[s]ettle once and forever the question of human rights, by giving [Negroes] equality before the law."[72] Republicans also insisted that citizens of the United States enjoyed—in whatever state they resided—"all the privileges and immunities secured, by the National Constitution, to a citizen of the United States."[73]

Never once did Republicans specify what those "national" privileges and immunities were, however. Certainly no Republicans ever suggested that the privileges and immunities clause of the Fourteenth Amendment included all the guarantees of the federal Bill of Rights, though the debate presented them with countless opportunities to make that point, had it been their understanding. Rather, they understood the privileges and immunities of citizenship as both fixed and fluid, or "natural and acquired," as Grey put it. Presumably they included both natural rights, some of which might also be found in the Bill of Rights, and statutory rights, as the state legislature from time to time enacted them.

Moreover, Arkansas Republicans did not think of the two concepts— privileges and immunities and equality before the law—as separate and distinct. They conflated the two in a formula that recognized the preeminence of the equality principle. The formula also made the principles of republican government the standard by which the substantive content of the two concepts was to be determined. The goal, they argued, was "equal and impartial citizenship, in accordance with the principles of the Constitution of the United States."[74] Indeed, they specifically cited Article IV, Section 2, and Section 1 of the pending Fourteenth Amendment on this point, cautioning their fellow delegates that any state constitutional provision which violated these sections would mean that "our government fails to be republican in form."[75]

Interestingly, the conservative Democratic delegates did not necessarily disagree with this philosophy, stated that generally and abstractly. They certainly considered themselves stalwart defenders of republican principles, including equality before the law. They also recognized that all citizens enjoyed certain privileges and immunities, which governments were obliged to respect. Understandably, they objected to any diminution in the power of the states to regulate those incidents of citizenship. That was their major—indeed, their only principled—objection to Section 1 of the Fourteenth Amendment.

Conservative Democrats in Arkansas did disagree that that philosophy required the state to grant the franchise to blacks or to recognize their right to marry whites. On the question of franchise, the Republicans and Democrats simply disagreed over a factual question: the fitness of blacks as a class to vote. At the outset of the debate, Mr. Cypert declared that the "elective franchise was not a universal right, but a class right."[76] He later elaborated:

[U]nder the doctrine of Jefferson, the elective franchise has been awarded to classes, *for the purpose of perpetuating a republican form of government*, and as *indispensable* to the attainment of that end. For it was only reasonable that the privilege of the ballot should be withheld, from negroes, or from any other class, not citizens of the United States, destitute of a knowledge of the principles and workings of our government, and not by nature qualified to exercise with sufficient judgment the privilege of the ballot. That privilege was consequently restricted to white men, citizens of the United States, and twenty-one years of age. That is the class known, to all the States, as voters. In some States there are some other classes who, under certain restrictions, are permitted to vote; but the class to which I refer exists in all the States. Now I know, *and every man in this house knows*, that, as a class, young men of the white race, from twelve to twenty-one, are more competent to exercise the elective franchise, than the negro race in the South. There is not an unprejudiced man in this house, but knows this to be true.[77]

Mr. Hicks reviewed the "barbarous" history of the African race and concluded that they had never developed, much less sustained, a republican government. He admitted that "some" blacks understood the principles of republican government, but they were too few in number to justify "granting the negro race the elective franchise."[78] Cypert concluded the debate by quoting an Englishman, an opponent of slavery who had visited Africa:

So long as it is generally considered that the negro and the white man are to be governed by the same laws and guided by the same management, so long will the former remain a thorn in the side of every community to which he may unhappily belong. When the horse and the ass shall be found to match in doubled harness, the white man and the African black will pull together under the same regime. It is the grand error of equalizing that which is unequal, that has lowered the negro character, and made the black man a reproach.[79]

Cypert added:

Let us not continue, as Mr. Baker says, that thorn in the flesh of the community. Let us afford them the same protection that our wives and our daughters have,—the right of liberty, the right of property, and of the pursuit of happiness. Let us afford to them the same rights enjoyed by the white man under the age of twenty-one. Let them be as minors. They *are* nothing but minors, as yet; and when they have proven, to a dispassionate people, that they constitute a fit element for incorporation . . . [there] will then be ample time to bring them in.[80]

Republicans insisted that the general mass of blacks were qualified or at least as qualified as many whites. Mr. Grey replied to Mr. Cypert: "Again, the gentleman denies us the right of suffrage, on the ground of our ignorance. Why, sir, every negro vote registered in this State I can duplicate with the vote of a white man that can neither read nor write; and still we are charged with ignorance. I do not deny it, but we are not isolated in that respect. If these men can vote, I see no injustice in permitting us to vote also."[81] Conservatives retorted that Republicans had a crasser political motive for extending voting rights to blacks, as an exchange between Messrs. Cypert and Wyatt showed:

Mr. CYPERT: Then why do you propose to enfranchise the negro race, as a class, and to keep unenfranchised the class of whites from twenty down to twelve, *known* to be more intelligent, and to be better informed concerning our form of government? What is your object? What can be the motive? I will tell you, sir! I was told, by one of the Republican members of this body, yesterday morning, or the evening before. In the course of conversation with him, on this subject, he told me, plainly, the motive. I asked him, as a citizen of Arkansas, whose interests were identified with those of the State,—"Your interests are all here; you want to perpetuate the government of the State and of the country, of which you are a citizen: why introduce, an element, the introduction of which you must *know* will tend to the ultimate dissolution of that government?"—"WE WANT THE NEGRO VOTE, TO CONTROL YOU REBELS!"

Mr. WYATT: I am the man you were talking to.
Mr. CYPERT: You are the man.
Mr. WYATT: That's what *I* want it for! [Laughter and applause.] [*In his seat.*] I want it, to control just such men as you![82]

Mr. Grey himself recognized that blacks were being given the vote "for the purpose of creating a . . . substratum upon which the loyal men of the South could build loyal government for the States of the South."[83]

This debate over voting rights for blacks did not turn on different interpretations of Section 1 of the Fourteenth Amendment, even though the philosophy embodied in that section framed the terms of the debates. The debate turned rather on the question of whether Congress or Arkansas *should* extend voting rights to blacks as a privilege of citizenship. The answer which delegates gave to that question of public policy turned on two considerations: (1) their assessment of the general intelligence of blacks and (2) their estimate of the political benefits to be derived from extending or denying the privilege to blacks.

Similarly, the debate over miscegenation did not turn on different estimates of the importance of the principle of equality before the law. Both sides recognized its fundamental importance. The debate did turn, however, on different senses of how far the equality principle extended. Even Republican delegates otherwise sympathetic to black concerns excluded intermarriage from the equality code:

I am here, intending to give the negro every right that God in heaven, upon His throne, has assigned him. I am ready to recognize his civil and political rights. . . .

I am ready to . . . build the rights of the black man upon a foundation which nothing but the fiat of God shall dissolve, until the thunders of the last great day. . . .

I have never belonged to a bleaching-machinery, and do not advocate the bleaching process. That is just what I want put down. I am astonished that gentlemen get up and say,—"Let it be a matter of taste!" It shows me a man's taste, when he wants no distinction, no partition, but wants the two races mixed in one common amalgamation. It shows me a taste that makes Heaven frown, and stinks in the nostrils of man! . . .

For God's sake let us build a wall! let it be understood as the organic law of the land that a white man shall be a white man, and a black man a black man, and that each shall have their rights in their respective spheres.[84]

Those who favored a constitutional bar to interracial marriage argued that amalgamation, or more pejoratively, mongrelization, was undesirable, and that the state could forbid it just as it forbade marriage between fathers and daughters.[85]

Those opposed to the constitutional bar characterized it as forbidden class legislation. Mr. Brooks declared himself "opposed to any class legislation"[86] and begged his fellow Republicans not to "break over all the great cardinal principles upon which . . . the country is founded."[87] And on this point they did invoke Section 1 of the Fourteenth Amendment.[88] Such class legislation was especially repugnant to some because it trenched on a free man's "right to marry as he pleases." Any infringement of that right was "contrary to the doctrine of inalienable rights [and] . . . to the doctrines of the Declaration of Independence" and would also be unconstitutional under Section 1 of the Fourteenth Amendment.[89]

Still others insisted that the bar could not be enforced because the prohibited classes could not be legislatively defined or legally proven with "scientific accuracy." Mr. Grey elaborated upon the point:

If we are to adopt this proposition [a bar to interracial marriages], the Legislature will have to pass an act creating a board of scientific physicians, or professors of anatomy, to discover who is a negro. There is the trouble. The purity of blood, of which the gentleman [MR. BRADLEY] speaks, has already been somewhat interfered with, in this country. When acts of the Legislature must be passed, making such a distinction as this, to define who is a negro, who is a mulatto, and so, *ad libitum* and *ad infinitum*, legislation becomes a farce. The insertion of a clause prohibiting negroes and whites from marrying, will not cover the case. You will have to define the point of intermixture of blood which shall constitute a mulatto, and so prevent him or her from intermarrying with the white race; and in the case of an octoroon, or of still further admixture of blood, I take it the distinction will grow very shadowy. The census of the United States shows that forty per cent. of us, already, have crossed the line. It is no fault of ours. No gentleman will lay it to our door. The intermixture has taken place illegitimately. Those gentlemen who so place themselves upon a pedestal of virtue, will not deny that this was wrong. Their own race has thus created the difficulty. I see no way, in the world, of putting an end to the evil by legislation. If you can show where the line can be drawn, I am perfectly willing.[90]

Finally, those opposed to the bar said they were content to let social mores govern intermarriage between blacks and whites: "The question before the Convention, and the question which will be before the people, is that of political equality merely. The people will arrange the question of social equality for themselves, irrespective of anything that we may do."[91] Mr. Brooks agreed with his colleague:

If gentlemen are sincere in desiring to prevent this intercourse of the races, either by marriage or illicitly, except as you may enact laws for the regulation of the *morals* of society with regard to intercourse between the sexes, then do nothing upon this subject. There is a more powerful regulation, to control these matters, if you leave them wholly to society. Let the philosophy of society, let the fitness of things, let the proprieties of life, let the social standard fixed by the people, without regard to race, color, or party, regulate this question.[92]

In the end the convention declined to put any prohibition into the constitution. It did, however, declare its opposition to "all amalgamation between the white and colored races" and invited the next session of the legislature to enact laws on the subject.[93]

What fascinates a contemporary student of these debates is their anticipation of modern equal protection analysis. For example, some delegates were very hostile to classifications that trenched on what today would be called fundamental rights like the right to vote or marry. Other delegates raised concerns that focused on the importance of the government's purpose in making the classification, the validity or reasonableness of the factual basis underlying the classification, and the effectiveness of the means used to enforce the classification. Analyzing the latter, delegates occasionally suggested alternative means. In the miscegenation debate, for instance, many delegates argued that social pressures alone would minimize interracial marriage.

The debate also revealed a common, core understanding of the equal protection clause. All agreed that it—or at least the equality principle which it presumably reflected—forbade class legislation. Yet all would also have conceded that legislation necessarily involved classification. At a minimum, a majority of the delegates would have agreed that all racial classifications were prohibited. Indeed, the delegates enshrined that policy in Section 3 of the new Bill of Rights: "The equality of all persons before the law is recognized, and shall ever remain inviolate; nor shall any citizen ever be deprived of any right, privilege or immunity, nor exempted from any burden or duty, on account of race, color, or previous condition."

That the delegates understood the equal protection clause to forbid racial preferences even if they were deemed beneficial is evident from Section 18 of the same Bill of Rights: "The General Assembly shall not grant to any citizen, or class of citizens, privileges or immunities which, upon the same terms, shall not equally belong to all citizens." The leading black delegate to the constitutional convention shared that view. Responding to the charge that the Freedmen's Bureau aided only blacks, he reminded the other delegates that it had also helped many poor whites.[94] An *opportunity* was all that Mr. Grey wanted: "Give us the right of suffrage; establish a school system that will give us opportunities to educate our children; leave ajar the door that leads to peace and power; and if by the next generation we do not place ourselves beyond the reach of mortal man, why, then take them away from us if not exercised properly."[95]

The third phase of reconstruction began in Arkansas on February 11, 1868, when the convention approved the new constitution forty-six to twenty and called for a vote to ratify it and elect new state officers and a new legislature. Conservatives fought to prevent adoption of the new constitution.[96] Declaring their intention to maintain a "WHITE MAN's government in a WHITE MAN's COUNTRY," they argued: "[I]f you vote [for]it [the constitution], you invite the nigger into your parlour—you invite him to ride in your carriage—you offer him one of your daughters in marriage."[97] The *Gazette* stated the conservative position succinctly: "We do not recognize that the negro has any political rights whatever." It added: "His existence in the country is only tolerated by white men on the score of humanity."[98]

From the beginning, black Arkansans had sought two rights in order to protect themselves: equality before the law and the right to vote. Petitioning the state and national legislatures in 1865, they sought those rights because they would "clothe us with the power of self-protection."[99] More particularly, blacks in Arkansas hoped to use their legal and political powers to secure protection from violence, education for their children, and farm land to support themselves.

While white Republicans endorsed these claims, they also emphasized internal improvements and fiscal responsibility.[100] In the bitterly fought election that spring, they won; and the new constitution was ratified.[101] The new legislature met on April 2, 1868, ratified the Fourteenth Amendment, elected two senators, petitioned Congress for readmission, and then adjourned. Two and a half months later, Arkansas was readmitted to the Union, two weeks before most of the other Southern states.

Over the next six years, Arkansan blacks struggled to achieve their political goals in an increasingly hostile environment. They achieved their greatest success in education. The newly elected Governor Powell Clayton demanded universal education:

Your attention is respectfully invited to a question that is perhaps more important than any other you may be called upon to consider. It is that of universal education. To the ears of the oppressor this is a startling and dangerous subject; for, wherever the ennobling influences of education are felt, the shackles fall from the limbs of the oppressed,—the slave becomes a freeman. To the lover of freedom it is the very "philosopher's stone" that changes the base metal of the ignorant and slavish mind to the pure ore upon which the light of liberty is caught and from which it is reflected to other minds until the whole becomes illumined. To us it is the keystone of the grand arch upon which rests the fair structure of our free government. No State founded upon the principles upon which our government is based can prosper where ignorance prevails. The people cannot rule successfully unless they are educated and informed.[102]

The school bill sailed through the legislature, largely because it provided that the schools be segregated. Governor Clayton later explained: "To have provided for mixed schools, under the existing conditions, would have been destructive of all we were laboring to accomplish. In making my recommendations to the Legislature I had to provide for conditions as they were and get the best results I could out of the new system, which provided for absolute segregation of the races."[103] In Arkansas, as in every other Southern state except Louisiana, the most ardent supporters of the Fourteenth Amendment thus mandated or accepted segregation in public education—in this case within a month of ratifying the amendment itself.

Blacks enjoyed mixed success in securing governmental protection from the maimings, burnings, and lynchings that Klansmen and their sympathizers used to intimidate the freedmen.[104] In those few counties where blacks outnumbered whites and controlled local governments, particularly the sheriff's office, they prevented or eliminated most of the terrorist activities.[105] In other areas they were dependent upon the governor's willingness to call out the militia and impose martial law. While Governor Powell Clayton did just that in November 1868, the decision proved to be politically unpopular. He did not repeat the "mistake."[106] Consequently, most Arkansan blacks were left unprotected. Vigilantes in many areas thus rendered the law in general and the Fourteenth Amendment in particular a dead letter.

Those who supported the Fourteenth Amendment believed that it had established a legal order within which free labor would flourish. Even before the war ended, army officers and officials of the Freedmen's Bureau in Arkansas had adopted policies by which they sought to promote free labor.[107] Despite the freedmen's ardent desire to acquire land and farm it,[108] these policies failed. The right to buy property meant little to blacks who had no money to buy land or who could find no owner willing to sell it to them.[109] The right to contract meant little in circumstances where blacks had no choice but to accept low wages or starve and where courts routinely construed contractual provisions against them. Thus economic and social realities also reduced many of the rights guaranteed by the Fourteenth Amendment to legal fictions.

Yet fifty years after the Civil War, the conservative black minister E. C. Morris would tell his Little Rock flock:

Let us turn back 50 years ago, and look at the condition of our people then, and see us later when we were emancipated, homeless, clotheless and many nameless, and then look at us today, free men and women, and in the places where once stood auction blocks for human slaves we find schoolhouses. We should all feel that we have much to be thankful for today and every other day. I have seen the whole because I have lived in the days of slavery and I know what freedom is.[110]

Whatever that freedom was, it was neither the freedom that Mr. Jefferson had declared the birthright of every human being nor the freedom Mr. Grey had so eagerly and eloquently sought for the advancement of his race.

NOTES

1. Augustus Garland to President Johnson, 24 October 1865. Paul H. Bergeron, ed., *The Papers of Andrew Johnson, vol. 9, September 1865–January 1866* (Knoxville: University of Tennessee Press, 1991), 276–77.

2. Thomas S. Staples, *Reconstruction in Arkansas, 1862–1874* (1964; reprinted Gloucester, Mass.: Peter Smith), 107.

3. Ibid.

4. Ibid., 106. Some conservatives did suggest that blacks might be reenslaved. Carl H. Moneyhon, *The Impact of the Civil War and Reconstruction on Arkansas: Persistence in the Midst of Ruin* (Baton Rouge: Louisiana State University Press, 1994), 195.

5. Paige E. Mulhollan, "Arkansas General Assembly of 1866 and Its Effect on Reconstruction," *Arkansas Historical Quarterly* 20 (Winter 1961): 331, 339–40.

6. Ibid., 331.

7. *Arkansas Daily Gazette*, 8 February 1866.

8. Ibid., 8 May 1866.

9. Ibid., 16 July 1866.

10. Ibid., 6 October 1866.

11. Ibid., 3 November 1866.

12. Ibid., 13 November 1866; see also 14 November 1866.

13. Ibid., 23 October 1866.

14. Ibid.

15. Ibid.

16. Ibid.

17. Ibid., 27 July 1866.

18. Ibid., 14 September 1866.

19. Ibid., 6 October 1866. Other papers carried far more pejorative characterizations.

20. Ibid., 13 November 1866.

21. Ibid., 2 November 1866.

22. Ibid., 21 June 1865.

23. See, e.g., *Arkansas Daily Gazette*, 23 March 1866 (U.S. Senator Wilson concedes Thirteenth Amendment did not grant blacks the right to vote or give Congress the power to make them voters); *Arkansas Daily Gazette*, 4 September 1865 (General Cox refuses to run on Republican platform in Ohio that endorses Negro suffrage); *Arkansas Daily Gazette*, 28 May 1866 (Governor Swann of Maryland quoted as saying, "I look upon Negro suffrage . . . as the virtual subordination of the white race to the ultimate control and domination of the negro").

24. *Arkansas Daily Gazette*, 13 November 1866.

25. *Des Arc Citizen*, 9 June 1866.

26. *Fort Smith Tri-Weekly Herald*, 18 December 1866.

27. *Van Buren Press*, 21 July 1866.

28. *Little Rock Daily Conservative*, 22 December 1866. See also *Little Rock Daily Conservative*, 25 October 1866.

29. *Des Arc Citizen*, 17 November 1866.

30. *Little Rock Daily Conservative*, 15 October 1866.

31. Ibid., 12 April 1867.

32. *Van Buren Press*, 7 April 1866.

33. Ibid., 16 November 1866.

34. *Fort Smith Tri-Weekly Herald*, 11 October 1866.

35. Ibid., 24 July 1866.

36. *Van Buren Press*, 16 November 1866.

37. *Van Buren Press*, 23 June 1866.

38. *Des Arc Citizen*, 14 July 1866.

39. *Pine Bluff Dispatch*, 30 November 1867.

40. *Little Rock Daily Conservative*, 5 June 1867.

41. *Van Buren Press*, 29 November 1867.

42. Ibid., 11 November 1867.

43. *Des Arc Citizen*, 2 June 1866.

44. *Van Buren Press*, 23 June 1866. See also *Little Rock Daily Conservative*, 8 June 1866.

45. Ibid., 21 July 1866.

46. *Arkansas Conservative*, 4 October 1866.

47. *Arkansas Daily Gazette*, 16 January 1867.

48. *Van Buren Press*, 21 July 1866; cf. *Fort Smith Tri-Weekly Herald*, 26 July 1866.

49. *Little Rock Daily Conservative*, 21 November 1866.

50. George C. Watkins to David Walker, 22 August 1868. David Walker Letters, Folder 2, Item 43, Special Collections Division, University of Arkansas Libraries, Fayetteville, Arkansas.

51. *Journal of the Senate of Arkansas, Sixteenth Session* (Little Rock: Price & Barton, State Printers, 1870), 50–51.

52. *Arkansas Daily Gazette*, 14 November 1866.

53. *Journal of the Senate of Arkansas, Sixteenth Session*, 260–62.

54. Ibid.

55. Ibid.

56. Ibid.

57. *Journal of the House of Representatives, Arkansas, Sixteenth Session* (Little Rock: Price & Barton, State Printers, 1870), 290–91.

58. Cf. *Arkansas Daily Gazette*, 12 January 1867 (the South has "refused the cup of degradation offered her").

59. The *Gazette* renamed the Reconstruction Acts the "destruction acts." *Arkansas Daily Gazette*, 15 March 1867.

60. On the eve of the Reconstruction Acts, the *Gazette* nevertheless bravely asserted: "We have heard the threats of worse alternatives, and have dared them boldly, trusting to the Supreme Court and the Executive, to sustain the right. We have looked the danger in the face and dared it. . . . When we rejected the constitutional amendment, we burnt our ships." *Arkansas Daily Gazette*, 8 March 1867.

61. *Fort Smith New Era*, 20 November 1866.

62. Cf. *Van Buren Press*, 21 December 1866.

63. *Journal of the Arkansas House of Representatives, Sixteenth Session*, 832–34.

64. Staples, *Reconstruction in Arkansas*, 129.

65. Ibid. Cf. *Fort Smith Tri-Weekly Herald*, 14 February 1867 ("Are We to Be Governed by African Votes or Bayonets?").

66. *Arkansas Daily Gazette*, 16 January 1867.

67. Ibid. See also *Pine Bluff Dispatch*, 19 January 1867 (the numerical superiority of whites will inexorably erode military control because "armed troops" cannot be placed in "every county and precinct").

68. Staples, *Reconstruction in Arkansas*, 130.

69. *Van Buren Press*, 19 April 1867.

70. *Debates and Proceedings of the Convention Which Assembled at Little Rock, January 7th, 1868, under the Provisions of the Act of Congress of March 2d, 1867, and the Acts of March 23d and July 19th, 1867, Supplementary Thereto, to Form a Constitution for the State of Arkansas* (Little Rock: J. G. Price, Printer to the Convention, 1868), 88.

71. Ibid., 363–88.

72. Ibid., 96.

73. Ibid., 499. See also comments of Delegate Brooks: "We claim . . . as citizens of the common country . . . all the privileges which pertain to that citizenship" (ibid., 107).

74. Ibid., 499.

75. Ibid., 502.

76. Ibid., 91.

77. Ibid., 146–47.

78. Ibid., 117.

79. Ibid., 151.

80. Ibid., 152.

81. Ibid., 93.

82. Ibid., 146–47.

83. Ibid., 443.

84. Ibid., 364 (comments of Mr. Bradley).

85. Ibid., 387 (comments of Mr. Gantt).

86. Ibid., 383 (comments of Mr. Brooks). Mr. Brooks was later quoted as saying he would make the state "all radical or all a waste, howling wilderness." He insisted that he said only that the laws should be followed, and the authority of the state respected, or the state made a "howling wilderness, for the habitation of only bats and owls."

87. Ibid., 382.

88. Ibid., 502 (comments of Mr. Hodges).

89. Ibid., 376 (comments of Mr. Langley).

90. Ibid., 366.

91. Ibid., 372 (comments of Mr. Montgomery).

92. Ibid., 383.

93. Ibid., 507.

94. Ibid., 439.

95. Quoted in Staples, *Reconstruction in Arkansas*, 231–32.

96. Moneyhon, *The Impact of the Civil War and Reconstruction on Arkansas*, 246.

97. Ibid., 247–48.

98. *Arkansas Daily Gazette*, 28 February 1868.

99. *Proceedings of the Convention of Colored Citizens of the State of Arkansas, Held in Little Rock, Thursday, Friday and Saturday, November 30, Dec. 1 and 2* (Helena, Arkansas: Clarion Office Print., 1866), 7.

100. In his inaugural address on 3 July 1868, Clayton said: "We should invite all classes to come here and we should greet everyone with a cordial welcome. Capital should be protected, industry fostered, and over each individual should be extended the strong and protecting arm of the law,—guaranteeing, upon the soil of Arkansas, equal rights to all men." Powell Clayton, *The Aftermath of the Civil War in Arkansas* (New York: Neale Publishing Company, 1915), 42.

101. The election results were disputed, both sides charging fraud. The commanding general acknowledged fraud on both sides but nevertheless recommended that the constitution be considered ratified. Staples, *Reconstruction in Arkansas*, 245.

102. Clayton, *The Aftermath of the Civil War in Arkansas*, 45.

103. Ibid., 226–27.

104. The Klan openly advertised in Democratic papers, declaring "[v]engeance is ours"; and one of those papers ridiculed the governor's attempt to defeat the Klan with "The Ethiopian militia." Orval Truman Driggs, Jr., "The Issues of the Powell Clayton Regime, 1868–1871," *Arkansas Historical Quarterly* 8 (Spring 1949): 1, 16–17.

105. David M. Tucker, *Arkansas: A People and Their Reputation* (Memphis: Memphis State University Press, 1985), 46.

106. See generally Otis A. Singletary, "Militia Disturbances in Arkansas during Reconstruction," *Arkansas Historical Quarterly* 15 (1956): 140, 143–45. The governor waited until after the 1868 election to call out the militia, sensing its use would offend

moderate whites and drive them into the conservative party. In a circular letter to registrars, he explained:

> The whole principle of the ballot is a free expression of the public will, and the use of a military force, either at the registration or election is not desirable.
>
> While I shall use every effort in my power to afford a fair registration, and to secure to all a free expression of their will at the ballot box, it can only be accomplished by the citizens of the respective counties manifesting a disposition to sustain the laws and to protect the registrar in the performance of his duties. In those counties where the people are not disposed to allow the civil authorities to execute the laws or to have a military force organized in them, they cannot expect a force to be furnished them for the purpose of enabling them to enjoy the privilege of an election. (*Weekly Herald*, 24 October 1868)

107. Moneyhon, *The Impact of the Civil War and Reconstruction on Arkansas*, 142–43, 150–51.

108. The following conversation between a freedman and a Union officer is particularly poignant:

> Freedman: "You set me free, but you left me there."
> Officer: "What do you want?"
> Freedman: "I want some land. I am helpless; you do nothing for me but give me freedom."
> Officer: "Is that not enough?"
> Freedman: "It is enough for the present; but I cannot help myself unless I get some land; then I can take care of myself and family; otherwise, I cannot do it."
>
> *House Reports*, 39th Cong., 1st Sess., No. 30, p. 77.

109. Gene W. Boyett, "The Black Experience in the First Decade of Reconstruction in Pope County," *Arkansas Historical Quarterly* 51 (1992): 119, 124 ("white opposition to black ownership of land posed the threat of physical harm to any white who sold even small parcels of land to blacks"). Cf. Donald G. Neiman, *To Set the Law in Motion: The Freedmen's Bureau and the Legal Rights of Blacks, 1865–1868* (Millwood, N.Y.: KTO Press, 1979), 43 ("A Louisiana plantation owner put the matter more bluntly, declaring that she 'would rather see her plantation grow up in weeds than let a Nigger cultivate it for his own use.'").

110. Tucker, *Arkansas: A People and Their Reputation*, 53.

11

Ratification in Texas

If I owned hell and Texas, I'd rent Texas and live in hell.

—General Philip Sheridan, exasperated by the violence
that racked the state throughout Reconstruction

The reorganization of civil government proceeded more slowly in Texas than in most other Southern states. Union troops moved into the state in June 1865. That same month President Johnson appointed Andrew Jackson Hamilton provisional governor. He was a loyal Texas Unionist who had fled north in 1862. Perhaps because his sojourn in the North had sensitized him to evolving Republican attitudes there, he delayed calling for an election that might return unrepentant rebels to power. In August 1865, Hamilton wrote President Johnson:

Districts remote from Military forces openly deny the negroes freedom—insist that the President's Proclamation of emancipation is but a military order which has Spent its force, and the laws of congress upon the Subject unconstitutional and void etc. etc. and exercising the most vigorous restraints upon the freedom of the Negroes. It is undoubtedly true that many freedmen have been killed by their late Masters and very many more greatly abused.[1]

In September 1865 he wrote a local military commander in Galveston that in several counties in the north and east portions of the state slave owners "openly declare that Slavery still exists, and in the most cruel manner force their late Slaves to obedience to their orders; and when their orders are not obeyed, the most atrocious cruelties are perpetrated, often resulting in Murder."[2] Fearing that such Texans would misjudge the North's determination to make the former slaves truly free, Hamilton presciently warned: "[T]here could not be devised a more successful mode of procrastinating our return to our original position in the Union than to deny the freedman, in our midst, those civil rights and privileges, without which, to call them free would be 'to keep the word of promise to the ear, and break it to the hope.'"[3] Pressured nevertheless to hold elections for a constitutional convention promptly, Governor Hamilton issued the call in mid-November for elections to be held on January 8, 1866, to select delegates to a convention the following month.

When the convention opened in Austin on February 7, 1866, Governor Hamilton addressed the delegates. He pointed out that the legal status of the Negro was "the most important question" they would need to address. He recommended that it would be "the better part of wisdom" to guarantee in the new constitution "that the freedmen . . . shall enjoy civil rights on an equality with [whites]." Lest the delegates misunderstand his recommendation, he made its scope quite clear: "By civil rights, I mean the right to sue . . . , to testify . . . , to acquire and hold property . . . , and to be placed upon an equality with white men in respect to the punishment of crimes."[4]

In short, Hamilton implored the convention not to constitutionalize the Black Codes that so many of its sister Southern states had already adopted. He went further: "I believe it would be unwise," he said, "to exclude the freedman . . . from the exercise of political privileges." Conceding that the "great mass of freedmen in our midst" were not presently "qualified by their intelligence to exercise the right of suffrage," he insisted that "progress is the great law . . . under every free government." He then rested his call for qualified suffrage on the broadest grounds of principle:

I do not believe that any policy can be enduring or permanent in this country which is based on accidental circumstances and the traditions of prejudice, instead of being founded on the eternal principles of truth and justice. . . . If . . . we fail to make political privileges depend upon rules of universal application, we will inevitably be betrayed into the error of legislating under the influence of ancient prejudice and with a view only to the present. [5]

Hamilton's was not the only voice calling upon the convention to grant civil and political equality to blacks. From a Union prison, John Reagan, a Texas congressman at the time of secession and the former postmaster general of the Confederacy, circulated a letter, advising Texans to grant full civil rights to blacks.[6] In September 1865, Hamilton's attorney general, William Alexander, wrote to the editor of the *Galveston News* in favor of civil and political equality.[7] At the state's 1866 constitutional convention, former Governor E. M. Pease argued for both. The preceding fall he had made the basis for his position quite clear in a private letter. Conceding to the Negro "all the rights that are given him by the great mass of the civilized world" would insure the "cooperation [of the North] in restoring us to an equal position in the Union."[8] A minority report from one of the convention's committees urged qualified suffrage for the freedmen.[9]

The attitudes of these Texas Unionists thus reflected the very same ideas that were simultaneously percolating through the congressional Reconstruction Committee in the spring of 1866. Had the delegates to the Texas convention heeded Hamilton's advice, their constitution would have anticipated both Section 1 of the Fourteenth Amendment and the Fifteenth Amendment. Unfortunately, the delegates rejected that advice. When they adjourned on April 2, 1866, they had adopted a constitution that accorded the newly freed blacks minimal civil rights but denied them citizenship, suffrage, certain testimonial privileges, access to public schools, and the right to hold office or even to be counted in legislative apportionments.

Admittedly, these provisions were less restrictive than the infamous Black Codes adopted by most of the other Southern states, for Texas had seen how angrily the North had reacted to their imposition. The new constitution nevertheless reflected the view that "the permanent preservation of the white race" was the "paramount object of the people of Texas."[10] To that end, the drafter of the article on freedmen insisted that the state legislature should have plenary authority to "pass all such laws relating especially to the African race within her limits."[11] Foreshadowing how that authority might be exercised, the delegates refused to include in the new constitution any prohibition against the institution of a compulsory labor system.[12]

These constitutional provisions reflected the prevailing racial attitudes of most white Texans.[13] Initially, these Texans scoffed at the notion that blacks might participate in government and society on equal terms with whites. W. C. Dalrymple, a conservative Democrat from Travis County, captured this attitude when he published a circular extolling a "white man's government" under which blacks would remain "hewers of wood and drawers of water."[14] Other conservatives saw "but little reason to doubt that whether or not slavery is perpetuated in name, there will be a return to . . . compulsory labor which will make the negro useful to society and subordinate to the white race."[15] The one liberty which conservatives were willing to concede to blacks was the liberty to seek another place to live if they did not like the fact that the government of Texas was a white man's government.[16]

The gubernatorial and legislative campaign that followed the constitutional convention confirmed this white hostility toward civil and political equality for blacks. The winning candidate was James Throckmorton, a prewar Unionist, who had nevertheless served in the Confederate Army. Allying himself with members of the antebellum Democratic Party, he and his colleagues tarred the Unionist candidate E. M. Pease with the frightful charge of radicalism. Pease did criticize the restrictions on Negro testimony and the exclusion of black children from the public schools. More generally, he pledged to "seek to ameliorate the condition of the freed people in our midst" and to accord the Negroes "not grudgingly, but willingly and heartily, the rights which are now, or may hereafter be, secured to them by the Constitution and the laws."[17] The universal conservative reaction to this platform was captured in an editorial, which described it as "a disgrace to the enlightenment of the age . . . [that] would debauch and destroy if carried into effect the moral and social condition of the South, and render it an abode fit alone for the habitation of brutes, negroes and negrophotists."[18]

So far from embracing Pease's call for equality, conservative whites were demanding the arrest of idle, vagrant, and suspicious Negroes. The *Galveston Weekly News* predicted that "if [the vagrancy laws are] properly enforced, we shall soon see the hordes of darkies congregated in dirty hovels in our alleys going somewhere else." It hoped that that "somewhere else" would be the plantation "where they are alone of any use."[19] No sooner had Throckmorton been elected governor than he wrote a friend:

I am for remaining under military rule allways [*sic*] rather than yielding anything but an acknowledgement that the negro has been freed by the act of the govn't and that we recognize it as an existing fact—and that we have no disposition to quarrell [*sic*] any more about it—or any desire to reestablish slavery—I am sure we will not be allowed even to contend for gradual emancipation—they look upon it as insulting. But I do believe we will be enabled to adopt a coercive system of labor. [20]

Even most white Republicans at that time favored a kind of second-class citizenship for blacks. Ferdinand Flake, an influential Unionist, wrote in his *Galveston Bulletin* that "[c]aste in society is an institution of heaven." He conceded that all men were "[f]ree and equal in the rights to life, liberty and the pursuit of happiness. But most unequal in their powers, capabilities and responsibilities. We could not if we would, we would not if we could, banish caste from our social economy." He concluded that "social equality has nothing to do with political rights."[21]

Judge Paschal similarly wrote:

In saying that the negro is free, and that he must be allowed all the rights of a freedman, let none understand me as meaning, that he is thereby entitled to social equality and political equality at the polls. . . . All men who have ever observed the working of society know that even social equality depends upon so many natural and artificial laws that it can not be said to absolutely exist in any community. Everyone must take his social position according to the circumstances of his case. These depend less upon political laws than upon the developments of mind, moral deportment, avocation and taste.[22]

Texas thus emphatically rejected the notion of equal citizenship for blacks at the very moment Congress adopted that policy in Section 1 of the Fourteenth Amendment. Indeed, the "content and meaning [of the Fourteenth Amendment] were very much a part of the [post-convention] debates."[23] Its passage by Congress was duly noted in the local press.[24] In Texas, as elsewhere in the South, the conservative press discounted the likelihood of its ever being ratified. In the first place, the radicals were said to intend the amendment only as a political ploy to exclude the South from the next presidential election. In the second place, its form was denounced as unconstitutional. Third, the procedures required for its ratification were also said to be unconstitutional.[25]

The conservative press nevertheless examined the substantive merits of the amendment throughout the summer and fall of 1866. They did not like what they saw. They saw an attempt "to permanently change the form of government," "to force negro equality and negro suffrage upon the country," and "to degrade the South by disenfranchising her best citizens."[26] Over the next few years these attacks would be repeated, elaborated, and illustrated. Never once, however, would an attack include any assertion that the due process clause (or any other clause of the proposed amendment) incorporated and thereby extended all the guarantees of the Bill of Rights to black Texans.

That such an assertion would have frightened and angered white Texans is clear from their racial attitudes. They recoiled at the prospect of armed blacks. They would not countenance blacks as their peers in the jury box. The right to petition would have implied active participation by blacks in the political process, and that was anathema. After all, Throckmorton had opposed an equal testimonial privilege for blacks because "it is an entering wedge to sitting on juries, suffrage, and, finally, to perfect social and political equality."[27]

In his inaugural address in August, Governor Throckmorton did not mention the Fourteenth Amendment, though he did pledge "to enact laws that will secure the freed people the full protection of all the rights of person and property guaranteed them [by the state constitution]." He also promised "due obedience to the Constitution and laws of the General Government"; but, hinting at what would become the decisive objection to Section 1 of the pending amendment, he also insisted on "a firm and just maintenance of the rights of the states."[28]

Between Throckmorton's inauguration and the legislature's subsequent decision to reject the amendment, Texans, like Southerners elsewhere, confronted the triumph of radicalism in the fall elections in the North. They were aghast. They recoiled at "radical fanaticism" that advocated "not only negro equality but negro superiority." They resented the proposed "disfranchisement of Southern whites and the confiscation of their estates." And they quaked at "the demoniac threats of the ultra," who, they predicted, would "[tear] down the super structure and [dig] up the very foundation stones of constitutional liberty."[29] They would not accept the Fourteenth Amendment.

Governor Throckmorton, "recommending unqualified rejection" of the amendment to the Texas legislature, did not condemn it for incorporating the Bill of Rights. In fact, the Governor declined to specify the grounds for his recommendation, except as to Section 3, which he claimed would "deprive the state for nearly a quarter of a century of the services of her ablest and best men." As to the other sections, he merely reminded the legislators that "other and equally impressive considerations [would] suggest themselves as reasons for rejection" without any need of his specifying them.[30]

The Texas Senate and House did specify their reasons for rejecting Section 1, and they did not include among them any concern that it incorporated the Bill of

Rights. The concerns expressed were rather the standard ones that had already been fully stated in the popular press. The House Committee on Federal Relations repeated the constitutional objections but did not rest its recommendation to reject Section 1 on them. Instead, it offered this analysis of the merits of the amendment:

The first section proposes to deprive the States of the right which they have possessed since the revolution of 1776 to determine what shall constitute citizenship of a State; and to transfer that right to the Federal Government. Its object is, provided the section shall become a part of the Constitution, under the color of a generality, to declare negroes to be citizens of the United States, and therefore, citizens of the several States, and as such entitled to all "the privileges and immunities" of white citizens; in these privileges would be embraced the exercise of suffrage at the polls, participation in jury duty in all cases, bearing arms in the militia, and other matters which need not be here enumerated.

There is scarcely any limit to the power sought to be transferred by this section from the States of the United States. Congress might declare almost any right or franchise whatever, to be the privilege or immunity of a citizen of the United States and it would immediately attach to every citizen of every State, whether white man or descendant of African. To estimate the comprehensive scope of the power herein sought for Congress—that body might declare miscegenation a privilege or immunity.[31]

The House committee did not denounce the due process and equal protection clauses, presumably because they were understood only to insure procedural fairness and equality before the law, a principle that would not have been thought to preclude at least some racial classifications. These clauses were thus inoffensive. The privileges and immunities clause was not, however, particularly when read in light of Section 5. Consequently, the committee focused its ire on the possibility that Congress might define those privileges and immunities so broadly as to impose political and social equality.

The Senate Committee on Federal Relations came to a similar conclusion, although its somewhat rambling report was more general. The committee insisted that the Texas constitution guaranteed the Negro every right of citizenship other than voting—a fact which precluded any quibbling about due process and equal protection. The committee did express shock at the power given Congress to define the privileges and immunities of citizenship:

These proposed amendments clothe Congress with the extraordinary power of declaring who are, and who are not citizens of the United States, and the several States thereof. Except by the process of naturalization, Congress cannot make a citizen. This is a sacred right reserved to the respective States. A man has heretofore been regarded as a citizen of the United States by virtue of his being a citizen of the State of his residence. A citizen of Ohio, or of Texas, is in virtue of that fact a citizen of the United States. And this has been the doctrine which has obtained from the remotest history of the Republic. If the subject is within the control of Congress, it must depend altogether upon the discretion of that body; for certainly the Constitution is as silent as the grave respecting any such powers. Being then within the discretion of Congress, as the amendments propose, it becomes a vast and dangerous power. If it be a fact that for the future no person can be an elector, or hold any office, or vote at any election, or enjoy any of the privileges of citizenship, except at the will of Congress, then in the hands of Congress, which is but the servant of the people, will be concentrated the entire power of the Federal Government.

Now, it has not escaped your Committee that these extraordinary powers, wielded by virtue of the 5th section of the proposed Article of amendment, whereby it is declared that "Congress shall have power to enforce, by appropriate legislation, the provisions of this Article," would utterly subvert the form of Government. What is "appropriate legislation?" The Constitution is silent; therefore, it is left for the Congress to determine. And this determination would be influenced in a greater or less degree by the prejudices and passions of the hour. If it rests with the Congress to declare first, who are citizens, and afterwards, by "appropriate legislation," to enforce the rights of citizenship, then by virtue of the same authority they can declare that the negro is a citizen, having the right to vote at any election, State or Federal, and by "appropriate legislation," enforce that right, either by the bayonet or otherwise. If these amendments are adopted it will radically change the form of the Government which we have inherited from our fathers, if it does not in its ultimate consequences destroy our boasted freedom, and extinguish the torch of republican liberty in this Western world. Destroy it here, and "I know not where is that Promethean heat / That will its light relume." [32]

Again, the objection to Section 1 was that it would consolidate in Congress the ultimate power to define state citizenship and its incidents and thereby "centralize all power in the Federal Congress, making the States mere appendages to a vast oligarchy, at the National Capitol." [33]

These and other legislative actions galvanized Texas loyalists. Convinced that the conservatives would never treat blacks fairly, they also feared that the conservatives intended to marginalize white Unionists as well. [34] Motivated by similar convictions and fears about the South's refusal to accept the implications of its defeat, congressional Republicans were already fashioning the Reconstruction Acts that would give blacks the right to vote. Texas Unionists like Hamilton had gone north following their defeat in June 1866 and urged universal suffrage, on the ground that it alone would insure a "loyal" reconstruction. [35] Pease summarized how these Texas Republicans viewed the Reconstruction Acts:

They meant to test the question, whether the government which had suppressed the rebellion could carry out, in good faith, the promises it had made to those who had aided and encouraged that government in the South. They meant to test the question, whether the government had the power to make citizens of the four million of slaves who had been emancipated as a result of the rebellion. They meant to test the question whether these freedmen were to live . . . without taking any part in the operations of the government. They were meant to test the question, whether these freedmen should be educated and raised to a condition that they could become useful to themselves and aid in sustaining the government in the future. [36]

An unsympathetic historian explained just how Republicans thought the freedmen could aid in sustaining the government: "'loyalist' politicians regarded the freedmen as political raw material which they hoped to mold into a winning voting machine."[37]

Once the Reconstruction Acts became law, Hamilton, Pease and their supporters began organizing Union or Loyal Leagues in earnest. Throughout April, May, and June 1867, mass meetings were held throughout the state.[38] One in Austin attracted two thousand persons, three-quarters of whom were black.[39] Throughout the Reconstruction period, the membership of the Republican Party in Texas was overwhelmingly black. One student of the period estimates that the ratio of black Republicans to white Republicans was three to one.[40] For both white and black Republicans, then, universal suffrage had become nonnegotiable. White Republicans needed black votes in order to secure public offices. Blacks understood that they could protect their interests only if they had the right to vote; as a black delegate to the 1868 constitutional convention explained to white critics of black suffrage: "If free men can live so well in a free country without a voice in the government, why not try it yourself for awhile? No, sir. Give us the ballot, and give it to us for all time; and then if you can outrun us in the race of life, all is well."[41] Blacks reconciled themselves to their virtual exclusion from positions of leadership within the party and the government because they had nowhere else to go.[42]

To pacify these blacks, white Texas Republicans repeatedly endorsed the doctrine of equal rights. They seldom specified what that meant, however. Specification was unnecessary because it was generally understood that the doctrine included equal civil and political rights but did not necessarily include social equality. Republicans explained: "No more can [laws] make [blacks] socially equal. Social equality depends on agreement. The laws cannot force it. I am no man's equal socially unless he agrees to the equality. No man has a right to demand against my consent; and this rule is universal and all pervading among men."[43] White Republicans consistently reassured their fellow citizens that social relationships were a matter of choice, not law. Their black allies agreed: "The majority of Negroes did not desire social integration, but they did maintain a claim to genuine civil rights as citizens."[44]

The Grand State Ball, held in the House chambers in May 1869, illustrated this sad reality. No blacks—not even the eleven black legislators who had been elected that spring—were invited.[45] Had blacks been invited, the Democrats would have pilloried the Republicans for promoting social equality. The white leadership of the party obviously preferred to disappoint their black supporters rather than risk public damnation for entertaining blacks as their social equals. Racial separation was thus the norm throughout Reconstruction in Texas.[46]

Besides, there is little evidence that these white Republicans themselves considered the freedmen their social equals. The differences in the economic and educational backgrounds of the two races were then so extreme that experience itself seemed to disprove to them the very idea of such equality. Nevertheless, white Republicans in Texas were at least willing to give blacks the opportunity to become their equals. Republicans reaffirmed this commitment when they held their initial state convention on July 4, 1867, in Houston. The conservative press dubbed it the "radico Congo" because the overwhelming majority of delegates were black. The leadership of the convention was largely white, however. The party adopted a platform that endorsed equal rights and demanded free schools and free homesteads.[47] The platform recognized the importance of incorporating into national legislation "as a living and fruitful principle, the declaration of our fathers, that all men are created equal."[48] Thus Republicans once again reiterated the plea for equality of rights.[49] And two years later the party platform called the Fourteenth and Fifteenth Amendments necessary to the "security of the equal civil and political rights of all classes of the people, the main object of civil government."[50] Shortly after his formal inauguration as governor, the radical Republican E. J. Davis confided in a private interview: "I do not want to see white or black named in any law whatsoever."[51] And on the eve of the state's "redemption" by conservative Democrats, a convention of Texas blacks issued this plaintive plea: "All we require of the [white] citizens of Texas is that they grant us all the rights guaranteed to them by the constitution and laws of Texas."[52]

Conservatives scoffed at the Republican commitment to "equal civil and political rights for all" because the party countenanced the disfranchisement of white men.[53] They accused white Republicans of "a mongrel connection with the inferior race among us"[54] and denounced "negrocracy": "[T]hey have placed four millions of the degraded and ignorant descendants, cannibals of Africa, to rule and dominate over eight millions of the blue-eyed, fair-faced and golden-haired race."[55] Indeed, in convention assembled, they said they accepted all the results of the war "except African domination."[56] They lamented the collapse of republican government.[57] And they continued to insist that the Fourteenth Amendment was a "most unjust oppression" upon the states because it would lead to "consolidation."[58] It caused bitterness through its unjust disfranchisement.[59] It was intended to force Negro suffrage on the state.[60] Nowhere, however, in this now-familiar litany of objections will be found any complaint that it bestowed on blacks every right guaranteed in the Bill of Rights.

Nor did the radical Republicans in Texas ever articulate that view. At their annual meeting in July 1868, the Republicans endorsed the Fourteenth Amendment "because we believe it right and just as well as necessary." They called themselves "the party of progress and liberal principles ... the friend of the poor and the defender of equal rights ... the only party under whose administration the misguided Southern states may hope for the capital and the aid" necessary to reconstruction.[61] An earlier resolution of the party had called for the fullest freedom of opinion on all subjects.[62] This ringing endorsement of free speech did not, however, include any statement that the Fourteenth Amendment, if ratified, would protect such speech. Surely such a statement would have been made if the amendment had been understood to incorporate the First Amendment.

Although Republicans dominated the constitutional convention that opened in June 1868, they split sharply over four issues: *ab initio*,[63] division,[64] disfranchisement, and civil rights for blacks. The latter issue generated the least discussion, in part because those who advocated additional rights beyond those guaranteed by the Fourteenth Amendment were few in number. Although all the black members of the convention supported broader rights' guarantees, theirs was the smallest of four competing Republican factions. This "civil rights" faction was headed by George Ruby, a black agent of the Freedmen's Bureau who had organized the Union Leagues the preceding year. Ruby and his allies insisted on including in the new constitution a provision that would require "equal treatment . . . in the private sector."[65] Specifically, they proposed that the fourth section of the proposed Texas Bill of Rights forbid discrimination on public conveyances, in places of business and public resort, and in establishments licensed by the state.[66] The proposal touched off an uproar. When it subsided, the delegates agreed only to a provision that embodied the party's traditional policy: it simply guaranteed the equality of all persons before the law. Specifically, Section 2 of the constitution declared that "[a]ll freemen . . . have equal rights." Section 21 elaborated: "The equality of all persons before the law is herein recognized, and shall ever remain inviolate; nor shall any citizen ever be deprived of any right, privilege, or immunity, nor be exempted from any burden or duty, on account of race, color, or previous condition." After all, the Fourteenth Amendment required that much—but only that much.

More generally, the Bill of Rights of the 1868 constitution is inconsistent with the notion that the Fourteenth Amendment required the state to observe all the particular strictures contained in the first eight amendments to the federal Constitution. For example, the Texas Bill of Rights permitted the prosecution of those charged with crime "on indictment or information." While it recognized the citizen's right to bear arms, it qualified that right, subjecting it to "such regulations as the legislature may prescribe." The Texas Bill of Rights also spelled out far more specifically what that state deemed to be the appropriate relationship between church and state:

All men have a natural and indefeasible right to worship God according to the dictates of their own consciences. No man shall be compelled to attend, erect, or support any place of worship, or to maintain any ministry, against his consent. No human authority ought, in any case whatever, to control or interfere with the rights of conscience in matters of religion; and no preference shall ever be given, by law, to any religious societies or mode of worship. But it shall be the duty of the legislature to pass such laws as may be necessary to protect every religious denomination in the peaceable enjoyment of their own mode of public worship.

In a subsequent memorial to Congress, the radical dissidents excoriated their moderate colleagues for striking out every provision in the draft constitution in favor of "equal civil and political rights for all" and urged that the "new Constitution . . . not . . . be submitted to the people."[67] The passionately worded memorial does not, however, contain any argument that these omissions were inconsistent with the dictates of the then-pending Fourteenth Amendment.

More generally, students of the 1869 constitution have never identified the national Bill of Rights as the principal source of its guarantees. Rather, they have emphasized its continuity with "the political traditions of Texas, both before the Civil War and after the end of Reconstruction."[68] Those traditions were philosophically rooted in a liberal ideology that preceded the American Constitution: Magna Carta, the English Bill of Rights, William Penn's Frame of Government and Pennsylvania's Charter of Privileges, the Declaration of Independence, and the Virginia Bill of Rights. "The Constitution . . . and some early state constitutions [did] contribute the basic framework of guarantees and rights" that were first set out in the 1836 Texas Declaration of Rights, but in subsequent revisions drafters "drew upon the provisions of earlier Texas constitutions" and the "organic laws" of other states. Significantly, a careful student of Texas's constitutional history concluded that "[n]o new guarantees were included in the . . . Reconstruction constitutions of 1866 and 1869."[69]

At the second session of the constitutional convention, the disfranchisement issue dominated discussions and precipitated "the final split in the Republican ranks."[70] By the end of 1868, the more moderate wing of the Republican Party had come to fear that "a coalition of divisionists, *ab initio* defenders, negroes, carpet-baggers, and Germans" might seize power.[71] Consequently, the moderates, who had previously demanded broad disfranchisement of former rebels, now insisted on a narrower disqualification clause. These forces, led now by Hamilton, outmaneuvered the Davis forces, both within and without the convention, and succeeded in thwarting the radical plan of disfranchisement.

Defeated in the convention and rebuffed by the Congress to whom they appealed, the radicals regrouped in Texas, held a convention that nominated Davis for governor, and persuaded President Grant and his friend J. J. Reynolds, the commanding general of the Fifth Military District, to support their campaign. Moderates persuaded A. J. Hamilton to run against Davis. The intense gubernatorial campaign shed only indirect light on the contemporary understanding of the Fourteenth Amendment. The radical Davis and his supporters did not emphasize their position on Negro rights. Although they ran on a platform that endorsed the Fourteenth and Fifteenth Amendments, they "played down even this mild commitment."[72] Though desperately needing every black vote, they never once in any campaign speech or circular praised the due process or privileges and immunities clauses of the Fourteenth Amendment for giving blacks all the protections of the federal Bill of Rights. And they never extolled the equal protection clause for permitting special legislation for the freedmen. Hamilton, now allied with more conservative forces, had no reason, of course, to emphasize his former commitment to black rights. Still, he frequently and severely criticized Davis for creating a black man's party. Yet in none of his criticism did he ever object to any "incorporation" or "class legislation" interpretation of the Fourteenth Amendment. One cannot reply to arguments that have not been made—or even imagined.

In the 1869 election, Texas voters elected Davis by the narrowest of margins (39,831 to 39,060 for Hamilton) and returned a Senate and House nearly divided between radical Republicans and a coalition of moderate Republicans and conservative Democrats. The radicals had a slim majority in the Senate and a slightly larger one in the House; but the moderate/conservative coalition voted more consistently as a bloc than did the radicals. This uncertain balance of power insured a thorough airing of issues. That airing demonstrates two facts. One, moderate and radical Republicans differed sharply on public policy questions that touched the interests of black Texans. Two, they nevertheless continued to share a common understanding of the Fourteenth Amendment. Part of their understanding was that the amendment permitted some range of legislative choice in matters of race. In fact, they split partly over the wisdom of certain choices in that area, as the conduct of the twelfth legislature makes clear.

One of the issues that then concerned black Texans was widespread violence. No sooner had Governor Davis taken office than he proposed organizing a militia and establishing a police force. Both were sorely needed. Texas was a frontier state, federal forces were thinly scattered about, and Ku Kluxers were waging a campaign of terror against blacks and their white sympathizers. By 1868, parts of Texas had degenerated into something like civil war.[73] In an official report to the adjutant general of the Army, the Union general in charge of Texas stated:

The civil law east of the Trinity river is almost a dead letter. In some counties the civil officers are all, or a portion of them, members of the Ku Klux Klan. In other counties the civil officers were compelled to leave their counties. In many counties where the officers have not been driven off, their influence is scarcely felt. . . .

Lawless men in large bands attend the political meetings held under the auspices of the Democratic clubs. The speakers indicate, by name, those elected for murder. The men thus pointed out have no course left them but to leave their homes, or to be murdered on the first convenient opportunity. The murder of negroes is so common as to render it impossible to keep an accurate account of them. Free speech and free press have never existed in Texas. The official reports of lawlessness and crime, so far from being exaggerated, do not tell the whole truth.[74]

This sorry state of affairs, which had existed since the end of the Civil War, prompted General Sheridan to remark that if he owned Texas and hell, he'd move to hell and rent Texas.[75]

Democrats nevertheless objected to the militia and police bills on two grounds. First, they argued that they violated certain provisions of the *state* constitution. Though some of the objectionable features of these bills might also have been challenged on the grounds that they violated guarantees contained in the federal Bill of Rights, the Democrats never made that argument though they might

have, had they any reason to suppose that its specific provisions now constrained state governments.

Second, and more importantly, Democrats objected to blacks serving in the
militia and police forces. Moreover, both bills envisaged blacks and whites
serving in the militia and police together. In fact, blacks dominated both.[76] The
prospect of integrated forces frightened many whites. The *Houston Telegraph*
predicted it would cause a race war.[77] Mathew Gaines, a black Senator, chided
his Democratic colleagues for objecting to the bills because "gentlemen of my
color [would be] armed and riding around after desperados."[78] Though supporters of the bills invoked general principles of equality in support of integration,
they never invoked any specific provision of the Fourteenth Amendment or the
federal Bill of Rights.

In another effort to reduce violence, Governor Davis persuaded the legislature
to adopt a statute that prescribed "severe penalties for keeping and bearing
deadly arms."[79] The governor, who attributed the frequency of murders in Texas
to "the universal habit of bearing arms," was pleased. Those who were dis-
pleased with the new restrictions did not invoke the Fourteenth Amendment as a
bar to the law as they surely would have, had they understood it to incorporate
the Second Amendment guarantee of the right to bear arms.

Education was another issue that might have been thought to raise questions
about the scope of the Fourteenth Amendment. Recognizing the importance of
free schools, Davis asked the legislature to establish a public school system consistent with the new state constitution. Article IX commanded the legislature to
establish and support "a uniform system of public free schools throughout the
state." It was deliberately silent about whether these schools must or could be
either segregated or integrated. Senator Gaines denounced the idea of separate
schools: "If negro men were good enough to occupy seats in the legislature
along with white men, their children were good enough to occupy seats in the
same school with white children."[80] Most of Gaines's colleagues disagreed. Indeed, the Senate refused to confirm the governor's nominee for superintendent
of public instruction because he would not "declare himself opposed to integrated schools in all cases."[81] What is surprising to a contemporary student of
this debate is the lack of any reference to the Fourteenth Amendment. The only
plausible explanation is that no one thought it specifically relevant. Education
was the responsibility of the states; and if a state constitution mandated a system
of public education, the state was free to provide separate or integrated schools,
so long as they afforded the children of both races an equal opportunity to obtain an education.

For nearly a century, the Davis record and that of the twelfth legislature and its
Republican-dominated successors would be denounced as corrupt, tyrannical,
and profligate. Today, revisionist historians evaluate the record differently.
They praise the radicals for trying to establish a public school system, to sup-
press violence, and to protect the civil and political rights of blacks.[82] The party
platforms, speeches, and private letters of Republicans do reflect a consistent

concern with all three challenges throughout the Reconstruction period.[83] One chronicler of radical rule summarizes the party's policy succinctly: "Believing themselves confronted with a choice between a rule of prejudice, bias, and local despotism, or a powerful government able to bring uniform security and freedom, they chose the latter."[84]

In making the latter choice, the Republican Party in Texas enthusiastically embraced the Fourteenth Amendment and the natural rights philosophy reflected in its first section. Though there is no evidence that they thought it incorporated the Bill of Rights, they clearly thought that the privileges and immunities of citizenship included both civil rights and natural rights. The latter category was scarcely self-defining, and Texas Republicans had little occasion in the rough-and-tumble of political debate to define it with philosophical precision. More generally, they believed passionately in the doctrine of equal rights, though the racial prejudices of most white Republicans blinded them to the full implications of that principle for blacks. They understood the Fourteenth Amendment to be consistent with their views because it did not guarantee the right to vote or other political rights, and it permitted reasonable legislative classifications.

Whatever the ambiguity inherent in Section 1, both friend and foe acknowledged that Congress had considerable discretion to eliminate that ambiguity with detailed legislation. Absent such legislation, Texas politicians acted as if that ambiguity permitted them substantial discretion in fashioning public policies; and they seldom exercised it on behalf of freedmen. A black state Senator complained after two years of radical rule that white Republicans still "refused to award blacks prominent offices and continued to discriminate against them in government."[85] In 1873 the Colored Men's Convention, meeting in Brenham, Texas, demanded "our Civil Rights" and vowed to "agitate until we can celebrate their acquisition."[86]

Conservative white Texans answered these complaints, demands, and vows swiftly. In December 1873 they elected a conservative Democrat governor. This conservative triumph had been predicted even as Davis had taken office four years earlier. In a state with one hundred fifty thousand voters, two-thirds to three-fourths of whom were white, radicals could not survive if the defeated Democrats unified the whites and controlled the blacks.[87]

To control blacks, Democrats adopted a dual strategy. The first was legal. The new governor told his cheering supporters that "the 40,000 Negro voters in Texas were simple and ignorant and should be eliminated from the polls."[88] The other strategy was extralegal, and involved the use of violence. Little more than a year after Davis's election, a band of white men invaded Houston's "Freedmen's Town" on a Sunday morning and slaughtered twenty-five blacks. "Stripping them of their coverings amid horrible jokes, and unfeeling laughter," a newspaper reported, "they disemboweled and quartered the poor victims, hanging them by the legs like hogs." One shocked newspaper correspondent noted that the mass lynching:

excited no comment from any of the ministers, no notice was taken of it in any of the congregations, save by a few men who, with glad and eager looks, left their pews, and a few women who, with smiles gave each other knowing nods.

... [The Negroes were] slain in the broad open daylight of the Sabbath morning, within the incorporate limits of the city of 20,000 inhabitants, and not an official raised his hand to prevent it, or to arrest the perpetrators of the deed; not a citizen raised his voice in protest. [89]

Certainly no one invoked the Fourteenth Amendment as a remedy for this and other violence; and the federal government, declining to exercise its power under Section 5, issued no rebuke. Conservative white Texans thus got what they had demanded "from the first, namely the right of self-government, unfettered and unwatched by the national authority; the right to deal with those among them who were 'traitors' to the Confederacy, and with the slaves according to the dictates of local public opinion."[90] Uttering this dire prophesy amidst the senatorial debate on Georgia's readmission, Texas's then radical Senator Morgan Hamilton begged his colleagues not to abandon the freedmen "to the rage of his long-chained and exasperated old master." It would be, he wept, "the most cold-blooded and deliberate piece of cruelty which history will have to record."[91]

NOTES

1. B. Ledbetter, "White Texans' Attitudes toward the Political Equality of Negroes, 1865–1870," *Phylon* 40 (September 1979): 253, 254. See also Sneed, "A Historiography of Reconstruction in Texas: Some Myths and Problems," *Southwest Historical Quarterly* 72 (1969): 435, 444 ("When federal troops first penetrated the interior of East Texas in September, 1865, they discovered most Negroes still bound in slavery. Masters had deceived their slaves by telling them that emancipation would not come until Christmas.").

2. Ibid., 253–54.

3. *Texas Republican*, 2 March 1866.

4. Ibid.

5. Ibid.

6. Reagan to the People of Texas, 11 August 1865, John H. Reagan Papers, University of Texas Archives, Austin, Texas. Reagan later changed his mind. In an 1868 address to the people of Texas, signed by Reagan and several other prominent Texans, he opposed a state constitutional convention, as required by the Reconstruction Acts of Congress, which would, he believed, support Negro suffrage. Because the radicals would control it, many white Texans would be disfranchised. To be unreconstructed was better than to allow Negro suffrage. He believed that he voiced the opinion of the entire South when he stated that white Southerners were unalterably opposed to Negro suffrage and that such a thing could never be forced upon them. "Address to the People of Texas," 23 January 1868.

7. *Galveston News*, 30 September 1865, cited in Carl H. Moneyhon, *Republicanism in Reconstruction Texas* (Austin: University of Texas Press, 1980), 27.

8. E. M. Pease to James H. Starr, 19 August 1865, J. H. Starr Papers, University of Texas Archives, Austin, Texas.

9. J. Carrier, "A Political History of Texas during Reconstruction" (Ph.D. diss., Vanderbilt University, 1971), 20.

10. Ibid.

11. Ibid.

12. Ibid. A Northern reporter who attended the convention described these constitutional provisions as "much the clearest and best thing that any of the seceded states have done for the Negro." *New York Times*, 18 March 1866.

13. Ledbetter, "White Texans' Attitudes," 258.

14. Circular of W. C. Dalrymple, Report of the Joint Committee on Reconstruction at the First Session, 39th Congress, Part IV, 95–96 (1866).

15. Charles W. Ramsdell, *Reconstruction in Texas* (1964; reprinted Gloucester, Mass.: Peter Smith), 46–47.

16. Carrier, "A Political History of Texas during Reconstruction," 20. White Texans were presumably not amused by the occasional suggestion in the North that Texas or parts of it be set aside as a colony for freedmen from all over the country.

17. *San Antonio Express*, 24 May 1866.

18. *Dallas Weekly Herald*, 19 May 1866.

19. *Galveston Weekly News*, 25 July 1866.

20. Ledbetter, "White Texans' Attitudes," 255.

21. Ibid., 257.

22. See *Austin Southern Intelligencer*, 11 August 1865; 16 November 1865.

23. Carrier, "A Political History of Texas during Reconstruction," 84.

24. See, e.g., *Texas Republican*, 9 June 1866.

25. Ibid.

26. *Galveston Weekly News*, 14 February 1866.

27. Throckmorton to R. S. Guy, 5 July 1865, in *Texas State Gazette*, 8 August 1865.

28. Message of Governor Throckmorton, *Journal of the Senate of the State of Texas, Eleventh Legislature. By Authority.* (Austin: Printed at the Office of the "State Gazette," 1866), 105–6.

29. The subsequent radical triumph in Texas was greeted with similar woeful outcries. Commenting on the radicals' narrow victory in December 1869, one newspaper moaned that "worth, patriotism, intelligence, property and virtue" were now prostrate "before as vile a collection of ignorance, vice, servility, barbarism, and cruelty" as ever seen. *Galveston Tri-Weekly News*, 1 January 1870. See also *Texas State Gazette*, 10 December 1869; *Dallas Weekly Herald*, 18 December 1869, 25 December 1869, and 20 February 1870.

30. Governor August Throckmorton, Address to the Texas State Senate, Eleventh Legislature (1866) (recommending that it reject the Fourteenth Amendment).

31. *Journal of the House of Representatives of the State of Texas, Eleventh Legislature, State of Texas. By Authority.* (Austin: Printed at the Office of the "State Gazette," 1866), 578.

32. *Journal of the Senate of the State of Texas, Eleventh Legislature,* 421–22.

33. Ibid., 422.

34. For example, the 1866 legislature revised judicial districts in order to eliminate Unionist judges. Randolph B. Campbell, "The District Judges of Texas in 1866–1867: An Episode in the Failure of Presidential Reconstruction," *Southwest Historical Quarterly* 93 (1990): 357, 367–75.

35. On December 3, 1866, Hamilton spoke to the Impartial Suffrage League in Boston. He made the following points:

1. Congress had the power and the duty under Article IV to guarantee every state a republican form of government.

2. Universal suffrage alone was consistent with "the great principle of republican equality."

3. The freedmen had or soon would have the same capacity for self-government that whites had.

In addition, he argued that universal suffrage would give "loyal black men" the power to help prevent the "leading spirits of the rebellion" from seizing power in the South. Andrew J. Hamilton, "An Address on 'Suffrage and Reconstruction,'" *The Duty of the People, the President, and Congress* (Boston: Impartial-Suffrage League, 1866).

36. Speech by E. M. Pease, July 12, 1880, quoted in J. Baggett, "The Rise and Fall of the Texas Radicals, 1867–1883" (Ph.D. diss., North Texas State University, 1972), 63–64.

37. H. Budd, "The Negro in Politics in Texas" (M.A. thesis, University of Texas, 1925), 3.

38. J. Dorsett, "Blacks in Reconstruction Texas, 1865–1877 (Ph.D. diss., University of Texas, 1985), 36.

39. *Southern Intelligencer*, 2 May 1867.

40. Baggett, *The Rise and Fall of the Texas Radicals*, 213.

41. *Weekly Austin Republican*, 28 December 1868, quoted in Dorsett, "Blacks in Reconstruction Texas," 50.

42. No blacks ever served Texas as congressmen or senators; none held executive office in the state government. There were two black senators and nine black representatives in the twelfth legislature; thereafter their numbers dwindled. Cf. Lerone Bennett Jr., *Black Power U.S.A.* (Chicago: Johnson Publishing Company, 1967), 281 (blacks provided "the lion's share of the vote" but received only "the lamb's share of the spoils").

43. *Texas State Gazette*, 14 September 1867.

44. Dorsett, "Blacks in Reconstruction Texas," 159. See also Barry A. Crouch, "'Unmanacling' Texas Reconstruction: A Twenty Year Perspective," *Southwest Historical Quarterly* 93 (1990): 275, 294 ("blacks sought equal treatment through the law").

45. Baggett, *The Rise and Fall of the Texas Radicals*, 127–28.

46. Barry A. Crouch, "'Unmanacling' Texas Reconstruction," 294. See generally Barry A. Crouch and L.J. Schultz, "Crisis in Color: Racial Separation in Texas During Reconstruction," *Civil War History* 16 (1970): 37.

47. Ernest W. Winkler, ed., *Platforms of Political Parties in Texas* (Austin: University of Texas, 1916), 99; *Galveston Daily News*, 5 July 1867.

48. Winkler, *Platforms of Political Parties in Texas*, 101.

49. *Southern Intelligencer*, 2 May 1867.

50. Winkler, *Platforms of Political Parties in Texas*, 121; *Houston Union*, 14 June 1869.

51. *Flake's Bulletin*, 13 May 1870, quoted in Moneyhon, *Republicanism in Reconstruction Texas*, 130. Davis was apparently a man of his word. When the legislature sent him "An Act to Incorporate the Leon County Colored Manual Labor School," he vetoed it because it included the word "colored." He asked the legislature to remove the word wherever it appeared.

52. *Galveston Daily News*, 4 July 1873, quoted in Dorsett, "Blacks in Reconstruction Texas," 72.

53. *Weekly Telegraph*, 30 July 1867.

54. *Harrison Flag*, 23 November 1867.

55. *Dallas Weekly Herald*, 7 March 1868.

56. Ibid., 1 February 1868.

57. *Texas State Gazette*, 20 July 1867.

58. *Weekly Telegraph*, 29 October 1868.

59. Ibid., 26 November 1868.

60. Ibid., 3 December 1868. See also *Texas Republican*, 30 June 1866.

61. Winkler, *Platforms of Political Parties in Texas*, 113.

62. *Galveston Republican*, 9 March 1868.

63. Following the end of the Civil War, each Southern state had to deal with this question: What laws passed by its legislature during the Confederate period remained valid? Though the answer proved troublesome in several states, it became a major issue only in Texas. Proponents of *ab initio* insisted that every law passed by the "rebel" Texas legislature was invalid. Moderates, including the A. J. Hamilton-Elisha [E. M.] Pease wing of the Republican Party, took the position that the wholesale invalidation of all state laws would be unfair and disruptive. The economic interests of many participants in the often bitter debates influenced the position they took on the issue. In the end, the *ab initio* movement was narrowly defeated.

64. Many Texans favored dividing Texas into two to four different states. Many rural Texans favored the idea because they chafed under the dominance of "East Texas," which included the major commercial centers of Houston and Galveston. Carving one or more separate states out of north Texas, west Texas, and southwest Texas was seen as a way of securing more funds for the development of these poorer areas of the state. Moreover, many radicals despaired of ever reconstructing all of Texas. They favored division because they thought that loyal governments could be established in the new state(s). Some also feared for their lives and imagined that the new state(s) would be a safe haven. In any case, division was a major issue in Texas during the early years of Reconstruction there. See generally Ernest Wallace, *The Howling of the Coyotes: Reconstruction Efforts to Divide Texas* (College Station: Texas A&M University Press, 1979).

65. Moneyhon, *Republicanism in Reconstruction Texas*, 90.

66. *Journal of the Reconstruction Convention, Which Met at Austin, Texas, June 1, A.D., 1868* (Austin: Tracy, Siemering & Co., Printers, 1870), 235.

67. *Memorial to the Senators and Representatives of the Forty-First Congress: Memorial from the Commissioners Elected by the Reconstruction Convention of the State of Texas* (Washington: J. L. Pearson, Printer, 1869), 4.

68. Sneed, "A Historiography of Reconstruction in Texas," 441.

69. J.E. Erickson, "Origins of the Texas Bill of Rights," *Southwest Historical Quarterly* 62 (1959): 457, 466.

70. Baggett, "The Rise and Fall of the Texas Radicals," 100.

71. See generally Wallace, *The Howling of the Coyotes*.

72. Moneyhon, *Republicanism in Reconstruction Texas*, 118.

73. See generally Otis A. Singletary, "The Texas Militia during Reconstruction," *Southwest Historical Quarterly* 60 (July 1956): 23.

74. See generally James Smallwood, *Time of Hope, Time of Despair: Black Texans during Reconstruction* (Port Washington, N.Y.: National University Publications, 1981), 128–58.

75. Quoted in Greg Cantrell, "Racial Violence and Reconstruction Politics in Texas, 1867–1868," *Southwest Historical Quarterly* 93 (1990): 333, 334.

76. Dorsett, "Blacks in Reconstruction Texas," 176. See generally Singletary, "The Texas Militia during Reconstruction," 27 (conservatives described the new forces as a "standing army of negro soldiers and mercenary hirelings").

77. *Houston Telegraph*, 14 July 1869.

78. Moneyhon, *Republicanism in Reconstruction Texas*, 139.

79. T. Johnson, *Texas and Texans,* vol. 1 (New York: American Historical Society, 1914), 565.

80. Dorsett, "Blacks in Reconstruction Texas," 67.

81. Moneyhon, *Republicanism in Reconstruction Texas*, 138.

82. See generally Sneed, "A Historiography of Reconstruction in Texas," 435.

83. See generally Philip J. Avillo, Jr., "Phantom Radicals: Texas Republicans in Congress, 1870–1873," *Southwest Historical Quarterly* 77 (April 1974): 431.

84. Baggett, *The Rise and Fall of the Texas Radicals*, 2–3.

85. Avillo, "Phantom Radicals," 444.

86. Ibid.

87. Carrier, "A Political History of Texas during Reconstruction," 403. Whites had been unified as early as 1871 when a Taxpayer Convention met in Austin to protest the financial extravaganza of the Davis regime.

88. Ledbetter, "White Texans' Attitudes," 263.

89. Crouch and Schultz, "Crisis in Color," 47–48. Unfortunately, this "incident" was not an isolated one, as Sneed concedes:

> The statistics on murder committed in Texas after the Civil War, compiled by a special committee of the 1868 Constitutional Convention, substantiate the charges of violent white hostility to Negroes and to Unionists. Ramsdell determines that about 500 whites and 500 Negroes were murdered in the first three postwar years; while 90 percent of the Negroes were killed by whites, only 1 percent of the whites were killed by Negroes. Probably the number of murders was far greater. These damning statistics leave no doubt. Texas was the scene of a race war in which Negroes and their protectors suffered great loss of life. (Sneed, "A Historiography of Reconstruction in Texas," 445).

90. *Congressional Globe*, 41st Cong., 2nd Sess. (15 April 1870), 2711–13.

91. Ibid.

12

Ratification in Georgia

When I thinks back, it warn't no good feelin' to be bound lak that. I sho'
had rather be free. I guess after all it's best dat slavery days is over.

—An elderly Georgia black man, reflecting on
a long and hard life during and after slavery

The good ship *Reconstruction* did not carry Georgia's freedmen to the promised land. It ran aground on the shoals of white defiance and Ku Klux violence. And then negrophobic torrents, fed by the social custom of generations, engulfed the stranded freedmen and swept them beyond the protection of the law, including the Fourteenth Amendment. Though the same racist flood reduced that amendment to legal flotsam, its waters did not destroy the record of the amendment's consideration and ratification in Georgia. Quite to the contrary, the swirling political eddies of the period illuminate rather than obscure that record, which shows that Georgians shared a common understanding of the amendment's meaning and potential scope. Moreover, their understanding paralleled the understanding of others elsewhere in the South.

Throughout the spring and summer of 1866, Georgians discussed the amendment only in the most general terms. Prior to its promulgation in May, discussion was necessarily speculative. It was nevertheless spirited. In early February, Georgia papers alerted readers to the prospect that an amendment might be designed "to compel the Southern states to admit the Negro population to the ballot box, under the penalty of losing a large portion of their Representatives."[1] Still another rumored possibility was an amendment "[t]o make all National and State laws apply equally to all men, without regard to color."[2] Also, Congress might insist, it was hinted, that every Southern state abolish "all distinctions with respect to all civil and religious rights."[3]

White Georgians were not well disposed toward any of these possibilities, save for the grant to the freedmen of the rights to buy and sell property, make contracts, and sue and be sued.[4] After all, white Georgians considered blacks ignorant and irresponsible:

[God] never designed that a race whose ancestors have been in all the past savages and cannibals, and whose brethren of today are the same, and who themselves have been taught all they know while slaves, and at this hour give no evidence of equality intellectually or morally with those who were their owners, but on the contrary prove by their very acts that they are not superior to their ancestors when the instruction imparted by the whites is deducted—we say God never intended such a race to govern such a land as this, while a superior race inhabits it. [5]

Political and social equality were unthinkable.

Negro suffrage was denounced in every forum. The "universal amnesty/universal suffrage" formula was called a "ruinous concession."[6] "Impartial or qualified suffrage" was equally dubious.[7] The *Daily Sun* ran articles depicting the unfortunate consequences of enfranchising blacks in Haiti[8] and Jamaica.[9] White Georgians naturally delighted in the president's firm rejection of Negro suffrage when a black delegation called on him in February 1866.[10] In the spring and fall of 1866, many Georgians sincerely believed that giving blacks the right to vote would ignite a war of the races.[11] Indeed, the *Macon Daily Telegraph* speculated that the radicals wanted a race war in order "to rid the country of the negro and put the white emigrant from the North and Europe in his place."[12]

White Georgians defied the North to reduce them "to the disgusting level of Negro Equality" or "compel [them] to live on a level with the sickening stench of a degraded humanity."[13] They insisted that: "[The black man] will never be allowed the elective franchise here; he shall not sit on our juries, or hold any office of trust or power within the jurisdiction of our State Governments; his testimony against a white person will always be a nonentity, and, while among us, he must keep his place."[14] "His place" was not with whites, for social equality was anathema. Abuse was heaped upon "negro-maniacs"[15] and "nigger lovers,"[16] who were told:

And since you professed to love the negro so much, we hope they will visit your theatres, sleep in your beds, run away with your daughters, fill up the family circle with "clay-bank" babies, swarm around your houses, until you can scent them on the water you drink, taste them in the bread you eat, then, perchance, you may learn, what God has tried to teach you, that the social equality of the two races were [sic] never intended.[17]

Persons who held these views—and virtually all white Georgians did hold them, albeit with varying degrees of intensity—could scarcely be expected to favor an amendment that curtailed their authority over blacks, encouraged Negro suffrage, and simultaneously disfranchised their heroes. "Never, *never* should the South adopt it—never till absolutely, literally, *forced* to do it!"[18]

Moreover, white Georgians revered the Constitution (as they understood it, of course). They had gone to war to preserve it, they thought; and they could not abide its amendment.[19] Quite aside from their substantive reservations to the radical ideas then being bruited about, they shared President Johnson's view that "propositions to amend the Constitution were becoming as numerous as preambles and resolutions of town meetings, called to consider the most ordinary questions connected with the administration of local affairs."[20] Such amendments trivialized the Constitution.

White Georgians had exhibited these same attitudes from the very beginning of presidential Reconstruction. Even as James Johnson, a one-term, prewar congressman who had approved secession, was being appointed provisional governor, Howell Cobb, one of the wealthiest and most influential citizens of the state, was writing General Wilson about the importance of the state's retaining its authority to control the freedmen:

By the abolition of slavery—which either has been—or soon will be accomplished, a state of things has been produced, well calculated to excite the most serious apprehensions with the people of the South. I regard the result as unfortunate both for the white and the black. The institution of slavery, in my judgment, provided the best system of labor that could be devised for the negro race. But that has passed away, and it will tax the ability of the best and wisest statesmen to provide a substitute for it. It is due both to the white population and the negroes that the present state of things should not remain. You will find that our people are fully prepared to conform to the new state of things;— and as a general rule will be disposed to pursue towards the negroes, a course dictated by humanity and kindness. I take it for granted, that the future relations, between the negroes and their former owners, like all other questions of domestic policy, will be under the control and direction of the State governments. [21]

In October 1865 a state convention met. Asked to comply with the demands of the president, the convention hedged. In abolishing slavery, it declared that it was not waiving its citizens' right to compensation. It refused to nullify the secession ordinance but did repeal it, thus implying that secession was merely unwise rather than unconstitutional. And it repudiated the state debt only after a bitter debate convinced the delegates that repudiation was necessary for restoration.[22]

The legislature met in December 1865. Dominated by conservatives, it had even fewer antisecessionists and Union sympathizers than had the constitutional convention.[23] The legislature was urged to grant the Negro the same civil rights the white man enjoyed.[24] Many white Georgians realized that "the unfortunate race who have recently been transferred by the dash of a pen from bondage to freedom" needed governmental protection.[25] Georgia did grant the freedmen certain civil rights, and the legislature was praised for making them secure in all their rights of person and property.[26] Consequently, the *Macon Daily Telegraph* professed not to understand why blacks had formed an Equal Rights Association:

The Legislature of our State has solemnly recognized all their civil rights, and placed them on an equal footing with the whites in person and property and before the courts. The negro vindicates his legal rights in the same tribunal with his former master, and each is amenable to the same punishment for the same offense. It is very clear, therefore, as the civil rights of the colored population are fully protected by law, that they need no further protection at the hands of Capt. Bryant or his association. [27]

Blacks thought otherwise. After all, the legislature had also denied freedmen the right to serve on juries, testify against whites, and intermarry with whites.[28] Moreover, it elected Alexander Stephens, the former vice-president of the Confederacy, and Herschel Johnson, a former Confederate senator, to represent Georgia in the United States Senate. Additionally, it sent Jefferson Davis a message, declaring "warm affections cluster around the fallen chief of a once dear, but now abandoned cause."[29]

These latter actions confirmed General Wilson's advice to his superiors six months earlier. Commenting on Mr. Cobb's letter, he had warned:

The people express an external submission to [slavery's] Abolition, but there is an evident desire on the part of some to get the matter within their own control, after the reorganization of the State. Others are anxious to substitute a gradual system of emancipation, or a modified condition of Slavery, similar to Peonage, and still others seem to doubt that the President's proclamation of freedom, and the laws of Congress have been final in disposing of the Slavery question. There must be no hesitation on any of these points either by military or civil authorities. The whole system of Slavery and slave labor must be effectually destroyed, and the Freedmen protected from the injustice of evil men, before the people of Georgia get the State Government under their own control. If a single particle of life is left in the institution, or the original guardians of it are allowed any influence in the reorganization of the State, they will resuscitate and perpetuate its iniquities if possible.[30]

Congress, sharing the same concerns, promulgated the Fourteenth Amendment the following spring.

In the first few weeks after the Reconstruction Committee reported on the amendment, Georgia newspapers tended to reduce its several provisions to a single-sentence summary rather than to analyze their language. In this vein, Section 1 was said to:

- acknowledge "the negro . . . [the] equal" of the white man;[31]
- insure the "civil rights and privileges of the person in all parts of the Republic";[32]
- mean "no state shall make or enforce statutes denying any person equality of rights under law";[33] and
- reaffirm "the chief provisions of the civil rights bill.[34]

These summaries obviously reflected somewhat different—though not inconsistent—emphases. None, however, reflected any understanding that Section 1 incorporated the Bill of Rights, though that, like the others, would have been a readily understood shorthand summary—had incorporation been understood to be the thrust of any of its provisions. In fact, very early in the debate in Georgia, a conservative wailed: "Whole sections of the Declaration of Independence may, in the matter of grievances set forth, be laid to the Radicals as things they have done, and still seek to do. Whole paragraphs of the Bill of Rights might be quoted as embodying principles now in danger."[35] One can well imagine his surprise—nay, shock—at the notion that the very embodiment of the most nefarious of radical schemes, the Fourteenth Amendment, included, rather than endangered, the guarantees of the Bill of Rights!

Initially, most detailed analysis was reserved for an examination of "the gross irregularity of the whole proceedings surrounding [the amendment's] adoption."[36] The first charge was that Congress had impermissibly bypassed the president when it failed to submit the amending resolution to him for his signature.[37] The second charge was that the amendment had not received the necessary approval of two-thirds of the Senate and House because representatives of the eleven Southern states had been excluded,[38] an exclusion which was characterized as "an anomaly in our Republican system."[39] A third charge was that the amendment was being rushed before state legislatures whose members were "elected without reference to" their views on its wisdom and desirability.[40] These critics drew sustenance from Senator Johnson's widely reprinted and oft-cited minority report on the Fourteenth Amendment, which likewise concluded that the Southern states were being deprived of their constitutional rights.[41]

This unwarranted deprivation was seen as fresh evidence of Congress's unremitting hostility to the South, and that rancorous attitude was much lamented.[42] It would only breed "eternal hate" because "[n]o people in God's green earth had ever submitted to inequality and degradation without hating those who imposed" such terms.[43] The terms themselves were resented, moreover, as yet new and additional conditions for restoration by a people who insisted they had already fulfilled all the conditions imposed upon them at the time of their surrender.[44]

Finally, white Georgians doubted that they would be restored even if they did agree to the "abominable measure."[45] Thus Georgians concluded without any need to analyze the amendment carefully that "[t]he North has nothing to grant that would compensate us for the loss of self-respect, and [the] surrender of all claims to the respect of mankind" entailed in ratification.[46] They would not grovel for "any crumb of comfort . . . thrown from the Congressional table."[47]

Most white Georgians hoped, of course, that the North would reject the fanaticism that bred such hostile attitudes and insulting measures or, as one editor put it, "rebuke the madness that rules the hour and come back to the support of . . . the Constitution."[48] These Georgians naturally supported the National Union Convention, which endorsed the president's Reconstruction program.[49] They regarded the Loyal National Convention as a "farce,"[50] staged by "nigger worshipping rowdies and rogues."[51]

The two conventions did clarify the issue which divided the country. It was not Negro suffrage, which neither convention endorsed. Rather, it was ratification of the Fourteenth Amendment:

What are the real differences as they now exist? We find by comparison they are narrowed down to certain constitutional amendments proposed by Congress. The Conservatives have declared that the National debt shall be paid—so say the Radicals. Under no circumstances shall the debt contracted in behalf of the rebellion be paid—and still they are in perfect accord. There shall be no indemnification for loss of slaves, and here again they agree. And so on until we come to two sections in the constitutional amendments proposed by Congress—the one basing representation on the voting population, and the other proscribing certain classes in the south, and denying them all participation in the State or Federal Government. Sifted of all untruths and misrepresentations this is the issue, and it will keep the country in a perpetual, dangerous ferment until it is settled. [52]

Disfranchisement and reduced representation were, as usual, the "sticking points."[53]

The first section of the amendment, standing alone, was apparently not considered divisive—presumably because everyone agreed that blacks were entitled to civil rights, including governmental protection. Had anyone thought that Section 1 had a broader ambit, it would have been divisive, too, because most white Georgians were loath to grant blacks political or social rights.

Section 1 was criticized, however, particularly when read in light of Section 5. Those who opposed ratification shared a pervasive fear of a "consolidated despotism."[54] Not surprisingly, white Georgians had objected to the Civil Rights Bill because it "obliterates State lines, and inaugurates consolidation—the concentration of the reserved powers of the States in the Federal government."[55] Similarly, white Georgians had objected to Congress's exercise of enforcement powers under Section 2 of the Thirteenth Amendment:

It matters little what construction the ratifying legislatures may have placed upon the 2d clause of the amendment. It is very clear that under it Congress claims the power to legislate for a portion of our population, and so far as they are concerned at least, to control the domestic affairs of the State. This power cannot be successfully resisted. The only question then is whether it is expedient for Congress to exercise it for the purpose at present avowed—the protection of the freedmen in their newly acquired rights of person and property. In our opinion there need be no necessity for such legislation as that proposed by Messrs. Trumbull & Wilson. The object aimed at can be better attained through the voluntary legislation of the States themselves than by either Congress or the Freedmen's Bureau.[56]

Opponents were thus alert to the dangers posed by the analogous section in the Fourteenth Amendment. Consequently, they concurred in the judgment of Kentucky's governor, who objected to the amendment because "[t]he just balance of power between the State and national Governments is sought to be destroyed, and the centralization of power to be established in the Federal Government, through amendments to the Constitution, which, if successful, will destroy those rights reserved to the States and people, and which are essential to the preservation of free Government."[57] Though white Georgians understood the general danger, there is no evidence that they understood that its scope might be amplified by an unarticulated and hence unknown doctrine of incorporation.

Some few critics were astute enough, however, to perceive danger from sources other than the Congress:

It [the amendment] imposes new prohibitions upon the power of the State to pass laws and interdicts the execution of such parts of the common law as the national judiciary may esteem inconsistent with the vague provisions of the said amendment, made vague for the purpose of facilitating encroachments upon the lives, liberties and property of the people.

It enlarges the judicial power of the United States so as to bring every law passed by the State, and every principle of the common law relating to life, liberty or property, within the jurisdiction of the Federal tribunals; and charges those tribunals with duties to the due performance of which they, from their nature and organization, and their distance from the people, are unequal.[58]

The critic was apparently not astute enough to anticipate that the federal courts would use the doctrine of incorporation to accomplish the results he feared. Had that doctrine been understood at the time, the critic surely would have reinforced his argument with some pointed illustrations, which the incorporation doctrine would have readily provided.

These Georgian critics of the Fourteenth Amendment declared themselves in favor of republican rather than democratic government, the "most stupid and execrable" of all forms of government.[59] They distinguished between the right to representation, which all should enjoy, and the right to vote, which was properly reserved to those "who from education, association and habits of thought, are most capable of exercising it with safety to the public welfare."[60] They thus simultaneously objected to reduced representation, which denied their white citizens the right to be fully represented, and negro suffrage, which conferred the right to vote on persons unfit to exercise it.

Governor Jenkins, a native son of South Carolina who had played a leading role in Georgia's constitutional convention the preceding year, sent the amendment to the state legislature on November 1, 1866. In his transmittal message, he made the same points that had emerged in the preceding public discussion. Describing the amendment as "equally novel and unjust" in its substantive provisions, he also pronounced it "unconstitutional, null, and void" because the Southern states had been excluded from the Congress that proposed it.[61] In analyzing the specific provisions of the amendment, he concentrated his fire on Sections 2 and 3. Section 2 posed a choice of evils: admit blacks to the vote or accept reduced representation in the Congress. The North faced no such choice because it had so few blacks. As a result, he complained, the South alone would suffer adverse consequences, whatever the choice it made. The governor also attacked Section 3 because of its differential impact on the North and South. The North could continue to rely upon its "best and brightest"; the South, however, would be deprived of hers. "Can Georgia," he asked, "spare all of these from her service?"[62] These sections were thus objectionable, not only because they invited Negro suffrage and disfranchised whites, but because they subverted the equality of the states.

The governor did not ignore Section 1 or 5. Of Section 1, he said simply: "The prominent feature of the first is, that it settles definitely the right of citizenship in the several States, as political communities, thereby depriving them in the future of all discretionary power over the subject within their respective limits, and with reference to their State governments proper. It makes all persons of color, born in the United States, citizens."[63] He did not even mention the equal protection or due process clauses. He worried only that Section 1 would deprive Georgia of the right to determine citizenship and its incidents. Section 5 made that concern especially acute:

The fifth, and last section empowers the Congress "to enforce, by appropriate legislation," the provisions of the amendment. It will be contended that they are the proper judges of what constitutes appropriate legislation. If therefore, the amendment be adopted, and a fractional Congress, from which the Southern States, chiefly interested in it, are excluded, be empowered "to enforce it by appropriate legislation," what vestige of hope remains to the people of those States? Nay, more, what semblance of Republican Government can the true patriot of the North discern in such a state of affairs?[64]

The governor clearly understood these sections to be revolutionary not because they incorporated the Bill of Rights, but because they infringed state sovereignty. Consolidation then, not incorporation, was the fear.

The House and Senate convened in Millegeville on November 3. Although neither presiding officer spoke explicitly of the Fourteenth Amendment, both expressed sentiments that foreshadowed their strong opposition. The president of the Senate praised President Johnson for preserving the Constitution and republican government, and the speaker of the House counseled against the sacrifice of manhood and honor in pursuit of restoration.[65] Although some advised the legislature to take no action on the amendment, others urged that it be referred to a committee of the "ablest and most discreet members" who could "point out the objections which the people of Georgia have to these propositions, and in fitting language lay before the people of the United States why the State of Georgia cannot give her consent to the changes sought to be made in the fundamental law."[66]

The amendment was referred to the aptly named "Committee on the State of the Republic."[67] The committee promptly produced a report in which it declined to discuss the substantive merits of the amendment.[68] The report did elaborate the thesis that the amendment was "presented without the authority of the Constitution."[69] The thesis was as simple as it was well known: either Georgia was not a state, in which case it had no right to pass on amendments to the Constitution; or it was a state, in which case Congress was improperly constituted when it passed the amendment.[70]

Though the report did not specify any substantive objections, they were well known and widely shared. Texas had already rejected the amendment, for example; and the report of its House Committee on Federal Relations had been published in the Georgia press on the eve of that state's consideration of the amendment.[71] The Texas report warned that Congress might read Section 1 expansively; and though its authors speculated at length on the numerous and horrific possibilities such an expansive reading might entail, they did not mention among them any danger that the provision of the first eight amendments to the federal constitution might also be imposed on the states, or that racial preferences of any kind might be established.

The decision of the legislature was never in doubt. On November 9, 1866, the Senate unanimously rejected the amendment; and the House rejected it with only two dissenting votes. There was some disappointment that the House's rejection was not unanimous. One observer consoled himself with the fact that the two persons who voted for ratification hailed "from counties notorious for ignorance and treason."[72]

Congressional Reconstruction ushered in a round of intense political activity in Georgia, as it did everywhere. For a time, conservative Georgians remained divided about how best to deal with congressional Reconstruction. Some thought they could stave it by belatedly "acquiescing in the amendment [they] had so defiantly repudiated only weeks ago."[73] Many, however, were not "disposed" to enter politics.[74] Governor Jenkins, for example, advocated a policy of "non-action," arguing that General John Pope's rule was "infinitely prefer[able]" to anything the Reconstruction convention might produce.[75] Others, however, urged "the good fight":

The most dangerous enemy to Republican institutions is political apathy—a failure, on the part of the populace to recognize the importance of political action. . . .
. . . [U]nless that spirit of apathy and despondency, which is so rapidly handing over the State—her government and varied interest—into the hands of an ignorant and vicious horde of Radicals and negroes is overcome, and the people brought to see and feel their true condition and dangers, there is but little hope for peace, prosperity and happiness, either for ourselves or those who are to come after us.[76]

Republicans were more decisive. Loyal Leagues, which had sprung up initially among white Georgians with Unionist sympathies, were organized to enlist and energize black Georgians and poor whites in defense of the "true principles" of popular government:

the establishment of equal liberty; the education and evaluation of the toiling masses of the republic; the preservation of the national honor and faith; the inculcation of a brotherly affection and true charity towards all; the complete and final overthrow of the ballot-box, as in the field, of the oligarchy of political leaders, who sought to ruin when they could not rule, and through whose errors and wrongs our country has been baptized in blood; the establishment here of an asylum for the distressed of other lands, and of a beacon light so prominent and endearing as to be seen by all nations for all time, and so unerring as to guide all people to the certain possession of national and true liberty.[77]

The Loyal League in Savannah, by way of example, was said to include sixteen hundred blacks and four hundred whites.[78] League members were accused of bloc voting,[79] and the Republican Party of Georgia was denounced as their spawn.[80] By mid-1867 the Republican Party of Georgia had been organized. The party platform, adopted by the Republican convention in July 1867, endorsed congressional Reconstruction, equal rights for all citizens, relief measures, and "free" schools.[81] Though the party included many moderates, radical voices predominated.[82]

The debate over ratification of the Fourteenth Amendment was now submerged in the larger issues of Reconstruction. The discussion of those larger issues nevertheless spotlighted how Georgians understood the concepts of privileges and immunities, equal protection, and due process. Freedom of the press became an issue in Georgia, for example, when General Pope ordered the state's civil officers to place governmental notices only in the "radical" press.[83] Even one of the papers authorized to receive such notices condemned the so-called "starvation order" as an "arbitrary interference with the sacred rights of the press . . . because it was intended to dictate what should be the political tone of the press of Georgia."[84] Early on, the Georgia press had criticized censorship by military commanders, as, for example, when General Schofeld ordered the office of the *Richmond Examiner* closed.[85] More generally, white Georgians objected to Congress "cloth[ing] their pro counsels [i.e., the military commanders] with power to silence all constitutional privileges."[86] The command of the First Amendment was thus well understood, and it was understood to circumscribe the power of federal officers to implement Reconstruction.

A number of issues also arose that implicated the equal protection guarantee. In general, that principle was understood to guarantee "*all* men . . . equal chance before the law."[87] White Georgians, for example, resented the accusation that they mistreated Unionists or Negroes, an accusation which was the most frequently invoked justification in the North for Section 1. While conceding "that individual instances of wrong and, perhaps, even outrage have been committed,"[88] white Georgians insisted that Unionists and Negroes there enjoyed "all the rights and privileges of citizens."[89] No one disagreed—in the abstract, at least—that every person was entitled to protection in person and property. Indeed, conservative whites themselves came to bemoan the fact that Reconstruction authorities tolerated physical assaults on blacks who voted the conservative ticket.

On more specific issues there was disagreement. These disagreements stemmed from varying assessments of what today would be called the reasonableness of the legislative classification or its disparate impact. Two issues—

Negro jury service and the permissibility of whipping as a punishment—are illustrative. Whipping was defined as a necessary punishment, particularly where there were no prisons and, hence, the state had to choose between imposing a death sentence or, in the alternative, some lesser penalty.[90] In Georgia, 90 percent of all crimes were punishable by whipping. The law which authorized whipping made no distinction between white and black perpetrators. In fact, "many of the persons likely to be punished in this way will be negroes" because "it has generally been considered very disgraceful for a white man to be whipped."[91] Blacks naturally objected to the infliction of a punishment that was primarily used against them.

Blacks also demanded the right to serve on juries. Whites generally thought them unfit, an attitude captured in the following news account from a local Georgia paper:

A negro man had hired himself to Mr. A. for $15 per month—and at the expiration of 10 months sued Mr. A. for $150. A. admitted the contract as alleged by the negro, and admitted that he (the negro) had worked for him the length of time for which the negro claimed wages. The case was submitted to the negro jury, under the charge of the court, and to the astonishment of all present, they brought in a verdict in favor of the plaintiff for $110. The Judge told them he did not see how they could render such a verdict; that the negro plaintiff was clearly entitled, by the admission of Mr. A., to $150. A large, dirty, greasy juryman raised up in the jury box, and with much gravity informed his Honor that $11 per month was all the negro's services were worth; that he knew the plaintiff to be a trifling, lazy scoundrel, and that the jury would not allow him any more! O tempora! O mores! The white man (Mr. A.) of course had no cause for complaint at the verdict. But this is a sample of their ideas of law and facts. God protect me from such juries! At the close of the first week of court in Houston, the negro jury were paid off at the rate of $2 per day for their services as jurors. And on the Monday morning following, when court opened, the negroes besieged the court house to get up on the jury. One old crippled negro stopped the Judge on his way to court and begged for a place on the jury, urging his crippled and almost helpless condition as a reason why he should be selected: and further proposed to take the job of sitting on the jury by the year. When the Judge informed him that the court would be in session only three or four weeks, he seemed to think this was an artful dodge of his Honor to avoid closing the contract, and ingenuously proposed to take the job by the year at one dollar per day! This is the pure and undefiled channel through which verdicts now flow. [92]

When General Pope ordered the civil courts of Georgia to include black jurors, the *Daily Sun* predicted that whites would simply refrain from using the courts, preferring to turn their disputes "over to the adjudication of honest and educated arbitrators" rather than "a dozen grinning and idiotic cuffees and Sambos."[93]

The discussion of these issues thus reflected two perspectives that illuminate the understanding of the Fourteenth Amendment among whites in Georgia by the fall of 1867. No one ever argued that the guarantees of the Fourteenth Amendment incorporated the Bill of Rights, and many continued to insist that its principles permitted "reasonable" legislative classifications. These same perspectives shaped the work of the constitutional convention, which was held in Atlanta from December 9, 1867, to March 11, 1868.

Though radicals dominated the leadership of the convention, they could not control it. Of the 165 delegates, 46 were "staunch Democrats"; and 59 of the Republican delegates were "moderates." There were only 35 black delegates and even fewer "carpetbaggers."[94] While such a convention might (and did) support relief measures, it could not be expected to embrace equal rights for the freedmen enthusiastically. It did not.

It did not even discuss issues like equal access to public accommodations; and while it did adopt a provision for public schools, no one suggested that they be integrated. The general silence on these issues may be attributable to the convention's expulsion of the most militant of the black delegates, Aaron Bradley of Savannah, who did call for an end to discrimination on public carriers.[95] Former Governor Joseph Brown's Atlanta paper, the *Daily New Era*, termed Bradley "a worthless and brawling negro . . . , obnoxious to both white and black [who was] a creator of discord among his race, an enemy to the black man, and a nuisance of which the people should be rid."[96]

The debate on the office-holding provision was especially revealing. Republicans did unite to block a Democratic proposal that would have disqualified freedmen from holding office. However, most Republican delegates acquiesced in the proposal to eliminate from the new constitution any explicit guarantee of the freedmen's right to hold office. Former Governor Brown, who may have engineered adoption of the moderate program, repeatedly cautioned the delegates against doing any more than the Reconstruction Acts and the Fourteenth Amendment required; and he clearly believed that the latter did not dictate the "speedy elevation of the Negro to full political privileges."[97]

While the black delegates had a different view, which they expressed privately, they nevertheless publicly supported the moderate strategy.[98] The black delegates also agreed to a vague clause that required jurors to be "upright and intelligent persons," a standard that obviously permitted the new constitution to be hawked by its supporters as both including and excluding Negro jurors, depending upon the audience.[99] Blacks, for example, predicted the fall of "the Jerichorian wall of prejudice."[100] Brown's Atlanta mouthpiece advised them to "quit dabbling in politics."[101]

The leader of the black delegates was Henry Turner. A minister-politician, he could speak with a conservative or radical voice. At the constitutional convention he talked a conservative line. He later said of his convention work: "So far as I am personally concerned, no man in Georgia has been more conservative than I. 'Anything to please the white folks' has been my motto."[102] The constitution which the convention submitted to the people of Georgia was thus among the more conservative of the Reconstruction constitutions. It did not stake out any advanced positions on equal rights for the freedmen, and its provisions belied any belief that the Fourteenth Amendment incorporated the federal Bill of Rights. Article I certainly recognized fundamental rights also found in the federal Constitution: freedom of speech (Section 9); the right to assemble and petition (Section 5); freedom of "religious sentiment" (Section 6); freedom from unreasonable searches (Section 10); jury trial rights (Section 7); and the right to bear arms (Section 14). Generally, however, these rights were not set out in the exact language of the Bill of Rights. Moreover, several were carefully circumscribed. Section 6, for example, declared that "the liberty of conscience hereby secured shall not be so construed as to excuse acts of licentiousness or justify practices inconsistent with the peace or safety of the people." Similarly, Section 14 authorized the General Assembly "to prescribe by law the manner in which arms may be borne."

Moreover, the Georgia Declaration of Fundamental Principles did not include every right guaranteed in the Bill of Rights. It was silent on the accused's right to a grand jury indictment, specifying only that he be "furnished, on demand, a copy of the accusation against him." The declaration did not forbid cruel and unusual punishment although it outlawed "whipping, as a punishment for crime" (Section 21) and insisted that "[a]ll penalties shall be proportional to the nature of the offense" (Section 22).

The most conclusive evidence that the delegates to the Georgia constitutional convention did not understand that the Fourteenth Amendment incorporated the Bill of Rights, however, is their inclusion in Sections 2 and 3 of the Georgian declaration the exact language of Section 1 of that amendment. If the language of Section 1 of the Fourteenth Amendment guaranteed the rights contained in the first eight amendments to the federal Constitution, any further specification of those rights would have been unnecessary. Furthermore, the subsequent inclusion of analogous rights would have injected unnecessary confusion into their meaning.

The constitution was narrowly approved after a "bitter and vituperative campaign,"[103] during which the people also elected a moderate to conservative legislature. During that campaign, Republicans had exploited the ambiguity of their position on the right of freedmen to hold office. In the upcountry they assured white farmers that Negroes did not have that right; in the Black Belt they assured the freedmen they could hold office. Again former Governor Brown led the way. In his widely quoted "Marietta Address," he conceded that blacks were now entitled to vote but added that the new constitution did not guarantee them the right to hold office.[104] While this position may have been a brilliant campaign strategy, it soon backfired.

Though the new legislature ratified the Fourteenth Amendment on July 21, 1868, it otherwise turned a deaf ear to radical demands. Indeed, that fall it stunned the North when it expelled "all the known Negro members"[105] on the theory that the right to vote did not include the right to hold office. It then seated conservative whites in their place. In this way did the Georgia legislature discharge its constitutional obligation "to protect every person in the due enjoyment of the rights, privileges, and immunities guaranteed [in Article I]," including, of course, the right to the equal protection of the laws.

The expulsion of black senators and representatives radicalized them. Calling the legislature a "lawless conclave," Representative Turner and the other expelled delegates formed a "Civil and Political Rights."[106] Blacks now publicly voiced the views they had expressed privately at the constitutional convention. They "wanted full and equal participation in every aspect of Georgia society . . . and expected equal political, civil and economic rights."[107] One black mass meeting adopted the following petition, "reminiscent of Jefferson's indictment of George III":

They have expelled our colored legislators in violation to the Constitution and laws. . . .
  They then refused to allow their protests to go on [sic] the Journals of the House.
  They have robbed us of the right to be Jurors. . . .
  They have inaugurated strife and discord between white and colored citizens.
  They have demoralized society. . . .
  They have refused to require common carriers to give us respectable accommodations, when we pay equal rates. . . .
  They have voted down every measure for the establishment of schools for the education of our children. . . .
  They have not only invaded our political rights, but nullified by prejudicial legislation, our civil rights.
  They have given indirect countenance to the murdering bands of the KKK.[108]

Blacks demanded federal intervention to correct these evils.[109] They got it in the form of a "force bill," passed in December 1869. It reimposed military rule though it permitted the governor to remain in office, albeit as a provisional governor. In early 1870 the purged Negroes were restored to their seats, and twenty-nine conservative whites were removed on the ground that they were ineligible under Section 3 of the Fourteenth Amendment. In their stead, the Republican runners-up were seated. Though the legislature now reflected a less conservative mien, it chose to concentrate on the economic development of the state rather than on the welfare of its newest citizens.

Black leaders did have a legislative agenda, summarized in a letter from one local black leader to state assemblyman James Porter: "[G]ive us the Militia Bill, the Jury Law, the Common School Law, and the Common Carrier Law, and all will be well in this portion of the state." [110] Unfortunately, they never secured sufficient support from their white allies to implement this agenda effectively. No militia bill was ever passed; and a jury bill, which required that the names of blacks be put in the "jury boxes" from which potential jurors' names were drawn, seldom resulted in blacks' actually sitting on juries. Invariably they were challenged. When frustrated blacks asked General Terry to order that some of their race be put on juries trying civil disputes between a black and a white, he refused. His explanation of the decision to General Sherman illuminates his understanding of the equal protection guarantee: "I don't like to be always sort of wet nurse to the negroes. . . . if with a majority in each branch favorable to them, they cannot pass measures for their protection they had better suffer for a time."[111]

Black advocacy of the public schools and public carrier bills illuminated their understanding of the equal protection clause. Though they succeeded in getting a public schools bill passed, they acquiesced in a separate but equal clause (which a subsequent legislature amended to require equality only so "far as practicable").[112] Similarly, the public carrier law, passed in 1870, required equal facilities but did not require integration. Custom dictated segregation, and in 1872 a United States commissioner ruled that a Savannah streetcar company could segregate passengers by race so long as it provided sufficient cars for blacks.[113]

By 1872 Georgia had been readmitted to the Union once again and "redeemed"—though there was precious little to redeem. Reconstruction had had little impact on Georgia, which never really slipped from the control of native whites. They systematically and successfully employed violence to reinforce their authority and return the freedmen to peonage.[114] Poor blacks who had lived through slavery would nevertheless say later, reflecting on the hard life that they endured after emancipation: "When I thinks back, it warn't no good feelin' to be bound lak that. I sho' had rather be free. I guess after all it's best dat slavery days is over."[115] But the plaintive cry of the most radical of Georgia's Reconstruction blacks must have echoed endlessly in the minds of their more educated brethren—Du Bois's "talented tenth": "Are we yet slaves or are we free American citizens?"[116]

NOTES

1. *Rome Tri-Weekly Courier*, 3 February 1866.

2. Ibid., 8 February 1866.

3. Ibid.

4. *Albany Patriot*, 8 June 1866.

5. *Newman Herald*, 30 March 1867; accord, *Daily Sun*, 9 June 1867 (the "irrepressible negro" is an "incomprehensible natural puzzle").

6. *Savannah Daily News-Herald*, 23 March 1866.

7. *Daily Constitutionalist*, 27 November 1866.

8. *Daily Sun*, 17 August 1867.

9. Ibid., 8 August 1867.

10. *Augusta Chronicle-Sentinel*, 16 February 1866.

11. *Albany Patriot*, 14 March 1866; 22 September 1866.

12. *Macon Daily Telegraph*, 11 February 1866.

13. *Rome Weekly Courier*, 27 April 1866.

14. *Albany Patriot*, 3 March 1866.

15. *Daily Constitutionalist*, 12 March 1868.

16. *Daily Sun*, 4 June 1868.

17. *Dawson Weekly Journal*, 8 June 1866; accord, *Macon Daily Telegraph*, 24 April 1866:

[N]egro equality will reign in all its transcendent beauties. Negroes and Yankees cheek by jowl in the churches, in the hotels, in the theatres, on the throughfares, everywhere, even in the nuptial bed. We wish them joy of the delightfully odorous sensations that await them. It will be a glorious consummation that the negro-worshippers will at last be in the full embrace of their idol, at least until they shall cry for mercy and the Supreme Court, a year or two hence, shall come to their relief.

18. *Southern Herald*, 22 October 1866.

19. *Daily Constitutionalist*, 3 March 1867.

20. *Albany Patriot*, 3 February 1866.

21. Howard Cobb to General Wilson, 14 June 1865, in James Johnson MSS, Library of Congress. See also *Loyal Georgian*, 3 March 1866 ("Most of the white citizens believe that the institution of slavery was right . . . [and] will believe that the condition, which comes nearest to slavery, that can now be established will be the best.").

22. E. Merton Coulter, *A Short History of Georgia* (Chapel Hill: University of North Carolina Press, 1960), 341. A year later, some Georgians would object to the same provision in Section 4 of the Fourteenth Amendment. See, e.g., *Savannah Daily Republican*, 4 July 1866.

23. *A History of Georgia*, ed. K. Coleman (Athens: University of Georgia Press, 1977), 208.

24. *Macon Daily Telegraph*, 22 February 1866.

25. Ibid., 13 January 1866.

26. Ibid., 4 March 1866.

27. Ibid., 5 May 1866; accord, *Augusta Chronicle-Sentinel*, 5 April 1866; *Daily Sun*, 20 April 1866. Initially, the Equal Rights Association advocated a moderate program. The January 1866 Convention of Georgia Freedmen, out of which it had grown, opposed universal suffrage and confiscation of rebel lands. Eliabeth S. Nathans, *Losing the Peace: Georgia Republicans and Reconstruction, 1865–1871* (Baton Rouge: Louisiana State University Press, 1968), 26.

28. Clara M. Thompson, *Reconstruction in Georgia: Economic, Social, and Political, 1865–1871* (New York: Columbia University Press, 1915), 159; *A History of Georgia*, 209.

29. Coulter, *A Short History of Georgia*, 343.

30. Bvt. Maj. Gen. J. H. Wilson to Brig. Gen. W. D. Whipple, 15 June 1865, James Johnson MSS, Library of Congress.

31. *Macon Daily Telegraph*, 5 May 1866. See also 4 October 1866.

32. *Rome Weekly Courier*, 15 June 1866.

33. *Daily Constitutionalist*, 12 May 1866.

34. *Savannah News-Herald*, 3 April 1867.

35. *Daily Constitutionalist*, 14 March 1866.

36. *Savannah News-Herald*, 23 June 1866.

37. *Augusta Chronicle-Sentinel*, 22 June 1866. Cf. *Savannah Daily News-Herald*, 14 June 1866 (Congress assumes that the president has "no authority under the law over the subject of reconstruction").

38. *Daily Constitutionalist*, 12 May 1866; accord, ibid., 29 June 1866: "[T]his so called Constitutional Amendment is indeed no amendment—is not worth, in its legal validity, the paper whereon it is written—and should be treated by every American legislature that cleaves to the Federal CONSTITUTION as so absolutely void as not to be entitled to the first word of legislative discussion."

39. *Macon Daily Telegraph*, 25 October 1866.

40. *Savannah Daily News-Herald*, 9 July 1866.

41. *Daily Sun*, 27 June 1866.

42. *Savannah Daily News-Herald*, 14 June 1866:

> Every excess at the South is charged to the general account of Southern society, instead of the locality and individual where and by whom the wrong is committed. The effect of this is both disheartening to Southern interests and shamefully unjust, and as the concealment of truth, next to the utterance of falsehood, becomes a crime, those in high places who indulge in either at the expense of their neighbors will be held to a fearful responsibility for the wrongs they do.

43. *Macon Daily Telegraph*, 11 November 1866.

44. Ibid., 26 May 1866; 2 November 1866.

45. *Daily Sun*, 12 January 1867; *Daily Constitutionalist*, 10 October 1866.

46. *Macon Daily Telegraph*, 2 October 1866.

47. *Daily Sun*, 8 April 1866.

48. Ibid., 6 November 1866.

49. *Savannah Daily News-Herald*, 25 August 1866 ("the success of the policy of the President . . . depends upon . . . an honest and zealous effort to sustain the measures of reconstruction in support of which we have been heretofore all of one mind"); *Macon Daily Telegraph*, 28 July 1866 ("Among honorable men, there can be no better test of loyalty to the Constitution than their willingness to go into a national convention, as equals and friends, with the men whom they so recently fought in the field.").

50. *Daily Sun*, 15 September 1866.

51. *Georgia Journal and Messenger*, 12 September 1866.

52. *Savannah Daily Republican*, 13 September 1866.

53. *Savannah Daily News-Herald*, 19 June 1866 ("We must demur to the division of the people of these States into two classes, the one favored and the other outlawed, which will inevitably lay the foundation for hates and fewds of which we fear this country would not witness the termination. There is no better mode than this to create and perpetuate feelings of disloyalty and irritation. The curse of test oaths, and all the rest of the apparatus for ascertaining men's loyalty, is that it breeds and perpetuates social hates"); *Macon Daily Telegraph*, 15 June 1866 ("We are called upon, in consideration of the privilege of sending members to Congress, to brand ourselves as rebels, to disfranchise our ablest and best men whom we put forward to fight the battles of Southern independence, and to write 'TRAITOR' upon the graves of our sons and brothers who fell fighting in defence of our homes and firesides); *Daily Sun*, 30 September 1866 (South should not purchase peace "by discarding and dishonoring the best and bravest of that band who survived the late conflict for their rights and their liberties"); *Macon Daily Telegraph*, 2 October 1866 ("[the amendment] is a mere party manœuvre, intended to save themselves at the North. They know full well that no such measure could command the support of any man at the South whose nature had not become thoroughly debased and brutalized").

54. *Macon Daily Telegraph*, 16 June 1866; accord, *Daily Constitutionalist*, 30 July 1867.

55. *Augusta Chronicle-Sentinel*, 27 March 1866.

56. *Savannah Daily News-Herald*, 1 January 1866.

57. *Daily Sun*, 9 January 1867.

58. *Newman Herald*, 7 March 1868.

59. *Daily Sun,* 24 October 1866.

60. *Macon Daily Telegraph,* 7 February 1866.

61. *Journal of the House of Representatives of the State of Georgia, at the Annual Session of the General Assembly, Commenced at Milledgeville, November 1st, 1866* (Milledgeville, Ga.: J. W. Burke & Co., Stationers and State Printers, 1866), 5–11. Newspapers published the governor's message. See, e.g., *Savannah Daily Republican,* 3 November 1866. And they praised him for recommending rejection. See, e.g., *Tri-Weekly Star,* 6 November 1866 ("we presume the legislature will have the good sense to follow the suggestions of the Governor").

62. Ibid., 9.

63. Ibid., 7.

64. Ibid., 9.

65. *Tri-Weekly Star,* 3 November 1866.

66. *Weekly Augusta Chronicle and Sentinel,* 31 November 1866.

67. *Daily Sun,* 7 November 1866.

68. *Journal of the Senate of the State of Georgia, at the Annual Session of the General Assembly, Begun and Held in Milledgeville, the Seat of Government, 1866* (Milledgeville, Ga.: J. W. Burke & Co., Stationers and State Printers, 1866), 65–71. The report was published in the local press. See, e.g., *Macon Daily Telegraph,* 11 November 1866.

69. *Journal of the Senate* (1866), 65.

70. *Macon Daily Telegraph,* 15 May 1866; 15 June 1866; *Savannah Daily News and Herald,* 9 June 1866.

71. *Macon Daily Telegraph,* 1 November 1866.

72. *Daily Sun,* 13 November 1866.

73. Nathans, *Losing the Peace,* 46.

74. *Daily Sun,* 22 November 1866.

75. *Augusta Constitutionalist,* 18 May 1867.

76. *Dawson Weekly Journal,* 6 December 1867. The most articulate spokesman for this position was Benjamin Hill, whose "Notes on the Situation" appeared in several Georgia newspapers between 19 June and 1 August 1867. He also gave an influential speech on the subject at Davis Hall in Atlanta on 16 July. See *Atlanta Daily Intelligencer,* 18 July 1867.

77. *Tri-Weekly Star,* 30 July 1867.

78. *Daily Constitutionalist,* 29 August 1867.

79. *Daily Sun,* 26 February 1867.

80. *Rome Weekly Courier,* 31 May 1867.

81. *Atlanta Opinion,* 5 July 1867.

82. In the effort to build a biracial coalition of poor blacks and whites, the Republicans advocated suffrage for colored voters and poor white persons without property, homestead exemptions, an eight-hour workday, and reduced taxes. Nathans, *Losing the Peace,* 43.

83. Ibid., 52.

84. *Daily Opinion,* 29 September 1867. *Savannah Daily Republican,* 3 December 1867.

85. *Daily Sun,* 27 February 1866.

86. Ibid., 1 May 1867.

87. *Daily Opinion,* 15 February 1868.

88. *Augusta Chronicle-Sentinel,* 6 March 1867.

89. *Daily Sun*, 16 February 1867.

90. *Augusta Chronicle-Sentinel*, 23 December 1866.

91. *Rome Tri-Weekly Courier*, 14 June 1866.

92. *Dawson Weekly Journal*, 12 July 1867.

93. *Daily Sun*, 23 August 1867.

94. Nathans, *Losing the Peace*, 56 and 64.

95. Edmund Drago, *Black Politicians and Reconstruction in Georgia* (Baton Rouge: Louisiana State University Press, 1982), 41.

96. Ibid., 42. See generally ed. Joseph P. Reidy, "Aaron A. Bradley: Voice of Black Labor in the Georgia Low Country," in *Southern Black Leaders of the Reconstruction Era*, ed. H. Rabinowitz (Champaign: University of Illinois Press, 1982), 281–300.

97. Nathans, *Losing the Peace*, 67.

98. Drago, *Black Politicians*, 40.

99. Ibid., 40–41.

100. *Freemen's Standard*, 13 June 1868.

101. *Daily New Era*, 25 April 1868.

102. E. Merton Coulter, "Henry M. Turner: Negro Preacher-Politician during the Reconstruction Era," *Georgia History Journal* 48 (December 1964): 371, 379.

103. *A History of Georgia*, 213.

104. Nathans, *Losing the Peace*, 91.

105. *A History of Georgia*, 213.

106. *Macon American Union*, 25 September 1868.

107. Drago, *Black Politicians*, 86.

108. Ibid., 73.

109. Ibid., 93.

110. R. W. White to James Porter, 16 July 1870, The Governor's Incoming Correspondence Records, Group 1–1–5, Georgia Department of Archives and History, Atlanta, Georgia.

111. General Terry to General William Sherman, 20 June 1870. Available in Sherman Papers, Library of Congress.

112. Drago, *Black Politicians*, 98.

113. Ibid., 100.

114. Nathans, *Losing the Peace*, 146 ("the Ku Klux Klan . . . operated as an effective adjunct to the Democratic party, securing by intimidation and violence at night whatever the party orators might have failed to win by day"). Allen W. Trelease, *White Terror: Ku Klux Klan Conspiracy and Southern Reconstruction* (New York: Harper & Row, 1971), 236 ("terror probably accomplished more in Georgia than in any other state to subvert the Republican party and Reconstruction").

In 1867 a Georgia Bureau agent wrote to his superior that one-third of the black children in Monroe County had been bound out to planters under the Apprentice Act of 1866. He added: "It would first be proper for me to denominate [the labor system] a system of slavery analoguis [*sic*] to the old Russian serfdom." Edwin Belcher to Caleb C. Sibley, 9 September 1867, Records of the Bureau of Refugees, Freedmen, and Abandoned Lands, Library of Congress.

115. Drago, *Black Politicians*, 140.

116. Reidy, "Aaron A. Bradley," 391.

13

The Imagined Future
of the Fourteenth Amendment

The Warren Court "imagined the past and remembered the future."

—Alexander Bickel, critiquing the Court's attempt
to construct the "Egalitarian Society"

People in the Southern states subjected the Fourteenth Amendment to unprecedented scrutiny. They studied it in committees, debated it in legislative chambers, discussed it around dinner tables, and wrangled over it during one political campaign after another. They dissected it section by section, clause by clause. They questioned the intentions of those who framed it, explored the implications that might be drawn from its language, and pondered the consequences that would follow its adoption. No other amendment has ever been examined so carefully or thoroughly at the state level.

The internal legislative history includes eight committee reports from five states, eleven messages from ten governors, and numerous newspaper accounts of various state legislative debates. The external legislative history is even more extensive, including, as it does, the historical context within which the amendment was first promulgated, then considered, and later implemented. That context thus begins with the South's adoption of the infamous Black Codes and ends with the actions of the "reconstructed" legislatures on issues involving the rights of black Americans. Between those two periods, the Southern states were required to enfranchise blacks and draft new constitutions, and the resulting election campaigns and convention deliberations also constitute an important part of the amendment's external legislative history. No other amendment has ever been ratified amidst such political turbulence, economic chaos, and social upheaval; and this dynamic context produced a complex but illuminating history of extraordinary richness.

What insight into the original understanding of the Fourteenth Amendment may be drawn from the South's intense study of it, as recorded in this voluminous legislative history? The fundamental lesson emerges with stark clarity: *the amendment was intended to nationalize the protection of individual liberty within the federal structure ordained by the original Constitution.* This lesson must be carefully qualified, however, lest it be thought to support a more general democratization and nationalizaton of the American republic. This caveat is critically important because the Supreme Court has perverted the Fourteenth Amendment to those very ends. First, the Court has undermined the federal structure by fastening the Bill of Rights upon the states through the fraudulent doctrine of incorporation.[1] It has further eroded state autonomy, second, by interpreting provisions of the Bill of Rights as if their general language embodied detailed statutory schemes, thus depriving the states of their traditional authority to define the incidents of those natural and civil rights that are due every person.[2] Third, the Court has given an unwarranted imprimatur to egalitarian doctrines through a latitudinarian interpretation of the equal protection clause, once again depriving the states of their traditional authority to make reasonable legislative classifications in support of legitimate public policies.[3]

The Southern ratification debates demonstrate that the Fourteenth Amendment was never intended to incorporate the Bill of Rights. In the entire record of the Southern debates there is not one shred of direct evidence—*not one*—which supports the theory that the due process clause incorporated the guarantees of the Bill of Rights. No committee report of any state legislature mentions the theory. No governor in any message articulates it. No legislator in any debate, no politician on the stump, refers to it. It cannot be found in any of the countless resolutions, declarations, or platforms that issued forth from persons and parties of every stripe; and no newspaper editor states it to praise it or to denounce it.

Had anyone even suspected, much less understood, that the due process clause or any other clause of Section 1 incorporated the Bill of Rights, that clause would have been *the* focus of the ratification debate on Section 1, for all the participants were concerned about the substantive rights the amendment gave the freedmen. Yet the due process clause was almost never discussed. That fact is scarcely surprising. Those concerned about the substantive rights which the amendment guaranteed would not worry about a clause that guaranteed nothing more than procedural fairness. Indeed, very early in the debate those opposed to the Fourteenth Amendment conceded that a state was obligated to treat all persons fairly (though their sense of what constituted fair treatment for blacks was shockingly unfair if judged by any reasonable contemporary standard).

Had the amendment's opponents suspected that the due process clause was a Trojan horse for the Bill of Rights, they would have attacked it venomously. After all, they speculated endlessly about the evil ends that the framers had allegedly concealed in other provisions of the amendment. Consider just three examples. Blacks felt the need to protect themselves; and they demanded the right to carry arms, to serve in the militia, and to sit on juries. Armed blacks terrified many whites, and they could not fathom how an "ignorant" black could discharge the functions of a juror. More generally, most Southern whites could not abide the prospect of blacks exercising control over them, as would have been the case if blacks sat on juries or served in militias. Though the debate on these issues was intense and particularly vituperative, no one ever suggested that the provisions of the Second and Sixth Amendments were relevant, as they surely would have been had the due process clause been understood to incorporate the Bill of Rights. The silence of conservative opponents on the due process clause proves it was not thought to protect any substantive rights, let alone all those contained in the Bill of Rights.

While the privileges and immunities clause did protect substantive rights, no one suggested that those rights included all the guarantees of the Bill of Rights. The privileges and immunities clause, unlike the due process clause, did excite comment, however. Indeed, argument over its scope raged as both proponents and opponents repeatedly tried to categorize the rights included within its ambit. None, however, ever stated that it was a concise summary of the Bill of Rights.

Proponents, who needed to explain the amendment in terms that their constituents could understand, would not have overlooked such a handy and compelling explanation. They would have cited the Fourteenth Amendment's incorporation of the Bill of Rights as evidence that it guaranteed blacks all the rights of American citizenship. Furthermore, they would have pointed out that incorporation protected blacks from the narrow definition, interpretation, or application of those rights by a state. And then they would have illustrated their general points with specific examples. "The Second Amendment guarantees us the right to carry arms," they would have shouted. They would have insisted, "The Sixth Amendment entitles us to sit on juries."

While radical blacks sometimes did claim that the Fourteenth Amendment guaranteed them the right to bear arms or the right to sit on juries, they invariably linked that claim, not to any guarantee found in the Bill of Rights, but rather to the more general equality of treatment principle, which they believed was embodied in the equal protection guarantee.[4] In other words, they wanted the same right to bear arms or sit on juries that their fellow white citizens enjoyed *under state law*. As the radical, black-owned *New Orleans Tribune* pointed out in justification of its opposing the disfranchisement of whites: "If we refuse the franchise to any class, it can as well be withheld from us."[5]

Even more telling, once again, is the silence of the amendment's opponents. They objected to the privileges and immunities clause precisely because it did confer substantive rights on blacks. They never asserted that it gave blacks all those rights listed in the Bill of Rights, however. Yet anyone familiar with the rhetoric of these debates can easily imagine how they could and would have framed these arguments, had incorporation been considered a plausible gloss on the meaning of privileges and immunities. While opponents might not have criticized the Bill of Rights, they would have lamented the sorry pass to which the country had come when those whom they caricatured as "Sambo and Delilah" could exercise the same rights as Madison, Jefferson, Randolph, and Calhoun. They would have thundered against incorporation as a usurpation of states' rights. And on the specific issues, they would have cried horror and wept tears. One accusation which they did make, for example, was that the privileges and immunities clause might be construed to give blacks the right to sit on juries. They did not base that fear on any theory of incorporation, however. Rather, they feared Congress would decree that blacks had the right to serve on juries through its enforcement powers under Section 5. Had these critics suspected that the clause incorporated the Bill of Rights, they could have supported their accusation with that suspicion because the Sixth Amendment guarantees one a jury of his peers. They did not. They did not because no one in these states, so far as one can tell from surviving records, ever contemplated the possibility that the privileges and immunities clause incorporated the Bill of Rights.

If the debates in the Southern states are carefully combed, one may pick out an occasional statement that might be construed, particularly if read out of context, to support the inference that the privileges and immunities of citizenship included some of the rights guaranteed in the Bill of Rights, especially those freedoms protected in the First Amendment. Once again, however, a closer examination of such statements reveals that the underlying claim was the right to equal protection in the exercise of speech rights, however defined by the state. Moreover, one must remember that these debates were not conducted in the dignified chambers of an appellate court; they took place in the rough and tumble of the political trenches. Unfortunately, wretched hyperbole was sometimes substituted for careful analysis. Proponents of the Fourteenth Amendment often invoked the principles of the Declaration and expiated on the many glories of liberty. Caught up in their own rhetoric, they occasionally coupled the concept of citizenship with the concept of fundamental liberties in a way that suggested they were either coterminous categories or that one was a subset of the other.

Three points need to be made about these eloquent waxings. First, and again, none explicitly stated that the privileges and immunities clause of Section 1 incorporated the first eight amendments to the Constitution. Invariably, the wording of such statements was general, opaque, vague. Consequently, any conclusion that these statements revealed an understanding that the Bill of Rights was incorporated into Section 1 would necessarily be a matter of inference.

Second, and as a matter of inferences, the probabilities greatly favor the conclusion that the privileges and immunities clause was not understood to include the Bill of Rights. The privileges and immunities of citizenship was after all a hoary legal concept, included in both the national and many state constitutions. In both contexts, it was intended to prevent discrimination: in the one, against outsiders; and in the other, among citizens of the state. While the privileges and immunities clause of Article IV arguably included some substantive rights, courts had consistently rejected the notion that it imposed substantive limits on how a state might treat its own citizens.[6] That is why those who attacked Section 1 focused on Congress's Section 5 power to define and enforce the privileges and immunities of citizenship. The Fourteenth Amendment was revolutionary, not because it redefined privileges and immunities to include the guarantees of the Bill of Rights, but because it gave Congress the power to define and therefore expand the privileges and immunities of citizenship, which states were obliged to respect.

Opponents of the Fourteenth Amendment in the South repeatedly stressed the dangers of giving Congress such power; they routinely paraded the horrid possibilities, the most shocking being the right of blacks to vote, followed by miscegenation, mixed schools, and integrated saloons and railway cars. The latter was no imaginary horrible; Congress had done just that in the Civil Rights Bill.[7] Alert as the opponents were to the danger of federal power, they never once mentioned that it included the power to enforce the Bill of Rights against the states.

The third point is that the substantive rights protected by the privileges and immunities clause would not have been thought coextensive with those guaranteed in the Bill of Rights because the privileges and immunities of citizenship did not include political rights; and the Bill of Rights jumbled together natural rights (like those found in the First Amendment), civil rights (like due process), and political rights (like those found in Amendments Five and Six). Consequently, incorporation cannot be inferred from the text of the amendment or the tenor of the debate over that text.

What rights did the participants in the Southern ratification debates think were embraced within the privileges and immunities of citizenship? To answer that question, one must first understand their philosophical conception of rights. Both the proponents and the opponents of the Fourteenth Amendment subscribed to a hierarchical view of rights. Inalienable rights, summarized in the Declaration as "life, liberty, and the pursuit of happiness," were at the apex of this hierarchy. Rights of conscience like those embodied in the First Amendment were often included in any fuller litany of these human or natural rights. The distinguishing characteristic of such rights was that they were substantive and were derived from personhood rather than from the political community. The political community could regulate the exercise of these rights but could not prohibit or abridge them.

Civil rights were the next important category of rights. These, too, were due every free person because they were essential to the exercise of one's natural right to life, liberty, and property. These rights are thus most accurately described as "facilitators" and were therefore at the core of the privileges and immunities of citizenship. Civil rights included the right to buy and sell, contract, and sue and be sued, as well as the right to equal protection and due process of law. These rights, unlike natural rights, were wholly procedural—except insofar as the definition of their incidence conferred particular privileges and immunities in a given political community.

Political rights constituted the third category of rights. Voting was of course the primary political right. Others included the right to hold office and the right to sit on juries, which at that time was regarded as an especially important political function. The distinguishing characteristic of political rights is that they are not due every person merely by virtue of birth, personhood, or even citizenship. The political community alone confers political rights and may limit their exercise to particular classes of persons. According to then prevailing theories of republican government, a wise political community would limit political rights to those fit to exercise them. While members of the community might fight over who was fit to exercise political rights, all conceded that the decision remained the community's. In one sense, then, Reconstruction was simply a fight about whether the relevant community for these purposes was the state or the nation, and whether blacks were fit to exercise certain rights.

Social rights were the last category of rights. Today these rights would probably be lumped together as associational rights. This was the least well-defined category of rights, in part because it was more fluid, reflecting, as it did, changing mores about the appropriateness of particular social relationships and the scope of the government's power to regulate them. Thus, for example, most white Southerners insisted that no government could force social equality upon them by requiring them to sit next to blacks in saloons and railway cars. At the same time, they expected their government to enforce the taboo against interracial marriage.

Admittedly, ratification arguments were not usually cast in such philosophical terms. Moreover, those engaged in the debates occasionally confused these categories of rights when they did invoke them. Still, the general philosophy of rights described above permeated the ratification debates in the South. Indeed, those debates can only be understood in that philosophical context. Understood in that context, the privileges and immunities clause guaranteed only the first two categories of rights: natural rights and civil rights. That guarantee, stated abstractly, was unobjectionable to most Southern whites, who conceded that blacks were human and therefore imbued with natural rights and, once free, entitled to civil rights as well.

The evidence that Section 1 was understood to protect natural rights is overwhelming. Advocates of Section 1 repeatedly invoked the Declaration of Independence as evidence that all persons enjoyed natural rights which no government could abridge, and they insisted that the privileges and immunities clause protected those rights. General Hancock, upon assuming command of the military district that included Texas and Louisiana, issued the following order: "[T]he great principles of American liberty are still the lawful inheritance of this people, and ever should be. The right of trial by jury, the habeas corpus, the liberty of the press, the freedom of speech, the natural rights of persons, and the rights of property must be preserved."[8] The general's statement succinctly captures the prevailing sense of the natural and civil rights included within the privileges and immunities of citizenship.

Contrary to the Supreme Court's holding in the *Slaughter-House Cases*,[9] advocates of the Fourteenth Amendment never implied that Section 1 guaranteed only those privileges and immunities peculiar to national citizenship, in contra-distinction to some different set of privileges and immunities peculiar to state citizenship. Section 1, which made them citizens of the state in which they re-sided, necessarily embraced the privileges and immunities of that status as well. A citizen was a citizen, and advocates of Section 1 intended to cloak every citi-zen with all the traditional privileges and immunities of that status. Republicans fretted continuously that Southern states systematically denied blacks the privi-leges and immunities of citizenship. They would not have adopted a guarantee that only prevented those states from abridging a limited number of privileges and immunities, derived solely from their status as citizens of the United States. Again, the critics understood that Section 1 was intended to protect citizens in the exercise of all the privileges and immunities of citizenship, whether they derived from the state or the nation.

The evidence is equally overwhelming that the privileges and immunities clause was also understood to include those civil rights which persons needed in order to protect and exercise their natural rights. Even those opposed to ratifica-tion of the Fourteenth Amendment generally conceded that blacks were entitled to the same basic civil rights as whites. In fact, Southerners believed that their state governments had conferred those "civil rights" on blacks even as they im-posed the infamous Black Codes:

The freedman was admitted to every right that was necessary for him. In the eye of the law, he was entitled to the same justice which was given to the whites. He was not only entitled to this justice, but, as a rule, he received it. Judge, magistrate, jury, and justice of the peace generally looked upon the shortcomings of the emancipated Negro with pitying indulgence. They made excuses for him that he would have made for himself; they took into consideration his former condition, the temptations to which he had been exposed, the inducements that were held out to him indirectly to become a vagabond upon the face of the earth; they made allowance for all these things, and it is not too much to say that in almost every case in this State, and, as far as is known, in every Southern State, in which a freedman has been concerned, he has been treated at least with justice.[10]

Though such statements might be dismissed as self-serving, some Northern ob-servers agreed. Mr. Truman, after surveying conditions in eight Southern states, confirmed to President Johnson that the Southern states had acted "to secure the colored race in their rights of person and property."[11]

The Southern Compromise Amendment,[12] which some white Southerners proffered in early 1867, reinforces the conclusion that they did not fear recog-nizing that blacks enjoyed natural rights or granting them civil rights. In fact, the language of Section 3 of that amendment tracks the language of Section 1 of the Fourteenth Amendment. Had the drafters of the Southern Compromise Amend-ment understood any of those phrases to guarantee political or social rights, they would have balked at including them. As they understood them, however, those phrases were so innocuous that they could be "given away" in exchange for concessions on Sections 2 and 3 of the Fourteenth Amendment, especially if

Congress was denied the power to enforce the Section 1 guarantees and the definition of their scope was left exclusively to the states.

Concern about the scope of Congress's enforcement power under Section 5 was thus the central issue in the debate over Section 1. That concern was justified because the Section 1 guarantees were stated broadly and were therefore inherently ambiguous, at least at the margin. Understanding the insight of Bishop Hoadley's dictum that "he who hath the power to interpret the law is truly the lawgiver,"[13] most white Southerners were loath to give Congress that power. They naturally feared that the national government would read the Section 1 guarantees too broadly and substitute its judgment for theirs on a wide range of public policy issues involving the definition of those rights and the regulation of their exercise.

Their warnings about the right to vote and to intermarry both dramatized this concern and underscored the extent to which many traditional notions of federalism survived adoption of the Fourteenth Amendment. Its opponents, pandering to the negrophobia prevalent among whites, never tired of predicting that Congress could declare either the right to vote or the right to intermarry a privilege and immunity of citizenship. Admittedly, the amendment was designed to encourage the extension of the franchise to blacks. Nevertheless, that decision was left to the states under Section 2. After all, the states had always determined the eligibility of voters. Moreover, advocates of the amendment, many of whom had initially opposed giving blacks the vote, continually reassured the people that voting was not a privilege and immunity of citizenship. When they later urged Negro suffrage, they never based their arguments for it on the text of the Fourteenth Amendment. Ultimately, of course, they secured adoption of another amendment—the Fifteenth—to accomplish that goal. The states had also always determined the incidence of the marital relationship. Even if the right to marry were deemed a natural right within the privileges and immunities of citizenship, the states presumably retained broad discretion to regulate the exercise of that right.

The constitutions adopted by the Southern states in the very midst of ratifying the Fourteenth Amendment reinforced that presumption. These constitutions were clearly intended to protect a wide range of rights, some of which might be denominated natural or fundamental. The rights guaranteed in these constitutions were not modeled specifically on those found in the federal Bill of Rights, however. Rather, they were derived from prior state constitutions stretching back to the Revolution. The federal Bill of Rights itself was derived from the same sources. Drawn from this common philosophical spring, the new constitutions obviously protected many of the same rights; and those rights were sometimes described in language identical to that found in the national Bill of Rights. All that proves, however, is the obvious: nineteenth-century American constitution makers shared the same historical experiences and worked in the same political tradition, of which the national Constitution was a significant part.

Every one of the eleven constitutions begins with a Bill or Declaration of Rights, and each appears to be intended as a comprehensive statement of the rights of the person as against the state government. Though they all guarantee a common core of rights, they often describe those rights differently; and each differs in the range, as well as in the scope, of the rights protected. These constitutions do not reflect the work of delegates who thought themselves obliged to follow some master plan. Rather, they reflect the work of delegates who shared a general philosophical heritage (of which the Bill of Rights would clearly have been a part) but who believed themselves generally free to work out the implications of that heritage as they saw fit.

In some cases, for example, Southern states were unwilling to recognize rights as broad as those guaranteed in the Bill of Rights. Some explicitly provided that persons were responsible for abusing freedom of speech or the press. Others specified that petitions for redress must be made in a peaceable manner. Many did not include a takings clause, and several permitted the state to proceed in criminal prosecutions by information rather than by indictment.

These constitutions were carefully reviewed by the Congress before it voted to restore the Southern states to the Union. Charles Fairman succinctly summarizes the import of that review:

While the constitutions had been examined in detail, and one provision had been annulled, no member of Congress had evinced the slightest interest in comparing the respective bills of rights with Amendments I to VIII—though as we have seen some marked disparities were to be observed. Representative Bingham and Senator Howard were very happy about the outcome. We may conclude that neither one had any desire to hold the states to an actual conformity to the federal Bill of Rights. Bingham said that the new constitutions were "in accordance with the spirit and letter of the Constitution . . . as it stands amended," and insisted that Congress had no proper concern about "local details" which did not "touch the general safety of the Republic."[14]

It is impossible to reconcile the incorporation theory with the fact that the same men who enthusiastically endorsed the Fourteenth Amendment drafted constitutions that contained some guarantees inconsistent with those found in the national Bill of Rights. It is equally impossible to reconcile the incorporation theory with the fact that congressmen who had drafted the Fourteenth Amendment approved these same constitutions, containing, as they did, these inconsistent guarantees. The only plausible explanation for the conduct of both sets of drafters is that they understood that the states would continue to be the primary guarantors of their citizens' rights, and that the states enjoyed substantial latitude in defining the scope of those rights, or, more precisely, the incidents of those rights. All Senator Wilson demanded, for example, was that "these constitutions . . . be like our constitutions"—a demand that precludes any inference that their Bills of Rights had to be conformed precisely to that of the national Constitution.[15]

A handful of contemporary scholars have nevertheless tried to reconcile the irreconcilable. William Crosskey simply asserts that the plain language of Section 1 clearly indicates that Section 1 incorporates the Bill of Rights.[16] Akhil Reed Amar parses the language similarly, though he at least concedes that the drafters could have stated the proposition more clearly.[17] The latter concession may fairly be described as an understatement, since the allegedly clear import of Section 1 escaped the Court for nearly a century; and its allegedly plain language has baffled generation after generation of scholars. If the incorporation of the Bill of Rights is found in the language of Section 1, it must then be written in invisible ink, discernible only to the incorporation faithful.

Amar also rests his argument for incorporation on the somewhat surprising ground that the very absence of any discussion of the incorporation doctrine during the ratification debates proves that that doctrine was so uncontroversial that it was an accepted article of faith among Republicans.[18] The "doubting Thomas" might wonder why, if that were so, no one ever mentioned it, even in passing. After all, politicians often fill the air with platitudinous "truths" to rally the party faithful. Amar has an answer: "Many informed men were not thinking carefully about the words of Section 1 at all."[19] Many of them in the South, however, thought carefully enough to point out that Section 1 overruled *Dred Scott*. Yet none of them ever added: "And it also overrules *Barron v. Baltimore*,"[20] as would have been the case had Section 1 imposed the Bill of Rights upon the states. While *Barron* was not as well known as *Dred Scott*, it must have been known to distinguished lawyers like Judge Simrall, who wrote Mississippi's legislative report on the proposed amendment. In that report, he carefully and thoughtfully analyzed how the federal judiciary might subvert state autonomy by exploiting the ambiguous language of Section 1 but never once illustrated his point by referring to the possibility that the federal judiciary could pervert the language of the Bill of Rights to that end.[21]

David Richards goes even further and argues that the privileges and immunities clause was intended to authorize federal courts to enforce, not only the Bill of Rights, but a vast and ever expanding universe of unenumerated rights currently demanded by, among others, the Congressional Black Caucus, the National Organization of Women, and the Gay and Lesbian Task Force.[22] The idea that those who ratified the Fourteenth Amendment in the Southern states not only anticipated such claims but embraced them is self-evidently silly. The assertion that they at least understood the Fourteenth Amendment to embody a theory that—in its evolutionary development—could include such rights is equally implausible to anyone who has studied the period, even casually. To conclude, as has one reviewer of Richards's thesis, that it ignores "the broader historical context" is thus an understatement.[23] The thesis is untethered to anything other than the writer's political agenda.

Crosskey, Amar, and Richards focus primarily and exclusively on the congressional debate. Admittedly, it contains some evidence, however thin, that a few members of the House and Senate thought that the privileges and immunities of citizenship included the first eight amendments to the Constitution. Only Michael Curtis, among contemporary supporters of incorporation theory, deigns to look for an echo of such remarks in the state debates; and he finds the echo deafening. Specifically, Curtis argues that the state ratification debates support the incorporation thesis because many "Republicans read [Section 1 of the Fourteenth Amendment] to cover a broad range of fundamental rights, including liberties set out in the Bill of Rights."[24] He "proves" his point by citing, from the multitudinous pronouncements on the meaning of Section 1, those statements that emphasize its guarantee of fundamental rights. Not one of those statements, however, explicitly equates the scope of that guarantee with the Bill of Rights. The more lengthy statements that Curtis cites often list specific rights, but those lists invariably include some rights found in the Bill of Rights and others not found there.

Curtis nevertheless revels in the very generality of these statements because they permit him to pour into them whatever specific content he likes, and he likes incorporation. He neglècts to mention the three most common explanations, given in the Southern ratification debates, for Section 1:

- Section 1 overrules *Dred Scott*;
- Section 1 constitutionalizes the Civil Rights Act;
- Section 1 requires equality of rights.

Whether Curtis would consider these, too, mere general phrases, they seem less susceptible to an incorporation gloss than the grandiloquent declamations he quotes.

How in any case does one explain the absence of similar, succinct explanations like these:

- Section 1 incorporates the Bill of Rights;
- Section 1 requires every state to respect the first eight amendments to the Constitution;
- Section 1 declares that a state cannot abridge the guarantees of the Bill of Rights because they are the privileges and immunities of every citizen.

The answer to that question is reasonably clear. The universe of fundamental rights was unclear, at least at the margin, and included, at a level of abstract statement, rights both within and without the Bill of Rights. While Section 1 did impose an affirmative obligation on a state to protect those rights, it also left each state broad discretion to define their incidents. Incorporationists simply refuse to acknowledge that fact.

They also overlook another, equally important fact: the equal protection clause was intended to insure that a state's exercise of its discretion to define those incidents did not compromise its obligation to protect its citizens in the exercise of the rights guaranteed by Section 1. Certainly those who supported the Fourteenth Amendment in the South viewed the equality of rights principle as the key to the preservation of their liberties. President Jackson had emphasized the critical importance of equal protection in 1832 when he vetoed the bill to re-charter the Bank of the United States. "There are no necessary evils in government. Its evils exist only in its abuses. If it would confine itself to equal protection, and, as Heaven does its rains, shower its favors alike on the high and the low, the rich and the poor, it would be an unqualified blessing."[25] Section 1 embodied that insight, which Justice Robert Jackson elaborated more than a century later in the *Railway Express* case:

Invocation of the equal protection clause . . . does not disable any governmental body from dealing with the subject at hand. It merely means that the prohibition or regulation must have a broader impact. I regard it as a salutary doctrine that [governments] must exercise their powers so as not to discriminate between their inhabitants except upon some reasonable differentiation fairly related to the object of regulation. This equality is not merely abstract justice. [T]here is no more effective practical guaranty against arbitrary and unreasonable government than to require that the principles of law which officials would impose upon a minority must be imposed generally. Conversely, nothing opens the door to arbitrary action so effectively as to allow those officials to pick and choose only a few to whom they will apply legislation and thus to escape the political retribution that might be visited upon them if larger numbers were affected. Courts can take no better measure to assure that laws will be just than to require that laws be equal in operation.[26]

In other words, a state enjoyed broad discretion to define the rights of its citizens so long as it applied those definitions to all.

The idea that the privileges and immunities clause was a shorthand statement of the guarantees of the Bill of Rights, however defined by the Supreme Court of the United States, would thus have surprised—nay, stunned—those who debated its meaning in the Southern states. That idea would have contradicted their understanding of fundamental rights, violated their belief in state autonomy, and confounded their sense of the appropriate role of the Supreme Court. It is then hardly surprising that the argument is never made explicitly. It can be teased out of general statements today only if they are, first, ripped out of the historical context that alone explains them, and second, pumped full of airy assumptions about what their authors must have known and thought—assumptions more congenial to the mind of twentieth-century liberals, who believe in government by judges, than to the mind of the nineteenth-century Americans, who still believed in a federated government of the people, by the people, for the people.

The guarantee of equal protection, like the privileges and immunities clause, did pose major interpretative challenges to those who participated in the Southern ratification debates. As that debate evolved in those states, advocates of ratification repeatedly invoked the Declaration of Independence as evidence that all persons should enjoy equal rights. The centrality of the Declaration to the political philosophy of the freedmen and white Unionists is captured in the poignant account of James Tebbetts's admonition to his children on July 4, 1861. Isolated in northern Arkansas among enthusiastic "rebs," Mr. Tebbets called his children into a candlelit room and conducted a solemn ceremony before an American flag. He admonished them:

Children, this is the fourth of July, 1861. I want you to remember that you heard your father read the "Declaration of Independence" on this day; and it is my wish that you either read aloud or hear aloud this great paper on every fourth of July that comes into your life. Also, I want you to remember that during this stress of war and danger, your father and mother are still loyal to this flag before you and to the government for which it stands.[27]

If Section 1 incorporated any of the foundational documents of the American republic, it incorporated the truths of the Declaration of Independence rather than the provisions of the Bill of Rights, from whose provisions those truths had been deliberately excluded.[28]

Equality of rights was thus the more critical concept, as a less selective quotation of statements by Curtis would have demonstrated. Consider, for example, this demand from an Alabama convention of blacks in 1867: "We claim exactly *the same rights, privileges and immunities as are enjoyed by white men*—we ask nothing more and will be content with nothing less. . . . The law no longer knows white nor black, but simply men, and consequently we are entitled to ride in public conveyances, hold office, sit on juries and do everything else which we have in the past been prevented from doing solely on the ground of color."[29] The same attitudes and demands emerged in all the Southern states as blacks began to assert themselves. By 1867, Republican parties in all the Southern states had embraced the equality of rights principle.

Did the injunction against any state denying a person within its jurisdiction the equal protection of the laws reflect this broad equality principle, or did it reflect a somewhat narrower concept? Answering that question is difficult for three reasons. Although the government's obligation to protect its citizens was a long-standing and well understood duty, equal protection lacked the historical pedigree of privileges and immunities and due process. Consequently, the community could not rely on traditional usage as a guide to meaning. Second, both proponents and opponents occasionally treated the privileges and immunities and equal protection clauses as if they protected the same set of rights. By confusing these two separate clauses, the discussants sometimes obscured the independent meaning they may have attributed to equal protection. Third, the discussants usually concentrated on concrete, specific problems. Because politicians geared their analysis to the particular concerns of their constituents, they seldom articulated any comprehensive understanding of equal protection. That understanding must then necessarily be inferred from their discussion of particular issues like public conveyances, the militia, common schools, and intermarriage.

As with privileges and immunities, one can confidently conclude what was included in and what was excluded form the equal protection guarantee only at the margin. At a minimum, the clause guaranteed equal treatment before the courts.

Supporters frequently cited differential punishments and the ban on Negro testimony as violations of the equal protection principle. More broadly, supporters condemned all laws that discriminated against blacks solely on account of their race. According to this view, the equal protection clause would proscribe laws that imposed harsher penalties on blacks or subjected them to different legal procedures. The Court's initial application of the Fourteenth Amendment equal protection guarantee in *Strauder v. State of West Virginia*[30] confirms this understanding of its scope. In that case the Court struck down a state statute barring blacks from jury service.

A miscegenation statute would not necessarily come within that same proscription, however, because it did not discriminate against blacks—at least formally. On its face, it affected whites and blacks identically. While the Supreme Court invalidated miscegenation statutes in *Loving v. Virginia*,[31] it rested its decision on non-originalist grounds. If the right to marry were considered a fundamental or civil right rather than a social right, the answer would have been reasonably clear: a state could not deny it to those otherwise eligible. The debate was not cast in those terms, however. Supporters of the amendment simply denied the charge that it guaranteed the right to marry regardless of race; opponents continuously decried the dangers of "mongrelization."

However racial intermarriage is classified, there is no evidence—viewed generally—that supports the proposition that the equal protection clause guaranteed equality in social or associational relationships. The difficulty was that persons disagreed over what relationships fit into the category of social rights. The one that vexed Southerners the most was access to public accommodations. Those who favored state-mandated access pointed to both the common law and state licensure as justifications for public accommodation laws. Those who opposed such laws relied on tradition and invoked concerns about public safety should those traditions be violated.

No one supposed that the state could or should dictate social mores. Opponents recognized this fact. Their arguments thus amounted to a warning, not an interpretation. If blacks were admitted to civil and political equality with whites, conservatives reasoned, blacks would inevitably intermingle socially with whites. One ought not to confuse sociological prediction with constitutional interpretation, however. On the other hand, evolving social mores might lead to legislative reconsideration of such issues. Furthermore, widespread legislative acquiescence in new social attitudes might justify judicial recognition of a redefined or expanded fundamental right like the right of public access.

All those who favored the Fourteenth Amendment agreed that the equal protection principle was fundamental because it forbade class legislation and required instead that the government treat all within its jurisdiction equally. They thus indignantly dismissed the accusation that Section 1 favored blacks or vouchsafed them special treatment. For example, South Carolina's Martin R. Delany, the "father of black nationalism," found it "dangerous to go into the country and speak of color in any manner whatever, without the angry rejoinder, 'we don't want to hear that; we are all one color now.'"[32]

Persons holding such views naturally sought to ban *all* class legislation. The debates in every Southern state are replete with praise for this laissez-faire principle of equality. The former military commander of Louisiana, General Butler, campaigning in 1866, explained the concept by quoting the late president:

I believe it is stated in the Constitution of Illinois that all men are born equal. Many eminent men have tried to define it, but their definitions have all needed some explanation. If you mean that all men are born with equal rights, then the Declaration of Independence is correct. But men are created differently. Some are born with different physical powers from others, and some with greater intellectual powers, and so on. Therefore, they are not exactly equal. But Abraham Lincoln, of Illinois, has stated this question with more clearness than any one who has heretofore attempted it, and in a manner which needs no explanation. With that peculiar terseness for which he was more renowned than anything else except patriotism and honesty, he says: 'Every man has the right to be the equal of every other man—if he can.' [Tremendous cheering.][33]

For precisely that reason Republicans generally rejected the radical demand for confiscation. Eric Foner describes the outraged reaction to Senator Sumner's proposal to provide the freedmen with homesteads: "To moderates, such proposals seemed a form of what Sen. James W. Grimes called 'class legislation'— singling out one group of citizens for special government favors. 'That is more than we do for white men,' declared Fessenden in opposing the land proposal."[34]

This explanation of the equal protection clause thus leaves little doubt that advocates of the amendment would have condemned governmentally mandated affirmative action programs. Such programs embody the very evil which those advocates insisted it was designed to prevent. Occasionally a radical voice did demand preferential treatment or insist that public offices be filled on a quota basis. Invariably, however, such voices were ignored or shouted down.[35]

The late Justice Thurgood Marshall, ironically echoing racist criticisms of the Freedmen's Bureau, once cited it as evidence that the framers of the Fourteenth Amendment endorsed race-conscious programs to ameliorate the condition of black Americans.[36] The justice's comment reflects both a misunderstanding of the act's legislative history and an ignorance of the Bureau's actual operations. The Freedmen's Bureau Bill passed Congress only after its sponsors assured their colleagues that the Bureau would help white refugees as well. Indeed, the full name of the Bureau was the Bureau of Refugees, Freedmen and Abandoned Lands. Moreover, Bureau field officers in the early months of its operation gave substantial help to white refugees.[37]

Between equality before the law, which the equal protection clause included, and social equality, which it excluded, its perceived scope is unclear from the public record. Perhaps the safest conclusion is that Southerners initially attributed a somewhat narrower meaning to the equal protection clause than they gave to the more general equality principle that Republicans later advocated.

This conclusion would explain why the state legislatures after 1868 acted as if they retained some discretion to regulate relationships between the races. In this view of the equal protection clause, a state could cleanse its statutes of any reference to race and impose a color-blind public order. Alternatively, a state could preserve some racial classifications so long as (1) it had a rational basis for doing so, and (2) the classification did not disadvantage one race. The legislature could choose from among these competing policies. The Fourteenth Amendment by its own terms commanded neither but, rather, permitted either.

This understanding alone explains the actions of Southern state legislatures in the years immediately following their ratification of the Fourteenth Amendment. At one time or another, all confronted the issue of public schools; and almost all dealt with the public accommodations issue. On the public schools issue, all in fact permitted segregated schools. Most insisted that the formal authorization, whether statutory or constitutional, be color-blind. In practice, however, the schools were segregated. Even Louisiana, which alone formally prohibited segregated schools, operated segregated schools outside New Orleans.

The practice with respect to public accommodations was less uniform. Many states adopted public accommodation laws. Others did not. In some states there was also, again, a sharp divergence between the formal law and actual practice. White opposition to integration often intimidated blacks from exercising their rights under these statutes. Additionally, a few states explicitly authorized segregation in public accommodations. This widely varying pattern not only supports the inference that state legislatures assumed they enjoyed broad policy-making discretion in these matters; it dramatizes once again the extent to which traditional notions of federalism survived adoption of the Fourteenth Amendment.

One needs to remember that the North fought the Civil War, primarily, to preserve the Union and, secondarily, to free the slaves. More to the point, it did not fight the war to abolish the federal structure of the American government. And yet the victors were confronted with a perplexing reality: though the North had succeeded in preserving the Union and freeing the slaves, their former masters seemed unwilling to accord the freedmen their rights as free persons. Moreover, conservative white majorities in the Southern states seemed indifferent to the truly horrific violence all too routinely inflicted upon the freedmen and their white allies.

Section 1 of the Fourteenth Amendment, viewed through the prism of the Southern ratification debates, emerges as an adroit compromise, intended to resolve these problems.[38] It rejected the radical demand to reduce the Southern states to administrative provinces governed by military commanders. It also rejected the conservative demand to accept "the Constitution as it is, the Union as it was, and the Negroes where they are." Instead, it established what can fairly be described as a default system for the protection of civil liberty. First, it preserved the state's traditional authority to define both the rights of its citizens and the procedures by which those rights would be protected. Second, it simultaneously obliged the state to exercise that authority in ways that preserved the privileges and immunities of citizenship for all by commanding that all persons should receive both due process and the equal protection of the laws. Third and finally, it made the national government the ultimate guarantor of those rights. This threefold scheme thus discharged Congress's obligation under Article IV to insure that every state enjoyed a republican government.

The Fourteenth Amendment did embrace a new notion of federalism. By giving Congress the power "to enforce" Section 1 by "appropriate legislation," the amendment significantly altered the distribution of governmental authority within that system. Both its advocates and its critics understood that fact. The precise scope of Congress's enforcement powers was never clearly defined in the ratification debates, however. Opponents certainly harped on the authority that Section 1, combined with Section 5, conferred on the national government. Before the war, belief in states' rights had been an article of political faith among most Southern whites; and a majority zealously clung to it after the war. Moreover, many whites doubtlessly wished to preserve state power as a check against radical congressional legislation. Thus they covered their naked racism with the fig leaf of states' rights. When conservatives invoked the specter of Negro suffrage or social equality, the Republicans immediately denounced them and refuted their claims. When conservatives invoked the specter of consolidation, Republicans usually said nothing. They implicitly conceded the argument. After all, they had come into office in the South under the protective cloak of national authority; and they knew that they would survive there only if the national government continued to protect them. There is, then, substantial support for the proposition that the Fourteenth Amendment nationalized questions about individual rights and deprived the states of either exclusive or final authority on those questions.

There are nevertheless substantial reasons to suppose that most Republicans did not anticipate that Congress would legislate routinely or broadly in matters traditionally reserved to the states. They probably expected or at least hoped that the mere specter of federal intervention would encourage the Southern states to legislate fairly. More realistically, Republicans anticipated that Southern blacks would be able to protect themselves in the rough-and-tumble of the political process, especially after they were guaranteed the right to vote. Blacks themselves routinely insisted that they could take care of themselves if they were only given the vote.

If national intervention were nevertheless required to preserve individual liberties from state infringement, both proponents and opponents assumed that Congress rather than the Supreme Court would exercise that authority. Despite occasional warnings uttered by law-trained politicians, there is little evidence that Southerners anticipated that federal courts would routinely circumscribe the policymaking discretion of their state legislatures, much less deprive them of it entirely. The chief concern about judicial intervention was that federal courts might enforce the equality of rights principle too stringently and thereby unduly circumscribe a state's authority to enact legislative classifications it deemed desirable. Opponents of ratification rarely expressed the fear that federal courts would create new rights. Courts were, after all, less activist in the nineteenth century. Additionally, the Supreme Court's effort to impose a final constitutional answer to the slavery question had proven disastrous. That decision alone counseled the wisdom of the Court's leaving political questions to political institutions. Section 5 appeared to contemplate that result as well. While the Courts could not forego their obligation to decide questions otherwise properly before them, they would have been expected to defer to state legislative judgments—unless those judgments clearly violated Section 1 guarantees.[39]

Whatever shape America might have assumed, had the courts hewed to this understanding of the Fourteenth Amendment, the country presently bears little resemblance to the one whose most pressing problems the Fourteenth Amendment was intended to address. Daniel Webster's indestructible union of indestructible states has been transformed into a centralized government in which the states act primarily as administrative minions of the national government. The states, once praised as laboratories for social and political experimentation,[40] now exercise only such discretion as the national government permits. In short, federalism is dead—though a handful of five-to-four decisions in the two most recent terms of the Supreme Court suggest that such reports, like those of Mr. Twain's death, may be exaggerated.[41]

The apparent demise of federalism has been slow and painful. It began at least as early as 1913 when the Seventeenth Amendment was adopted, and the state government ceased to be the senator's key constituency. Freed of that political obligation, a senator could ignore the interests of the state government. Consequently, state governments could no longer effectively protect through the political process those powers reserved to them in the Tenth Amendment. The direct election of senators thus grievously undermined the concept of federalism upon which the Republic had been founded.

Countless additional wounds were inflicted by the Supreme Court's interpretation of the commerce clause from 1937 onward. Having abandoned the states to the political whims of the Congress in the regulation of commercial matters, the Court sounded the death knell for federalism in the 1960s when it seized from the states virtually all responsibility for protecting the civil rights and liberties of their citizens. It cast itself in the role of guarantor, not of republican government and the fundamental rights of all persons, but of the rights of racial and other minorities and criminal defendants. Using the Fourteenth Amendment as a garrote about the necks of the states, it strangled the last vestiges of diversity that had once been the hallmark of federalism. In its stead, the Court imposed a uniform policy on race, religion, and gender, and a common code of criminal procedure.

The Court's authority to impose that policy and that code—whatever their intrinsic merits—is questionable, however. It rests primarily on a single linchpin: the assertion that the due process clause of the Fourteenth Amendment incorporates most (though not all) of the provisions of the Bill of Rights and thereby subjects the states to their restraints. To a lesser degree, the Court's Fourteenth Amendment jurisprudence rests on a latitudinal construction of those provisions and, until the very recent past, an increasingly egalitarian interpretation of the equal protection clause. That understanding of the Fourteenth Amendment thus turns the original understanding of the amendment—at least as manifested in the Southern ratification debates—on its head.

- The Court has gutted the one clause that was intended to guarantee substantive rights.
- It has transformed a procedural guarantee into a fertile source of substantive rights.
- It purports to determine the scope of those rights by reference to a body of law never intended to have any legal relationship to the Fourteenth Amendment.
- It has until very recently construed a provision originally thought to bar class legislation to permit—and in some cases even require—racial quotas and minority set-asides.

Whatever may be said of this Fourteenth Amendment, it is not the one the Southern states thought they ratified at the close of the Civil War. Its proponents thought that they had ratified an amendment that would insure what later came to be called "ordered liberty."[42] They understood that to mean that the states remained free to govern in matters traditionally reserved to them so long as they respected the fundamental rights of their citizens and treated all persons fairly and equally.

Today's Fourteenth Amendment is not even the one its most savage critics in those states dreaded. They did warn their people about the dangers of a consolidated despotism, and in the last fifty years Congress has begun to act as if it were the county, city, and village government for the whole nation. What these critics did not anticipate, even in their bleakest despair, was the awful possibility that the Supreme Court would both license and expand that consolidated despotism through perverse interpretations of the very guarantees its justices were sworn to uphold.

As Alexander Bickel so shrewdly pointed out in *The Supreme Court and the Idea of Progress*,[43] the Warren Court's assault on federalism and its egalitarian reinterpretation of the Bill of Rights were inspired by its commitment to a particular vision of progress. Believing that that vision was destined to triumph, it wished to be seen by future generations as having both anticipated and facilitated that triumph. The Court thus imagined a past that would justify the future it remembered. The unanswered question for each new generation of Americans is, of course, whether the future they imagine will come to pass. There is increasing evidence that many Americans, on the cusp of an approaching millennium, imagine a future with a smaller national government and reinvigorated state and local governments; a future with less overt judicial intervention in the legislative process at all levels; and a future in which the law takes no account of a person's race, but respects every person's natural rights to life, liberty, and the pursuit of happiness.

That future cannot come to pass, however, until the United States Supreme Court begins to reimagine the Fourteenth Amendment in light of the dreams and aspirations of the freedmen who embraced it so enthusiastically. They had survived all the horrors of slavery; they knew there would be no easy walk to freedom. Looking about for some guide on the dangerous and uncertain journey before them, the freedmen—simple, uneducated fieldhands fresh from plantation cabins and sophisticated, learned newspaper editors in Mobile and New Orleans alike—reached out for the eternal truths of the Declaration of Independence.

They saw those truths revealed in the three great clauses of Section 1 of the Fourteenth Amendment. And they believed that the implementation and enforcement of those simple commands would transport them to the promised land in which they imagined all white Americans lived. Just as the American revolutionaries demanded nothing more than the rights of Englishmen, the freedmen demanded nothing more than the rights of white Americans.

Moreover, the freedmen subscribed to the then prevailing beliefs in individualism and limited government. They wanted only two things from the government. First, they wanted the legal right to seize whatever opportunities a free society offered its members. Second, they wanted the government to protect their right to keep and use whatever they gained from exploiting those opportunities. They thought Section 1 of the Fourteenth Amendment embodied that legal regime.

It thus should come as no surprise that the Supreme Court's most articulate spokesperson for those dreams is himself the child of poverty and a descendant of the freedman. Justice Clarence Thomas's voice is the singularly authentic voice of those men and women, whose simple but eloquent pleas still call us, as did Mr. Grey of Arkansas in 1867, to fulfill that contract written "by the hand of an angel" and guaranteeing all persons their inalienable rights to life, liberty, and the pursuit of happiness.

Concurring in *Adarand Constructors v. Pena*,[44] Justice Thomas eloquently reiterates his commitment to a color-blind principle of equality before the law in the same cadences the freedmen themselves used:

I write . . . to express my disagreement with the premise . . . that there is a racial paternalism exception to the principle of equal protection. I believe that there is a "moral [and] constitutional equivalence" . . . between laws designed to subjugate a race and those that distribute benefits on the basis of race in order to foster some current notion of equality. Government cannot make us equal; it can only recognize, respect, and protect us as equal before the law.[45]

Recognizing the relevance of the Declaration to any interpretation of the Constitution, Justice Thomas explains:

There can be no doubt that the paternalism that appears to lie at the heart of this program is at war with the principle of inherent equality that underlies and infuses our Constitution. . . .

These programs . . . undermine the moral basis of the equal protection principle. Purchased at the price of immeasurable human suffering, the equal protection principle reflects our Nation's understanding that such classifications ultimately have a destructive impact on the individual and our society. Unquestionably, "invidious [racial] discrimination is an engine of oppression" . . . It is also true that "remedial" racial preferences may reflect "a desire to foster equality in society." But there can be no doubt that racial paternalism and its unintended consequences can be as poisonous and pernicious as any other form of discrimination.[46]

After explaining the unfortunate policy consequences of affirmative action programs, Justice Thomas concludes by reemphasizing the fundamental principle that "government-sponsored racial discrimination based on benign prejudice is just as noxious as discrimination inspired by malicious prejudice. In each instance, it is racial discrimination, plain and simple."[47]

Justice Thomas has spoken with equal insight about the importance of the federal structure of American government to the preservation of individual liberty, which was also "purchased at the price of immeasurable human suffering." Dissenting in *U.S. Term Limits v. Thornton*,[48] Justice Thomas articulated the concept of federalism succinctly:

Our system of government rests on one overriding principle: all power stems from the consent of the people. To phrase the principle in this way, however, is to be imprecise about something important to the notion of "reserved powers." The ultimate source of the Constitution's authority is the consent of the people of each individual State, not the consent of the undifferentiated people of the Nation as a whole. . . .

When they adopted the Federal Constitution, of course, the people of each State surrendered some of their authority to the United States (and hence to entities accountable to the people of other States as well as to themselves). They affirmatively deprived their States of certain powers . . . and they affirmatively conferred certain powers upon the Federal Government. . . . Because the people of the several States are the only true source of power, however, the Federal Government enjoys no authority beyond what the Constitution confers: the Federal Government's powers are limited and enumerated. In the words of Justice Black, "the United States is entirely a creature of the Constitution. Its power and authority have no other source." . . .

As far as the Federal Constitution is concerned, then, the States can exercise all powers that the Constitution does not withhold from them. The Federal Government and the States thus face different default rules: where the Constitution is silent about the exercise of a particular power—that is, where the Constitution does not speak either expressly or by necessary implication—the Federal Government lacks that power and the States enjoy it.[49]

Like the freedmen and others who supported ratification of the Fourteenth Amendment in the South, Justice Thomas does not understand it to have undermined the fundamental structure of Madison's "extended Republic."

Rather, Justice Thomas has indicated that he understands, as did the freedmen and their allies, that the states retain extensive police powers under the Fourteenth Amendment. Concurring in *Lopez v. United States,*[50] Justice Thomas reminded his colleagues that the Court had never read the Constitution to grant Congress any general police power. He then added with respect to the specific facts of the case before the Court:

[T]he power to regulate "commerce" can by no means encompass authority over mere gun possession, any more than it empowers the Federal Government to regulate marriage, littering, or cruelty to animals, throughout the 50 States. Our Constitution quite properly leaves such matters to the individual States, notwithstanding these activities' effects on interstate commerce.[51]

Turning to the post-1937 commerce clause decisions of the Court, he minced no words about their questionable constitutional paternity, describing them as ungrounded "in the original understanding of the Constitution" because they "appear to grant Congress a police power over the Nation,"[52] police powers which the freedmen understood the states would continue to exercise so long as they respected the equality of rights principle.

Whether Justice Thomas's voice will recall America to its republican heritage and the powerful promise of the Fourteenth Amendment is uncertain, dependent as it is on a history whose unfolding can now only be imagined. What is certain is that Justice Thomas has remembered accurately the tortured history of the Fourteenth Amendment's ratification in the Southern states. Unlike his fierce and savage critics among the black intellectual elite, he remembers his roots; he knows that his forebears understood far more keenly than does the contemporary liberal establishment that the fundamental values of liberty and equality can be reconciled in the American experience only in a republic committed to the rule of law. The Fourteenth Amendment, understood as those who ratified it in the Southern states understood it, is an indispensable bulwark of that legal regime. And if its guarantees were interpreted as the freedmen imagined them in their dreams, the Fourteenth Amendment may yet be the answer to Lincoln's prayer for a new birth of freedom.

NOTES

1. Hugo Black, *A Constitutional Faith* (New York: Knopf, 1968). The scholarly debate on incorporation is voluminous. See, e.g., Charles Fairman, "Does the Fourteenth Amendment Incorporate the Bill of Rights?" *Stanford Law Review* 2 (1949): 5; Felix Frankfurter, "Memorandum on Incorporation of the Bill of Rights into the Due Process Clause of the Fourteenth Amendment," *Harvard Law Review* 78 (1965): 746; and W. Brennan, "The Bill of Rights and the States," *New York University Law Review* 36 (1961): 761.

2. The most egregious example of this phenomenon is *Roe v. Wade*, 410 U.S. 113 (1973), and its progeny.

3. See generally Raoul Berger, "New Deal Symposium: The Activist Legacy of the New Deal Court," *Washington Law Review* 59 (1984), 751, 781; Alexander M. Bickel, *The Supreme Court and the Idea of Progress* (New Haven and London: Yale University Press, 1978), 11–42.

4. See Chapter 5, p. 112.

5. *New Orleans Tribune*, 25 November 1866.

6. Earl M. Maltz, "Fourteenth Amendment Concepts in the Antebellum Era," *American Journal of Legal History* 32 (1988): 305, 334–39.

7. See generally Earl M. Maltz, "The Civil Rights Act and the *Civil Rights Cases*: Congress, Court, and Constitution," *Florida Law Review* 44 (1992): 605.

8. *The Civil Record of Major General Winfield S. Hancock during His Administrations in Louisiana and Texas* (n.p., 1880), 5. Available at the Harry Ransom Human Research Center, University of Texas, Austin, Texas.

9. 83 U.S. 36 (1872).

10. Report of Benjamin C. Truman in "Message of President Communicating Report on Condition of Southern People and States in Which Rebellion Existed," 39th Cong., 1st sess., Senate Exec. Doc. No. 43.

11. Ibid.

12. See generally Joseph B. James, "Southern Reaction to the Proposal of the Fourteenth Amendment," *Journal of Southern History* 22 (1956): 477, 494–96.

13. "Bishop Hoadley's dictum" was first delivered by Benjamin Hoadley, Bishop of Bangor, in a sermon preached before the king of England in 1717. Reprinted in John Chipman Gray, *The Nature and Sources of the Law* (New York: Macmillan, 1921), 125.

14. Fairman, "Does the Fourteenth Amendment Incorporate the Bill of Rights?" 5.

15. *Congressional Globe*, 40th Cong., 1st Sess., 144.

16. William W. Crosskey, "Charles Fairman, 'Legislative History,' and the Constitutional Limitations on State Authority," *Chicago Law Review* 22 (1954): 1, 3.

17. Akhil Reed Amar, "The Bill of Rights and the Fourteenth Amendment," *Yale Law Journal* 101 (1992): 1193, 1218–26.

18. Ibid., 1253.

19. Ibid., 1250.

20. 32 U.S. (7 Pet.) 243 (1833).

21. See Chapter 3, 52–53. See also *Journal of the House of Representatives of the State of Mississippi at a Called Session, October 1866* (Jackson: J. J. Shannon & Co., 1866), Appendix, 78–79.

22. David A. J. Richards, *Conscience and the Constitution: History, Theory, and Law of the Reconstruction Amendments* (Princeton: Princeton University Press, 1993).

23. Roberta Sue Alexander, book review, *American Historical Review* (April 1995): 570, 571.

24. Michael Curtis, *No State Shall Abridge: The Fourteenth Amendment and the Bill of Rights* (Durham, N.C.: Duke University Press, 1986), 145.

25. Robert J. Reinstein, "Completing the Constitution: The Declaration of Independence, Bill of Rights, and Fourteenth Amendment," *Temple Law Review* 66 (1993): 361, 403.

26. 336 U.S. 106, 112–13 (1949) (concurring opinion).

27. David M. Tucker, *Arkansas: A People and Their Reputation* (Memphis: Memphis State University, 1985), 29.

28. Reinstein, "Completing the Constitution," 362–63.

29. Foner, *Reconstruction*, 288.

30. 100 U.S. 303 (1879).

31. 388 U.S. 1 (1967).

32. Quoted in Foner, *Reconstruction*, 308.

33. *Danville Plain Dealer*, 1 November 1866.

34. *Regents of University of California v. Bakke,* 438 U.S. 265 (1978) (Marshall, J., dissenting).

35. See Chapter 8, pp. 223–24.

36. See Justice Marshall's dissenting opinion in *Regents of University of California v. Bakke*, 438 U.S. 265 (1978).

37. See Paul Skeels Pierce, *The Freedmen's Bureau: A Chapter in the History of Reconstruction* (Iowa City: University of Iowa, 1904), 99–100.

38. Cf. Earl M. Maltz, "The Fourteenth Amendment as Political Compromise—Section One in the Joint Committee on Reconstruction," *Ohio State Law Journal* 45 (1984): 933.

39. See generally Earl M. Maltz, "Individual Rights and State Autonomy," *Harvard Journal of Law and Public Policy* 12 (1989): 163.

40. *New State Ice Co. v. Liebmann*, 285 U.S. 262, 311 (1932) (Brandeis, J. dissenting).

41. See, e.g., *U.S. v. Lopez*, 115 S. Ct. 1624 (1995).

42. *Palko v. Connecticut*, 58 S. Ct. 149 (1937).

43. Alexander M. Bickel, *The Supreme Court and the Idea of Progress.*

44. 115 S. Ct. 2097 (1995).

45. Ibid., 2119.

46. Ibid.

47. Ibid.

48. 115 S. Ct. 1842 (1995).

49. Ibid., 1875–76.

50. 115 S. Ct. 1624 (1994).

51. Ibid., 1642.

52. Ibid., 1649.

Selected Bibliography

BOOKS AND ARTICLES

Abbott, Martin. *The Freedman's Bureau in South Carolina, 1865–1872.* Chapel Hill: University of North Carolina Press, 1967.

Ackerman, Philip D. "Florida Reconstruction from Walker through Reed 1865–1873." Ph.D. diss., University of Florida, 1948.

Alcorn, James Lusk. Papers. Mississippi Department of Archives and History, Jackson, Mississippi.

Alexander, Roberta Sue. Book review, *American Historical Review* (April 1995): 570.

Alexander, Thomas B. "Persistent Whiggery in Alabama and the Lower South, 1860–1867." *Alabama Review* 12 (1959): 35.

———. "Persistent Whiggery in Mississippi Reconstruction." *Journal of Mississippi History* 23 (April 1961): 71.

———. *Political Reconstruction in Tennessee.* New York: Russell & Russell, 1968.

———. "Whiggery and Reconstruction in Tennessee." *Journal of Southern History* 16 (1950): 291.

Amar, Akhil Reed. "The Bill of Rights and the Fourteenth Amendment." *Yale Law Journal* 101 (1992): 1193.

Ambler, Charles H. *Francis H. Pierpont, Union War Governor of Virginia and Father of West Virginia.* Chapel Hill: University of North Carolina Press, 1937.

Aptheker, Herbert. "South Carolina Negro Conventions, 1865." *Journal of Negro History* 31 (1946): 91.

Atkinson, S. "Emerson Etheridge as a Candidate in the Tennessee Gubernatorial Election of 1867." M. A. thesis, University of Tennessee, 1969.

Avillo, Philip J., Jr. "Phantom Radicals: Texas Republicans in Congress, 1870–1873." *Southwest Historical Quarterly* 77 (April 1974): 431.

Baggett, J. "The Rise and Fall of the Texas Radicals, 1867–1883." Ph.D. diss., North Texas State University, 1972.

Bailey, O. "Black Legislators during the Reconstruction of Alabama, 1867–1878." Ph.D. diss., Kansas State University, 1984.

Baker, Vaughan and Amos E. Simpson. "Michael Hahn: Steady Patriot." *Louisiana History* 13 (1972): 229.

Balanoff, Elizabeth. "Negro Legislators in the North Carolina General Assembly, July 1868–February 1872." *North Carolina Historical Review* 49 (1972): 22.

Banning, Lance. *The Sacred Fire of Liberty: James Madison and the Founding of the Federal Republic.* Ithaca, N.Y.: Cornell University Press, 1996.

Barrett, John G. *Sherman's March through the Carolinas.* Chapel Hill: University of North Carolina Press, 1956.

Basler, Roy P. (ed.). *The Collected Works of Abraham Lincoln, vol. 7.* New Brunswick, N.J.: Rutgers University Press, 1953.

Beale, Howard K. *The Critical Years: A Study of Andrew Johnson and Reconstruction.* New York: F. Unger Publishing Company, 1958.

Belz, Herman. *A New Birth of Freedom: The Republican Party and Freedmen's Rights, 1861–1866.* Westport, Conn.: Greenwood Press, 1976.

Bennett, Lerone, Jr. *Black Power U.S.A.* Chicago: Johnson Publishing Company, 1967.

Bentley, George R. *A History of the Freedmen's Bureau.* Philadelphia: University of Pennsylvania Press, 1955.

———. "The Political Activity of the Freedmen's Bureau in Florida." *Florida Historical Quarterly* 28 (1949): 28.

Berger, Raoul. "New Deal Symposium: The Activist Legacy of the New Deal Court." *Washington Law Review* 59 (1984): 751.

Bergeron, Paul H. (ed.). *The Papers of Andrew Johnson, vol. 9, September 1865–January 1866.* Knoxville: University of Tennessee Press, 1991.

Bernstein, Contra Leonard. "The Participation of Negro Delegates in the Constitutional Convention of 1868 in North Carolina." *Journal of Negro History* 34 (1949): 391.

Bethel, Elizabeth. "The Freedman's Bureau in Alabama." *Journal of Southern History* 14 (1948): 49.

Bickel, Alexander M. *The Supreme Court and the Idea of Progress.* New Haven and London: Yale University Press, 1978.

Black, Hugo. *A Constitutional Faith.* New York: Knopf, 1968.

Blaine, James G. *Twenty Years of Congress: From Lincoln to Garfield, vol. 2.* Norwich, Conn.: Henry Hill Publishing Company, 1884–86.

Bond, Horace Mann. "Social and Economic Forces in Alabama Reconstruction." *Journal of Negro History* 23 (1938): 290.

Bond, James E. "The Original Understanding of the Fourteenth Amendment in Illinois, Ohio, and Pennsylvania." *Akron Law Review* 18 (1985): 435.

———."Ratification of the 14th Amendment in North Carolina." *Wake Forest Law Review* 20 (Spring 1984): 89.

Borden, Morton. *The Antifederalist Papers.* East Lansing: Michigan State University Press, 1965.

Boyett, Gene W. "The Black Experience in the First Decade of Reconstruction in Pope County." *Arkansas Historical Quarterly* 51 (1992): 119.

Brennan, W. "The Bill of Rights and the States." *New York University Law Review* 36 (1961): 761.

Brent, J. "No Surrender: Mobile, Alabama, during Presidential Reconstruction, 1865–1867." M.A. thesis, University of Southern Alabama, 1988.

Budd, H. "The Negro in Politics in Texas." M.A. thesis, University of Texas, 1925.

Burgess, John W. *Reconstruction and the Constitution.* New York: C. Scribner's Sons, 1982.

Cahill, A. "Gilbert Carelton Walker: Virginia's Redeemer Governor." M.A. thesis, University of Virginia, 1956.

Cahill, M. "The Negro in Florida during Reconstruction 1865–1877." M.A. thesis, University of Florida, 1954.

Campbell, James B. *Two Letters from the Hon. James B. Campbell, U.S. Senator Elect from South Carolina, on Public Affairs and our Duties to the Colored Race.* Charleston: Walker, Evans & Cogswell, Stationers and Printers, 1868.

Campbell, Randolph B. "The District Judges of Texas in 1866–1867: An Episode in the Failure of Presidential Reconstruction." *Southwest Historical Quarterly* 93 (1990): 357.

Cantrell, Greg. "Racial Violence and Reconstruction Politics in Texas, 1867–1868." *Southwest Historical Quarterly* 93 (1990): 333.

Carrier, J. "A Political History of Texas during Reconstruction." Ph.D. diss., Vanderbilt University, 1971.

Chamberlain, Daniel H. "The Facts and Figures: The Practical and Truthful Record of the Republican Party of South Carolina." Columbia, n.p. 1870: 2 (available at the South Caroliniana Library, University of South Carolina, Columbia, South Carolina).

Clayton, Powell. *The Aftermath of the Civil War in Arkansas.* New York: Neale Publishing Company, 1915.

Cobb, H. "Negroes in Alabama during the Reconstruction Period, 1865–1875." Ph.D. diss., Temple University, 1952.

Coleman, K. (ed.). *A History of Georgia.* Athens: University of Georgia Press, 1977.

Cook, M. "Restoration and Innovation: Alabamians Adjust to Defeat, 1865–1867." Ph.D. diss., University of Alabama, 1968.

Cooper, Walter Raymond. "Parson Brownlow: A Study of Reconstruction in Tennessee." *Southwestern Bulletin* 19 (1908): 3.

Coulter, E. Merton. *A Short History of Georgia.* Chapel Hill: University of North Carolina Press, 1960.

———. "Henry M. Turner: Negro Preacher-Politician during the Reconstruction Era." *Georgia History Journal* 48 (December 1964): 371.

Coulter, Ellis M. *William G. Brownlow, Fighting Parson of the Southern Highlands.* Chapel Hill: University of North Carolina Press, 1937.

Crosskey, William W. "Charles Fairman, 'Legislative History,' and the Constitutional Limitations on State Authority." *Chicago Law Review* 22 (1954): 1.

Crouch, Barry A. "'Unmanacling' Texas Reconstruction: A Twenty Year Perspective." *Southwest Historical Quarterly* 93 (1990): 275.

Crouch, Barry A. and L. J. Schultz. "Crisis in Color: Racial Separation in Texas during Reconstruction." *Civil War History* 16 (1970): 37.

Curtis, Michael. *No State Shall Abridge: The Fourteenth Amendment and the Bill of Rights.* Durham, N.C.: Duke University Press, 1986.

Dabney, Virginius. *Virginia: The New Dominion.* Charlottesville: University Press of Virginia, 1971.

Davis, William W. *The Civil War and Reconstruction in Florida.* New York: Columbia University Press, 1913.

DeMunro, A. "'We Are Men'—Black Reconstruction in North Carolina, 1865–1870." M.A. thesis, University of North Carolina, 1979.

Donald, David. "The Scalawag in Mississippi Reconstruction." *Journal of Southern History* 10 (November 1944): 447.

Dorman, L. "The Free Negro in Alabama from 1819 to 1861." M.A. thesis, University of Alabama, 1916.

Dorsett, J. "Blacks in Reconstruction Texas, 1865–1877." Ph.D. diss., University of Texas, 1985.

Drago, Edmund. *Black Politicians and Reconstruction in Georgia.* Baton Rouge: Louisiana State University Press, 1982.

Driggs, Orval Truman, Jr. "The Issues of the Powell Clayton Regime, 1868–1871." *Arkansas Historical Quarterly* 8 (Spring 1949): 1.

Eckenrode, Hamilton J. *The Political History of Virginia during the Reconstruction.* Baltimore: Johns Hopkins University Press, 1904.

Ellem, Warren A. "Who Were the Mississippi Scalawags?" *Journal of Southern History* 38 (May 1972): 217.

Erickson, J. E. "Origins of the Texas Bill of Rights." *Southwest Historical Quarterly* 62 (1959): 457.

Everett, Donald E. "Demands of the New Orleans Free Colored Population for Political Equality, 1862–1865." *Louisiana Historical Quarterly* 38 (April 1955): 41.

Fairman, Charles. "Does the Fourteenth Amendment Incorporate the Bill of Rights?" *Stanford Law Review* 2 (1949): 5.

Feistman, Eugene G. "Radical Disfranchisement and the Restoration of Tennessee, 1865–1866," *Tennessee Historical Quarterly* 12 (1953): 135.

Fertig, James W. *Secession and Reconstruction in Tennessee.* New York: A.M.S. Press, 1972.

Ficklen, John R. *A History of Reconstruction in Louisiana, through 1868.* 1910. Reprint, Gloucester, Mass.: Peter Smith.

Fischer, R. *The Segregation Struggle in Louisiana, 1862–1877.* Champaign: University of Illinois Press, 1974.

Fitchett, E. Horace. "The Tradition of the Free Negro in Charleston, South Carolina." *Journal of Negro History* 25 (1940): 139.

Fitzgerald, Michael William. "The Union League Movement in Alabama and Mississippi: Politics and Agricultural Change in the Deep South during Reconstruction." Ph.D. diss., University of California at Los Angeles, 1986.

Fleming, Walter L. *Civil War and Reconstruction in Alabama.* New York: Columbia University Press, 1905.

———. "The Peace Movement in Alabama during the Civil War," (parts 1 and 2). *South Atlantic Quarterly* (April/July 1903): 114, 246.

Folmsbee, Stanley J. *Tennessee: A Short History.* Knoxville: University of Tennessee Press, 1969.

Foner, Eric. *Nothing but Freedom: Emancipation and Its Legacy.* Baton Rouge: Louisiana State University Press, 1983.

———. *Reconstruction: America's Unfinished Revolution, 1863–1877.* New York: Harper & Row, 1973.

Frankfurter, Felix. "Memorandum on Incorporation of the Bill of Rights into the Due Process Clause of the Fourteenth Amendment." *Harvard Law Review* 78 (1965): 746.

Fraser, Walter J. "William Henry Ruffner and the Establishment of Virginia's Public School System." *Virginia Magazine of History and Biography* 79 (1971): 259.

Garner, James W. *Reconstruction in Mississippi.* New York: Macmillan, 1901.

Glass, R., and C. Glass. *Virginia Democrats: A History of the Achievements of the Party and Its Leaders in the Mother of Commonwealths, the Old Dominion.* Springfield, Ill.: Democratic Historical Association, Inc., 1937.

Graham, Howard J. "The Early Anti-Slavery Backgrounds of the Fourteenth Amendment." *Wisconsin Law Review* (1950): 479.

Gray, John Chipman. *The Nature and Sources of the Law.* New York: Macmillan, 1921.

Hamilton, Alexander, James Madison, and John Jay. *The Federalist Papers* (Introduction, Table of Contents, and Index of Ideas by Clinton Rositer). New York: New American Library, 1961.

Hamilton, Andrew J. "An Address on 'Suffrage and Reconstruction.'" *The Duty of the People, the President, and Congress.* Boston: Impartial-Suffrage League, 1866.

Hamilton, Joseph G. *Reconstruction in North Carolina.* New York: Columbia University, 1914.

Hamilton, Joseph G. (ed.). *Correspondence of Jonathan Worth, vol. 2.* Raleigh, N.C.: Edwards & Broughton, 1909.

Harding, Vincent. *There Is a River: The Black Struggle for Freedom in America.* San Antonio: Harcourt Brace Jovanovich, 1981.

Harlan, Louis R. "Desegregation in New Orleans Public Schools." *American Historical Review* 67 (April 1962): 663.

Harris, William C. *The Day of the Carpetbagger: Republican Reconstruction in Mississippi.* Baton Rouge: Louisiana State University Press, 1979.

———. "Formulation of the First Mississippi Plan: The Black Code of 1865." *Journal of Mississippi History* 29 (August 1967): 181.

———. *Presidential Reconstruction in Mississippi.* Baton Rouge: Louisiana State University Press, 1967.

———. "The Reconstruction of the Commonwealth." In *A History of Mississippi*, ed. Richard A. McLemore. Jackson: University and College Press of Mississippi, 1973.

Hoffman, R. "The Republican Party in North Carolina 1867–1871." M.A. thesis, University of North Carolina, 1960.

Holden, William W. *The President's Plan Considered; The Proposed Constitutional Amendment Explained, and Its Adoption Urged: The Union the Paramount Good to the People of North Carolina.* Raleigh, N.C.: F. Broadside, 1866.

Holt, Thomas C. *Black over White: Negro Political Leadership in South Carolina during Reconstruction.* Champaign: University of Illinois Press, 1977.

Horn, Stanley F. *Invisible Empire: The Story of the Ku Klux Klan, 1865–1871.* Boston: Houghton Mifflin, 1939.

Houzeau, Jean-Charles. *My Passage at the New Orleans Tribune: A Memoir of the Civil War Era.* Ed. D. Rankin, Baton Rouge: Louisiana State University Press, 1984.

James, Joseph. *The Framing of the Fourteenth Amendment.* Macon, Ga.: Mercer University Press, 1984.

———. "Southern Reaction to the Proposal of the Fourteenth Amendment." *Journal of Southern History* 22 (1956): 477.

Johnson, T. *Texas and Texans, vol. 1.* New York: American Historical Society, 1914.

Johnston, Frank. "Conference between General George and Governor Ames." *Publications of the Mississippi Historical Society, vol. 6.* Jackson, 1902.

Klingman, P. "Josiah Walls: Florida's Black Congressman of Reconstruction." Ph.D. diss., University of Florida, 1972.

Kolchin, Peter. *First Freedom: The Response of Alabama's Blacks to Emancipation and Reconstruction.* Westport, Conn.: Greenwood Press, 1972.

Lander, Ernest M. *A History of South Carolina, 1865–1900.* Chapel Hill: University of North Carolina Press, 1960.

Leavens, F. "*L'Union* and the New Orleans *Tribune* and Louisiana Reconstruction." M.A. thesis, Louisiana State University, 1966.

Ledbetter, B. "White Texans' Attitudes toward the Political Equality of Negroes, 1865–1870." *Phylon* 40 (September 1979): 253.

Lonn, Ella. *Reconstruction in Louisiana after 1868.* 1918. Reprint Gloucester, Mass.: Peter Smith.

Lovett, Bobby. "The Memphis Race Riot and Its Aftermath." *Tennessee Historical Quarterly* 38 (1979): 9.

Lowe, R. "Republicans, Rebellion, and Reconstruction: The Republican Party in Virginia, 1856–1870." Ph.D. diss., University of Virginia, 1968.

Maddex, Jack. *The Virginia Conservatives, 1867–1879.* Chapel Hill: University of North Carolina Press, 1970.

Maddox, Virginia. "The Persistence of Centrist Hegemony." In *Reconstruction and Redemption in the South*, ed. Otto H. Olsen. Baton Rouge: Louisiana State University Press, 1980.

Maltz, Earl M. "The Civil Rights Act and the Civil Rights Cases: Congress, Court, and Constitution." *Florida Law Review* 44 (1992): 605.

———. "The Fourteenth Amendment as Political Compromise—Section One in the Joint Committee on Reconstruction." *Ohio State Law Journal* 45 (1984): 933.

———. "Fourteenth Amendment Concepts in the Antebellum Era." *American Journal of Legal History* 32 (1988): 305.

———. "Individual Rights and State Autonomy." *Harvard Journal of Law and Public Policy* 12 (1989): 163.

McBride, W. "Blacks and the Race Issue in Tennessee Politics, 1865–1876." Ph.D. diss., Vanderbilt University, 1989.

McDonough, James. *Schofield: Union General in the Civil War and Reconstruction.* Tallahassee: Florida State University Press, 1972.

McGee, E. "North Carolina Conservatives and Reconstruction." Ph.D. diss., University of North Carolina, 1972.

McLaughlin, J. "John R. Lynch: The Reconstruction Politician." Ph.D. diss., Ball State University, 1981.

Moneyhon, Carl H. *The Impact of the Civil War and Reconstruction on Arkansas: Persistence in the Midst of Ruin.* Baton Rouge: Louisiana State University Press, 1994.

———. *Republicanism in Reconstruction Texas.* Austin: University of Texas Press, 1980.

Morrill, James Roy. "North Carolina and the Administration of Brevet Major General Sickles." *North Carolina Historical Review* 42 (1965): 291.

Morton, Richard L. *The Negro in Virginia Politics, 1865–1870.* Charlottesville: University of Virginia Press, 1919.

Morton, Richard L., Philip A. Bruce, and Lyon G. Tyler. *History of Virginia, vol. 3.* New York: American Historical Society, 1924.

Mulhollan, Paige E. "Arkansas General Assembly of 1866 and Its Effect on Reconstruction." *Arkansas Historical Quarterly* 20 (Winter 1961): 331.

Nathans, Elizabeth S. *Losing the Peace: Georgia Republicans and Reconstruction, 1865–1871.* Baton Rouge: Louisiana State University Press, 1968.

Nero, C. "'To Develop Our Manhood': Free Black Leadership and the Rhetoric of the New Orleans *Tribune*." Ph.D. diss., Indiana University, 1991.

Nieman, Donald G. *To Set the Law in Motion: The Freedmen's Bureau and the Legal Rights of Blacks, 1865–1868.* Millwood, N.Y.: KTO Press, 1979.

Olsen, Otto H. "A. U. Tourgee: Carpetbagger." *North Carolina Historical Review* 40 (1963): 434.

Patton, James W. *Unionism and Reconstruction in Tennessee.* 1934. Reprint Gloucester, Mass.: Peter Smith.

Pearson, Charles Chilton. "William Henry Ruffner: Reconstruction Statesman of Virginia." *South Atlantic Quarterly* 20 (1921): 137.

Peek, Ralph. "Military Reconstruction and the Growth of Anti-Negro Sentiment in Florida, 1867." *Florida Historical Quarterly* 47 (1969): 380.

Pereyra, Lillian A. *James Lusk Alcorn: Persistent Whig.* Baton Rouge: Louisiana State University Press, 1966.

Phillips, Paul D. "White Reaction to the Freedmen's Bureau in Tennessee." *Tennessee Historical Quarterly* 25 (1966): 50.

Pierce, Paul Skeels. *The Freedmen's Bureau: A Chapter in the History of Reconstruction.* Iowa City: University of Iowa Press, 1904.

Pike, James S. *The Prostrate State: South Carolina under Negro Government.* New York: D. Appleton, 1874.

Pittman, P. "The Mississippi Constitutional Convention of 1868." M.A. thesis, University of Mississippi, 1949.

Pyburn, Nita Katherine. "David Selby Walker: Educational Statesman of Florida." *Florida Historical Quarterly* 34 (1955): 159.

Rainwater, P. L. (ed.) "The Autobiography of Benjamin Grubb Humphreys." *Mississippi Valley Historical Review* 21 (September 1934): 231.

Ramsdell, Charles W. *Reconstruction in Texas.* 1964. Reprint Gloucester, Mass.: Peter Smith.

Raper, H. "William Woods Holden: A Political Biography." Ph.D. diss., University of North Carolina, 1951.

Reidy, Joseph P. (ed.). "Aaron A. Bradley: Voice of Black Labor in the Georgia Low Country." In *Southern Black Leaders of the Reconstruction Era*, ed. H. Rabinowitz. Champaign: University of Illinois Press, 1982.

Reinstein, Robert J. "Completing the Constitution: The Declaration of Independence, Bill of Rights, and Fourteenth Amendment." *Temple Law Review* 66 (1993): 361.

Remonstrance by "The White People of South Carolina." (1868) Fitz William McMaster Collection, South Caroliniana Library, University of South Carolina. Columbia, South Carolina.

Richards, David A. J. *Conscience and the Constitution: History, Theory, and Law of the Reconstruction Amendments.* Princeton: Princeton University Press, 1993.

Richardson, Joe M. "Florida Black Codes." *Florida Historical Quarterly* 47 (1969): 365.

———. "The Freedman's Bureau in Florida." M.A. thesis, Florida State University, 1959.

———. "Memphis Riots: White Reaction to Blacks in Memphis, May 1865–June 1866." *Tennessee Historical Quarterly* 24 (1964): 63.

———. *The Negro in the Reconstruction of Florida, 1865–1877.* Tallahassee: Florida State University, 1965.

Ripley, C. Peter. *Slaves and Freedmen in Civil War Louisiana.* Baton Rouge: Louisiana State University Press, 1976.

Robertson, Alexander F. *Alexander Hugh Holmes Stuart, 1807–1891: A Biography.* Richmond: William Byrd Press, Inc., 1925.

Rouzan, L. "A Rhetorical Analysis of Editorials in *L'Union* and the New Orleans *Tribune*." Ph.D. diss., Florida State University, 1989.

Russ, William A. "Radical Disfranchisement in North Carolina 1867–1868." *North Carolina Historical Review* 11 (1934): 271.

Rutherford, Robert E. "Florida's First Reconstruction Legislature (A Letter of William H. Gleason to C. W. Holmes, dated October 10, 1890)." *Florida Historical Quarterly* 32 (1953): 41.

Sansing, William. "Congressional Reconstruction." In *A History of Mississippi*, ed. Richard A. McLemore. Jackson: University and College Press of Mississippi, 1973.

Schofield, John M. *Forty-Six Years in the Army.* New York: Century, 1897.

Sears, Alfred B. "Presidential Address: Slavery and Retribution." *Southwestern Social Science Quarterly* 41 (1960): 3.

Shapiro, Herbert. "Ku Klux Klan during Reconstruction: The South Carolina Episode." *Journal of Negro History* 49 (1964): 34.

Shofner, Jerrell H. "The Constitution of 1868." *Florida Historical Quarterly* 41 (1963): 356.

———. "A Failure of Moderate Republicanism." In *Reconstruction and Redemption in the South*, ed. Otto H. Olsen. Baton Rouge: Louisiana State University Press, 1980.

———. *Nor Is It Over Yet: Florida in the Era of Reconstruction, 1863–1877.* Gainesville: University Presses of Florida, 1974.

———. "Political Reconstruction of Florida." *Florida Historical Quarterly* 45 (October 1966): 145.

Simkins, Francis Butler. "Election of 1876 in South Carolina." *South Atlantic Quarterly* 21 (1922): 225.

Simkins, Francis Butler, and Robert-Hilliard Woody. *South Carolina during Reconstruction.* 1966. Reprint Gloucester, Mass.: Peter Smith.

Singletary, Otis A. "Militia Disturbances in Arkansas during Reconstruction." *Arkansas Historical Quarterly* 15 (1956): 140.

———. "The Texas Militia during Reconstruction." *Southwest Historical Quarterly* 60 (July 1956): 23.

Smallwood, James. *Time of Hope, Time of Despair: Black Texans during Reconstruction.* Port Washington, N.Y.: National University Publications, 1981.

Smith, D. "Black Reconstruction in Mississippi, 1862–1870." Ph.D. diss., University of Kansas, 1985.

Smith, George Washington. "Carpetbag Imperialism in Florida 1862–1868." *Florida Historical Quarterly* 27 (July 1948): 99.

Smith, J. "Virginia during Reconstruction, 1865–1870." Ph.D. diss., University of Virginia, 1960.

Smith, William Russell, Papers. Library of Congress.

Sneed, Edgar P. "A Historiography of Reconstruction in Texas: Some Myths and Problems." *Southwest Historical Quarterly* 72 (1969): 435.

Stahl, Annie Lee West. "The Free Negro in Ante-Bellum Louisiana." *Louisiana Historical Quarterly* 25 (April 1942): 301.

Staples, Thomas S. *Reconstruction in Arkansas, 1862–1874.* 1964. Reprint Gloucester, Mass.: Peter Smith.

Sydnor, Charles S. "The Free Negro in Mississippi before the Civil War." *American Historical Review* 32 (1927): 769.

Taylor, Alrutheus A. *The Negro in the Reconstruction of Virginia.* Washington, D.C.: Association for the Study of Negro Life and History, 1926.

———. *The Negro in South Carolina during the Reconstruction.* Washington, D.C.: Association for the Study of Negro Life and History, 1924.

————. *The Negro in Tennessee, 1865–1880.* Spartanburg, S.C.: Associated Publishers, 1941.

Taylor, Joe G. "Louisiana: An Impossible Task." In *Reconstruction and Redemption in the South,* ed. Otto H. Olsen. Baton Rouge: Louisiana State University Press, 1980.

————. *Louisiana Reconstructed 1863–1877.* Baton Rouge: Louisiana State University Press, 1974.

Ten Broeck, Jacobus. *Equal under Law.* New York: Collier, 1965 (originally published in 1951 under the title *The Anti-Slavery Origins of the Fourteenth Amendment*).

Thomas, J. "The Alabama Constitutional Convention of 1867." M.S. thesis, Alabama Polytechnic Institute, 1947.

Thompson, Clara M. *Reconstruction in Georgia: Economic, Social, and Political, 1865–1871.* New York: Columbia University Press, 1915.

Trelease, Allen W. "Republican Reconstruction in North Carolina: A Roll-Call Analysis of the State House of Representatives 1868–1870." *Journal of Southern History* 42 (1976): 319.

————. *White Terror: The Ku Klux Klan Conspiracy and Southern Reconstruction.* New York: Harper & Row, 1971.

Tribe, Lawrence. *American Constitutional Law.* Mineola, N.Y.: Foundation Press, 1978.

Trowbridge, John J. *The South: A Tour of Its Battlefields and Ruined Cities, A Journey through the Desolated States.* New York: Arno Press and the New York Times, 1969.

Tucker, David M. *Arkansas: A People and Their Reputation.* Memphis: Memphis State University Press, 1985.

Tunnell, Ted. *Crucible of Reconstruction: War, Radicalism and Race in Louisiana, 1862-1877.* Baton Rouge: Louisiana State University Press, 1984.

Ullman, Victor. *Martin R. Delany: The Beginning of Black Nationalism.* Boston: Beacon Press, 1971.

Walker, J. "The Negro in Tennessee during the Reconstruction Period." M.A. thesis, University of Tennessee, 1933.

Wallace, David D. *The History of South Carolina, vol. 3.* New York: American Historical Society, Inc., 1934.

————. *South Carolina; A Short History, 1520–1948.* Columbia: University of South Carolina Press, 1961.

Wallace, Ernest. *The Howling of the Coyotes: Reconstruction Efforts to Divide Texas.* College Station: Texas A & M University Press, 1979.

Wallace, John. *Carpet-bag Rule in Florida: The Inside Workings of the Reconstruction of Civil Government in Florida after the Close of the Civil War.* Jacksonville, Fla.: Da Costa Printing and Publishing House, 1888.

Warmouth, Henry C. *War, Politics and Reconstruction: Stormy Days in Louisiana.* New York: Macmillan, 1930.

Wharton, Vernon L. *The Negro in Mississippi, 1865–1890.* Chapel Hill: University of North Carolina Press, 1947.

Wiggins, Sarah W. "Alabama: Democratic Bulldozing and Republican Folly." In *Reconstruction and Redemption in the South.* ed. Otto Olsen. Baton Rouge: Louisiana State University Press, 1980.

————. *The Scalawag in Alabama Politics, 1865–1881.* University, Ala.: University of Alabama Press, 1977.

Wikramanajake, I. "The Free Negro in Antebellum South Carolina." Ph.D. diss., University of Wisconsin, 1966.

Williams, T. "The Louisiana Unification Movement of 1873." *Journal of Southern History* 11 (August 1945): 347.
Williamson, Joel. *After Slavery: The Negro in South Carolina during Reconstruction, 1861–1877.* Hanover, N.H.: University Press of New England, 1965.
Wilson, Theodore B. *The Black Codes of the South.* University, Ala.: University of Alabama Press, 1965.
Winkler, Ernest W. (ed.). *Platforms of Political Parties in Texas.* Austin: University of Texas Press, 1916.
Wood, George A. "The Black Codes of Alabama." *South Atlantic Quarterly* 13 (January 1916): 356.
Woodward, C. Vann. *The Burden of Southern History.* Baton Rouge: Louisiana State University Press, 1968.
————. *Origins of the New South.* Baton Rouge: Louisiana State University Press, 1951.
————. (ed.). *Mary Chestnut's Civil War.* New Haven: Yale University Press, 1981.
Wynes, Charles E. *Race Relations in Virginia, 1870–1962.* Totowa, N.J.: Rowman and Littlefield, 1961.

NEWSPAPERS

Abbeville (S.C.) Press, 2 March 1866–28 February 1868.
Abingdon (Va.) Virginian, 30 March 1866–8 May 1868.
Albany (Ga.) Patriot, 3 February–22 September 1866.
Alexandria Gazette, 13 June–8 July 1865.
American Citizen (Miss.), 5 January 1865–28 April 1866.
American Union (Va.), 16 June 1866.
Anderson (S.C.) Intelligencer, 25 January–8 February 1866.
Arkansas Conservative, 4 October 1866.
Arkansas Daily Gazette, 21 June 1865–28 February 1868.
Asheville News, 12 March 1868.
Asheville Pioneer, 26 September 1867–21 May 1868.
Athens (Ga.) Post, 9 June 1867–2 April 1868.
Augusta (Ga.) Chronicle-Sentinel, 16 February 1866–1 May 1867.
Austin Southern Intelligencer, 11 August 1865–2 May 1867.
Baton Rouge Tri-Weekly, 9 January 1866.
Baton Rouge Weekly Advocate, 12 May–4 August 1866.
Beaufort (S.C.) Republican, 19 February 1874.
Bolivar (Tenn.) Bulletin, 28 April–30 June 1866.
Bossier (La.) Banner, 16 February 1867–23 May 1868.
Bristol (Va.) News, 17 April–1 May 1868.
Carolina Watchman (N.C.), 1 October 1866.
Carroll (La.) Reader, 18 July–19 July 1868.
Charleston Daily Courier, 22 March 1865–9 April 1868.
Charleston Daily Republican, 24 June 1870.
Charleston Mercury, 30 June 1866–30 June 1868.
Charlotte Daily Bulletin, 13 January–23 March 1868.
Charlottesville (Va.) Chronicle, 9 October 1866–26 May 1868.
Cincinnati Commercial, 15 June 1866.
Clarke County (Ala.) Democrat, 13 December 1866–5 December 1867.
Clarke County (Ala.) Journal, 10 May–28 June 1866.

Clarksville (Tenn.) Weekly Chronicle, 15 June–6 July 1866.
Cleveland (Tenn.) Banner, 10 February 1866–20 April 1867.
Coahomian (Miss.), 3 November 1865.
Columbia (Tenn.) Herald, 2 May 1866.
Crescent (S.C.), 28 November 1866–5 February 1868.
Daily Advance (Tenn.), 22 June 1867.
Daily Constitutionalist (Ga.), 14 March 1866–12 March 1868.
Daily New Era (Ga.), 25 April 1868.
Daily Opinion (Ga.), 15 February 1868.
Daily South Carolinian, 7 March–23 March 1866.
Daily State Sentinel (Ga.), 22 August–29 August 1867.
Daily Sun (Ga.), 8 April 1866–4 June 1868.
Dallas Weekly Herald, 19 May 1866–20 February 1870.
Danville (Ill.) Plain Dealer, 1 November 1866.
Dawson (Ga.) Weekly Journal, 8 June 1866–12 July 1867.
Des Arc Citizen (Ark.), 2 June–17 November 1866.
East Florida Banner, 12 October 1867.
Elmore (Ala.) Standard, 10 October–20 December 1867.
Fayetteville (N.C.) News, 8 May 1866–12 February 1867.
Fayetteville (Tenn.) Observer, 1 March–28 June 1866.
Florida Union, 7 March 1868.
Floridian, 26 September 1865.
Forest Register Weekly, 17 November 1869.
Fort Smith (Ark.) New Era, 20 November 1866.
Fort Smith (Ark.) Tri-Weekly Herald, 26 July 1866–14 February 1867.
Fredericksberg (Va.) New Era, 27 June–18 July 1865.
Freemen's Standard (Ga.), 13 June 1868.
Galveston Daily News, 5 July 1867.
Galveston News, 30 September 1865.
Galveston Republican, 9 March 1868.
Galveston Tri-Weekly News, 1 January 1870.
Galveston Weekly News, 14 February–25 July 1866.
Georgia Journal and Messenger, 12 September 1866.
Greensboro Patriot, 15 February 1866–23 July 1868.
Greensboro Times, 13 February–21 May 1868.
Harper's Weekly, 10 June 1865
Hinds County (Miss.) Gazette, 22 June 1866–28 June 1871.
Houston Telegraph, 14 July 1869.
Huntsville (Ga.) Daily Independent, 9 May 1866.
Iberville (La.) South, 11 August–20 October 1866.
Jackson Clarion, 8 November 1865–28 September 1866.
Jackson News, 14 November 1865.
Jackson Weekly Clarion, 10 October 1866.
Knoxville Whig, 11 January 1865–19 December 1866.
L'Union (La.), 9 April 1864.
Lancaster (S.C.) Ledger, 7 March 1866–10 July 1867.
Liberty Advocate (Miss.), 22 December 1866.
Little Rock Daily Conservative, 8 June 1866–5 June 1867.
Louisiana Democrat, 6 February 1866–4 December 1867.

Loyal Georgian, 3 March 1866.
Macon American Union, 25 September 1868.
Macon Daily Telegraph, 13 January–11 November 1866.
Marion (S.C.) Star, 21 November 1866–22 November 1868.
Memphis Argus, 9 August 1865.
Memphis Daily Post, 27 February 1867.
Meridian (Miss.) Clarion, 22 October 1865.
Mississippian, The, 18 August 1865.
Mobile Advertiser and Register, 1 January–18 August 1867.
Monroe (Ga.) Eagle, 27 May 1868.
Montgomery Daily Advertiser, 26 November 1867–30 June 1874.
Montgomery Daily Mail, 27 February 1866–26 November 1867.
Moulton (Ga.) Advertiser, 9 February 1867.
Nashville Daily Gazette, 11 June 1866.
Nashville Daily Press-Times, 5 January–22 November 1866.
Nashville Daily Union, 22 October–2 December 1865.
Nashville Daily Union and American, 14 September–16 September 1866.
Nashville Democrat, 21 June 1866.
Nashville Dispatch, 4 May–20 July 1866.
Nashville Republican Banner, 1 June 1866–6 July 1867.
Nashville Union, 13 February 1866.
Nashville Union and American, 27 June 1866.
Nashville Union and Dispatch, 7 February 1867.
Natchez (Miss.) Daily Courier, 14 June 1866.
Natchez (Miss.) Tri-Weekly Democrat, 1 October 1867.
Nationalist (Ga.), 5 April 1866–22 February 1869.
New Bern (N.C.) Daily Journal of Commerce, 12 February–21 May 1867.
New Era (Tenn.), 7 July 1866.
New Orleans Bee, 26 January–5 March 1866.
New Orleans Picayune, 29 May 1866–6 June 1873.
New Orleans Times, 6 November 1863–1 July 1877.
New Orleans Tribune, 11 August 1864–25 November 1866.
New South, The (S.C.), 29 September 1866.
New York Times, 25 September 1865–18 March 1866.
New York Tribune, 12 April 1867.
Newman (Ga.) Herald, 30 March 1867.
News and Courier (S.C.), 11 April 1877.
Norfolk Virginian, 3 December 1866.
Old North State (N.C.), 26 June–11 October 1866.
Opelousas (La.) Courier, 21 December 1867–29 February 1868.
Oxford (Miss.) Falcon, 3 May–11 November 1866.
Page News-Courier (Va.), 15 January 1869.
Paris (Tenn.) Post-Intelligencer, 20 April–29 June 1866.
People's Press (Miss.), 28 June–10 October 1866.
Pine Bluff (Ark.) Dispatch, 19 January–30 November 1867.
Pulaski (Tenn.) Citizen, 27 April–22 June 1866.
Quanchita (La.) Telegraph, 23 August 1866–21 June 1873.
Raleigh Daily Standard, 9 February 1866.
Raleigh Sentinel, 4 April 1866–4 July 1868.

Raleigh Standard, 4 April 1866–12 February 1869.
Reconstructionist (Ga.), 6 June 1868.
Republican Banner (Tenn.), 9 June–20 July 1866.
Richmond Daily Whig, 19 March–30 April 1869.
Richmond Dispatch, 2 February 1866–3 August 1867.
Richmond Enquirer, 1 January 1867–8 April 1868.
Richmond Enquirer and Examiner, 6 April 1868.
Richmond Examiner, 3 May 1866.
Richmond Whig, 4 January–13 December 1867.
Roanoke Times, 11 November 1866–12 February 1867.
Rome (Ga.) Tri-Weekly Courier, 3 February–14 June 1866.
Rome (Ga.) Weekly Courier, 27 April–15 June 1866.
St. Augustine (Fla.) Examiner, 8 September 1866–7 December 1867.
Salisbury (N.C.) Tri-Weekly Banner, 6 March 1867.
San Antonio Express, 24 May 1866.
Savannah Daily News, 12 December 1866.
Savannah Daily News-Herald, 23 March–3 April 1867.
Savannah Daily Republican, 4 July–13 September 1866.
Selma Daily Messenger, 29 September–15 November 1866
Selma Messenger, 12 September 1867.
Selma Morning Times, 17 February–12 June 1866.
Semi-Weekly Floridian, 11 May–2 October 1866.
Semi-Weekly Times (La.), 7 February 1866–13 April 1867.
South Carolina Leader, 15 November 1865.
South Western (Louis.), 14 February 1866–8 April 1868.
Southern Advertiser (Ala.), 11 May 1866–18 January 1867.
Southern Herald (Miss.), 25 August–10 October 1866.
State Line Gazette (Va.), 22 June 1866–13 February 1867.
Sugar Planter (La.), 14 April–8 September 1866.
Tallahassee Sentinel, 9 September 1867–13 August 1868.
Texas Republican, 2 March–30 June 1866.
Texas State Gazette, 8 August 1865–10 December 1869.
True Index (Va.), 14 April 1866–28 September 1867.
Tuscaloosa Independent Monitor, 30 October 67
Union Springs (Ga.) Times, 11 April 1866–11 September 1867.
Van Buren (Ark.) Press, 7 April 1866–29 November 1867.
Vicksburg (Miss.) Daily Herald, 1 November 1865–24 July 1868.
*Vicksburg (Miss.) Daily Times,*20 June–17 October 1866.
Vicksburg (Miss.) Herald, 27 January 1866.
Vicksburg (Miss.) Journal, 21 September 1865–19 May 1866.
Virginia Sentinel, 12 April 1866.
Wadesboro (N.C.) Argus, 16 May 1866–20 February 1868.
Washington (D.C.) Chronicle, 14 June 1865.
Washington (D.C.) Herald, 15 June 1866.
Weekly Floridian, 18 January 1867–24 March 1868.
Weekly Gazette and Comet (La.), 28 August 1866–2 May 1868.
Weekly Panola Star (Miss.), 28 October 1865–2 November 1867.
Weekly Standard (Miss.), 3 April–7 April, 1866
Weekly Telegraph (Tex.), 30 July 1867–3 December 1868.

Western Democrat (N.C.), 1 May 1866–26 March 1867.
Wilmington Daily Dispatch, 11 April–31 October 1866.
Wilmington Daily Herald, 24 January 1866.
Wilmington Journal, 28 June 1866–15 February 1867.

Index

About the Author

JAMES E. BOND is the Dean of and Professor at the School of Law at Seattle University. He has taught constitutional law for two decades and is the author of four other books, including *I Dissent*, a biography of Justice James Clark McReynolds, and *The Art of Judging*, a critique of how judges decide cases. A brief sojourn as a civil rights worker in Mississippi in the summer of 1964 sparked his initial interest in the 14th Amendment and Reconstruction.

ISBN 0-275-95703-9

EAN

9 780275 957032

HARDCOVER BAR CODE